WORLD GEOGRAPHY

Guided Reading Workbook

Contents

Guided Reading Workbook

How to Use This Book

The *Guided Reading Workbook* was developed to help you get the most from your reading. Using this workbook alongside your textbook will help you master geography content while developing your reading and vocabulary skills. Reviewing the next few pages before getting started will make you aware of the many useful features in this book.

Lesson summary pages allow you to interact with the content and key terms and places from each section of a module. The summaries explain each section of your textbook in a way that is easy to understand.

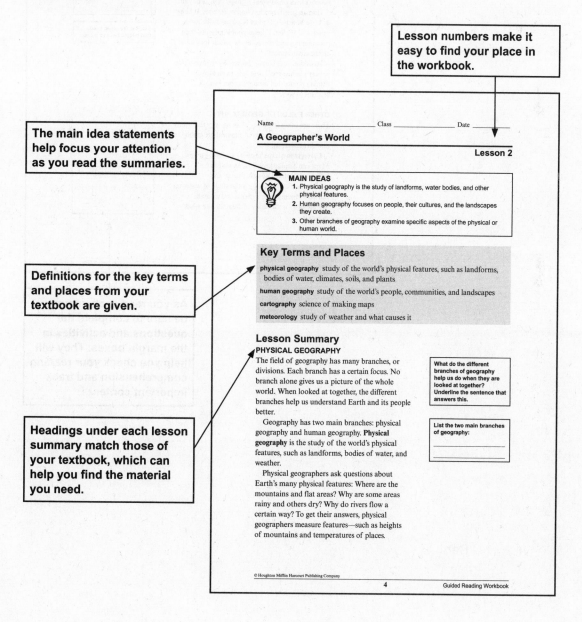

The main idea statements help focus your attention as you read the summaries.

Definitions for the key terms and places from your textbook are given.

Headings under each lesson summary match those of your textbook, which can help you find the material you need.

Lesson numbers make it easy to find your place in the workbook.

Name _____ Class _____ Date _____

A Geographer's World

Lesson 2

MAIN IDEAS
1. Physical geography is the study of landforms, water bodies, and other physical features.
2. Human geography focuses on people, their cultures, and the landscapes they create.
3. Other branches of geography examine specific aspects of the physical or human world.

Key Terms and Places

physical geography study of the world's physical features, such as landforms, bodies of water, climates, soils, and plants

human geography study of the world's people, communities, and landscapes

cartography science of making maps

meteorology study of weather and what causes it

Lesson Summary
PHYSICAL GEOGRAPHY

The field of geography has many branches, or divisions. Each branch has a certain focus. No branch alone gives us a picture of the whole world. When looked at together, the different branches help us understand Earth and its people better.

Geography has two main branches: physical geography and human geography. **Physical geography** is the study of the world's physical features, such as landforms, bodies of water, and weather.

Physical geographers ask questions about Earth's many physical features: Where are the mountains and flat areas? Why are some areas rainy and others dry? Why do rivers flow a certain way? To get their answers, physical geographers measure features—such as heights of mountains and temperatures of places.

What do the different branches of geography help us do when they are looked at together? Underline the sentence that answers this.

List the two main branches of geography:
_____
_____

© Houghton Mifflin Harcourt Publishing Company

4   Guided Reading Workbook

The key terms and places from your textbook have been boldfaced, allowing you to quickly find and study them.

Name _____ Class _____ Date _____

Lesson 2, *continued*

Physical geography has important uses. It helps us understand how the world works. It also helps us predict and prepare for dangerous storms.

HUMAN GEOGRAPHY

Human geography is the other main branch of geography. It is the study of people and their communities and landscapes.

Human geographers study people in the past or present. They ask questions such as why people choose to live in certain places. They might investigate what kinds of work people do.

People all over the world are very different, so human geographers often study a smaller topic. They might study people in one region, such as central Africa. They might study one part of people's lives in different regions, such as city life.

Human geography has important uses. It helps us learn how people meet basic needs for food, water, and shelter. It helps people improve their communities and measures the effects they have on the environment.

Historians use human geography to investigate patterns in history. These help them identify turning points that brought about historic changes to society.

> Why do human geographers often study one smaller topic?
> _____
> _____
> _____

> Circle three basic needs that people have to meet.

OTHER FIELDS OF GEOGRAPHY

There are other branches of geography that study smaller specialized parts of physical geography or human geography.

Cartography is the science of making maps. Maps can display locations, as well as information about people, places, and environments. Hydrology is the study of water on Earth, including river systems and rainfall. **Meteorology** is the study of weather and what causes it.

> What is meteorology?
> _____
> _____
> _____

© Houghton Mifflin Harcourt Publishing Company

5   Guided Reading Workbook

As you read each summary, be sure to complete the questions and activities in the margin boxes. They will help you check your reading comprehension and track important content.

Each lesson has activities that allow you to demonstrate your understanding of the lesson's key terms and places. Use the lesson summaries and your textbook to answer these activities.

The challenge activity provides an opportunity for you to apply important critical thinking skills using the content that you learned in the lesson.

A variety of activities helps you check your knowledge of key terms and places.

Some pages have a word bank. You can use it to help find answers or complete writing activities.

Writing activities require you to include key words and places in what you write. Remember to check to make sure you are using the terms and places correctly.

Name _____ Class _____ Date _____

Lesson 2, *continued*

CHALLENGE ACTIVITY

Critical Thinking: Draw Inferences Examine a map of an unfamiliar city using a road atlas or an online map. Write a paragraph telling a visitor what physical and human features to look for in each quadrant (NE, SE, NW, SW).

DIRECTIONS Read each sentence, and fill in the blank with the word in the word pair that best completes the sentence.

1. _____ is the study of weather and what causes it. **(Cartography/Meteorology)**

2. Geographers might study _____ if they want to know how Victoria Falls was formed. **(physical geography/human geography)**

3. Without _____, geographers would not be able to use maps to study where things are in the world. **(cartography/meteorology)**

4. The study of Earth's people, including their ways of life, homes, cities, beliefs, and customs, is called _____. **(physical geography/human geography)**

5. Studying the world's river systems and how to protect the world's water supply are important parts of _____. **(hydrology/meteorology)**

| cartography | human geography | hydrology |
| meteorology | physical geography | |

DIRECTIONS Look up the vocabulary terms in the word bank in a dictionary. Write the dictionary definition of the word that is closest to the definition used in your textbook.

_____

_____

_____

_____

_____

© Houghton Mifflin Harcourt Publishing Company

6

Guided Reading Workbook

A Geographer's World

MAIN IDEAS
1. Geography is the study of the world, its people, and the landscapes they create.
2. Geographers look at the world in many different ways.

Key Terms and Places

geography study of the world, its people, and the landscapes they create

landscape human and physical features that make a place unique

social science field that studies people and the relationships among them

region part of the world with one or more common features distinguishing it from surrounding areas

Lesson Summary
WHAT IS GEOGRAPHY?

For every place on Earth, you can ask questions to learn about it: What does the land look like? What is the weather like? What are people's lives like? Asking questions like these is how you study geography. **Geography** is the study of the world, its people, and the physical and human **landscapes** that make a place unique.

Geographers (people who study geography) ask questions about how the world works. For example, they may ask why a place gets tornadoes. To find answers, they gather data by observing and measuring. Then they study and interpret the data. In this way, geography is like science.

Geography can also be like a social science. **Social science** studies people and how they relate to each other. This information cannot be measured in the same way. To study people, geographers may visit places and talk to the people about their lives.

> Underline the sentences that state how geography is like science.

Lesson 1, *continued*

LOOKING AT THE WORLD

Geographers must look carefully at the world around them. Depending on what they want to learn, they look at the world at different levels.

Geographers may study at the local level, such as a city or town. They may ask why people live there, what work they do, and how they travel. They can help a town or city plan improvements.

Geographers may also study at the regional level. A **region** is an area with common features. A region may be big or small. Its features make it different from areas around it. The features may be physical (such as mountains) or human (such as language).

Sometimes geographers study at the global level. They study how people interact all over the world. Geographers can help us learn how people's actions affect other people and places. For example, they may ask how one region influences other regions.

> Circle the three levels that geographers study.

CHALLENGE ACTIVITY

Critical Thinking: Evaluate Find a map of your state. Determine the state's different regions based on physical characteristics. Are there regions with mountains, ones near important bodies of water, regions that rely on farming, or areas with lots of cities? Make a list of the regions and each one's characteristics. Which region do you live in?

Lesson 1, *continued*

DIRECTIONS On the line provided before each statement, write **T** if the statement is true and **F** if the statement is false. If the statement is false, write the correct term on the line after each sentence that makes the sentence a true statement.

_____ 1. The study of the world, its people, and the landscapes they create is called <u>geography</u>.

_____

_____ 2. Geography is sometimes called a <u>social science</u> because it studies people and the relationships among them.

_____

_____ 3. An example of a small <u>region</u> that geographers might study is Chinatown in San Francisco.

_____

_____ 4. The combination of human and physical features that make a place unique is called a <u>landscape</u>.

_____

_____ 5. When geographers study how people live on a <u>global level</u>, they look at a single city or town.

Guided Reading Workbook

A Geographer's World

MAIN IDEAS
1. Physical geography is the study of landforms, water bodies, and other physical features.
2. Human geography focuses on people, their cultures, and the landscapes they create.
3. Other branches of geography examine specific aspects of the physical or human world.

Key Terms and Places

physical geography study of the world's physical features, such as landforms, bodies of water, climates, soils, and plants

human geography study of the world's people, communities, and landscapes

cartography science of making maps

meteorology study of weather and what causes it

Lesson Summary
PHYSICAL GEOGRAPHY

The field of geography has many branches, or divisions. Each branch has a certain focus. No branch alone gives us a picture of the whole world. When looked at together, the different branches help us understand Earth and its people better.

Geography has two main branches: physical geography and human geography. **Physical geography** is the study of the world's physical features, such as landforms, bodies of water, and weather.

Physical geographers ask questions about Earth's many physical features: Where are the mountains and flat areas? Why are some areas rainy and others dry? Why do rivers flow a certain way? To get their answers, physical geographers measure features—such as heights of mountains and temperatures of places.

> What do the different branches of geography help us do when they are looked at together? Underline the sentence that answers this.

> List the two main branches of geography:
>
> _____
>
> _____

Guided Reading Workbook

Physical geography has important uses. It helps us understand how the world works. It also helps us predict and prepare for dangerous storms.

HUMAN GEOGRAPHY

Human geography is the other main branch of geography. It is the study of people and their communities and landscapes.

Human geographers study people in the past or present. They ask questions such as why people choose to live in certain places. They might investigate what kinds of work people do.

People all over the world are very different, so human geographers often study a smaller topic. They might study people in one region, such as central Africa. They might study one part of people's lives in different regions, such as city life.

Human geography has important uses. It helps us learn how people meet basic needs for food, water, and shelter. It helps people improve their communities and measures the effects they have on the environment.

Historians use human geography to investigate patterns in history. These help them identify turning points that brought about historic changes to society.

OTHER FIELDS OF GEOGRAPHY

There are other branches of geography that study smaller specialized parts of physical geography or human geography.

Cartography is the science of making maps. Maps can display locations, as well as information about people, places, and environments. Hydrology is the study of water on Earth, including river systems and rainfall. **Meteorology** is the study of weather and what causes it.

> Why do human geographers often study one smaller topic?
>
> _____
> _____
> _____

> Circle three basic needs that people have to meet.

> What is meteorology?
>
> _____
> _____
> _____

CHALLENGE ACTIVITY

Critical Thinking: Draw Inferences Examine a
map of an unfamiliar city using a road atlas or
an online map. Write a paragraph telling a visitor
what physical and human features to look for in
each quadrant (NE, SE, NW, SW).

DIRECTIONS Read each sentence, and fill in the blank with the
word in the word pair that best completes the sentence.

1. _____ is the study of weather and what causes it.
   (**Cartography/Meteorology**)

2. Geographers might study _____ if they want to know
   how Victoria Falls was formed. (**physical geography/human geography**)

3. Without _____, geographers would not be able to use
   maps to study where things are in the world. (**cartography/meteorology**)

4. The study of Earth's people, including their ways of life, homes, cities, beliefs,
   and customs, is called _____. (**physical geography/human
   geography**)

5. Studying the world's river systems and how to protect the world's water supply
   are important parts of _____. (**hydrology/meteorology**)

cartography	human geography	hydrology
meteorology	physical geography	

DIRECTIONS Look up the vocabulary terms in the word bank in a
dictionary. Write the dictionary definition of the word that is closest
to the definition used in your textbook.

_____

_____

_____

_____

_____

A Geographer's World

MAIN IDEAS
1. The five themes of geography help us organize our studies of the world.
2. The six essential elements of geography highlight some of the subject's most important ideas.

Key Terms and Places

absolute location specific description of where a place is

relative location general description of where a place is

environment an area's land, water, climate, plants and animals, and other physical features

Lesson Summary
THE FIVE THEMES OF GEOGRAPHY

Geographers use themes in their work. A theme is a topic that is common throughout a discussion or event. Many holidays have a theme, such as the flag and patriotism on the Fourth of July.

There are five major themes of geography: Location, Place, Human-Environment Interaction, Movement, and Regions. Geographers can use these themes in almost everything they study.

Location describes where a place is. This may be specific, such as an address. This is called an **absolute location.** It may also be general, such as saying the United States is north of Central America. This is called a **relative location.**

Place refers to an area's landscape. The landscape is made up of the physical and human features of a place, such as the land, climate, or people. Together, these features give a place its own identity apart from other places.

Human-Environment Interaction studies how people and their environment affect each other. The **environment** includes an area's physical

> List the five major themes of geography:
>
> _____
>
> _____
>
> _____
>
> _____

features, such as land, water, weather, and animals. Geographers study how people change their environment (by building dams or towns, for example). They also study how the environment causes people to adapt (by dressing for the weather, for example).

Movement involves learning about why and how people move. Do they move for work or pleasure? Do they travel by roads or other routes?

Studying Regions helps geographers learn how places are alike and different. This also helps them learn why places developed the way they did.

> **Describe two ways that people and their environment affect each other.**
> _____
> _____
> _____
> _____

THE SIX ESSENTIAL ELEMENTS

It is important to organize how you study geography so you get the most complete picture of a place. Using the five major themes can help you do this. Using the six essential elements can, too.

Geographers and teachers created the six elements from 18 basic ideas, called standards. The standards say what everyone should understand about geography. Each element groups together the standards that are related to each other.

The six elements are The World in Spatial Terms (*spatial* refers to where places are located), Places and Regions, Physical Systems, Human Systems, Environment and Society, and Uses of Geography. The six elements build on the five themes, so some elements and themes are similar. Uses of Geography is not part of the five themes. It focuses on how people can use geography to learn about the past and present and plan for the future.

> **What do the five themes and six elements of geography help you do? Underline the sentence that explains this.**

CHALLENGE ACTIVITY

Critical Thinking: Analyze Analyze a place you regularly visit, such as a vacation spot or a park in your neighborhood. Write a question about the place for each geography theme to help someone not familiar with the themes to understand them.

DIRECTIONS Write a word or phrase that has the same meaning as
the term given.

1. absolute location _____

_____

2. element _____

_____

3. environment _____

_____

4. interaction _____

_____

5. relative location _____

_____

absolute location	element	environment
interaction	relative location	

DIRECTIONS Choose at least four of the vocabulary words from the
word bank. Use these words to write a story or poem that relates to
the lesson.

_____

_____

_____

_____

_____

_____

_____

_____

_____

A Geographer's World

MAIN IDEA

1. Maps and globes are the most commonly used tools of geographers.
2. Many geographers study information gathered by satellites.
3. Geographers use many other tools, including graphs, charts, databases, and models in their work.

Key Terms and Places

map flat drawing that shows part of Earth's surface

globe spherical model of the entire planet

Global Positioning System (GPS) tool that uses satellites to transmit locations of objects on Earth

Geographic Information System (GIS) information from many geographic data sources

Lesson Summary
MAPS AND GLOBES

Geographers need tools to do their work. Often, they use maps and globes. A **map** is a flat drawing that shows Earth's surface. A **globe** is a spherical (round) model of the whole planet.

Maps and globes both show what Earth looks like. Because a globe is round, it can show Earth as it really is. To show the round Earth on a flat map, some details have to change. For example, a place's shape may change a little. But maps have benefits. They are easier to work with. They can also show small areas, such as cities, better.

> Underline two sentences that tell the benefits of using maps.

SATELLITES

Geographers also use images and information from satellites. These images help geographers see what Earth looks like from far above.

Satellites are part of a **Global Positioning System (GPS).** This system uses 24 satellites to transmit information about locations of objects on Earth. Many people use GPS in their cars to find out how to get to a new place.

> Why do drivers use GPS in their cars?
>
> _____
>
> _____
>
> _____

OTHER GEOGRAPHIC TOOLS

Geographers use many other tools, including notebooks and voice recorders to take notes. They also work with computers, which lets them use a **Geographic Information System (GIS).** GIS makes it possible to get information from many data sources.

Geographers can ask GIS a question such as, "What are the most important geographic characteristics of an airport site?" GIS answers the question with different kinds of information, including maps.

> Circle the tools geographers use to take notes.

CHALLENGE ACTIVITY

Critical Thinking: Develop Pick a city you would like to study. You want to develop the most complete picture possible of this place and its people. Make a list of questions to ask and tools you would use to find the answers.

DIRECTIONS Circle the word or statement that relates most closely to the vocabulary word.

1. **globe:** spherical, city streets, drawing

2. **map:** entire planet, changed shapes, round

3. **Global Positioning System (GPS):** close-up images, satellites, regional languages

4. **Geographic Information System (GIS):** notebooks, driving directions, computer data

A Geographer's World

Lesson 5

MAIN IDEAS

1. When creating maps, cartographers use a pattern of latitude and longitude lines that circle Earth.
2. Cartographers have created map projections to show the round surface of Earth on a flat piece of paper.
3. Cartographers provide features to help users read maps.
4. There are different kinds of maps for different uses.
5. There are many kinds of landforms and other features on Earth.

Key Terms and Places

grid imaginary lines that circle Earth in east–west and north–south directions

latitude east–west lines in the grid

parallels lines of latitude

longitude north–south lines in the grid

meridians lines of longitude

degrees units of measurement that locate lines of latitude and longitude

minutes unit of measurement that is 1/60 of a degree

equator imaginary line that circles the globe halfway between the North and South Poles

prime meridian imaginary line that divides the globe into east and west halves

hemispheres northern and southern or eastern and western halves of the globe

continents seven large landmasses on Earth's surface

map projections ways that our round planet can be shown on a flat map

Lesson Summary
LATITUDE AND LONGITUDE

Geographers created a pattern of imaginary lines that circle the globe. These lines are called a **grid.** East–west lines are lines of **latitude.** They are also called **parallels** because they are always parallel to each other. North–south lines are called lines of **longitude,** or **meridians.** They pass through the poles.

> **Why are lines of latitude called parallels?**
> _____
> _____

The location of latitude and longitude is measured using **degrees,** or a ° symbol. Degrees are divided into 60 smaller measurements called **minutes.** Degrees and minutes help geographers locate any place on Earth.

Lines of latitude are north and south of the equator. The **equator** is an imaginary line that circles the globe halfway between the North and South Poles. Lines of longitude are east and west of an imaginary line called the **prime meridian.** The prime meridian divides the globe into east and west halves.

Lines of latitude start at 0° at the equator. North of the equator, they are labeled with an *N*. For example, the North Pole is located at 90°N. South of the equator, they are labeled with an *S*. The South Pole is located at 90°S.

Lines of longitude start at 0° at the prime meridian. They go up to 180°, which is the middle of the Pacific Ocean. Meridians west of the prime meridian to 180° are labeled with a *W*. Meridians east of the prime meridian to 180° are labeled with an *E*.

The equator and prime meridian divide the globe into **hemispheres,** or halves. The equator divides the world into the Northern Hemisphere and Southern Hemisphere. The prime meridian divides it into the Eastern Hemisphere and Western Hemisphere.

Earth's surface is further divided into seven large landmasses, called **continents.** Earth's major ocean region is divided into five smaller oceans.

> **Underline the sentence that states how degree measurements help geographers.**

> **What are the latitudes of the most northern and most southern points on Earth?**
>
> _____
>
> _____

> **Circle the imaginary line that divides the globe into Northern and Southern Hemispheres.**

MAP PROJECTIONS

Mapmakers use **map projections** to show our round planet on a flat map. All flat maps are distorted in some way. Mapmakers use one of three map projections: cylindrical, conic, or flat-plane.

Cylindrical projections are based on a cylinder wrapped around a globe at the equator. These maps pull the meridians apart so they are parallel to each other and do not meet at the poles. This makes the land areas at the poles look larger.

Conic projections are based on a cone placed over a globe. It is most accurate along the lines of latitude where the cone touches the globe.

Flat-plane projections are based on a flat shape touching the globe at only one point, such as the North Pole. It shows true direction and true area. That can help navigators. However, it distorts the shapes of land areas.

> Circle the three types of map projections.

> Underline the sentence that explains why navigators might want to use a flat-planed map.

MAP FEATURES

Most maps include four features that help us understand them and what they present. The first feature we usually see is a title. The map title tells you what the map is trying to show. Another feature is a compass rose. This has arrows that show which way north, south, east, and west lie on the map. A third feature is a scale. It is used to measure the distance between points on a map. The fourth important feature is a legend. It explains what symbols and colors represent on the map. For example, roads might be different colors, showing whether they are highways or two lanes.

Some maps include a locator map as a fifth feature. This shows where the area on the map is located in the larger world.

> Circle the four features you are likely to find on most maps.

DIFFERENT KINDS OF MAPS

Political and physical maps are two of the most common maps, but there are also many types of thematic maps. Political maps use different colors to show borders of countries, capital cities, and other places in a region. Physical maps show features like mountain ranges, rivers, and deserts in a region. They often use different colors to represent different elevations. Thematic maps focus on one topic, like climate, resources, or population. They may show the information using different colors, arrows, or other symbols.

Name three kinds of thematic maps.
_____
_____
_____

EARTH'S SURFACE FEATURES

Landforms are features on Earth's surface that are formed by nature. There are many kinds of landforms and water features on Earth. Landform features include hills, valleys, and mountains, while water features include oceans, rivers, and lakes.

CHALLENGE ACTIVITY

Critical Thinking: Design a Map Create a small map of your school. Add a title, compass rose, scale, and legend to explain what the map is about and how to understand its colors and symbols.

DIRECTIONS On the line provided before each statement, write **T** if
the statement is true and **F** if the statement is false. If the statement
is false, write the correct answer on the line after each sentence that
makes the sentence a true statement.

_____ 1. Lines of <u>longitude</u> are also called <u>meridians</u>.

_____

_____ 2. Geographers created a <u>grid</u> to help find locations on the globe.

_____

_____ 3. <u>Minutes</u> are divided in smaller units called <u>degrees</u>.

_____

_____ 4. Lines of <u>latitude</u> meet at the poles.

_____

_____ 5. The <u>equator</u> divides the globe into a Northern <u>Hemisphere</u> and a
Southern Hemisphere.

_____

_____ 6. The location of the <u>prime meridian</u> is 0°.

_____

_____ 7. Lines of <u>latitude</u> run in parallel east–west paths around the globe.

_____

_____ 8. Mapmakers use a <u>compass rose</u> to show our round planet on a flat
map.

_____

_____ 9. The seven large landmasses on Earth's surface are called <u>continents</u>.

_____

The Physical World

MAIN IDEAS
1. Earth's movement affects the amount of energy we receive from the sun.
2. Earth's seasons are caused by the planet's tilt.

Key Terms and Places

solar energy energy from the sun

rotation one complete spin of Earth on its axis

revolution one trip of Earth around the sun

tropics regions close to the equator

Lesson Summary
EARTH'S MOVEMENT

Energy from the sun, or **solar energy,** is necessary for life on Earth. It helps plants grow and provides light and heat. Several factors affect the amount of solar energy Earth receives. These are rotation, revolution, tilt, and latitude.

Earth's axis is an imaginary rod running from the North Pole to the South Pole. Earth spins around on its axis. One complete **rotation** takes 24 hours, or one day. It looks as if the sun is moving, but it is really the planet's rotation that creates that effect.

Solar energy reaches only half of the planet at a time. The half that faces the sun receives light and warmth, creating daytime. In the half that faces away from the sun, it is nighttime, which is darker and cooler.

As Earth rotates, it also moves around the sun. It takes Earth a year, 365 1/4 days, to complete one **revolution** around the sun. Every four years, an extra day is added to February. This makes up for the extra quarter of a day.

Earth's axis is tilted, not straight up and down. At different times of year, some locations tilt toward

> **List the four factors that affect the amount of solar energy Earth receives.**
> _____
> _____

> **What would happen if Earth did not rotate?**
> _____
> _____
> _____

> **Underline the sentence that describes Earth's revolution around the sun.**

the sun. They get more solar energy than locations tilted away from the sun.

Latitude refers to imaginary lines that run east and west around the planet, north and south of Earth's equator. Areas near the equator receive direct rays from the sun all year and have warm temperatures. Higher latitudes receive fewer direct rays and are cooler.

> **Why are areas near the equator warmer than those in higher latitudes?**
>
> _____
>
> _____

THE SEASONS

Many locations on Earth have four seasons: winter, spring, summer, and fall. These are based on temperature and how long the days are.

The seasons change because of the tilt of Earth's axis. In summer, the Northern Hemisphere is tilted toward the sun. It receives more solar energy than during the winter, when it is tilted away from the sun.

Because Earth's axis is tilted, the hemispheres have opposite seasons. Winter in the Northern Hemisphere is summer in the Southern Hemisphere. During the fall and spring, the poles point neither toward nor away from the sun. In spring, temperatures rise and days become longer as summer approaches. In fall, the opposite occurs.

> **What would the seasons be like in the Northern and Southern Hemispheres if Earth's axis weren't tilted?**
>
> _____
>
> _____

In some regions, the seasons are tied to rainfall instead of temperature. One of these regions, close to the equator, is the **tropics.** There, winds bring heavy rains from June to October. The weather turns dry in the tropics from November to January.

> **Circle the name of the warm region near the equator.**

CHALLENGE ACTIVITY

Critical Thinking: Draw Conclusions Imagine that you are a travel agent. One of your clients is planning a trip to Argentina in June, and another is planning a trip to Chicago in August. What kinds of clothing would you suggest they pack for their trips and why?

Lesson 1, *continued*

latitude	rainfall	revolution
rotation	solar energy	tropics

DIRECTIONS On the line provided before each statement, write **T** if a statement is true and **F** if a statement is false. If the statement is false, write the term from the word bank that would make the statement correct on the line after each sentence.

_____ 1. The hemisphere of Earth that is tilted away from the sun receives less direct <u>rainfall</u> than the other hemisphere receives.

_____

_____ 2. An umbrella might be more useful to a person in the <u>tropics</u> than a winter coat.

_____

_____ 3. Earth's path, or orbit, around the sun is its <u>rotation</u>.

_____

_____ 4. One <u>revolution</u> of Earth takes 24 hours.

_____

_____ 5. Plants in an area of high latitude receive less direct solar energy during the year than plants at a <u>lower latitude</u> because they are farther from the equator.

_____

The Physical World

Lesson 2

MAIN IDEAS
1. Salt water and freshwater make up Earth's water supply.
2. In the water cycle, water circulates from Earth's surface to the atmosphere and back again.
3. Water plays an important role in people's lives.

Key Terms and Places

freshwater water without salt

glaciers large areas of slow-moving ice

surface water water that is stored in Earth's streams, rivers, and lakes

precipitation water that falls to Earth's surface as rain, snow, sleet, or hail

groundwater water found below Earth's surface

water vapor water that occurs in the air as an invisible gas

water cycle the circulation of water from Earth's surface to the atmosphere and back

Lesson Summary
EARTH'S WATER SUPPLY

Approximately two-thirds of Earth's surface is covered with water. There are two kinds of water: salt water and **freshwater.** About 97 percent of Earth's water is salt water. Most of it is in the oceans, seas, gulfs, bays, and straits. Some lakes, such as the Great Salt Lake in Utah, also contain salt water.

> Circle the places where we find salt water.

Salt water cannot be used for drinking. Only freshwater is safe to drink. Freshwater is found in lakes and rivers and stored underground. Much is frozen in the ice found in **glaciers,** as well as the Arctic and Antarctic regions.

> Underline the places where we find freshwater.

One form of freshwater is **surface water.** This is stored in streams, lakes, and rivers. Streams form when **precipitation** falls to Earth as rain, snow, sleet, or hail. These streams then flow into larger

Guided Reading Workbook

streams and rivers. Less than 1 percent of Earth's water supply comes from surface water.

Most freshwater is stored underground. **Groundwater** bubbles to the surface in springs or can be reached by digging deep holes, or wells.

THE WATER CYCLE

Water is the only substance on Earth that can take the form of a liquid, gas, or solid. In its solid form, water is snow and ice. Liquid water is rain or water found in lakes and rivers. **Water vapor** is an invisible form of water in the air.

> **Underline the words that define water vapor.**

Water is always moving. When water on Earth's surface heats up, it evaporates and turns into water vapor. It then rises from Earth into the atmosphere. When it cools down, it changes from water vapor to liquid. Droplets of water form clouds. When they get heavier, these droplets fall to Earth as precipitation. This process of evaporation and precipitation is called the **water cycle.**

> **What are the two main processes of the water cycle?**
> _____
> _____

Some precipitation is absorbed into the soil as groundwater. The rest flows into streams, rivers, and oceans.

WATER AND PEOPLE

Water is crucial for survival. It is a problem when people lack freshwater because of shortages. Shortages are caused by overuse and by drought, when there is little or no precipitation for a long time. Water shortages can lead to less food. Another problem is pollution. Chemicals and waste can pollute water, making it dangerous to use. Lack of water can lead to conflicts when countries fight over who controls water supplies.

> **Circle two words that are causes of water shortages.**

Water can affect the physical environment. For example, sinkholes are formed when water dissolves the surface layer of the ground. Heavy rains can cause flooding that damages property and threatens lives.

> **How does water cause sinkholes?**
> _____
> _____

Water has many benefits, too. It quenches our thirst and allows us to have food to eat. Flowing water is an important source of electric energy. Water also provides recreation, making our lives richer and more enjoyable.

Water is essential for life on Earth. Cities and even nations are now working together to manage freshwater supplies. For example, Central Florida Water Initiative works with businesses and many other groups to protect the water resources in that region.

> **How does the Central Florida Water Initiative help water supplies?**
> _____
> _____
> _____
> _____
> _____

CHALLENGE ACTIVITY

Critical Thinking: Solve Problems You are campaigning for public office. Write a speech describing three actions you plan to take to protect supplies of freshwater.

DIRECTIONS Read each sentence, and fill in the blank with the word in the word pair that best completes the sentence.

1. Some freshwater is locked in Earth's _____. (**water vapor/ glaciers**)

2. Less than 1 percent of Earth's water supply comes from _____ stored in streams, rivers, and lakes. (**surface water/ groundwater**)

3. Water can be a solid (ice), a liquid, or a gas called _____. (**precipitation/water vapor**)

4. The water brought to the surface from deep holes is _____. (**freshwater/groundwater**)

5. _____ is water that falls from clouds as rain, snow, sleet, or hail. (**Precipitation/Water cycle**)

6. Surface water is a form of _____. (**glacier/freshwater**)

freshwater	glacier	groundwater	precipitation
surface water	water cycle	water vapor	

DIRECTIONS Use the terms from the word bank to write a summary of what you learned in the lesson.

_____

_____

_____

_____

_____

_____

_____

The Physical World

Lesson 3

MAIN IDEAS
1. Earth's surface is covered by many different landforms.
2. Forces below Earth's surface build up our landforms.
3. Forces on the planet's surface shape Earth's landforms.
4. Landforms influence people's lives and culture.

Key Terms and Places

landforms shapes on Earth's surface, such as hills or mountains

continents large landmasses

plate tectonics theory suggesting that Earth's surface is divided into more than 12 slow-moving plates, or pieces of Earth's crust

lava magma, or liquid rock, that reaches Earth's surface

earthquakes sudden, violent movements of Earth's crust

weathering process of breaking rock into smaller pieces

erosion movement of sediment from one location to another

alluvial deposition process by which rivers create floodplains and deltas when they flood and deposit sediment along the banks

Lesson Summary
LANDFORMS

Geographers study **landforms** such as mountains, valleys, plains, islands, and peninsulas. They study how landforms are made and how they affect human activity.

> **Give two examples of landforms.**
> _____
> _____
> _____

FORCES BELOW EARTH'S SURFACE

The planet is made up of three layers. Below the top layer, or crust, is a layer of liquid. Earth's center, the third layer, is a solid core. The planet has seven **continents,** large landmasses that are part of Earth's crust. Earth's crust is divided into 12 pieces, called plates. These plates move very slowly. Geographers have a theory called **plate tectonics,** which explains how plates' movements shape our landforms.

> **What are plates?**
> _____
> _____

Energy from deep inside the planet makes the plates move at different speeds and in different directions. As they move, they shift the continents. This is known as continental drift. Plates move in three ways: they collide, they separate, and they slide past each other.

The energy of colliding plates creates new landforms. When two ocean plates collide, they may form deep valleys on the ocean's floor. When ocean plates collide with continental plates, mountain ranges are formed. Mountains are also created when two continental plates collide.

When plates separate, usually on the ocean floor, they cause gaps in the planet's crust. Magma, or liquid rock, rises through the cracks as **lava.** As it cools, it forms underwater mountains or ridges. Sometimes these mountains rise above the surface of the water and form islands.

Plates can also slide past each other. When they grind past each other, they cause **earthquakes.** Earthquakes often happen along faults, or breaks in Earth's crust.

> **Underline the sentence that lists the three different ways in which Earth's plates move.**

> **Underline what happens when two ocean plates collide with one another.**

> **What causes earthquakes?**
> _____
> _____

PROCESSES ON EARTH'S SURFACE

As landforms are created, other forces work to wear them away. **Weathering** breaks larger rocks into smaller rocks. Changes in temperature can cause cracks in rocks. Water then gets into the cracks, expands as it freezes, and breaks the rocks. Rocks eventually break down into smaller pieces called sediment.

Another force that wears down landforms is **erosion.** Erosion takes place when sediment is moved by water, ice, and wind. The most common cause of erosion is water. Rivers can flood their banks and deposit sediment, a process called **alluvial deposition.** This creates floodplains and river deltas.

> **Circle the three elements that cause erosion.**

LANDFORMS INFLUENCE LIFE

Landforms influence where people live. For example, people might want to farm in an area with good soil and water. Mineral deposits may create jobs in mining. People also change landforms in many ways. For example, engineers build tunnels through mountains to make roads. Farmers build terraces on steep hillsides.

CHALLENGE ACTIVITY

Critical Thinking: Draw Inferences Find out about a landform in your area that was changed by people. Write a report explaining why and how it was changed.

DIRECTIONS Look at each set of four vocabulary terms. On the line provided, write the letter of the term that does not relate to the others.

_____ 1. a. erosion   b. weathering   c. landform   d. continent

_____ 2. a. lava   b. alluvial depositions   c. earthquake   d. plate tectonics

alluvial depositions	continents	earthquake	erosion
landforms	lava	plate tectonics	weathering

DIRECTIONS Answer each question by writing a sentence that contains at least one word from the word bank.

3. What are two ways that the movements of tectonic plates affect Earth?

_____

_____

4. What is the most common cause of erosion?

_____

_____

DIRECTIONS Choose four of the terms from the word bank. Look
them up in a dictionary. Write the definition of the word that is
closest to the definition that is used in your textbook.

_____

_____

_____

_____

The Physical World

MAIN IDEAS

1. While weather is short term, climate is a region's average weather over a long period.
2. The amount of sun at a given location is affected by Earth's tilt, movement, and shape.
3. Wind and water move heat around Earth, affecting how warm or wet a place is.
4. Mountains influence temperature and precipitation.

Key Terms and Places

weather short-term changes in the air for a given place and time

climate region's average weather conditions over a long period

prevailing winds winds that blow in the same direction over large areas of Earth

ocean currents large streams of surface seawater

front place where two air masses of different temperature or moisture content meet

Lesson Summary
UNDERSTANDING WEATHER AND CLIMATE

Weather is the temperature and precipitation at a specific time and place. **Climate** is a region's average weather over a long period of time. Climate and weather are affected by the sun, location on Earth, wind, water, and mountains.

> Circle the forces that affect climate and weather.

SUN AND LOCATION

The parts of Earth tilted toward the sun get more solar energy than the parts tilted away from the sun. This changes during the year, creating seasons. While some locations are having a warm summer, others are having a cold winter.

Energy from the sun falls more directly on the equator, so that area has warm temperatures all year. It gets colder as you move away from the low latitude of the equator. The coldest areas are at the poles, the highest latitudes.

> Underline the sentence that explains why the equator has warm temperatures year-round.

Guided Reading Workbook

Lesson 4, *continued*

WIND AND WATER

Heat from the sun moves around Earth, partly because of winds. Winds blow in great streams around the planet. They are caused by the rising and sinking of air. Cold air sinks and warm air rises. More air flows in to take the place of the air that has moved.

Prevailing winds are winds that blow in the same direction over large areas of Earth. Hot air rises at the equator and flows toward the poles. Cold air at the poles sinks and moves toward the equator. The planet's rotation curves the winds east or west. Prevailing winds control an area's climate. They make regions warmer or colder, drier or wetter. They pick up moisture from water and dry out as they pass over land.

Large bodies of water also affect temperature. **Ocean currents** are large streams of surface water that carry warm water from the equator toward the poles and cold water from the poles toward the equator. Water heats and cools more slowly than land. Therefore, water helps to moderate the temperature of nearby land, keeping it from getting very hot or very cold.

Storms happen when two large bodies of air collide. A **front** is a place where two air masses with different temperatures or moisture collide. In the United States and other regions, warm and cold air masses meet often, causing severe weather. These can include thunderstorms, blizzards, and tornadoes. Tornadoes are twisting funnels of air that touch the ground. Hurricanes are large tropical storms that form over water. They bring strong winds and heavy rain. Tornadoes and hurricanes are both dangerous and destructive.

What causes wind?
_____
_____

Which heats and cools more slowly—land or water?
_____

What often happens when warm and cold air masses meet?
_____
_____
_____

Lesson 4, *continued*

MOUNTAINS

Mountains also affect climate. The higher areas
are colder than the lower elevations. Warm air
blowing against a mountainside rises and cools.
Clouds form, and precipitation falls on the side
facing the wind. However, there is little moisture
on the other side of the mountain. This effect
creates a rain shadow, a dry area on the side of
the mountain facing away from the direction of
the wind.

> **Which areas are colder—
> lower or higher elevations?**
> _____

CHALLENGE ACTIVITY

Critical Thinking: Sequence Write a short
description of the process leading up to the
formation of a rain shadow. Draw and label a
picture to go with your description.

Guided Reading Workbook

DIRECTIONS On the line provided before each statement, write **T** if a statement is true and **F** if a statement is false. If the statement is false, write the correct term on the line after each sentence that makes the sentence true.

_____ 1. <u>Climate</u> describes the atmospheric conditions in a place at a specific time. It changes rapidly.

_____

_____

_____ 2. <u>Precipitation</u> falls on the side of a mountain that faces the wind.

_____

_____ 3. <u>Fronts</u> may form when air masses of different temperatures come together.

_____

_____ 4. <u>Ocean currents</u> affect the temperature of nearby land.

_____

_____ 5. Warm air at the <u>poles</u> rises, causing prevailing winds that travel toward the <u>equator</u>.

_____

_____

| climate | equator | front | ocean currents |
| poles | precipitation | prevailing winds | weather |

DIRECTIONS Choose five of the vocabulary words from the word bank. On a separate sheet of paper, use these words to write a summary of what you learned in the lesson.

_____

_____

_____

_____

_____

The Physical World

MAIN IDEAS
1. Geographers use temperature, precipitation, and plant life to identify climate zones.
2. Tropical climates are wet and warm, while dry climates receive little or no rain.
3. Temperate climates have the most seasonal change.
4. Polar climates are cold and dry, while highland climates change with elevation.

Key Terms and Places

monsoons winds that shift direction with the seasons and create wet and dry periods

savannas areas of tall grasses and scattered trees and shrubs

steppes semidry grasslands or prairies

permafrost permanently frozen layers of soil

Lesson Summary
MAJOR CLIMATE ZONES

We can divide Earth into five climate zones: tropical, temperate, polar, dry, and highland. Tropical climates appear near the equator, temperate climates are found in the middle latitudes, and polar climates occur near the poles. Dry and highland climates can appear at different latitudes.

> Underline the names of the five climate zones.

TROPICAL AND DRY CLIMATES

Humid tropical climates occur near the equator. Some are hot and humid throughout the year. Rain forests need this type of climate to thrive and support thousands of species. Other tropical areas have **monsoons**—winds that shift directions and create wet and dry seasons.

Moving away from the equator, we find tropical savanna climates. A long, hot dry season is followed by short periods of rain. This climate supports **savannas,** an area of tall grasses and scattered trees and shrubs.

> What happens when monsoon winds change direction?
>
> _____
>
> _____

Guided Reading Workbook

Lesson 5, *continued*

Deserts are hot and dry. At night, the dry air cools quickly; desert nights can be cold. Only a few tough plants and animals survive in a desert. Sometimes **steppes**—semidry grasslands—are found near deserts.

TEMPERATE CLIMATES

Temperate, or mild, climates occur in the middle latitudes. In this climate, weather often changes quickly when cold and warm air masses meet. Most temperate regions have four distinct seasons, with hot summers and cold winters.

A Mediterranean climate has hot, sunny summers and mild, wet winters. They occur near the ocean, and the climate is mostly pleasant. People like to vacation in these climates. Only small, scattered trees survive in these areas.

East coasts near the tropics have humid subtropical climates because winds bring moisture from the ocean. They have hot, wet summers and mild winters, with storms year-round. Marine west coast climates occur farther north on the west coast. They also get moisture from the sea, which causes mild summers and rainy winters. Inland or east-coast regions in the upper-middle latitudes often have humid continental climates. These have short, hot summers, a mild spring and fall, and long, cold winters.

POLAR AND HIGHLAND CLIMATES

There are three polar climates. Subarctic climate occurs south of the Arctic Ocean. Winters are long and very cold; summers are cool. There is enough precipitation to support forests. At the same latitude near the coasts, tundra climate is also cold, but too dry for trees to survive. In parts of the tundra, soil is frozen as **permafrost.**

> **Circle the name of the climate that can have four distinct seasons.**

> **What do people typically like to do in Mediterranean climates?**
>
> _____

> **What kind of climate do you live in?**
>
> _____
>
> _____

> **Can there be forests in subarctic climates? Explain.**
>
> _____
>
> _____
>
> _____

Ice cap climates are the coldest on Earth. There is little precipitation and little vegetation. Even though it is a harsh place, penguins and polar bears live there.

Highland, or mountain, climate changes with elevation. As you go up a mountain, the climate may go from tropical to polar.

CHALLENGE ACTIVITY

Critical Thinking: Compare and Contrast

Create a table showing the differences and similarities between any two types of climate.

DIRECTIONS Write three words or phrases that describe the term.

1. savanna _____

2. steppe _____

3. monsoon _____

_____

4. permafrost _____

_____

DIRECTIONS Look at each set of four terms. On the line provided, write the letter of the term that does not relate to the others.

_____ 5. a. humid continental
     b. marine west coast
     c. Mediterranean
     d. steppe

_____ 6. a. subarctic
     b. tundra
     c. desert
     d. permafrost

_____ 7. a. monsoon
     b. muggy
     c. prairies
     d. rain forest

_____ 8. a. forest
     b. steppes
     c. savannas
     d. grassland

Guided Reading Workbook

The Physical World

MAIN IDEAS
1. The environment and life are interconnected and exist in a fragile balance.
2. Soils play an important role in the environment.

Key Terms and Places

environment plant or animal's surroundings

ecosystem any place where plants and animals depend upon each other and their environment for survival

biome area much larger than an ecosystem and possibly made up of several ecosystems

habitat place where a plant or animal lives

extinct to die out completely

humus decayed plant or animal matter

desertification slow process of losing soil fertility and plant life

Lesson Summary
THE ENVIRONMENT AND LIFE

Plants and animals cannot live just anywhere. They must have an **environment,** or surroundings, that suits them. Climate, land features, and water are all part of a living thing's environment. Plants and animals adapt to specific environments. For example, kangaroo rats do not need to drink much water and are adapted to a desert environment.

An **ecosystem** is the connection between a particular environment and the plants and animals that live there. They all depend on each other for survival. Ecosystems can be as small as a garden pond or as large as a forest. **Biomes** are much larger than ecosystems. They may contain several ecosystems.

Each part of an ecosystem fills a certain role in a cycle. For example, the sun provides energy to plants, which use it to make food. These plants

> Which is larger, a biome or an ecosystem?
>
> _____

> Underline the sentences that describe the steps in an ecosystem's cycle.

Guided Reading Workbook

Lesson 6, *continued*

then provide energy and food to other plants and animals. When these life forms die, their bodies break down and give nutrients to the soil so more plants can grow.

A small change in one part of an ecosystem can affect the whole system. Many natural events and human actions affect ecosystems and the habitats in them. A **habitat** is the place where a plant or animal lives. Natural events include forest fires, disease, and climate changes.

> **Circle the natural events that can affect ecosystems.**

Human actions such as clearing land and polluting can destroy habitats. For example, people are clearing Earth's rain forests for farmland, lumber, and other reasons. As a result, these diverse habitats are being lost. If a change to the environment is extreme, a species might become **extinct,** or die out completely.

> **What two human actions are destroying habitats?**
>
> _____
>
> _____

Many countries are passing laws to protect the environment. Although these laws do not please everyone, they can have good results. The U.S. Endangered Species Act of 1973 has saved 47 species from becoming extinct.

SOIL AND THE ENVIRONMENT

An environment's soil affects which plants can grow there. Fertile soils have lots of humus and minerals. **Humus** is decayed plant or animal matter.

> **Circle two things found in fertile soil.**

Soils can lose fertility from erosion when wind or water sweeps topsoil away. Soil can also lose fertility from planting the same crops repeatedly. When soil becomes worn out and can no longer support plants, **desertification** can occur. The spread of desert conditions causes problems in many parts of the world.

Guided Reading Workbook

CHALLENGE ACTIVITY

Critical Thinking: Draw Inferences Consider the interconnections in your environment. As you go through a normal day, keep a list of the sources you rely on for energy, food, and water.

DIRECTIONS Read each sentence and fill in the blank with the word in the word pair that best completes the sentence.

1. Organic material called _____ enriches the soil. **(biomes/humus)**

2. When soil gets worn out, it may lead to _____. **(erosion/desertification)**

3. A rainforest is a/an _____, which can contain many different ecosystems. **(biome/environment)**

4. If there are too many changes in conditions, a species may die out, or become _____. **(consequence/extinct)**

5. Plants and animals are adapted to the specific _____ where they live. **(environment/humus)**

6. Laws have been passed to protect _____ from human activities that could destroy them. **(habitats/nutrients)**

biome	desertification	ecosystem	environment
erosion	extinct	fertile soils	habitat
humus	nutrients		

DIRECTIONS Choose five of the words from the word bank. On a separate sheet of paper, use these words to write a poem or story that relates to the lesson.

The Physical World

MAIN IDEAS
1. Earth provides valuable resources for our use.
2. Energy resources provide fuel, heat, and electricity.
3. Mineral resources include metals, rocks, and salt.
4. Resources shape people's lives and countries' wealth.

Key Terms and Places

natural resource any material in nature that people use and value

renewable resources resources that can be replaced naturally

nonrenewable resources resources that cannot be replaced

deforestation loss of forestland

reforestation planting trees to replace lost forestland

fossil fuels nonrenewable resources formed from the remains of ancient plants and animals

hydroelectric power production of electricity by moving water

Lesson Summary
EARTH'S VALUABLE RESOURCES

Anything in nature that people use and value is a **natural resource.** Earth's most important natural resources are air, water, soils, forests, and minerals. We often use these resources to make something new. For example, we make paper from trees. Resources such as trees are called **renewable resources** because another tree can grow in its place. Resources that cannot be replaced, such as oil, are called **nonrenewable resources.**

Even though forests are renewable, we can cut down trees faster than they can grow. For example, in Brazil, illegal logging is destroying rain forests. The loss of forests is called **deforestation.** When we plant trees to replace lost forests, we call it **reforestation.**

> Circle the natural resources that are most important.

> Underline the sentence that explains why there is deforestation even though trees are renewable resources.

ENERGY RESOURCES

Most of our energy comes from **fossil fuels,** which are formed from the remains of ancient living things. These include coal, oil, and natural gas.

We use coal mostly for electricity, but it causes air pollution. Since there is a lot of coal, people are trying to find cleaner ways to use it. Another fossil fuel is petroleum, or oil. It is used to make different kinds of fuels and heating oil. Oil can also be turned into plastics, cosmetics, and other products.

> **Circle four products made from oil.**

We depend on fossil fuels for much of our energy, so they are very valuable. However, fuel from oil can cause air and land pollution. Oil spills pollute the water and hurt wildlife. The cleanest fossil fuel is natural gas, which is used mainly for cooking and heating.

> **What is the cleanest-burning fossil fuel?**
> _____

Many scientists believe that burning fossil fuels causes climate change. They believe Earth's temperature is rising. More than 190 countries have signed the Kyoto Protocol, an agreement adopted in 1997 that sets targets to reduce emissions from burning fossil fuels. They hope this will reduce pollution from fossil fuels.

Renewable energy resources include **hydroelectric power**—the creation of electricity from the motion and movement of running water. This is accomplished mainly by building dams on rivers. Other renewable energy sources are wind and solar energy. Wind produces electricity with windmills, and solar energy uses the power of sunlight to generate electricity.

> **Underline the sentence that explains why some people do not want to use nuclear energy.**

One nonrenewable resource is nuclear energy. This type of energy is created by splitting atoms, small particles of matter. Although nuclear energy does not pollute the air, it does produce dangerous waste material that must be stored for thousands of years.

MINERAL RESOURCES

Like oil, minerals are nonrenewable and can be very valuable. Minerals include metals, salt, rocks, and gemstones. Minerals like iron are used to make steel. We make buildings from stone and window glass from quartz. We also use minerals to make jewelry, coins, and many other common objects. Recycling minerals like aluminum in cans can make these resources last longer.

List four uses of minerals.
_____
_____
_____

RESOURCES AND PEOPLE

Natural resources vary from place to place. Some places are rich in natural resources. Resources such as fertile farmland, forests, and oil have helped the United States become a powerful country with a strong economy. Places with fewer resources do not have the wealth and choices of Americans.

Some countries use their resources to trade for resources they do not have. For example, many Middle Eastern countries are rich in oil but do not have water to grow food. They must use their oil profits to import food. Some of these countries are part of The Organization of the Petroleum Exporting Countries (OPEC). This group of 13 countries helps control oil prices so oil-producing countries can use the wealth to buy products they need.

What is OPEC?
_____
_____
_____

CHALLENGE ACTIVITY

Critical Thinking: Draw Inferences Write a short essay explaining how America's natural resources have helped it become a powerful country.

deforestation	electricity	fossil fuels
hydroelectric power	natural resources	nonrenewable resources
petroleum	reforestation	renewable resources

DIRECTIONS Answer each question by writing a sentence that contains at least one word from the word bank.

1. What problem is caused when trees are cut down faster than they can grow back? How can this problem be fixed?

_____

_____

_____

2. What are some examples of energy resources we can use instead of fossil fuels? List two types, and explain how they work.

_____

_____

_____

3. What may happen to a country that has only a few natural resources?

_____

_____

_____

DIRECTIONS Write three examples of each term.

4. natural resources _____

5. renewable resources _____

6. fossil fuels _____

The Human World

MAIN IDEAS
1. Culture is the set of beliefs, goals, and practices that a group of people share.
2. The world includes many different culture groups.
3. New ideas and events lead to changes in culture.
4. The features common to all cultures are called cultural universals.
5. All societies have social institutions that help their groups survive.
6. Every culture expresses itself creatively in a variety of ways.
7. All societies use technology to help shape and control the environment.

Key Terms and Places

culture set of beliefs, values, and practices a group of people have in common

culture trait activity or behavior in which people often take part

culture region area in which people have many shared culture traits

ethnic group group of people who share a common culture and ancestry

multicultural society society that includes a variety of cultures in the same area

cultural diffusion spread of culture traits from one region to another

cultural universals features societies have developed that are common to all cultures

social institutions organized patterns of belief and behavior that focus on meeting societal needs

heritage wealth of cultural elements that has been passed down over generations

universal theme message about life or human nature that is meaningful across time and in all places

technology use of knowledge, tools, and skills to solve problems

Lesson Summary
WHAT IS CULTURE?

Culture is the set of beliefs, values, and practices a group of people have in common. Everything in day-to-day life is part of culture, including language, religion, clothes, music, and foods.

> Underline the sentence that lists some examples of culture.

People everywhere share certain basic cultural features, such as forming a government, educating children, and creating art or music. However, people practice these things in different ways, making each culture unique.

Culture traits are activities or behaviors in which people often take part, such as language and popular sports. People share some culture traits but not others. For example, people eat using forks, chopsticks, or their fingers in different areas.

Cultures are often passed from one generation to the next. They may be based on family traditions, like holiday customs, or laws and moral codes passed down within a society. Other factors that influence how cultures develop include immigrants moving to a new country, historical events, and the environment where people live and work.

> What are three factors that influence how a culture develops?
>
> _____
> _____
> _____
> _____
> _____

CULTURE GROUPS

There are thousands of different cultures in the world. People who share a culture are part of a culture group that may be based on things like age or religion.

A **culture region** is an area in which people have many shared culture traits such as language, religion, or lifestyle. A cultural region can extend over many countries. For example, most people in North Africa and Southeast Asia share the Arabic language and Muslim religion. Some countries, like Japan, may be a single culture region. Other countries may have several different culture regions.

> Circle the country that is also a single cultural region.

Often, cultural regions within a country are based on ethnic groups. An **ethnic group** is a group of people who often share cultural traits like language, foods, or religion. Sometimes, though, people who have the same religion are still in different ethnic groups, and different ethnic groups can have different religious beliefs.

Countries or areas with many ethnic groups are **multicultural societies**. Multiculturalism can create an interesting mix of ideas and practices, but it can also lead to conflict. In Canada, French Canadians want to separate from the rest of Canada. In Rwanda, a 1990s ethnic conflict led to extreme violence. In some countries, like the U.S., different ethnic groups cooperate and live side by side. That is because so many people have migrated to the country from all over the world and they celebrate their ethnic heritage.

Why are different ethnic groups likely to cooperate in the U.S.?

_____

_____

_____

_____

_____

_____

CHANGES IN CULTURE

Cultures change constantly, sometimes quickly and sometimes over years. Two main causes of change are new ideas or contact with other societies. New technology like motion pictures and the Internet have changed how people spend their time and how they communicate. Contact with another culture may cause both to change. For example, both Spanish and Native American cultures changed when the Spanish arrived in the Americas.

Underline two sentences that describe examples that cause cultures to change.

Cultural diffusion is the spread of culture traits from one part of the world to another. It occurs when people bring their culture to another country. This happens when people immigrate or when people trade goods in different regions. People also move to other countries to escape conflicts and wars.

What are three ways cultural diffusion occurs?

_____

_____

_____

_____

WHAT DO ALL CULTURES HAVE IN COMMON?

All people have the same basic needs, such as food, clothing, and shelter. Geographers believe that all societies have developed **cultural universals**—specific features that meet basic needs. Three important cultural universals are social institutions, creative expressions, and technology.

Lesson 1, *continued*

BASIC SOCIAL INSTITUTIONS

Social institutions are organized patterns of belief and behavior that focus on meeting the needs of the society's members. The most basic social institutions are family, education, religion, government, and economy. These institutions are shaped by a group's cultural values and principles, which vary from culture to culture.

Family is the most basic social institution. The family cares for the children and provides support. They also teach the culture's values and traditions, often through elders. Family members may live together under one roof or be part of a whole village. Societies also pass on values and knowledge through education. For example, U.S. schools teach students how to be good citizens.

Although there are many religions, they all help explain the meanings of life and death and the difference between good and bad behavior. Religions' practices and traditions make them the source of many cultures' beliefs and attitudes. In all world regions, religion has inspired great works of devotion, including art and architecture.

Government is a system of leaders and laws that help people live together in their community or country. It defines standards, protects property and people's rights, and helps settle conflicts. A society's economy is its system of using resources to meet needs. Economic principles guide the way a nation does business.

CREATIVE EXPRESSIONS

Societies, like individuals, express themselves creatively. There are three main types of creative expression. Performing arts include music, theater, and dance. Visual arts include painting, sculpture, and architecture. Literary arts are related in words and language such as literature and folklore.

> **Circle the most basic social institutions.**

> **What do all religions have in common?**
> _____
> _____
> _____
> _____
> _____
> _____
> _____
> _____

> **What are the three main types of creative expressions?**
> _____
> _____

Creative expressions reflect a specific **heritage,** or wealth of cultural elements that have been passed down through generations. Creative expressions also express individual choices, as well as universal themes. A **universal theme** is a message about life that is true throughout time and in all places. This is true of art masterpieces that continue to speak to people everywhere.

SCIENCE AND TECHNOLOGY

Technology is the use of knowledge, tools, and skills to solve problems. Science is a way of understanding the world through observation and the testing of ideas. Technology is often developed to solve problems posed by the environment we live in. Its use is influenced by factors such as politics, economics, and belief systems. For example, some countries restrict Internet use. Advances in science and technology have made life easier and have changed society. Vaccines have prevented diseases. Electricity and computers have transformed daily life and work for most of the world's people.

What are three examples of technology that have changed lives?
_____
_____
_____

CHALLENGE ACTIVITY

Critical Thinking: Make Inferences Consider all of the parts of your culture that have been influenced by other cultures. During a normal day, keep a list of all the things you use or do that you think have been influenced by other cultures.

DIRECTIONS On the line provided before each statement, write **T** if a statement is true and **F** if a statement is false. If the statement is false, write the term that would make the statement correct on the line after each sentence.

_____ 1. The language you speak and the sports you play are examples of <u>culture traits</u>.

_____

_____ 2. <u>Cultural universals</u> can create an interesting mix of ideas but sometimes can lead to conflict.

_____

_____ 3. When more than one cultural group lives in an area, this is called a <u>cultural diffusion</u>.

_____

_____ 4. A great masterpiece of art, music, or literature has a <u>universal theme</u>.

_____

_____ 5. Family, education, religion, and government are all examples of basic <u>ethnic groups</u>.

_____

_____ 6. A <u>culture region</u> can be one country or many countries.

_____

cultural diffusion	culture region	culture trait	cultural universal
ethnic group	multicultural society	social institutions	universal theme

DIRECTIONS On a separate sheet of paper, use four of the terms from the word bank to write a summary of what you learned in the lesson.

The Human World

Lesson 2

MAIN IDEAS
1. The study of population patterns helps geographers learn about the world.
2. Population statistics and trends are important measures of population change.

Key Terms and Places

population total number of people in a given area

population density measure of the number of people living in an area, usually expressed as persons per square mile or square kilometer

birthrate annual number of births per 1,000 people

migration process of moving from one place to live in another

Lesson Summary
POPULATION PATTERNS

Population is the total number of people in a given area. Population patterns show how human populations change over time and tell us much about our world.

Population density is a measure of the number of people living in an area, expressed as persons per square mile or square kilometer. The more people per square mile, the more crowded it is and more limited space is. In places with a high density, land is expensive, buildings are taller, and roads are more crowded. However, there are usually more resources and jobs. Places with low density have more space, less traffic, and more open land, but goods and services may be in short supply.

Areas that are less populated are usually difficult to live in. They may be deserts or mountains or have harsh climates that make survival harder. Large clusters of people tend to live in places with good agricultural climates, plenty of vegetation, minerals, and reliable water sources.

Underline the two sentences that describe the effects of high population density on a place.

What are conditions like in areas of low population density?

_____
_____

Often, desirable areas attract so many people that there is too much demand for resources. This can change the environment. For example, as regions make room for more people, the amount of available farmland shrinks and local ecosystems are in danger. There is more demand for food and water, which can lead to shortages.

What are three problems caused by population growth?
_____
_____
_____

POPULATION CHANGE

The number of people living in an area affects jobs, housing, schools, medical care, available food, and many other things. Geographers track population changes by studying important statistics, movement of people, and population trends.

Three statistics are important to studying a country's population over time. **Birthrate** is the annual number of births per 1,000 people. Death rate is the annual number of deaths per 1,000 people. The rate of natural increase is the rate at which a population is changing. It is determined by subtracting the death rate from the birthrate.

Underline the sentence that tells how to calculate the rate of natural increase.

A population is shrinking if the death rate is higher than the birthrate. In most countries, the birthrate is higher than the death rate, and those populations are growing. The United States has a low rate of natural increase and is growing slowly. Other countries, like Mali, have a high natural increase that could double its population in 20 years.

High rates can make it hard for countries to develop economically because they need to provide jobs, education, and medical care for a growing population. Many governments track population patterns so they can better address the needs of their citizens.

Migration is a common cause of population change. It is the process of moving from one place to live in another. People may be pushed to leave a place because of problems there, such as war,

Why do high rates of natural increase make it hard for a country to develop economically?
_____
_____
_____
_____

famine, drought, or lack of jobs. Other people
may be pulled to move to find political or
religious freedom or economic opportunities in a
new place.

   For thousands of years, Earth's population
growth was slow and steady. In the last 200 years,
it has grown very rapidly due to better health
care and improved food production. Currently,
many industrialized countries have low rates of
natural increase, while countries that are less
industrialized often have very high growth. Fast
growth can put a strain on resources, jobs, and
government aid.

Why has the world's population grown faster in the last 200 years?
_____
_____
_____

CHALLENGE ACTIVITY

Critical Thinking: Identify Cause and Effect Find
out the population density of your city or town.
Write down ways that this density affects your life
and the lives of others.

DIRECTIONS Read each sentence, and fill in the blank with the word in the word pair that best completes the sentence.

1. The study of human _____ focuses on the total number of people in a given area. (**population/migration**)

2. Studying the _____ is one way to track the percentage of natural increase in the population. (**population density/birthrate**)

3. Calculating _____ can tell us whether a population is growing or shrinking. (**natural increase/population density**)

4. _____ is a common cause of population change. (**Birthrate/Migration**)

5. Land is more expensive in areas with higher _____. (**population density/population patterns**)

birthrate	migration	natural increase
population	population density	population patterns

DIRECTIONS Look up three terms from the word bank in a dictionary. On a separate sheet of paper, write the dictionary definition of the term that is closest to the definition used in your textbook. Then write a sentence using each term correctly.

The Human World

MAIN IDEAS
1. Natural resources and trade routes are important factors in determining location for settlements.
2. Areas can be defined as urban or rural.
3. Spatial patterns describe ways that people build settlements.
4. New technology has improved the interaction of regions with nearby and distant places.

Key Terms and Places

settlement any place where a community is established

trade route path used by people for buying and selling goods

urban related to cities and their surrounding areas

suburb residential community immediately outside of a city

metropolitan area large urban area

megalopolis area where several metropolitan areas grow together

rural related to areas that are found outside of cities

spatial pattern placement of people and objects on Earth and the space between them

linear settlements communities grouped along the length of a resource

cluster settlements communities grouped around or at the center of a resource

grid settlements communities that are laid out according to a network of transportation routes

commerce substantial exchange of goods between cities, states, or countries

Lesson Summary
THE IMPORTANCE OF LOCATION

A **settlement** is any place where a community is started. Settlements can be as small as a remote island village or as large as a very populated city. People often settle near natural resources. Early settlements were near freshwater and good farmland. In the 1800s many cities started as mining centers near coal and iron resources.

> **Where do people often settle?**
> _____

Trade routes are also important to settlements. A **trade route** is a path people use to sell and buy goods. Many settlements started on trade routes, and they grew into important trading centers where major routes met. These centers also were important politically because of their wealth and the different groups that met there.

What two factors made some trading centers more important than others?

_____

_____

_____

_____

URBAN AND RURAL

Geographers classify settlements by certain patterns. **Urban** areas are cities and their surroundings. They are heavily populated and developed, with many buildings and roads. Most urban jobs are not related to the land. Small urban areas might include a city center and a **suburb,** which is a residential area just outside the city. A large urban area, called a **metropolitan area,** might include an entire city, a number of suburbs, and surrounding areas. When several metropolitan areas grow into each other, they form a **megalopolis.** An example of this is the cluster of cities that includes Boston, New York, Philadelphia, Baltimore, and Washington, DC.

How is population density different in rural and urban areas?

_____

_____

_____

_____

Rural areas are found outside of cities. They are usually lightly populated and their economies are tied to the land. Many are built around agriculture, forestry, mining, and recreation.

SPATIAL PATTERNS

Geographers use **spatial patterns** to classify different ways settlements form. They describe how people and objects on Earth are placed in relation to each other. **Linear settlements** are grouped along the length of resource, such as a river. They usually form long, narrow patterns. **Cluster settlements** are grouped around a resource or at its center. For example, many communities are grouped around coal mining operations. **Grid settlements** are laid out along a network of transportation routes. They are

usually in urban areas and may follow a grid
made of roads, water routes, or train routes.

REGIONS INTERACT

Commerce is the significant exchange of goods
between cities, states, or countries. Urban areas
are usually centers of commerce and trade, as
well as government. They are often hubs for
education, communication, transportation, and
innovation. That is why many people live in or
near urban areas.

Advances in television, satellites, computers,
and the Internet improved communication. This
made it easier for cities to create services aimed at
nearby regions. It helped them reach markets
around the world. Advances in transportation
have made the world seem smaller because it is
easier to travel great distances in a shorter
amount of time.

CHALLENGE ACTIVITY

Critical Thinking: Identify Cause and Effect

Look into the history of the place where you live
and answer the following questions. What was the
main source of commerce when your area was
first settled? How did that affect where the
settlement was first built and its spatial pattern?
How has the area changed over the years?

> **What type of area is most likely to have a grid settlement?**
>
> _____
>
> _____

> **Circle two important advancements that have helped commerce in cities grow.**

DIRECTIONS Read each sentence and fill in the blank with the word in the word pair that best completes the sentence.

1. A metropolitan area usually contains a(n) _____ area. (**megalopolis/urban**)

2. A rural community is likely to have started as a _____ near a river. (**linear settlement/suburb**)

cluster settlements	commerce	grid settlement	linear settlement
megalopolis	metropolitan area	rural	settlement
spatial pattern	suburb	trade route	urban

DIRECTIONS On the line provided before each statement, write **T** if the statement is true and **F** if the statement is false. If the statement is false, write the term from the word bank that would make the statement correct on the line after each sentence.

_____ 3. The substantial exchange of goods between cities, states, or countries is called <u>trade route</u>.

_____

_____ 4. Cluster settlements are an example of a <u>metropolitan area</u>.

_____

_____ 5. A <u>suburb</u> is usually part of an urban area.

_____

_____ 6. Economies of <u>rural</u> areas are often built around agriculture, forestry, mining, and recreation.

_____

_____ 7. A <u>grid settlement</u> is laid out according to a network of transportation routes.

_____

Guided Reading Workbook

The Human World

Lesson 4

MAIN IDEAS
1. Geographers examine how environmental conditions shape people's lives.
2. Human activity changes specific places, regions, and the world as a whole.

Key Terms and Places

terraced farming form of farming on steps carved into steep hillsides to create flat land for growing crops

slash-and-burn agriculture form of farming where trees and plants in heavily forested areas are cut down and burned to clear the land for growing crops

center-pivot irrigation system where a center sprinkler waters crops in a circular field

fracking process that uses large amounts of water and chemicals to break up rocks in order to extract gas or oil

Lesson Summary
RESPONDING TO THE ENVIRONMENT

Geographers are interested in how the environment shapes people's lives. They study human systems, like farming, to see how people respond to environmental conditions. Farming is an important example of the way humans respond to their environment. Over time, humans have developed practices that let them grow food in many types of environmental conditions.

Sometimes people have to change the land. For example, in Peru, ancient Inca carved steps into steep hillsides to create flat fields for crops. This is called **terraced farming**. In thickly forested areas, like the Amazon rain forest, some farmers use **slash-and-burn agriculture**. They cut down trees and then burn them so they can clear land to grow crops. And in the U.S., farmers in dry areas create circular fields so they can water them

> **What is an example of a human system?**
> _____

> **What is the practice of carving steps into hillsides called?**
> _____

with a central sprinkler system called **center-pivot irrigation.**

Sometimes the environment cannot be controlled by humans. Natural hazards like fires, tornados, earthquakes, and hurricanes can be deadly and cause a lot of damage. People prepare for them by building shelters, practicing emergency drills, and following strict building codes.

CHANGING THE ENVIRONMENT

People have always changed their environment by building roads, bridges, and dams. They clear land for farming and housing and dig to find natural resources that give them fuel. Many human activities improve people's lives, but they are not always good for the environment. A dam could destroy the ecosystem of a river. Large cities trap heat and make areas drier.

> Circle six examples of ways humans have changed their environment.

Geographers worry about how humans may create environmental problems like pollution, acid rain, land erosion, and global warming. One concern is the ozone layer, which protects Earth from the sun's harmful rays. The use of products with chemicals called chlorofluorocarbons (CFS) started thinning out the ozone layer. Even though most CFS use has been stopped, the ozone layer has not recovered. It may be one of the causes of global warming, severe storms, and rising sea levels.

> Underline the sentence that explains how the ozone layer helps the planet.

Another concern is **fracking.** This process breaks up rock by injecting large amounts of water and chemicals into cracks. Some people support this process because it supplies oil and natural gas for fuel. Others are against fracking because they are worried it will hurt the environment or pollute drinking water.

> Why do some people support fracking?
> _____
> _____

Governments and environmental groups try to create laws to protect the environment and preserve natural resources. Other groups believe that some practices are important for economic growth. No matter what the viewpoint, environmental issues affect everyone on Earth. That is why many countries are now coming together to improve the environment around the globe.

CHALLENGE ACTIVITY

Critical Thinking: Draw Conclusions Write a paragraph that explains why some people are for fracking and some are against it. Use these arguments to come up with your own conclusion about whether to support or oppose fracking.

DIRECTIONS Write three words or phrases to describe each term.

1. slash-and-burn agriculture _____

   _____

2. terraced farming _____

   _____

3. center-pivot irrigation _____

4. fracking _____

   _____

center-pivot irrigation	environment	fracking
ozone layer	slash-and-burn agriculture	terraced farming

DIRECTIONS On a separate sheet of paper, use at least three terms from the word bank to write a short story about what you learned in the lesson.

Government and Citizenship

MAIN IDEAS
1. The world is divided into physical and human borders.
2. The nations of the world interact through trade and foreign policy.
3. The nations of the world form a world community that resolves conflicts and addresses global issues.

Key Terms and Places

borders a country's political boundaries

sovereign nation government having complete authority over a geographic area

foreign policy a nation's plan for interacting with other countries of the world

diplomacy process of conducting relations between countries

national interest a country's economic, cultural, or military goals

United Nations an organization of the world's countries that promotes peace and security around the globe

human rights rights that all people deserve, such as rights to equality and justice

humanitarian aid assistance to people in distress

Lesson Summary
BOUNDARIES AND BORDERS

Every country has political boundaries, or **borders,** which mark its territory. Within a country, smaller political units such as cities, counties, and states each have their own borders. There are two main types of political boundaries: physical borders and human borders. Physical features such as mountains, deserts, lakes, and oceans make physical borders. These physical features rarely shift. Rivers are also used as boundaries, but the changing course of a river can create border difficulties.

There are two main types of human borders: cultural and geometric. A cultural boundary based on religion was used to divide Muslim Pakistan from mostly Hindu India. Geometric boundaries are borders that do not follow

> **What are the two main types of political boundaries?**
>
> _____
>
> _____

national or cultural patterns. Often, they are straight lines based on lines of latitude or longitude.

NATIONS OF THE WORLD

The establishment of borders is one of the characteristics of a **sovereign nation,** or a government that has complete authority over a geographic area. Sovereign nations rule independently from governments outside their borders. They rule over everyone in their territory and make decisions about domestic, or internal, affairs. They can also defend themselves against foreign invasion.

Sovereign nations interact with other nations through trade and **foreign policy.** Trade allows nations to get the goods they need in exchange for the goods they have or can make. A nation's foreign policy is its plan for interacting with other countries of the world. Foreign policy tools include **diplomacy** and foreign aid. Diplomacy is the process of conducting relations between countries. Diplomacy is used to maintain national security, prevent war, negotiate an end to conflicts, solve problems, and establish communication between countries. Foreign aid is economic or military assistance to another country. Each country shapes its foreign policy to help reach its economic, cultural, or military goals. These make up its **national interest.**

A WORLD COMMUNITY

Nations around the world are connected closely through trade, diplomacy, and foreign aid. What happens in one place affects others. The world community works together to promote cooperation between countries. When conflicts occur, countries from around the world try to settle them. The **United Nations** (UN) is an

> Underline the sentence describing a sovereign nation's authority within its borders.

> List two foreign policy tools.
>
> _____

association of nearly 200 countries dedicated to promoting peace and security. It also works to guarantee **human rights,** or rights that all people deserve. These rights include political rights, social and economic rights, freedom of expression, and equality before the law. The UN sometimes places sanctions, or penalties, on countries, groups, or individuals who have broken international laws.

> Underline the sentence that describes the main goals of the United Nations.

Some groups provide humanitarian and development assistance to conflict- and poverty-stricken countries around the world. Humanitarian organizations providing aid in areas of conflict are protected by the Geneva Conventions. The Geneva Conventions are international humanitarian laws that regulate the conduct of armed conflict in all nations. They protect civilians, medics, and aid workers, along with the wounded, sick, and prisoners of war.

> What are the Geneva Conventions?
>
> _____
> _____
> _____
> _____
> _____
> _____

Crises such as earthquakes, floods, droughts, or tsunamis can leave people in great need. Groups from around the world provide **humanitarian aid,** or assistance to people in distress. Some groups aid refugees or provide medical care and vaccinations.

CHALLENGE ACTIVITY

Critical Thinking: Draw Conclusions

Look at a map showing the border between Canada and the United States. Write a description of the border using the following words: physical borders, human borders, and geometric borders.

Name _____ Class _____ Date _____

Lesson 1, *continued*

DIRECTIONS Read each sentence, and fill in the blank with the word in the word pair that best completes the sentence.

1. There are two main types of _____, physical and human. (**borders/humanitarian aid**)

2. A government that rules over everyone in its territory and makes decisions about domestic affairs is a _____. (**sovereign nation/ United Nations**)

3. A nation's plan for interacting with other countries is its _____. (**diplomacy/foreign policy**)

4. A nation's economic, cultural, or military goals make up its _____. (**foreign policy/national interest**)

5. The process of conducting relations between countries is called _____. (**diplomacy/foreign policy**)

6. Freedom of expression and equality before the law are examples of _____. (**diplomacy/human rights**)

borders	diplomacy	foreign policy
human rights	humanitarian aid	national interest
sovereign nation	United Nations	

DIRECTIONS Answer each question by writing a sentence that contains at least two terms from the word bank.

7. What is the purpose of political boundaries?

_____

_____

8. How do sovereign nations interact with one another?

_____

_____

_____

9. How do countries around the world deal with conflict and disaster?

_____

_____

_____

© Houghton Mifflin Harcourt Publishing Company

Guided Reading Workbook

Government and Citizenship

MAIN IDEAS
1. Limited governments of the world include democracies.
2. Unlimited governments of the world include totalitarian governments.
3. Most human rights abuses occur under unlimited governments of the world.

Key Terms and Places

limited government government that has legal limits on its power

constitution written plan of government that outlines its purposes, powers, and limitations

democracy form of government in which the people elect leaders and rule by majority

direct democracy government in which citizens meet in popular assembly to discuss issues and vote for leaders

representative democracy indirect democracy in which citizens vote for representatives who decide on issues and make laws on their behalf

common good welfare of the community

unlimited government government in which power is concentrated in the hands of a single leader or small group

totalitarian government government that controls all aspects of society

Lesson Summary
LIMITED GOVERNMENT

Governments make and enforce laws, regulate business and trade, and provide aid to people. A **limited government** has legal limits on its power, usually in the form of a constitution. A **constitution** is a written plan outlining the government's purposes, powers, and limitations. A **democracy** is a form of limited government in which the people elect leaders and rule by majority. In a **direct democracy,** citizens meet regularly in assembly to discuss issues and vote for leaders.

Most democratic governments today are **representative democracies.** The citizens vote for representatives to decide on issues and make laws

What is a constitution?
_____
_____
_____
_____
_____

on their behalf. Two major forms of
representative democratic governments today are
presidential and parliamentary democracies. In a
presidential democracy, the president is elected
by the people and is directly accountable to them.
Power is shared among three branches of
government. In a parliamentary democracy, the
head of government is directly accountable to the
legislature, or parliament. The legislative branch
also holds executive functions. Most of the
world's democratic governments today are
parliamentary democracies. A few nations are
also constitutional monarchies.

> **Underline the two forms of representative democracies most common today.**

In a limited government, both the government
and individuals must obey the laws. These
governments balance the welfare of the
community, or the **common good,** with individual
welfare. Democracies have social welfare systems
that seek to improve the quality of their citizens'
lives, and they protect their citizens' rights and
freedoms.

> **What two things do limited governments balance?**
> _____
> _____
> _____
> _____

UNLIMITED GOVERNMENTS

In a limited government, everyone, including
leaders, must obey the law. In an **unlimited
government,** there are no limits on a ruler's power.
Power in an authoritarian government is
concentrated in the hands of a single leader or
group. A **totalitarian government** is authoritarian
rule at its most extreme. Totalitarian governments
exercise control over all aspects of society—the
government, economy, and even people's beliefs
and actions. In these societies, citizens have no
way to change the government. Examples of
totalitarian governments include China under
Mao Zedong and North Korea under Kim
Jong-un.

> **List two examples of totalitarian governments.**
> _____
> _____
> _____

In unlimited governments, the rights of citizens
are rarely recognized or protected, and citizens
may not be able to take part in government or

openly express their views. Rulers often use force to put down opposition movements. They ignore or change constitutions or laws intended to restrict their power.

Shortly after World War II, the Chinese government created an authoritarian Communist system, imprisoning or killing those who spoke out against its policies. Although plans for industrial development were instituted, widespread food shortages led to the deaths of tens of millions by the early 1960s.

A gradual retreat from many of these early policies began in the late 1970s, but there were limits to what officials would allow. In 1989 the government violently crushed a peaceful pro-democracy student demonstration in China's capital, Beijing. This became known as the Tiananmen Square Massacre.

China's government today is balancing authoritarian rule, economic growth, and slow political reform.

What was the name given to the 1989 pro-democracy demonstration in Beijing?
_____ _____

HUMAN RIGHTS ABUSES

People today believe that everyone has human rights, or rights that all people deserve. These rights include equality, justice, political rights, and social and economic rights. Human rights abuses are most common in countries that are not free or are only partially free. These abuses include torture, slavery, and murder. Abuses in democratic countries often occur as a result of inaction.

The United Nations (UN) is an international organization committed to guaranteeing human rights for all people. The United States recognizes that respect for human rights promotes peace and deters aggression.

What are some examples of human rights abuses?
_____ _____

CHALLENGE ACTIVITY
Critical Thinking: Compare and Contrast Write a
paragraph that compares and contrasts limited
and unlimited governments.

common good	constitution	democracy
direct democracy	unlimited government	representative democracy
totalitarian government		

DIRECTIONS On the line provided before each statement, write **T** if
a statement is true and **F** if a statement is false. If the statement is
false, write a term from the word bank that would make the
statement correct on the line after each sentence.

_____ 1. Korea under Kim Jong-un is an example of a <u>direct democracy</u>.

_____

_____ 2. <u>Democracy</u> is a form of government in which one person or a few
people hold power.

_____

_____ 3. A government in which the state has control over all aspects of society
is called a <u>totalitarian government</u>.

_____

_____ 4. In <u>unlimited governments,</u> people elect leaders and rule by majorities.

_____

_____ 5. A <u>constitution</u> enforces the legal limits of a government's power.

_____

_____ 6. A constitutional monarchy is an example of a <u>totalitarian government</u>.

_____

_____ 7. The welfare of a whole community is known as the <u>common good</u>.

_____

Government and Citizenship

MAIN IDEAS
1. The duties and roles of citizenship help to make representative government work.
2. Good citizens accept their responsibilities for maintaining a strong democracy.
3. Citizens influence government through public opinion.
4. The type of government in some societies influences the roles of the citizens in those societies.

Key Terms and Places

representative government system in which people are the ultimate source of government authority

draft law that requires men of certain ages and qualifications to join the military

jury duty required service of citizens to act as a member of a jury

political party group of citizens with similar views on public issues who work to put their ideas into effective government action

interest groups organizations of people with a common interest that try to influence government policies and decisions

public opinion the way large groups of citizens think about issues and people

nonrepresentative government a government in which government power is unlimited and citizens have few, if any, rights

Lesson Summary
DUTIES AND ROLES OF CITIZENSHIP

In the United States, citizens are the ultimate source of government authority. This is called a **representative government.** For this type of government to work, citizens must perform certain duties. One duty of citizens is to obey the law. A democracy needs educated citizens to choose leaders and understand issues. In the United States, you must attend school until the age of 16.

> Who is the source of government authority in a representative government?
>
> _____

Citizens must pay taxes. Taxes fund public services such as road repair, police protection, and national security. When the country needs people to fight wars, it may issue a **draft.** A draft requires men of certain ages and qualifications to serve in the military. Citizens must also serve on a jury if they are called to do so. This service is called **jury duty.** The Constitution guarantees citizens the right to a trial by their peers—their fellow citizens.

RIGHTS AND RESPONSIBILITIES

In a representative government, citizens also have responsibilities—tasks they should do as citizens but that are not required by law.

In order to give consent to our lawmakers in government, we should vote. Voting is a way to show our decision makers whether we agree with their opinions on issues. Becoming informed about key issues, candidates, and current events will help you make informed choices when you vote. You might also take part in government by joining a **political party.** Political parties nominate or select candidates to run for political office.

Citizens can also join an **interest group.** These are organizations made up of people sharing a common goal. Interest groups try to influence government policies and decisions.

Another way to help society is by volunteering in your community. By knowing your own rights as a citizen, you can make sure you respect the rights of the people around you. You should also know if someone else's rights are being violated.

CITIZENS AND THE MEDIA

The media plays an important role in free societies such as the United States. Newspapers, magazines, radio, television, film, the Internet, and books help to keep people informed. What citizens learn from the media shapes

> **Underline the three responsibilities of citizens.**

> **What are some of our responsibilities as citizens?**
>
> _____
> _____
> _____
> _____
> _____
> _____

> **Underline the influences that affect public opinion.**

public opinion, or the way large groups of citizens think about issues and people. Public opinion on any particular issue may be very diverse.

Opinions are also influenced by family, friends, teachers, and clubs. Citizens rely on mass media to help them decide how to vote on important issues or candidates. However, effective citizenship requires critical thinking about what you see, hear, and read.

CITIZENSHIP IN OTHER SOCIETIES

Other representative governments may have similar roles and responsibilities for their citizens. These may not be the same as those of U.S. citizens. **Nonrepresentative governments** are governments in which citizens have few, if any, rights. The government maintains all the power. At times, citizens become so dissatisfied that they revolt against their leaders.

CHALLENGE ACTIVITY

Critical Thinking: Explain Explain why representative government requires the involvement of the country's citizens.

What rights do citizens have under nonrepresentative governments?

_____

_____

_____

_____

| draft | interest group | jury duty | nonrepresentative government |
| political party | public opinion | representative government | |

DIRECTIONS Answer each question by writing a sentence that contains at least one term from the word bank.

1. How does a representative government work?

_____

_____

2. When might the United States issue a draft?

_____

_____

3. Name some duties and responsibilities of a United States citizen.

_____

_____

4. What is a nonrepresentative government?

_____

_____

5. Explain how the Constitution guarantees citizens a right to a trial by their peers.

_____

_____

6. How are candidates for political office usually chosen?

_____

_____

7. How can citizens in the United States influence the government?

_____

_____

Economics

MAIN IDEAS

1. There are three basic types of economic systems.
2. Contemporary societies have mixed economies.
3. The United States benefits from a free enterprise system.
4. Governments provide public goods.
5. Geographers categorize countries based on levels of economic development and range of economic activities.

Key Terms and Places

traditional economy people's work is based on long-established customs

command economy government controls the economy

market economy economy based on private ownership, free trade, and competition

mixed economy combination of traditional, market, and command economic systems

free enterprise system economic system in which few limits are placed on business activities

public goods goods and services provided by the government for public consumption

agricultural industries businesses that focus on growing crops and raising livestock

manufacturing industries businesses that make finished products from raw materials

wholesale industries businesses that sell to other businesses

retail industries businesses that sell directly to consumers

service industries businesses that provide services rather than goods

developed countries countries with strong economies and a high quality of life

developing countries countries with weak economies and a lower quality of life

gross domestic product (GDP) value of all goods and services produced within a country in a single year

Lesson Summary
MAIN TYPES OF ECONOMIC SYSTEMS

An economic system is the way in which a society organizes the production and distribution of goods and services. A **traditional economy** is based on long-established customs of who does what work. A **command economy** is controlled by

> Underline the three types of economic systems.

the government. A **market economy** is based on private ownership, free trade, and competition.

MODERN ECONOMIES

Most countries have one of three types of **mixed economies:** communist, capitalist, and socialist. In a communist society, the government owns all factors of production. In a capitalist economy, individuals and businesses own the factors of production. In socialist economies, the government controls some of the basic factors of production.

> **What are the three types of mixed economies?**
> _____
> _____

THE FREE ENTERPRISE SYSTEM

U.S. capitalism is sometimes called the **free enterprise system.** Individuals are free to exchange goods and services and to own and operate businesses with little government intervention. The ability to make a profit is one of the key advantages of this system. To function properly, the free enterprise system requires that people obey laws, be truthful, and avoid behaviors that harm others.

> **What is a free enterprise system?**
> _____
> _____
> _____
> _____
> _____
> _____

GOVERNMENT AND PUBLIC GOODS

Governments today provide expensive or important services to large groups of people who might otherwise have to do without the service. These government goods and services are called **public goods.** They include schools, highways, and police and fire protection. Public goods are paid for through taxes. Because scarcity affects government, too, a government must determine the opportunity cost of public goods.

Governments also use regulations, or rules, to control business behavior. These rules must be helpful and fair. The most common government regulations include protection for public health and safety and for the environment.

> **How are public goods paid?**
> _____
> _____

ECONOMIC ACTIVITIES AND DEVELOPMENT

There are three levels of economic activity, or areas in which people make a living. People in primary industries harvest products from the earth. An example is **agricultural industries,** in which people focus on growing crops and raising livestock. In secondary industries, the natural resources and raw materials are made into products. **Manufacturing industries** are secondary industries. In tertiary industries, people provide goods and services to customers. **Wholesale industries, retail industries,** and **service industries** are tertiary industries. Health care workers, mechanics, and teachers work in service industries.

> Circle three types of industries that are tertiary industries.

The world's most powerful nations are **developed countries,** countries with strong economies and a high quality of life. **Developing countries** have less productive economies and a lower quality of life. One indicator, or measure, of a country's wealth is **gross domestic product (GDP).** GDP is the value of all goods and services produced within a country in a single year. Literacy, life expectancy, and overall level of industrialization are other indicators of a country's wealth.

> Underline the four indicators of a country's wealth.

CHALLENGE ACTIVITY

Critical Thinking: Compare and Contrast How is the American free enterprise system different from communist and socialist economies? Write a paragraph explaining the differences.

DIRECTIONS Read each sentence, and fill in the blank with the word in the word pair that best completes the sentence.

1. Businesses known as _____ make finished products from raw materials. (**manufacturing industries/retail industries**)

2. In a _____, few limits are placed on business activities. (**command economy/free enterprise system**)

3. _____ industries focus on growing crops and raising livestock. (**Agricultural/Wholesale**)

4. Countries with less productive economies and a lower quality of life are known as _____. (**developing countries/developed countries**)

5. Police and fire protection are examples of _____. (**public goods/gross domestic product**)

agricultural industries	command economy
developed countries	developing countries
free enterprise system	gross domestic product
manufacturing industries	market economy
mixed economy	public goods
retail industries	service industries
traditional economy	wholesale industries

DIRECTIONS Look up three terms from the word bank in an encyclopedia or dictionary. On a separate sheet of paper, write the encyclopedia or dictionary definition of the term that is closest to the definition used in your textbook. Then write a sentence using each term correctly.

Economics

MAIN IDEAS
1. Money is used as a medium of exchange, a store of value, and a unit of account.
2. Banks are places to store money, earn money, and borrow money.
3. People can use their earnings to build wealth.

Key Terms and Places

barter trade a good or service for a good or service provided by someone else

money anything that people will accept as payment for goods and services

medium of exchange means through which goods and services can be exchanged

store of value something that holds its value over time

unit of account yardstick of economic value in exchanges

interest rate percentage of the total amount of money loaned or borrowed

assets things of economic value that a person or company owns

income money paid to a person or business for goods or services

savings income not spent on immediate wants

investment use of money today in a way that earns future benefits

Lesson Summary
PURPOSES OF MONEY

Without money, people must **barter,** or trade, for goods and services they want or need. Barter works when both people want to exchange particular goods or services at the same time. If only one wants to exchange, barter does not work. This difficulty led to the invention of money. **Money** is anything that people will accept as payment for goods and services. Today it is generally metal coins or paper currency, but other items have been used as money.

Money performs three functions. First, it serves as a **medium of exchange,** or means through which goods and services can be exchanged. Second, it serves as a **store of value,** something that holds its value over time. This

Why is money easier to use than barter?
_____
_____
_____
_____
_____
_____
_____

Underline the three functions of money.

allows money to be saved for use in the future. Third, money serves as a **unit of account.** It allows people to measure the relative costs of goods and services. In the United States, the economic value of all goods and services can be measured by the dollar, the nation's basic monetary unit.

BANKS AND THE ECONOMY

Banks are like money stores, where people buy (borrow) money and sell (lend) it. Customers store money, earn money, and borrow money at a bank. Banks are businesses, so they earn money by charging interest or fees for these services.

Banks have three main functions. First, they are safe places where people can store money. Second, customers can earn money when they store their savings in banks. Savings accounts and some checking accounts offer a payment, called interest. The bank is borrowing the money from the customer, and the customer is paid for the use of the money. Third, banks loan this money to other customers who want to borrow money for a purchase. These borrowers pay the bank interest for the use of the money. The amount of interest paid is based on an **interest rate.** When interest rates are high, people are more likely to save their money. When interest rates are low, they may borrow or shift their savings to investments with higher interest rates.

MONEY MANAGEMENT

People and businesses save and invest money in order to increase their financial resources. Savings and investments are good ways to gain **assets,** which are things a person or business owns that have economic value.

Every person who has a job that pays a wage earns **income.** Businesses also earn income by

> **How do banks earn money?**
>
> _____
> _____
> _____

> **Underline the three main functions of banks.**

selling goods and services. People can do two things with their income: spend it or save it. **Savings** is income not spent on immediate wants. Common options for saving money include savings accounts, certificates of deposit (CDs), and stocks. Money in a savings account can be used at any time, but the interest rate is low. CDs pay a higher interest rate, but the money is deposited for a set amount of time, so it is not easily available.

Investment in stock gives a person partial ownership in a company. If the stock price increases, the stock owner makes money. If the stock price drops, the stock owner can lose money. People decide whether to save or invest their money by choosing an investment goal. Generally, investments that carry a higher risk of losing some or all of the money are more likely to earn high rewards. Lower-risk investments such as savings accounts and CDs earn lower rewards. Inflation is another risk that savers must consider. Inflation affects the purchasing power of money, so the money saved may not buy as much in the future as it does in the present.

What two things can people do with their income?
_____

What happens to a stock owner if the stock price increases?
_____
_____
_____

CHALLENGE ACTIVITY

Critical Thinking: Make Inferences Banks charge a higher interest rate for loans than they pay for savings accounts. Why are the interest rates not the same for borrowing and lending?

DIRECTIONS Read each sentence, and fill in the blank with the word in the word pair that best completes the sentence.

1. Money serves as a _____ because it holds its value over time. **(medium of exchange/store of value)**

2. _____ is something that people accept as payment for goods or services. **(Barter/Money)**

3. People saving for retirement want to make wise investments so their _____ will grow and they can live comfortably. **(assets/income)**

4. Stocks are _____ that help people increase their assets. **(units of account/investments)**

5. _____ is the function of money that allows people to measure the relative costs of goods and services. **(Medium of exchange/Unit of account)**

assets	barter
income	interest rate
investment	medium of exchange
money	savings
store of value	unit of account

DIRECTIONS Answer each question by writing a sentence that contains at least one term from the word bank.

6. Which of the three functions of money is the most important, and why?

_____

_____

_____

7. What does a bank do with money it stores?

_____

_____

8. Why might a person invest in CDs rather than savings?

_____

Guided Reading Workbook

Economics

MAIN IDEAS
1. Globalization links the world's countries together through culture and trade.
2. Multinational corporations make global trade easier and allow countries to become more interdependent.
3. The world community works together to solve global conflicts and crises.

Key Terms and Places

globalization process in which countries are increasingly linked to each other through culture and trade

popular culture culture traits that are well known and widely accepted

trade barriers any law that limits free trade between nations

free trade trade without trade barriers between nations

Lesson Summary
GLOBALIZATION

People around the world are more closely linked than ever before. **Globalization** is the process in which countries are increasingly linked to each other through culture and trade. Improvements in transportation and communication have increased globalization.

Popular culture refers to culture traits that are well known and widely accepted. These traits can include food, sports, music, and movies. The United States has a great influence on popular culture through American products, television, and the English language. English has become the major global language. It is used for international music, business, science, and education around the world. The United States is, in turn, greatly influenced by other countries. Martial arts movies from Asia are quite popular in the United States, and many foreign words such as *sushi* and *croissant* have become common in the English language.

> Underline the sentence that describes two ways countries are linked together.

> What are four traits that can be considered part of popular culture?
> _____
> _____
> _____
> _____

Lesson 4, *continued*

GLOBAL TRADE

Globalization also connects businesses and affects trade. Global trade takes place at a much faster pace than ever because of faster transportation and communication technologies. Telecommunication, computers, and the Internet have made global trade quick and easy.

The expansion of global trade has increased interdependence among the world's countries. Interdependence is a relationship between countries in which they rely on one another for resources, goods, or services. Companies that operate in a number of different countries are called multinational corporations. For their manufacturing plants, these companies select locations where raw materials or labor is cheapest. They often produce different parts of their products on different continents. Many developing nations want multinational corporations to invest in them because they create jobs.

What four improvements have made global trade faster and easier?
_____
_____
_____

GLOBAL ECONOMIC ISSUES

Countries trade with each other to obtain resources, goods, and services. Developing nations still struggle to gain economic stability because they lack the necessary technologies, well-trained workers, and money for investments. Developed nations provide aid to developing nations through the work of international organizations. The World Bank provides loans for large projects, health care, education, or infrastructure such as roads or power plants. The International Monetary Fund (IMF) offers emergency loans to countries in financial trouble.

Sometimes, governments pass laws to protect their countries' jobs and industries. **Trade barriers** such as quotas, tariffs, and embargoes limit **free trade** between nations. Quotas limit the number of lower-priced products that can be imported. A tariff, or tax on imported goods, protects the

Why do many developing nations want multinational corporations to invest in them?
_____
_____
_____

What are two international organizations that aid developing nations?
_____
_____
_____

price of domestic goods. An embargo is a law that cuts off most or all trade with a specific country. Many countries, however, encourage free trade. The World Trade Organization (WTO) has worked with other nations to help trade among nations flow as smoothly and freely as possible.

What are three types of trade barriers?
_____
_____

CHALLENGE ACTIVITY

Critical Thinking: Make Inferences Why do developed nations provide aid to developing nations?

DIRECTIONS Read each sentence, and fill in the blank with the word in the word pair that best completes the sentence.

1. Tariffs, quotas, and embargoes are examples of _____.
   (interdependence/trade barriers)

2. _____ occurs when countries depend on each other for resources, goods, or services. **(Telecommunications/Interdependence)**

3. The _____ provides loans to developing nations so they can build such things as power plants and roads. **(World Bank/World Trade Organization)**

DIRECTIONS On the line provided before each statement, write **T** if the statement is true and **F** if the statement is false. If the statement is false, write the term that would make the statement correct on the line after each sentence.

_____ 4. The process in which countries are linked to one another through culture and trade is called <u>popular culture</u>.

_____

_____ 5. Culture traits such as food, music, movies, and sports are examples of <u>globalization</u>.

_____

_____ 6. As a result of globalization, there is more <u>interdependence</u> among countries.

_____

_____ 7. The World Trade Organization works to create <u>trade barriers</u> between nations.

_____

Guided Reading Workbook

The United States

MAIN IDEAS
1. Major physical features of the United States include mountains, rivers, and plains.
2. The climate of the United States is wetter in the East and South and drier in the West.
3. The United States is rich in natural resources such as farmland, oil, forests, and minerals.

Key Terms and Places

Appalachian Mountains main mountain range in the East

Great Lakes largest group of freshwater lakes in the world

Mississippi River North America's largest and most important river

tributary smaller stream or river that flows into a larger stream or river

Rocky Mountains enormous mountain range in the West

continental divide area of high ground that divides the flow of rivers toward opposite ends of a continent

Lesson Summary
PHYSICAL FEATURES

The United States is one of the largest countries in the world. On the eastern coast of the United States, the land is flat and close to sea level. This area is called the Atlantic Coastal Plain. Moving west, the land rises to a region called the Piedmont. The land rises higher in the **Appalachian Mountains,** the main mountain range in the East. The highest peak in the Appalachians is about 6,700 feet (2,042 m).

West of the Appalachian Mountains are the Interior Plains. The plains are filled with rolling hills, lakes, and rivers. The main physical features of the Interior Plains are the **Great Lakes.** The Great Lakes are the largest freshwater lake system in the world. They are also an important waterway for trade between the United States and Canada.

Where is the Atlantic Coastal Plain?
_____
_____

What is special about the Great Lakes?
_____
_____
_____

The **Mississippi River** lies west of the Great Lakes. It is the largest and most important river in North America. **Tributaries** of the Mississippi River deposit rich silt that produces fertile farmlands. These farmlands cover most of the Interior Plains.

West of the Mississippi River lie the Great Plains. These are vast areas of grasslands. Further west, the land begins to rise, eventually leading to the **Rocky Mountains.** Many of these mountains reach higher than 14,000 feet (4,267 m). Along the crest of the Rocky Mountains is a ridge that divides North America's rivers. This is called a **continental divide.** Rivers east of the divide mostly flow eastward, and most rivers west of the divide flow westward.

Farther west, mountain ranges include the Cascade Range and the Sierra Nevada. Mountains also stretch north along the Pacific coast. Alaska's Denali, which used to be called Mount McKinley, is the highest mountain in North America.

What is special about the Mississippi River?   _____   _____   _____

About how high are the highest mountains in the Rocky Mountains?   _____   _____

What is the highest mountain in North America?   _____   _____

CLIMATE

The eastern United States is divided into three climate regions. The Northeast has a humid continental climate. To the south, the climate is humid subtropical. Farthest south, most of Florida is warm all year.

The climate in the Interior Plains varies. It is hot and dry in the Great Plains. But in most of the Midwest, the climate is humid continental. In the West, climates are mostly dry. Alaska has subarctic and tundra climates, while Hawaii is tropical.

Circle the names of the climate regions in the eastern United States.

NATURAL RESOURCES

Our lives are affected by natural resources every day. Much of our paper, food, gas, and electricity come from natural resources in the United States.

List four products that come from natural resources found in the United States.   _____   _____

CHALLENGE ACTIVITY

Critical Thinking: Draw Inferences Write three paragraphs describing what makes the physical geography of the United States so diverse.

DIRECTIONS Read each sentence and fill in the blank with the word in the word pair that best completes the sentence.

1. Grasslands cover most of the _____, making the region a good place to grow wheat and other grains. **(Rocky Mountains/Great Plains)**

2. The Missouri and Ohio Rivers are two major tributaries of the _____. **(Great Lakes/Mississippi River)**

3. The _____ separates the flow of North America's rivers, sending some water east into the Mississippi River and some water west into the Pacific Ocean. **(tributary/continental divide)**

Appalachian Mountains	continental divide	Great Lakes
Great Plains	Mississippi River	Rocky Mountains
tributary		

DIRECTIONS On the line provided before each statement, write **T** if a statement is true and **F** if a statement is false. If the statement is false, write the term from the word bank that would make the statement correct on the line after each sentence.

_____ 4. The <u>Rocky Mountains</u> are the main mountain range in the East.

_____

_____ 5. The <u>Mississippi River</u> is (are) an important waterway for trade between the United States and Canada.

_____

DIRECTIONS Write three words or phrases that describe the term.

6. tributary _____

_____

Guided Reading Workbook

The United States

Lesson 2

MAIN IDEAS

1. The United States, the world's first modern democracy, expanded from the Atlantic coast to the Pacific coast over time.
2. In the United States, different levels of government have different roles, but all levels require the participation of the citizens.
3. The people and culture of the United States are very diverse.

Key Terms and Places

colony territory inhabited and controlled by people from a foreign land

Boston major seaport in the British colonies during the mid-1700s

New York major seaport in the British colonies during the mid-1700s

plantation large farm that grows mainly one crop

pioneers first settlers in the West

U.S. Constitution document spelling out the powers and function of the branches of the federal government

legislative branch responsible for making laws

executive branch carries out and enforces laws

judicial branch interprets the laws in court cases

bilingual people who speak two languages

Lesson Summary
FIRST MODERN DEMOCRACY

Europeans began settling in North America in the 1500s and setting up **colonies.** New cities such as **Boston** and **New York** became major seaports in the British colonies. Thousands of enslaved Africans were brought to the colonies and forced to work on **plantations.**

In the 1770s many British colonists were unhappy with British rule. As a result, colonial representatives adopted the Declaration of Independence in July 1776. To win independence, colonists fought the British in the Revolutionary War. The British were defeated in 1781 at the Battle of Yorktown in Virginia.

> Name two major seaports in the British colonies.
>
> _____

> What happened in July 1776?
>
> _____
> _____
> _____
> _____

Lesson 2, *continued*

After the war, the United States began to expand west. The first settlers in the West were called **pioneers.** Many sought land, others were looking for gold. By 1850 the country stretched all the way to the Pacific Ocean. The United States faced two world wars during the 1900s. After World War II, the United States and the Soviet Union became rivals in the Cold War, which lasted until the 1990s.

> **By 1850 the United States stretched from the Atlantic coast to which ocean?**
>
> _____

GOVERNMENT AND CITIZENSHIP

The United States is a representative democracy. It is a limited government based on the **U.S. Constitution.** The Bill of Rights, a part of the Constitution, protects individual rights such as the freedoms of speech, press, and religion and the right to a fair trial.

> **Underline four individual rights protected by the Constitution.**

The federal government has three branches. Congress, the **legislative branch,** makes laws. The **executive branch,** which includes the president and vice-president, enforces the laws. The **judicial branch** interprets the laws in court cases. Each state has its own constitution and government. Counties and cities have their own local governments. All levels of government require the participation of the citizens. Participation includes voting, paying taxes, and jury service.

> **What are the three branches of the federal government?**
>
> _____
>
> _____
>
> _____

PEOPLE AND CULTURE

Many Americans are descendants of European immigrants. The United States is also home to people of many different cultures and ethnic groups. The United States is a diverse nation, where many languages are spoken, different religions are practiced, and a variety of foods are eaten.

For thousands of years, Native Americans were the only people living in the Americas. Descendants of enslaved Africans live throughout the country, with the highest population of African Americans living in the South. Asian Americans are descendants of people who came from Asian countries. Many Hispanic Americans originally migrated to the United States from Mexico, Cuba, and other Latin American countries.

When people migrate to the United States, they bring parts of their culture with them, including their religions, food, and music. Some Americans are **bilingual.** Other than English, Spanish is the most widely spoken language in the United States. People of different ethnic groups make the United States a very diverse country.

> Underline the sentence that explains where many Hispanic Americans originally migrated.

> What parts of their culture do people bring with them when they migrate to the United States?
>
> _____

CHALLENGE ACTIVITY

Critical Thinking: Draw Inferences

Imagine that you are about to turn 18. Make a list of ways you, as a U.S. citizen, can participate in the state, local, and federal government.

DIRECTIONS Look at the set of three terms following each number.
On the line provided, write the letter of the term that does not relate
to the others.

_____ 1. a. cotton   b. plantation   c. bilingual

_____ 2. a. seaport   b. pioneers   c. New York

_____ 3. a. legislative branch   b. West   c. pioneers

_____ 4. a. Boston   b. judicial branch   c. New York

_____ 5. a. U.S. Constitution   b. Boston   c. executive branch

bilingual	Boston	colony	executive branch
judicial branch	legislative branch	New York	pioneers
plantation	U.S. Constitution		

DIRECTIONS Answer each question by writing a sentence that
contains at least one term from the word bank.

_____ 6. What is one reason that the population of the United States is so
culturally diverse today?

_____

_____ 7. What was America like before the Revolutionary War?

_____

_____

_____

_____ 8. What makes the government of the United States a limited
democracy?

_____

_____

The United States

Lesson 3

MAIN IDEAS
1. The United States has four regions—the Northeast, the South, the Midwest, and the West.
2. The United States has a strong economy and a powerful military but is facing the challenge of world terrorism.

Key Terms and Places

Washington, DC the United States capital

Chicago one of the busiest shipping ports on the Great Lakes

Detroit located in Michigan and is the nation's leading automobile producer

Seattle Washington's largest city and home to technology and aerospace companies

terrorism violent attacks to intimidate or cause fear

Lesson Summary
REGIONS OF THE UNITED STATES

Geographers often divide the United States into four main regions. These are the Northeast, the South, the Midwest, and the West.

The Northeast is the smallest region in the United States, as well as the most densely populated. Natural resources in the Northeast include rich farmland, coal, and fishing. Major seaports make it possible to ship products to markets around the world.

The Northeast is covered by a string of large cities called a megalopolis. It stretches from Boston to **Washington, DC.** Other major cities are New York, Philadelphia, and Baltimore.

The South includes coastlines along the Atlantic Ocean and the Gulf of Mexico. The coastal plains provide farmers with rich soils for growing cotton, tobacco, and citrus fruits.

Technology, education, and oil are also important industries in the South. Warm weather and beautiful beaches make tourism an important part of the South's economy.

> **What are the four main regions of the United States?**
> _____
> _____

> **List five cities that make up the megalopolis in the Northeast.**
> _____
> _____
> _____
> _____

> **Underline the sentences that describe the industries that contribute to the South's economy.**

The Midwest is one of the world's most productive farming regions. Rich soils deposited by the region's rivers are perfect for raising livestock and producing corn, dairy products, and soybeans.

Most of the major cities in the Midwest, such as **Chicago** and **Detroit,** are located on rivers or the Great Lakes. This makes it easier to transport farm products, coal, and iron ore.

The West is the largest region. California's mild climate and wealth of resources make it home to more than 10 percent of the country's population.

Ranching, farming, coal, oil, gold, silver, copper, forestry, and fishing are important industries in the West. **Seattle,** Washington's largest city, is home to many industries, including technology and aerospace.

Where are the major cities of the Midwest located?
_____
_____

What is the largest region in the United States?
_____

CHANGES IN THE NATION

The United States has faced many challenges in recent years. Trade, technology, and an abundance of natural resources have helped make the U.S. economy strong. However, by the end of 2007, the United States faced a recession, or a sharp decrease in economic activity. The housing market collapsed, some banks and businesses failed, and millions of jobs were lost.

Terrorism continued to threaten the nation's safety. After the deadliest terrorist attack in U.S. history on September 11, 2001, the United States and other world leaders began working together to combat terrorism.

In 2008 Barack Obama became the nation's first African American president. In 2016 Donald Trump, a businessman, defeated the Democratic candidate, Hillary Clinton.

What are two major issues the United States has faced in recent years?
_____
_____

CHALLENGE ACTIVITY

Critical Thinking: Explain Think about the physical features, climates, natural resources, industries, and economies of the regions in the United States. Choose the region you would most like to live in and explain why.

Chicago	Detroit	megalopolis	Seattle
South	terrorism	Washington, DC	

DIRECTIONS On the line provided before each statement, write **T** if a statement is true and **F** if a statement is false. If the statement is false, write the term from the word bank that would make the statement correct on the line after each sentence.

_____ 1. <u>Seattle</u> and New York are part of a megalopolis in the northeastern region of the United States.

_____

_____ 2. Most major cities in the Midwest, such as Detroit and <u>Chicago</u>, are located on rivers or the Great Lakes.

_____

_____ 3. The <u>South</u> includes coastlines along the Atlantic Ocean and the Gulf of Mexico.

_____

_____ 4. Terrorist acts in the United States have encouraged leaders around the world to work together to combat the problem of <u>terrorism</u>.

_____

_____ 5. Forestry and fishing are two important economic activities in the <u>Detroit</u> area.

_____

DIRECTIONS Choose four of the terms from the word bank. On a separate sheet of paper, use these terms to write a description of the United States.

Canada

Lesson 1

MAIN IDEAS
1. A huge country, Canada has a wide variety of physical features, including rugged mountains, plains, and swamps.
2. Because of its northerly location, Canada is dominated by cold climates.
3. Canada is rich in natural resources like fish, minerals, fertile soils, and forests.

Key Terms and Places

Rocky Mountains mountains that extend north from the United States into western Canada

St. Lawrence River important international waterway that links the Great Lakes to the Atlantic Ocean

Niagara Falls falls created by the waters of the Niagara River

Canadian Shield region of rocky uplands, lakes, and swamps

Grand Banks large fishing ground off the Atlantic coast near Newfoundland and Labrador

pulp softened wood fibers

newsprint cheap paper used mainly for newspapers

Lesson Summary
PHYSICAL FEATURES

Canada is the second-largest country in the world. Only Russia is larger. The United States and Canada share several physical features. Among them are the mountains along the Pacific coast and the **Rocky Mountains** as well as broad plains that stretch across both countries. The two nations also share a natural border formed by the **St. Lawrence River**.

Niagara Falls is another physical feature that the two countries share. The falls are created by the Niagara River as it drops over a rocky ledge.

One of Canada's unique features is the **Canadian Shield**. This rocky region covers about half of the country. Canadian territory extends north to the Arctic Ocean where the land is

> Underline the sentence that describes Canada's size compared to other countries in the world.

> List three physical features that are in both Canada and the United States.
>
> _____
> _____
> _____
> _____
> _____

covered with ice all year. Very few people live in
this harsh environment.

CLIMATE

Canada's climate is greatly affected by its
location. The country is far to the north of the
equator. It is also at higher latitudes than the
United States. Because of this, it generally has
cool to freezing temperatures year round.

The coldest part of Canada is close to the
Arctic Circle. Both central and northern Canada
have subarctic climates. The far north has tundra
and ice cap climates. More than 80 percent of
Canadians live in urban areas. Many of these
cities are located in provinces that border
the United States, where the weather is
relatively mild.

How has Canada's location influenced its climate?
_____
_____
_____
_____
_____

RESOURCES

Canada has many natural resources. These
resources include fish, minerals, and forests. One
of Canada's richest fishing areas is the **Grand
Banks** near Newfoundland and Labrador, off the
Atlantic coast. Large schools of fish once swam
there, but too much fishing has reduced the
number of fish in this part of the ocean.

Canada has many mineral resources. It also
has oil and gas. Many of Canada's mineral
resources come from the Canadian Shield, a
region of rocky uplands, lakes, and swamps.
Canada is a main source of the world's nickel,
zinc, and uranium. Alberta produces most of
Canada's oil and natural gas.

All across Canada, forests provide lumber and
pulp to make paper. The United States, the
United Kingdom, and Japan get much of their
newsprint from Canada.

Circle the names of three types of natural resources that Canada has.

CHALLENGE ACTIVITY

Critical Thinking: Draw Inferences How are Canada's natural resources connected to its climate and physical features? Write two paragraphs explaining the connections.

DIRECTIONS Read each sentence and fill in the blank with the word in the word pair that best completes the sentence.

1. The _____ forms a natural border between the United States and Canada. (**Canadian Shield/St. Lawrence River**)

2. _____ refers to softened wood fibers used to make paper. (**Pulp/Newsprint**)

3. The _____ extend from the western United States into western Canada. (**Grand Banks/Rocky Mountains**)

4. The Canadian Shield is a region of lakes, swamps, and rocky _____. (**tundra/uplands**)

5. _____ is a physical feature that the United States and Canada share. (**Hudson Bay/Niagara Falls**)

Canadian Shield	Grand Banks	Hudson Bay
newsprint	Niagara Falls	pulp
Rocky Mountains	St. Lawrence River	tundra
uplands		

DIRECTIONS Choose five of the terms from the word bank. Use these terms to write a summary of what you learned in the lesson.

_____

_____

_____

_____

_____

Canada

MAIN IDEAS

1. Beginning in the 1600s, Europeans settled the region that would later become Canada.
2. Immigration and migration to cities have shaped Canadian culture.

Key Terms and Places

Quebec province of Canada, first settled by the French

provinces administrative divisions of a country

British Columbia province of Canada on the Pacific Coast

Toronto Canada's largest city

Lesson Summary

HISTORY

Native peoples such as the Inuit were the first people to live in Canada. Over time, some of these native peoples divided into groups known as the First Nations. The Cree, one of those groups, lived on the plains. They survived by hunting bison. The Inuit lived in the far north. They learned to survive in the harsh, cold climate by hunting seals, whales, and other animals.

The Vikings were the first Europeans to come to Canada, but they did not stay. European explorers and fishermen came in the late 1400s. Europeans soon began to trade with Native Canadians. The French built the first permanent settlements in what became Canada. They called the lands they claimed New France. In the 1700s Britain defeated France in the French and Indian War. Although the British took control, most French settlers stayed. Their way of life did not change much. Many descendants of these French settlers live in **Quebec** today.

The British divided their territory into two colonies called Upper and Lower Canada. Canada stayed divided until 1867, when the

> **Circle two groups that are part of the First Nations.**

> **How did the French and Indian War affect the French colonists in New France?**
>
> _____
> _____
> _____

British passed a law making it a dominion, a territory or area of influence. This act gave Canada its own government. The British also divided the country into **provinces**. In 1885, Canadians completed a railroad across Canada. It connected **British Columbia** with the eastern provinces. Canada increased in size by buying lands in the north where many Native Canadians lived.

What is a dominion?
_____
_____

CULTURE

Canadians come from many places. Some are descendants of early settlers from France and Britain. In the late 1800s and early 1900s many immigrants came from Europe. Most were from Britain, Russia, and Germany. Some came from the United States. Most farmed, while others worked in mines, forests, and factories. Some hoped to find gold in Canada's Yukon Territory. Many Asian immigrants have come to Canada, especially from China, Japan, and India. Many Chinese immigrants came to work on the railroads. Immigrants helped Canada's economy grow. British Columbia was the first Canadian province to have a large Asian minority.

Circle the countries where some of Canada's immigrants came from prior to World War II.

After World War II a new wave of immigrants came to large cities like **Toronto**. Many came from Asia. Others came from Europe, Africa, the Caribbean, and Latin America. Like earlier immigrants, they came for jobs and new opportunities. In recent years, Canadians have also moved from farms in rural areas to large cities like Vancouver and Montreal. Many of these people have moved to cities to find jobs.

CHALLENGE ACTIVITY

Critical Thinking: Make Inferences How has immigration helped Canada's economy grow? Imagine that you are a person preparing to move to Canada. Write a letter to a friend explaining

your reasons for moving and how you expect to
contribute to the Canadian economy.

DIRECTIONS On the line provided before each statement, write **T** if
a statement is true and **F** if a statement is false. If the statement is
false, write the term that would make the statement correct on the
line after each sentence.

_____ 1. Since World War II, <u>Quebec</u> has become one of the most culturally
diverse cities in the world.

_____

_____ 2. Quebec and Ontario are examples of Canadian <u>colonies</u>.

_____

_____ 3. The Canadians built a transcontinental railroad to connect <u>British
Columbia</u> with eastern Canada.

_____

_____ 4. <u>Toronto</u> remains a mainly French-speaking region.

_____

_____ 5. A <u>dominion</u>, such as the Dominion of Canada, is a territory or area of
influence.

_____

DIRECTIONS Write three adjectives or descriptive phrases that
describe the term.

6. British Columbia _____

7. New France _____

8. Canadian Pacific Railroad _____

_____

9. Canadian Cities _____

10. First Nations _____

_____

Canada

Lesson 3

MAIN IDEAS

1. Canada has a democratic government with a prime minister and a parliament.
2. Canada has four distinct geographic and cultural regions.
3. Canada's economy is largely based on trade with the United States.

Key Terms and Places

regionalism strong connection that people feel toward their region

maritime on or near the sea

Montreal Canada's second-largest city, one of the world's largest French-speaking cities

Ottawa Canada's national capital

Vancouver city on the Pacific coast with strong trade ties to Asia

Lesson Summary
CANADA'S GOVERNMENT

Canada has a democratic central government led by a prime minister. This job is like that of a president. The prime minister is the head of Canada's national government. The prime minister also leads Parliament, Canada's governing body. Parliament is made up of the House of Commons and the Senate. Canadians elect members of the House of Commons. The prime minister appoints senators. Provincial governments are like state governments. A premier leads each province.

> Circle the title of the person who is the leader of Canada's national government.

CANADA'S REGIONS

Canada has four regions. Each has its own cultural and physical features. In Quebec province, located in the Heartland region, **regionalism** has created problems between French and English speakers.

The Eastern Provinces are on the Atlantic coast region. They include three **Maritime** Provinces—

> Underline the names of the three Maritime Provinces.

Guided Reading Workbook

New Brunswick, Nova Scotia and Prince Edward Island—as well as Newfoundland and Labrador. Most people live in cities near the coast. Forestry and fishing are the major economic activities.

More than half of all Canadians live in the Heartland region in the provinces of Ontario and Quebec. This region includes **Montreal**, Toronto, and **Ottawa**. Quebec is a center of French culture. Ontario is Canada's top manufacturing province.

The Western region includes British Columbia on the Pacific coast and the prairie provinces— Manitoba, Saskatchewan, and Alberta. Farming is important there, especially growing wheat. In British Columbia, **Vancouver** is a major center for trade with Asia.

The Canadian North region consists of the Yukon and Northwest Territories and Nunavut, the Inuit homeland. The region is very cold and not many people live there. Nunavut has its own local government.

List two ways in which the Eastern and Heartland provinces are different from each other.

_____
_____
_____
_____
_____
_____
_____
_____
_____
_____
_____
_____

CANADA'S ECONOMY

Many of Canada's economic activities are connected to its natural resources. Mining and manufacturing are key industries along with producing minerals. Most Canadians hold service jobs. Tourism is the fastest-growing service industry. Trade is also important. The United States is Canada's leading trading partner. The United States buys much of its lumber from Canada.

Which type of economic activity employs the most workers?

_____
_____

CHALLENGE ACTIVITY

Critical Thinking: Draw Conclusions Why do you think Canada and the United States are such strong trading partners? What are the advantages and disadvantages of this strong trading relationship? Explain your answer in a one-page essay.

DIRECTIONS Look at each set of four vocabulary terms. On the line provided, write the letter of the term that does not relate to the others.

_____ 1. a. culture
   b. regionalism
   c. connection
   d. industrial

_____ 2. a. coast
   b. heartland
   c. Atlantic
   d. maritime

_____ 3. a. Montreal
   b. Toronto
   c. Ottawa
   d. Vancouver

_____ 4. a. Yukon
   b. Maritime
   c. Nunavut
   d. tundra

_____ 5. a. Alberta
   b. Manitoba
   c. Saskatchewan
   d. Nova Scotia

Heartland	Inuit	Maritime
Montreal	motto	Ottawa
Regionalism	Toronto	Vancouver

DIRECTIONS Choose five terms from the word bank. On the lines below use these terms to write a poem or story that relates to the lesson.

_____

_____

_____

_____

_____

_____

_____

_____

Early Civilizations of Latin America

MAIN IDEAS

1. The Olmec were the first complex civilization in Mesoamerica and influenced other cultures.
2. Geography helped shape the lives of the early Maya.
3. During the Classic Age, the Maya built great cities linked by trade.
4. Maya culture included a strict social structure, a religion with many gods, and achievements in science and the arts.
5. The decline of Maya civilization began in the 900s.

Key Terms and Places

civilization organized society within a specific area

maize corn

Palenque Maya city in which the king Pacal had a temple built to record his achievements

observatories buildings from which people could study the sky

Lesson Summary
THE OLMEC

Mesoamerica extends from central Mexico to the northern part of Central America. A people called the Olmec developed the first complex **civilization** in Mesoamerica around 1200 BC. The region is hot and humid with abundant rainfall and rich, fertile soil. The Olmec grew **maize**, beans, squash, peppers, and avocados.

The Olmec built towns which were religious and government centers with temples and plazas. They built the first pyramids in the Americas and made sculptures of huge stone heads. They created one of the first writing systems in the Americas, but no one today knows how to read it. Their influence and culture spread through a large trading network. Olmec civilization ended around 400 BC, but it influenced the Maya.

> Underline the sentence that gives the location of Mesoamerica.

> Why are there no translations of Olmec writing?
>
> _____
> _____
> _____

GEOGRAPHY AND THE EARLY MAYA

The Maya settled in thick tropical forests of
what is now northern Guatemala. They cleared
areas to farm beans, squash, avocados, and
maize. The forests provided animals for food and
plants for building materials. By AD 200, the
Maya had begun building large cities in
Mesoamerica.

> **What crops did the Maya grow?**
> _____
> _____

THE CLASSIC AGE

Maya civilization was at its peak between AD
250 and 900, a period called the Classic Age.
There were more than 40 Maya cities. These cities
sometimes fought one another for control of land
and resources. The Maya established trade
routes throughout Mesoamerica and traded for
the supplies they needed to build their grand
cities.

    The Maya built large stone pyramids, temples,
palaces, and plazas. Some buildings honored
local kings. A temple built in the city of **Palenque**
(pah-LENG-kay) honored its builder, the king
Pacal (puh-KAHL). The Maya built canals and
shaped hillsides into flat terraces for crops.
Volcanoes and volcanic eruptions influenced
Maya civilization during this period.

> **How did Maya cities relate to one another?**
> _____
> _____
> _____
> _____
> _____
> _____

> **How was the Maya king Pacal honored?**
> _____
> _____

MAYA CULTURE

Social structure and religion were the main forces
influencing Maya life. Kings held the highest
position, both in politics and religion. Priests,
warriors, and rich merchants were in the upper
class. Most Maya belonged to lower class
farming families. Maya farmers had to "pay" the
rulers with some of their crops and with goods
such as cloth and salt. They also had to help
build temples and other buildings and serve in
the army.

> **Which groups made up the upper class of the Maya social structure?**
> _____
> _____

Guided Reading Workbook

The Maya worshipped many gods. They tried to keep their gods happy by giving them blood. They did this by piercing their tongues or skin. Maya achievements in art, architecture, math, science, and writing were remarkable. They built **observatories** for priests to study the stars. They developed a calendar that had 365 days. The Maya developed a writing system and a number system. They were among the first people with a symbol for zero.

> **What was special about the Maya number system?**
> _____
> _____

DECLINE OF MAYA CIVILIZATION

Maya civilization began to collapse in the AD 900s. They stopped building large structures and left the cities for the countryside. Historians are not sure why this happened, but there are several theories. Some historians believe that Maya farmers kept planting the same crop over and over, which weakened the soil. This may have caused more competition and war between the cities. The people may have decided to rebel against their kings' demands. Droughts may have played a part as well. There were probably many factors that led to the decline of the Maya civilization.

> **List two factors that may have contributed to the decline of the Maya civilization.**
> _____
> _____
> _____
> _____
> _____
> _____

CHALLENGE ACTIVITY

Critical Thinking: Make Inferences One source of information about the Maya comes from kings like Pacal, who dedicated a temple to his achievements. Draw a building that honors our culture. Include details that would help future historians reconstruct 21st century life.

DIRECTIONS Read each sentence and fill in the blank with the word in the word pair that best completes the sentence.

1. The Maya's religious beliefs led them to make impressive advances in science, using _____ to study astronomy. (**observatories/Palenque**)

2. The Maya grew a variety of crops, including _____, which is corn. (**avocados/maize**)

3. Pacal, a Maya king, had a temple built in _____ to honor his achievements. (**observatories/Palenque**)

4. The _____ developed the first complex civilization in Mesoamerica. (**Maya/Olmec**)

5. The Maya were influenced by Olmec _____. (**civilization/ Palenque**)

civilization	maize
Maya	observatories
Olmec	Palenque

DIRECTIONS Look up three terms from the word bank in an encyclopedia or dictionary. On a separate sheet of paper, write the encyclopedia or dictionary definition of the term that is closest to the definition used in your textbook. Then write a sentence using each term correctly.

Early Civilizations of Latin America

MAIN IDEAS
1. The Aztecs built a rich and powerful empire in central Mexico.
2. Social structure, religion, and warfare shaped life in the empire.
3. Hernán Cortés conquered the Aztec Empire in 1521.

Key Terms and Places

Tenochtitlán island city and capital of the Aztec Empire

causeways raised roads across water or wet ground

conquistadors Spanish conquerors

Lesson Summary

THE AZTECS BUILD AN EMPIRE

The first Aztecs were farmers who migrated south to central Mexico. Other tribes had taken the good farmland, so the Aztecs settled on a swampy island in Lake Texcoco (tays-KOH-koh). In 1325, they began building their capital there.

War was key to the Aztecs' rise to power. The Aztec warriors conquered many towns and made the conquered people pay tribute with cotton, gold, or food. The Aztecs also controlled a large trade network.

The Aztecs' power and wealth was most visible in the capital, **Tenochtitlán** (tay-nawch-teet-LAHN). The Aztecs built three **causeways** to connect the island city to the lakeshore. They grew food on floating gardens, called *chinampas*. At its peak, Tenochtitlán had about 200,000 people. The city had temples, a palace, and a busy market.

LIFE IN THE EMPIRE

Aztec society had clearly defined social classes. The king was the most important person. He was in charge of law, trade, tribute, and warfare. The nobles, including tax collectors and judges,

> Why did the Aztecs settle on an island in Lake Texcoco?
>
> _____
> _____
> _____

> How were the Aztecs able to become wealthy?
>
> _____
> _____
> _____
> _____

> Underline the sentence that lists the responsibilities of the king.

helped the king with his duties. Below the king and nobles were priests and warriors. Priests had great influence over the Aztecs. Warriors were highly respected. Below priests and warriors were merchants and artisans, and then farmers and laborers. Slaves were lowest in society.

The Aztecs believed that gods ruled all parts of life and human sacrifice was necessary to keep the gods happy. In rituals, priests cut open victims' chests to give blood to the gods and sacrificed nearly 10,000 humans a year.

The Aztecs studied astronomy. Their calendar was much like the Maya calendar. The Aztecs had a rich artistic tradition and a writing system. They also had a strong oral tradition.

What did the Aztecs believe was necessary to keep the gods happy?
_____
_____
_____
_____

CORTÉS CONQUERS THE AZTECS

In 1519 Hernán Cortés (er-NAHN kawr-TEZ) led a group of Spanish conquerors called **conquistadors** into Mexico. Their motives were to seek gold, claim land, and spread their religion. The Aztec ruler, Moctezuma II (MAWK-tay-SOO-mah), thought Cortés was a god. Moctezuma gave Cortés many gifts, including gold. Wanting more gold, Cortés took Moctezuma prisoner. Enraged, the Aztecs attacked the Spanish. They drove the Spanish out of the city, but Moctezuma was killed.

To defeat the Aztecs, the Spanish allied with people who did not like the Aztec rulers. The Spanish used guns and rode horses. They also carried diseases like smallpox that killed many Aztecs. In 1521 the Spanish brought the Aztec Empire to an end.

What factors contributed to the Aztecs' defeat?
_____
_____
_____
_____

CHALLENGE ACTIVITY

Critical Thinking: Make Inferences Do you think
Cortés's actions toward the Aztecs were fair?
Write two paragraphs defending your opinion.
Give examples to support your opinion.

DIRECTIONS Write a word or phrase that explains the term or
name given.

1. Tenochtitlán _____

2. causeway _____

   _____

3. conquistadors _____

4. Hernán Cortés _____

5. Moctezuma II _____

6. tribute _____

7. chinampas _____

Early Civilizations of Latin America

MAIN IDEAS
1. Prior to the Inca Empire, several civilizations grew in the Andes and along the Pacific coast of South America.
2. The Inca created an empire with a strong central government in South America.
3. Life in the Inca Empire was influenced by social structure, religion, and the Inca's cultural achievements.
4. Francisco Pizarro conquered the Inca and took control of the region in 1537.

Key Terms and Places

Cuzco capital of the Inca Empire, located in present-day Peru

Quechua official language of the Inca

masonry stonework

Lesson Summary
GEOGRAPHY AND EARLY ANDEAN CIVILIZATIONS

The Andes Mountains run along the western side of South America. Between the mountain ridges lie high plains, called *altiplano*. A narrow desert lies between the mountains and rich fishing waters in the Pacific Ocean. Rivers from the Andes drain into the Pacific and into the Amazon River to the east. The climate varies with latitude and altitude. Within this region, many civilizations grew, adapting to the land around them.

South America's first major civilization developed in what is now northern and central Peru. People of the Chavín culture grew maize and potatoes, wove textiles, carved stone monuments, and produced animal and human-shaped pottery. They were followed by the Moche in northern coastal Peru. The Moche irrigated their fields of corn, built adobe pyramids, and produced pottery and metalwork. Along the coast to the south, the Nazca used

What is the *altiplano*?
_____
_____
_____

Circle the names of the four early Andean civilizations.

irrigation to farm their dry region. They built cisterns to hold water. Their artifacts include large designs of animals, plants, and geometric shapes which are best seen from the air. The Chimú followed the Moche in northern coastal Peru. They built irrigation systems, roads, and a large capital. They were conquered by the Inca around 1460.

THE INCA CREATE AN EMPIRE

The Inca began as a small tribe in the Andes. They built their capital, **Cuzco**, in what is now Peru. Inca territorial expansion began in the mid-1400s under the ruler Pachacuti. By the early 1500s, the Inca Empire stretched from Ecuador to central Chile.

> Underline the sentence that describes the Inca's beginnings.

To rule this vast empire, the Inca formed a strong central government. The Inca replaced local leaders of conquered areas with new people loyal to the Inca government. The Inca established an official language, **Quechua**. The Inca paid taxes in the form of labor. This labor tax system was called the *mita*. There were no merchants or markets. Instead, government officials would distribute goods collected through the mita. Leftover goods were stored in the capital for emergencies. If a natural disaster struck, or if people simply could not care for themselves, the government provided supplies to help them.

> How did Inca get food, clothing, and other goods?
>
> _____
> _____
> _____
> _____

LIFE IN THE INCA EMPIRE

Inca society had two main social classes. The emperor, priests, and government officials were the upper class. The upper class lived in Cuzco and did not pay the labor tax. The lower class included farmers, artisans, and servants. Most Inca were farmers. They grew maize and peanuts

in the warmer valleys and potatoes on terraced
hillsides in the mountains.

Inca religion was based on the belief that Inca
rulers were related to the sun god and never really
died. Inca ceremonies often included sacrifice of
llamas, cloth, or food. They also believed certain
natural landforms had magical powers.

Inca are known for their expert **masonry**, or
stonework. They cut stone blocks so precisely
that no cement was needed to hold them
together. Some of their stone buildings and roads
have lasted until today. Inca artisans made
beautiful pottery, jewelry, and textiles. The Inca
had no written language, but they kept records
with knotted cords called *quipus*. They passed
down stories and songs orally.

> To whom did the Inca
> believe their rulers were
> related?
>
> _____
>
> _____
>
> _____

> The Inca excelled in the
> use of what building
> material?
>
> _____
>
> _____

PIZARRO CONQUERS THE INCA

In the late 1520s a civil war began between an
Inca ruler's two sons, Atahualpa and Huáscar.
Atahualpa won, but the war had weakened the
Inca army. On his way to be crowned king,
Atahualpa heard that conquistadors led by
Francisco Pizarro had arrived in the Inca Empire.
When Atahualpa came to meet them, the Spanish
captured him. They attacked and killed thousands
of Inca soldiers. Although the Inca brought gold
and silver to pay for Atahualpa's return, the
Spanish killed him. The Spanish defeated the Inca
and ruled their lands for the next 300 years.

> Circle the name of the
> leader who led the Spanish
> conquistadors in their
> defeat of the Inca.

CHALLENGE ACTIVITY

Critical Thinking: Make Inferences The Inca used labor as a form of
taxation. Write two paragraphs explaining the advantages and
disadvantages of this practice.

DIRECTIONS Read each sentence and fill in the blank with the word in the word pair that best completes the sentence.

1. High plains, called _____, lie between the mountain ridges of the Andes. **(altiplano/mita)**

2. The Inca capital was called _____. **(Cuzco/Quechua)**

3. The _____ created large designs best seen from the air. **(Chimú/ Nazca)**

4. The official language of the Inca was _____. **(quipu/Quechua)**

5. The _____, or Inca labor tax system, was not paid by the upper class. **(mita/masonry)**

DIRECTIONS Write a paragraph describing the Inca Empire using the words *Cuzco*, *Quechua*, and *masonry*.

> **MAIN IDEAS**
> 1. Mexico's physical features include plateaus, mountains, and coastal lowlands.
> 2. Mexico's climate and vegetation include deserts, tropical forests, and cool highlands.
> 3. Key natural resources in Mexico include oil, silver, gold, and scenic landscapes.

Key Terms and Places

Río Bravo river, known in the United States as the Rio Grande, that forms part of Mexico's border with the United States

peninsula piece of land surrounded on three sides by water

Baja California peninsula stretching from northern Mexico into the Pacific Ocean

Yucatán Peninsula land separating the Gulf of Mexico from the Caribbean Sea

Gulf of Mexico body of water that forms Mexico's eastern border

Sierra Madre "mother range" made up of three mountain ranges in Mexico

Lesson Summary
PHYSICAL FEATURES

Mexico shares a long border with the United States. Part of this border is formed by a river called the **Río Bravo,** known as the Rio Grande in the United States. Mexico's western border is the Pacific Ocean, where a long **peninsula** called **Baja California** stretches south from northern Mexico. In the east, the **Yucatán Peninsula** separates the **Gulf of Mexico** from the Caribbean Sea.

> Underline the names of Mexico's two peninsulas.

The interior of Mexico is mostly the high, rugged Mexican Plateau, which rises in the west to the Sierra Madre Occidental. In the east it meets the Sierra Madre Oriental. **Sierra Madre** means "mother range." The country's capital, Mexico City, lies at the southern end of the plateau in the Valley of Mexico. The city has earthquakes, and to the south there are active volcanoes.

> Where is Mexico City located?
>
> _____
>
> _____

From the central highlands, the land slopes down to Mexico's sunny beaches. In the east the Gulf coastal plain is wide, and there are many farms.

The Yucatán Peninsula is mostly flat. The limestone rock there has eroded to form caves and steep depressions called sinkholes, many of which are filled with water.

> **How is the terrain in the Yucatán Peninsula different from that of the Sierra Madre?**
>
> _____
>
> _____

CLIMATE AND VEGETATION

Mexico has many climates with different types of vegetation. The mountains and plateaus are cool, and freezing temperatures can reach all the way to Mexico City. The mountain valleys are mild, and the southern coast is also pleasant. Summer rains support tropical rain forests, where animals such as jaguars, monkeys, and anteaters live. The Yucatán Peninsula is hot and dry, supporting only scrub forests. The north is also dry, much of it covered by desert.

> **Underline the words that describe the many climates of Mexico.**

NATURAL RESOURCES

Petroleum, or oil, is an important resource. Mexico sells a lot of oil to the United States. Before oil was discovered, minerals were the most valuable resource. Today, Mexico mines more silver than any other country. Copper, lead, gold, and zinc are also mined.

Another important resource is water. Unfortunately, this resource is scarce in many parts of Mexico. However, the water surrounding Mexico draws many tourists to the country's scenic beaches.

> **What is Mexico's most important mineral product?**
>
> _____

CHALLENGE ACTIVITY

Critical Thinking: Make Predictions Write a paragraph making a prediction about which of Mexico's resources will be most important in Mexico's future. Support your prediction with information you learned in the lesson.

DIRECTIONS On the line provided before each statement, write **T** if
a statement is true and **F** if a statement is false. If a statement is
false, write the term that would make the statement correct on the
line after each sentence.

_____ 1. In the Yucatán Peninsula, erosion of limestone rock has created many
caves and <u>sinkholes</u>.

_____

_____ 2. The climate in southern Mexico is mostly warm and humid, or
<u>peninsula.</u>

_____

_____ 3. Baja California is a narrow <u>plateau</u> that stretches into the Pacific
Ocean.

_____

_____ 4. <u>Petroleum</u> is one of Mexico's most important natural resources.

_____

_____ 5. The <u>Gulf of Mexico</u> is Mexico's eastern border.

_____

DIRECTIONS Write three words or phrases that describe the term.

6. peninsula _____

7. Río Bravo _____

8. plateau _____

9. Sierra Madre _____

10. Yucatán Peninsula _____

Mexico

MAIN IDEAS

1. Early cultures of Mexico included the Olmecs, the Mayas, and the Aztecs.
2. Mexico's period as a Spanish colony and its struggles since independence have shaped its culture.
3. Spanish and native cultures have influenced Mexico's customs and traditions today.

Key Terms and Places

empire land with different territories and peoples under a single ruler

mestizos Spanish name for people of mixed European and Indian ancestry

mulattoes Spanish name for people of mixed European and African ancestry

missions church outposts

haciendas huge expanses of farm or ranch land

Lesson Summary
EARLY CULTURES

People of Mexico grew corn, beans, peppers, and squash as early as 5,000 years ago. Around 1500 BC the Olmecs settled on the southern coast of the Gulf of Mexico. They built temples and statues. About AD 250 the Mayas built cities in Mexico and Central America. They were astronomers and left written records. Maya civilization collapsed after AD 900.

Later, the Aztecs moved into central Mexico. In 1325 they founded their capital, Tenochtitlán. They built an **empire** through conquest of other tribes.

> Circle the achievements of the Olmecs and Mayas.

COLONIAL MEXICO AND INDEPENDENCE

In 1519 a Spanish soldier, Hernán Cortés, arrived in Mexico with guns, horses, and about 600 soldiers. The Spanish also brought diseases that killed many Aztecs. This helped Cortés defeat the Aztecs in 1521.

> How long did it take Cortés to conquer the Aztecs?
> _____

Many people in colonial Mexico were of mixed European and Indian ancestry and were called **mestizos**. When Africans were brought to America as slaves, they added to the mix of people. The Spaniards called people of mixed European and African ancestry **mulattoes**. The Catholic Church was important in the colony. Priests tried to convert the Indians, traveling far north to build **missions**.

Spain was eager to mine gold and silver in Mexico. The native people and enslaved Africans did most of the mining. They also worked the huge farms and ranches, called **haciendas**, that were owned by wealthy people of Spanish ancestry.

Mexico gained independence in 1821. Miguel Hidalgo started the revolt in 1810 by asking for equality. Later, Texas broke away from Mexico and joined the United States. The two countries fought over their border in the Mexican-American War. Mexico lost the war and almost half its territory.

In the mid-1800s, the popular president Benito Juárez made many reforms. But in the early 1900s the government helped the hacienda owners take land from the peasants. People were angry and started the Mexican Revolution in 1910. In 1920 a new government took land from the large landowners and gave it back to the peasants.

Who owned the haciendas?
_____
_____

What did the government do that made people angry?
_____
_____
_____

CULTURE

In Mexico language is tied to ethnic groups. Speaking an American Indian language identifies a person as Indian. Mexicans have combined Indian religious practices with Catholic practices. One example is a holiday called Day of the Dead. On this day, Mexicans follow native traditions for remembering ancestors. The holiday is celebrated on November 1 and 2—the same dates as similar Catholic holidays.

Underline the Indian aspects of the Day of the Dead

CHALLENGE ACTIVITY

Critical Thinking: Sequence Make a timeline with important dates and events in Mexican history.

DIRECTIONS Read each sentence and circle the word in the word pair that best completes each sentence.

1. Through conquest of neighboring tribes, the (**Olmec/Aztecs**) built an empire.

2. The term that the Spanish used for people in colonial Mexico with both European and Indian ancestry was (**mestizos/mulattoes**).

3. During colonial times, Catholic priests at (**haciendas/missions**) taught the Indians Spanish and learned their language.

4. To seek independence from Spain, Miguel Hidalgo began a/an (**revolt/empire**) in 1810.

DIRECTIONS Look at each set of four vocabulary terms. On the line provided, write the letter of the term that does not relate to the others.

_____ 5. a. haciendas   _____ 6. a. ancestors
   b. ranches   b. Day of the Dead
   c. peasants   c. chinampas
   d. mulattoes   d. celebration

| chinampas | conquistadors | empire | haciendas |
| mestizos | missions | mulattoes | revolt |

DIRECTIONS Choose five of the words from the word bank. On a separate sheet of paper, use these words to write a summary of what you have learned in the lesson.

Mexico

MAIN IDEAS
1. Government has traditionally played a large role in Mexico's economy.
2. Mexico has four distinct culture regions.

Key Terms and Places

inflation rise in prices that occurs when currency loses its buying power

indigenous original or native resident of a specific region

slash-and-burn agriculture practice of burning forest to clear land for planting

cash crop crop that farmers grow mainly to sell for a profit

Mexico City world's second-largest city and Mexico's capital

smog mixture of smoke, chemicals, and fog

maquiladoras U.S.- and foreign-owned factories in Mexico

Lesson Summary
GOVERNMENT

Mexico's government has made improvements over the years. Today people in Mexico can vote in certain elections. People can find jobs in cities and buy a home. More children can attend school. However, that was not always true. Although Mexico is a democracy, one political party ran the government for 71 years. This ended in 2000 when Vicente Fox was elected president. He represented a different political party.

> Underline the improvements people in Mexico enjoy today.
> _____

ECONOMY

Like other developing countries, Mexico has foreign debts, unemployment, and **inflation**. Due to the North American Free Trade Agreement (NAFTA), Mexico now sells more products to the United States and Canada. Although exports have helped the economy, some Mexicans believe NAFTA has not helped the **indigenous** people, or

> How did NAFTA change trade for Mexico?
> _____
> _____
> _____

native Indians, who mostly farm on communal lands.

Agriculture is a key part of the Mexican economy. Some farmers who do not own much land and only grow enough to feed their families use **slash-and-burn agriculture**. Other farmers specialize by growing **cash crops**, such as fruits and vegetables. Trucks often bring these cash crops to the United States.

Mexicans work in oil fields and in factories. Many Mexicans also come to the United States looking for work. Tourists visit Mexico to enjoy its attractions.

MEXICO'S CULTURE REGIONS

Mexico has four culture regions that differ from one another in population, resources, and climate.

The Greater **Mexico City** region includes the capital and about 50 nearby cities. More than 19 million people make Mexico City one of the world's largest cities. Many people move there to look for work, and air pollution has become a problem. The mountains trap the **smog**—a mixture of smoke, chemicals, and fog. Poverty is also a problem.

Many cities in Mexico's central region were colonial mining or ranching centers. Mexico's colonial heritage can be seen today in the churches and public squares of this region. Family farmers grow vegetables and corn in the fertile valleys. In recent years, cities such as Guadalajara have attracted new industries from Mexico City.

> **Underline information about the current economy of Mexico's central region. Circle information about its past economy.**

Trade with the United States has helped northern region cities like Monterrey and Tijuana grow. Foreign-owned factories, called **maquiladoras**, have been built in this region. Many Mexicans cross the border to shop, work, or live in the United States. Some cross the

> **What has helped Monterrey and Tijuana grow?**
>
> _____
>
> _____

border legally. The U.S. government tries to prevent illegal immigration.

Many people in the southern Mexico region speak Indian languages and follow traditional customs. Sugarcane and coffee, two major export crops, grow well in the humid southern climate. Oil production in the region has brought population growth to southern Mexico. Maya ruins, sunny beaches, and clear blue waters make tourism a major industry in the Yucatán Peninsula. Many of today's cities were tiny villages just 20 years ago.

> **Underline information about the people in Mexico's southern region.**

CHALLENGE ACTIVITY

Critical Thinking: Compare and Contrast Make a four-columned chart—one column for each cultural region in Mexico. Make three rows and write information for each region about History, Population and Economy, and Geography and Natural Resources. When you have completed the chart, circle items that are similar among the regions.

cash crop	indigenous	inflation
maquiladoras	Mexico City	slash-and-burn agriculture
smog		

DIRECTIONS Answer each question by writing a sentence that contains at least one term from the word bank.

1. How has Mexico's economy struggled?

   _____

   _____

   _____

2. Why is northern Mexico's economy growing today?

_____

_____

_____

3. Why were some Mexicans unhappy with the North American Free Trade Agreement (NAFTA)?

_____

_____

_____

4. What types of agriculture do farmers practice in southern Mexico?

_____

_____

_____

DIRECTIONS Your family is planning a trip to Mexico City. On a separate sheet of paper, write a paragraph describing what you expect to see when you get there.

Central America and the Caribbean

MAIN IDEAS
1. Physical features of the region include volcanic highlands and coastal plains.
2. The climate and vegetation of the region include forested highlands, tropical forests, and humid lowlands.
3. Key natural resources in the region include rich soils for agriculture, a few minerals, and beautiful beaches.

Key Terms and Places

isthmus narrow strip of land that connects two larger land areas

Caribbean Sea sea surrounded by Central America, the Greater and Lesser Antilles, and South America

Lesser Antilles group of small islands in the Caribbean Sea

archipelago large group of islands

Greater Antilles group of large islands in the Caribbean Sea

cloud forest moist, high-elevation tropical forest where low clouds are common

Lesson Summary
PHYSICAL FEATURES

Central America is an **isthmus** that connects North and South America. It is made up of seven small countries: Belize, Guatemala, El Salvador, Honduras, Nicaragua, Costa Rica, and Panama. At its widest, the isthmus separates the Pacific Ocean and the **Caribbean Sea** by 125 miles (200 km). A chain of mountains and volcanoes runs through the middle of the isthmus. On both sides, a few short rivers run through the coastal plains to the sea. The lack of good water routes and ruggedness of the land make travel difficult.

The Caribbean islands separate the Atlantic Ocean from the Caribbean Sea. On the east lie the **Lesser Antilles**, an **archipelago** of islands that stretch from the Virgin Islands to Trinidad and Tobago. West and north of these are the **Greater Antilles**, which include Cuba, Jamaica, Puerto Rico, and Hispaniola. The Bahama Islands,

> Underline the names of the seven countries that make up Central America.

> What two bodies of water are separated by the Caribbean islands?
> _____
> _____

located in the Atlantic Ocean, southeast of Florida, include nearly 700 islands and thousands of reefs. Many of these islands are actually the tops of underwater volcanoes. They are located along the edges of tectonic plates that move against each other, causing earthquakes and volcanic eruptions.

> **What causes earthquakes and volcanoes in the region?**
> _____
> _____
> _____

CLIMATE AND VEGETATION

Most of the region is generally sunny and warm. Most of Central America's Pacific coast, where plantations and ranches are found, has a tropical savanna climate. The Caribbean coast has areas of tropical rain forest. The inland mountains are cool and humid. Some mountainous areas have dense **cloud forests**, or moist, high-elevation tropical forests where low clouds are common. Many animal and plant species live there.

> **Where are cloud forests found?**
> _____
> _____

Temperatures in the region do not change much from day to night or from winter to summer. Change in seasons is marked by changes in rainfall. Winters are generally dry, but it rains nearly every day in the summer. From summer to fall, hurricanes bring heavy rains and wind, which occasionally cause flooding and great destruction.

RESOURCES

The region's best resources are its land and climate, which make tourism an important industry. Warm climate and rich volcanic soil make the region a good place to grow coffee, bananas, sugarcane, and cotton. However, the region has few mineral or energy resources.

> **What two factors make the region a good place to grow crops?**
> _____
> _____

CHALLENGE ACTIVITY

Critical Thinking: Compare and Contrast Write a description of the year-round climate in your region and compare and contrast it with that of the Central American and Caribbean region.

DIRECTIONS Read each sentence and fill in the blank with the word
in the word pair that best completes the sentence.

1. The land that the seven countries of Central America are on is an
   _____, a narrow strip of land that connects two larger
   land areas. (**archipelago/isthmus**)

2. A large group of islands, such as the Caribbean Islands, is called an
   _____. (**archipelago/isthmus**)

3. The _____ is the body of water between Central
   America and the Caribbean Islands. (**Greater Antilles/Caribbean Sea**)

4. Cuba is part of the _____, one of the two main island
   groups in the Caribbean. (**Greater Antilles/Caribbean Sea**)

5. The many smaller islands of the Caribbean are called the
   _____. (**Lesser Antilles/Greater Antilles**)

6. A _____ is a moist, high-elevation tropical forest where
   low clouds are common. (**cloud forest/tropical savanna**)

archipelago	Caribbean Sea	cloud forest	Greater Antilles
isthmus	Lesser Antilles	reefs	volcanic ash

DIRECTIONS On a separate sheet of paper, write a letter to
someone who lives in a desert region. Describe how the geography
of the Central America and Caribbean area differs from the desert.
Include at least four terms from the word bank to describe the
Central America and Caribbean region.

Central America and the Caribbean

> **MAIN IDEAS**
> 1. The history of Central America was mostly influenced by Spain.
> 2. The culture of Central America is a mixture of Native American and European traditions.
> 3. Today, the countries of Central America have challenges and opportunities.

Key Terms and Places

civil war conflict between two or more groups within a country

ecotourism practice of using an area's natural environment to attract tourists

Panama Canal waterway connecting the Pacific Ocean, the Caribbean Sea, and the Atlantic Ocean

Lesson Summary
HISTORY

The Maya people built a civilization in the region from about AD 250 to 900. Many of their descendants, and some of their customs, can still be found. In the 1500s Spain controlled the entire region except for Belize, which became a British colony. The Europeans established gold mines and large tobacco and sugarcane plantations and forced the Central American Indians to do the hard work. They also brought enslaved Africans to work.

In 1821 Honduras, El Salvador, Costa Rica, Guatemala, and Nicaragua gained independence and were a single country until 1839. Panama was part of Colombia until 1903. Belize separated from Britain in 1981. Independence did not help most people, as wealthy landowners took control. In the early to mid-1900s the U.S.-based United Fruit Company controlled most of the banana production in the region. Many people resented the role of foreign companies and thought it was unfair for a few people to have so much power. In the mid- to late 1900s

> Underline the country that controlled most of the region in the 1500s.

> Underline the sentence that explains why people in the region objected to large foreign companies.

people fought for land reform in Guatemala, El Salvador, and Nicaragua.

CULTURE

Most people in Central America are mestizos, people of mixed Indian and European ancestry. Some Indian people live in areas such as the highlands, and people of African ancestry live mainly along the eastern coast. English is the official language in Belize. Spanish is also spoken there and in the other countries. Many people speak Indian languages.

The Spanish brought Roman Catholicism to people in the region, but Indian traditions are also followed. Corn, tomatoes, chocolate, and hot peppers are foods of the region.

> Underline the languages that are spoken in the region.

CENTRAL AMERICA TODAY

Guatemala has the region's largest population. Most people are mestizos, but many are descendants of the Mayas. Conflict there killed some 200,000 people from 1960 to 1996. Coffee is the most important crop.

Honduras is mountainous, making transportation difficult. It has little farmland, but fruit is exported.

In the 1980s the poor people of El Salvador fought a **civil war** against the few rich families that owned much of the best land, which is very fertile. The war ended in 1992, and people are rebuilding.

Nicaragua was ruled by Sandinistas from 1979 to 1990. After a civil war, it became a democracy.

Costa Rica has been more peaceful than most of its neighbors, which helps its economy. Coffee, bananas, and tourism are its largest industries.

Belize has the region's lowest population. Recently, **ecotourism** has become a large industry, as more people visit the Maya ruins and coral reefs.

> Underline the countries that fought a civil war in the last century.

> Which country has been more peaceful than most of the other countries in the region?
> _____

Most Panamanians live near the **Panama Canal**,
built and controlled by the United States. In 1999
the United States gave control to Panama.

CHALLENGE ACTIVITY
Critical Thinking: Sequence Make a timeline that
shows important events in Central American
history.

DIRECTIONS On the line before each statement, write **T** if the
statement is true and **F** if the statement is false. If the statement is
false, change the underlined term to make the sentence true. Then
write the correct term on the line after the sentence.

_____ 1. The <u>Europeans</u> began building large cities with pyramids and temples
in many Central American countries.

_____

_____ 2. Most of Central America came under the control of Europeans, who
established <u>ecotourism</u> to grow crops such as tobacco and sugarcane.

_____

_____ 3. The Spanish colonies declared <u>independence</u> from Spain, but little
changed, leading to wars more than a century later.

_____

_____ 4. As agreed to with the United States, Panama took over the <u>Maya,</u>
which links the Pacific Ocean, Caribbean Sea, and Atlantic Ocean.

_____

_____ 5. Belize is one country that supports its economy with <u>plantations,</u> using
its natural environment to attract tourists.

_____

civil wars	ecotourism	Europeans	independence
Mayas	Panama Canal	plantations	

DIRECTIONS Write a poem or short story about the history or culture
of Central America. Use at least four terms from the word bank.

Central America and the Caribbean

MAIN IDEAS
1. The history of the Caribbean islands includes European colonization followed by independence.
2. The culture of the Caribbean islands shows signs of past colonialism and slavery.
3. Today the Caribbean islands have distinctive governments with economies that depend on agriculture and tourism.

Key Terms and Places

Columbian Exchange movement of people, animals, plants, ideas, and diseases between Europe and the Americas

dialect regional variety of a language

commonwealth self-governing territory associated with another country

refugee someone who flees to another country, usually for political or economic reasons

Havana capital of Cuba

cooperative organization owned by its members and operated for their benefit

Lesson Summary
HISTORY

The Caribbean islands were the first land Christopher Columbus saw in 1492, though he thought he had sailed to islands near India. By the 1700s the islands were colonized by the Spanish, English, French, Dutch, and Danish. They brought enslaved Africans to work on their sugarcane plantations.

Much of the sugar grown in this area was exported to Europe, along with other crops. Colonists then imported products, food, and even animals from Europe. This movement of people, animals, plants, ideas, and diseases between Europe and the Americas came to be known as the **Columbian Exchange**.

> Underline the sentence that tells who colonized the Caribbean islands.

Haiti gained independence in 1804. Cuba became independent in 1902. Other islands became independent after World War II. Some, such as Martinique and Guadeloupe, never did. Most people on these French islands do not want independence.

CULTURE

Most islanders are descended from Europeans, Africans, or a mixture of the two. There are also some Asians. Some people speak English, French, or Spanish—others speak Creole, a **dialect**, or regional variety of a language.

Today, islands colonized by France and Spain have many Catholics. Elsewhere, people practice a blend of Catholicism and traditional African religion called Santería. Caribbean people enjoy the Carnival holiday. It comes before the Christian season of Lent and features parades and costumes. Some of the region's foods, such as okra and yams, were brought to the area by enslaved Africans. They also made souse, a dish made from the leftover pork given to them by slaveholders.

THE CARIBBEAN ISLANDS TODAY

Puerto Rico is a **commonwealth**, a self-governing territory associated with the United States. Some Puerto Ricans are happy about this, while others would like to become a state or a separate country. Though richer than others in the region, Puerto Ricans are not as well off as other U.S. citizens.

Haiti, occupying the western part of Hispaniola, is the poorest country in the Americas. Dishonest governments have caused violence, which many Haitians have tried to escape by becoming **refugees**.

> Underline the sentence that describes the general economic status of people living in Puerto Rico.

> What is the poorest country in the Americas?
> _____

The eastern part of Hispaniola is the Dominican Republic. Its industries are tourism and agriculture.

Havana is the capital of Cuba, the largest, most populous island in the Caribbean. Cuba has been run by a Communist government since Fidel Castro came to power in 1959. The government runs the economy, newspapers, and television. Most farms are organized as **cooperatives**, owned by the people who work on them and run for their benefit.

> Underline the sentences that describe Cuba's government.

Some of the remaining Caribbean islands, such as Jamaica, are independent countries. Others, such as the Virgin Islands, are territories of other countries. Most rely on tourism for their income.

CHALLENGE ACTIVITY

Critical Thinking: Make Inferences Imagine you are a Haitian refugee. Write a paragraph describing the reasons you left Haiti and your hopes for the future.

DIRECTIONS Look at each set of words. On the line provided, write the letter of the term that does not relate to the others.

_____ 1. a. dialect   b. language   c. religion   d. Creole

_____ 2. a. treasury   b. territory   c. Puerto Rico   d. commonwealth

_____ 3. a. refugee   b. poverty   c. tourism   d. violence

_____ 4. a. Hispaniola   b. Havana   c. Cuba   d. Castro

_____ 5. a. cooperative   b. territory   c. members   d. organization

_____ 6. a. Columbian Exchange b. movement c. people   d. dialect

| Columbian Exchange | commonwealth | cooperative | dialect |
| Havana | Hispaniola | refugee | revolt |

DIRECTIONS Write a summary of what you learned in Lesson 3.
Use five of the terms from the word bank.

_____

_____

_____

_____

_____

_____

_____

_____

South America

MAIN IDEAS
1. Coastal lowlands, mountains and highlands, and river systems shape much of Caribbean South America.
2. Atlantic South America's rain forests are its major source of natural resources.
3. The Andes mountains are Pacific South America's main physical feature.

Key Terms and Places

Andes mountains on the western side of Colombia

cordillera mountain system made up of roughly parallel ranges

Llanos plains region between the highlands and Andes

Orinoco River longest river in the region, flows through Venezuela to the Atlantic Ocean

Amazon River 4,000-mile-long river that flows eastward across northern Brazil

estuary partially enclosed body of water where freshwater mixes with salty seawater

Río de la Plata estuary that connects the Paraná River and the Atlantic Ocean

Pampas wide, grassy plains in central Argentina

deforestation action of clearing trees

soil exhaustion soil that has become infertile because it has lost nutrients needed by plants

altiplano broad, high plateau that lies between the ridges of the Andes

El Niño ocean weather pattern that affects the Pacific coast

Lesson Summary
CARIBBEAN SOUTH AMERICA

Caribbean South America includes rugged mountains, highlands, and plains drained by huge river systems. The region's highest point is in western Colombia, where the snow-capped **Andes** reach 18,000 feet. These mountains form a **cordillera**, or a system of roughly parallel mountain ranges. The **Llanos** is mostly grassland

> Underline the sentence that describes the Llanos.

and often floods. The **Orinoco River** and its
tributaries drain the plains and highlands. Two
other rivers, the Cauca and the Magdalena, drain
the Andean region.

Most of the region is warm year round since it
is near the equator. However, higher elevations
are cooler. The grassy Llanos has low elevation.
It has a tropical savanna climate with wet and dry
seasons. Humid tropical rain forests cover much
of southern Colombia. Heavy rainfall produces
huge trees and vegetation so thick that sunlight
barely reaches the jungle floor. Resources include
agriculture, oil, timber, and plentiful hydroelectric
power.

> **Describe the climate of southern Colombia.**
>
> _____
>
> _____
>
> _____

ATLANTIC SOUTH AMERICA

The Atlantic South America region includes
Brazil, Argentina, Uruguay, and Paraguay. The
Amazon River extends from the Andes
Mountains in Peru to the Atlantic Ocean. The
Paraná River drains much of the central part of
South America. It flows into an **estuary** called the
Río de la Plata and the Atlantic Ocean. The
region's landforms mainly consist of plains and
plateaus. The Amazon Basin in northern Brazil is
a huge, flat floodplain. Farther south are the
Brazilian Highlands and an area of high plains
called the Mato Grosso Plateau. The low plains
region, Gran Chaco, stretches across parts of
Paraguay and northern Argentina. The grassy
plains of the **Pampas** are found in central
Argentina. Patagonia is a region of dry plains
and plateaus south of the Pampas. These plains
rise in the west to form the Andes Mountains.

> **Underline the names of four plains regions in Atlantic South America.**

Atlantic South America has many climates.
Southern and highland areas tend to have cool
climates. Northern and coastal areas generally
have tropical and moist climates. The Amazon
rain forest provides food, wood, rubber, plants
for medicines, and other products. **Deforestation**

> **What threatens this region?**
>
> _____
>
> _____

Guided Reading Workbook

threatens the resources of the rain forest. Land near the coastal areas in the region is used for commercial farming but some areas face **soil exhaustion**. Other resources include gold, silver, copper, iron, oil, and hydroelectric power from the rivers.

PACIFIC SOUTH AMERICA

The Andes Mountains run through all of the Pacific South American countries. In the south, the mountains are rugged and covered by ice caps. In the north, they are rounded and the range splits into two ridges. A high plateau, called the **altiplano**, lies between the two ridges. Rivers flowing into the altiplano never reach the sea, but fill two large lakes. At the southern tip of the continent, the Strait of Magellan links the Atlantic and Pacific oceans.

> Underline the sentences that compare the Andes Mountains in the south and in the north.

Climate, vegetation, and landscapes all vary widely in Pacific South America. In this region, elevation has the biggest effect on climate and vegetation. Bananas and sugarcane are grown in the hot and humid elevations near sea level and in the Amazon basin. In the moist climates of the mountain forests, coffee is grown. In the forests and grasslands, potatoes and wheat are grown. At the higher altitudes, vegetation is limited. In the Atacama Desert of northern Chile, rain falls only about once every 20 years. A recurring weather pattern called **El Niño** causes extreme and unusual weather around the world. The region's natural resources include lumber, gold and other metals, and oil and natural gas. The lack of good farmland means there are few agricultural exports.

> What is the main reason climate varies in the region?
>
> _____

CHALLENGE ACTIVITY

**Critical Thinking: Compare and
Contrast** Compare the resources of the three
regions of South America. How are they similar
and how are they different?

DIRECTIONS Read each sentence and fill in the blank with the word
in the word pair that best completes the sentence.

1. The Andes mountains form a _____, or system of roughly

   parallel mountain ranges. (**cordillera/estuary**)

2. The _____ extends from the Andes Mountains in Peru to the

   Atlantic Ocean. (**Amazon River/Orinoco River**)

3. An _____ is a partially enclosed body of water where freshwater

   and seawater mix. (**altiplano/estuary**)

4. The _____ are grassy plains of central Argentina.

   (**Llanos/Pampas**)

5. _____, a recurring weather pattern, causes extreme and unusual

   weather around the world. (**El Niño/Río de la Plata**)

6. The _____ is a high plateau between the two ridges of the An-

   des. (**altiplano/cordillera**)

altiplano	Amazon River	Andes	cordillera
deforestation	El Niño	estuary	Llanos
Orinoco River	Pampas	Río de la Plata	soil exhaustion

DIRECTIONS Answer each question by writing a sentence that contains at least two terms from the word bank.

7. Into what body of water does the Paraná River flow?

   _____

8. What problems are affecting the natural resources of Atlantic South America?

   _____

   _____

South America

MAIN IDEAS

1. Brazil's history has been affected by Brazilian Indians, Portuguese settlers, and enslaved Africans.
2. Brazil's society reflects a mix of people and cultures.
3. Brazil today is experiencing population growth in its cities and new development in rain forest areas.

Key Terms and Places

São Paulo largest urban area in South America, located in southeastern Brazil

megacity giant urban area that includes surrounding cities and suburbs

Rio de Janeiro Brazil's second-largest city, located northeast of São Paulo

favelas huge slums

Brasília capital of Brazil

Manaus major port and industrial city, located 1,000 miles from the mouth of the Amazon River

Lesson Summary
HISTORY

Brazil is the largest country in South America. It has a population of more than 211 million people. The first people in Brazil were American Indians who arrived in the region thousands of years ago.

In 1500 Portuguese explorers became the first Europeans to find Brazil. Colonists brought Africans to the region to work as slaves on sugar plantations. These plantations helped make Portugal rich.

Gold and precious gems were discovered in the late 1600s and early 1700s in the southeast. The resulting mining boom drew people to Brazil from all over the world. Brazil became a major coffee producer in the late 1800s. Brazil gained independence from Portugal without a fight in 1822. Since the end of Portuguese rule, Brazil has been governed by both dictators and elected

> Who were the first people to live in Brazil?
>
> _____

> What discovery brought people to Brazil from all over the world?
>
> _____

officials. Today Brazil has an elected president
and legislature.

PEOPLE AND CULTURE

Nearly 40 percent of Brazil's people are of mixed
African and European descent. Brazil also has
the largest Japanese population outside of Japan.
Brazil's official language is Portuguese.

Brazil has the world's largest population of
Roman Catholics. Some Brazilians practice
macumba, a religion that combines beliefs and
practices of African and Indian religions with
Christianity.

Brazilians celebrate Carnival, a celebration
that mixes traditions from Africa, Brazil, and
Europe.

> **What percentage of Brazil's people are of mixed African and European descent?**
>
> _____

> **What is macumba?**
>
> _____
> _____
> _____
> _____

BRAZIL TODAY

Brazil can be divided into four regions. The
southeast is the most populated. About
21 million people live in and around the city of
São Paulo. São Paulo is considered a **megacity**,
or giant urban area that includes surrounding
cities and suburbs. **Rio de Janeiro**, Brazil's former
capital and second-largest city, is also located in
the southeast. The southeast has a good
economy, but it also has poverty. Many people
live in city slums, or **favelas**.

The northeast is Brazil's poorest region.
Drought has made farming difficult. However,
many tourists are attracted to the region.
Tourism is an important industry.

The interior region is a frontier land, with
much potential for farming. The capital of
Brazil, **Brasília**, was built there in the mid-1950s.

The Amazon region covers the northern part
of Brazil. **Manaus** is a major port and industrial
city 1,000 miles from the mouth of the Amazon
River. The Amazon rain forest is a valuable
resource to people who live and work there, but

> **What is Brazil's second-largest city?**
>
> _____

> **Circle the word describing an important industry in northeast Brazil.**

> **What are the four regions of Brazil?**
>
> _____
> _____
> _____

deforestation threatens the wildlife and Brazilian
Indians living there.

CHALLENGE ACTIVITY

Critical Thinking: Draw Conclusions Why do
most Brazilians live in the southeast? Write a
paragraph to explain your answer.

Brasília	Carnival	favelas
macumba	Manaus	megacity
Rio de Janeiro	São Paulo	

DIRECTIONS Read each sentence and choose the correct term from
the word bank to replace the underlined phrase. Write the term in
the space provided and then define the term in your own words.

1. This city was built in the interior region in the mid-1950s. _____

   Your definition: _____

   _____

2. These areas within Brazil's southeastern cities are marked by poverty.

   _____

   Your definition: _____

   _____

3. This cultural event mixes traditions from Africa, Brazil, and Europe.

   _____

   Your definition: _____

   _____

4. Popular with tourists, <u>this major port city</u> was once Brazil's capital.

_____

Your definition: _____

_____

5. São Paulo is a <u>giant city</u>. _____

_____

Your definition: _____

_____

_____

South America

MAIN IDEAS
1. European immigrants have dominated the history and culture of Argentina.
2. Argentina's capital, Buenos Aires, plays a large role in the country's government and economy today.
3. Uruguay has been influenced by its neighbors.
4. Paraguay is the most rural country in the region.

Key Terms and Places

gauchos Argentine cowboys

Buenos Aires capital of Argentina

Mercosur organization that promotes trade and economic cooperation among the southern and eastern countries of South America

informal economy part of the economy based on odd jobs that people perform without government regulation through taxes

landlocked completely surrounded by land with no direct access to the ocean

Lesson Summary
ARGENTINA'S HISTORY AND CULTURE

Argentina was originally home to groups of Indians. In the 1500s Spanish conquerors spread into southern South America in search of silver and gold. They built settlements in Argentina. Spanish monarchs granted land to the colonists. Landowners forced Indians living there to work.

During the colonial era, the Pampas became an important agricultural region. Argentine cowboys, called **gauchos**, herded cattle and horses there.

Argentina gained independence in the 1800s. Many Indians were killed. Immigrants from Italy, Germany, and Spain began to arrive in Argentina.

During the 1970s, many Argentines were tortured and killed after being accused of disagreeing with the government. Argentina's

> **Why did Spanish conquerors come to the region in the 1500s?**
> _____
> _____

> **Immigrants began to arrive from what European countries?**
> _____
> _____

Lesson 3, *continued*

military government gave up power to an elected
government in the 1980s. Argentina's historical
ties to Europe still affect its culture. Most
Argentinians are Roman Catholic.

ARGENTINA TODAY

Buenos Aires is the capital of Argentina. It is the
second-largest urban area in South America. In
the 1990s, government leaders made economic
reforms to help businesses grow. Argentina joined
Mercosur—an organization that promotes trade
and economic cooperation among the southern
and eastern countries of South America.
However, heavy debt and government spending
brought Argentina into an economic crisis. Many
people lost their jobs and joined the **informal
economy**—a part of the economy based on odd
jobs that people perform without government
regulation through taxes.

What is the purpose of Mercosur?
_____
_____
_____
_____

URUGUAY

Uruguay lies between Argentina and Brazil. Its
capital is Montevideo. Portugal claimed Uruguay
during the colonial era, but the Spanish took
over in the 1770s. Few Uruguayan Indians
remained. Uruguay declared its independence
from Spain in 1825. Today Uruguay is a
democracy. The economy is based on agriculture
and some manufacturing.

What is the capital of Uruguay?
_____

PARAGUAY

Paraguay is **landlocked**, which means completely
surrounded by land with no direct access to the
ocean. It was claimed by the Spanish in the
mid-1530s and remained a Spanish colony until
1811, when it won independence. Today Paraguay
is a democracy. Ninety-five percent of
Paraguayans are mestizos. People of European
descent and Indians make up the rest of the

Underline the definition of landlocked.

What type of government do Uruguay and Paraguay have today?
_____

Guided Reading Workbook

population. Most Paraguayans speak both Spanish and Guarani, an Indian language. Agriculture is an important part of the economy.

CHALLENGE ACTIVITY

Critical Thinking: Make Inferences Which Atlantic South American country do you think has the strongest economy? Write a paragraph giving reasons supporting your answer.

DIRECTIONS Read each sentence and fill in the blank with the word in the word pair that best completes the sentence.

1. Cowboys in Argentina are known as _____. (**gauchos/Guarani**)

2. The _____ in Argentina is based on odd jobs performed without government regulation through taxes. (**Mercosur/informal economy**)

3. Portugal claimed _____ during the colonial era. (**Argentina/Uruguay**)

4. _____ is completely surrounded by land with no direct access to the ocean. (**Paraguay/Uruguay**)

5. The capital of Argentina is _____. (**Buenos Aires/Montevideo**)

DIRECTIONS Look at each set of four terms following each number. On the line provided, write the letter of the term that does not relate to the others.

_____ 6. a. Argentina   b. Montevideo   c. gauchos   d. Buenos Aires

_____ 7. a. trade   b. Mercosur   c. cooperation   d. rural

_____ 8. a. Paraguay   b. Guarani   c. coastal   d. landlocked

_____ 9. a. agriculture   b. urban   c. Buenos Aires   d. Uruguay

_____ 10. a. economy   b. Spanish   c. mestizo   d. Portuguese

South America

MAIN IDEAS
1. Native cultures, Spanish conquest, and independence shaped Colombia's history.
2. In Colombia today, the benefits of a rich culture and many natural resources contrast with the effects of a long period of civil war.
3. Spanish settlement shaped the history and culture of Venezuela.
4. Oil production plays a large role in Venezuela's economy and government today.
5. The Guianas have diverse cultures and plentiful resources.

Key Terms and Places

Cartagena major Caribbean naval base and port during the Spanish empire

Bogotá capital of Colombia, located high in the eastern Andes

guerrillas members of an irregular military force

Caracas capital of Venezuela and the economic and cultural center of the country

llaneros Venezuelan cowboys

Lake Maracaibo lake near the Caribbean Sea, rich in oil deposits

strike group of workers stopping work until their demands are met

Lesson Summary
COLOMBIA'S HISTORY

In ancient times, the Chibcha people lived in Colombia. They had a well-developed civilization. They made pottery, wove fabrics, and made fine objects from gold and other metals. The Spanish claimed the land, started a colony, and built large estates. They forced the Chibcha and enslaved Africans to work on them. The Spanish also built a large naval base and commercial port at the city of **Cartagena**. Even after independence from Spain, there was trouble in Colombia. Part of the problem is Colombia's rugged geography, which isolates people into separate regions. Many people identify with their region more than their nation.

> Who were the inhabitants of Colombia in ancient times?
>
> _____

COLOMBIA TODAY

Most Colombians live in the fertile valleys and river basins among the mountain ranges, where the climate is moderate. **Bogotá**, the capital, is located high in the eastern Andes. Each region has a distinct geography as well as a distinct culture. Colombia's major export is oil. Its most famous agricultural product is coffee. Today, **guerrillas** have seized land from farmers and are involved in growing the illegal coca plant, which is used to make the dangerous drug cocaine. Colombia's government continues to fight the guerrillas with laws and military action.

> What is Colombia's most famous agricultural product?
>
> _____

VENEZUELA'S HISTORY

The Spanish came to Venezuela in the early 1500s looking for gold, but found little. In the early 1800s the Venezuelan people, led by Simon Bolívar, revolted against their Spanish rulers and fought for independence, which they officially gained in 1830. Military dictators ran the country throughout the 1800s. Oil was discovered in the 1900s but brought wealth only to the powerful.

> Who led the Venezuelan fight for independence?
>
> _____

VENEZUELA TODAY

Venezuelans are of native Indian, African, and European descent. European descendants tend to live in the cities, and African descendants tend to live on the coast. Most people are Spanish-speaking Roman Catholics, but Indian languages and religious beliefs have been kept alive. **Caracas**, Venezuela's capital, is the country's economic and cultural center. It has modern subways and buildings, but it is surrounded by slums. Many people in rural Venezuela are farmers or ranchers. Cattle on the ranches are herded by **llaneros**, or cowboys of the Llanos. The Orinoco River basin and **Lake Maracaibo** are rich in oil. The oil industry has made some people wealthy, but the vast majority of the population lives in poverty.

> Why do you think there is significant poverty in Venezuela?
>
> _____

Guided Reading Workbook

After years of military dictators, the first president was elected in 1959. In 2002 President Hugo Chavez started to distribute the country's oil income equally among all Venezuelans. Oil workers went on **strike** to protest the president's actions. The country's economy suffered greatly.

How did oil workers protest the actions of President Chavez?
_____

THE GUIANAS

The Guianas consist of the countries of Guyana, Suriname, and French Guiana. Dense tropical rain forests cover much of this region. These countries have diverse populations with many people descended from Africans, but each country is different. Guyana has many immigrants from India who came to work on sugarcane plantations. Today most people run small farms or businesses. Suriname's population includes Creoles, or people of mixed heritage, and people from China, Indonesia, Africa, and South Asia. Suriname's economy is similar to Guyana's. French Guiana is a territory of France. Most people live in coastal areas, and the country relies heavily on imports.

Circle the names of the countries that make up the Guianas.

CHALLENGE ACTIVITY

Critical Thinking: Draw Conclusions Did President Hugo Chavez help his country? Write a short paragraph explaining your answer.

Bogotá	Caracas	Cartagena
guerrillas	Lake Maracaibo	llaneros
strike		

DIRECTIONS On the line provided before each statement, write **T** if a statement is true and **F** if a statement is false. If the statement is false, write the term from the word bank that would make the statement correct on the line after each sentence.

_____ 1. The Orinoco River Basin and <u>Lake Maracaibo</u> are particularly rich in oil.

_____

_____ 2. <u>Guyana</u> is the economic center and capital city of Venezuela.

_____

_____ 3. In 2002 oil workers protested their president's control of oil by calling for a <u>strike.</u>

_____

_____ 4. <u>Guerrillas</u> are cowboys who herd cattle on ranches in the Llanos region.

_____

DIRECTIONS Answer each question by writing a sentence that contains at least one term from the word bank.

5. Why is civil war a major problem in Colombia today?

_____

_____

6. What did the Spanish do after conquering the Chibcha culture?

_____

_____

7. Where is Colombia's capital city located?

_____

South America

MAIN IDEAS

1. The countries of Pacific South America share a history influenced by the Inca civilization and Spanish colonization.
2. The culture of Pacific South America includes American Indian and Spanish influences.
3. Ecuador struggles with poverty and political instability.
4. Bolivia's government is trying to gain stability and improve the economy.
5. Peru has made progress against poverty and violence.
6. Chile has a stable government and a strong economy.

Key Terms and Places

viceroy governor of a Spanish colony

Creoles American-born descendants of Europeans

Quito capital of Ecuador

La Paz one of Bolivia's two capital cities

Lima capital of Peru

coup sudden overthrow of a government by a small group of people

Santiago capital of Chile

Lesson Summary
PACIFIC SOUTH AMERICA'S HISTORY

Thousands of years ago, people in Pacific South America learned how to adapt to and modify their environments. They built stone terraces into the steep mountainsides so they could raise crops. In coastal areas, people created irrigation systems to store water and control flooding. Eventually, the Inca Empire came to rule most of the region. They built stone-paved roads and used irrigation to turn the desert into farmland. Their civilization was destroyed by Spanish explorers seeking gold and silver. The Spanish **viceroy**, or governor, made the Indians follow Spanish laws and customs. By the early 1800s people began to revolt against Spanish rule. **Creoles**, American-born descendants of Europeans, were the main

> **How did people in Pacific South America farm on rugged land?**
>
> _____
> _____
> _____

leaders. These revolts helped Chile, Ecuador, Bolivia, and Peru gain independence by 1825.

PACIFIC SOUTH AMERICA'S CULTURE

Most people in the region speak Spanish, an official language in every country in the region. However, millions of South American Indians speak a native language. Bolivia, which has the highest percentage of Indians in South America, has three official languages: Spanish and two Indian languages. The religion of this region also reflects both Spanish and native Indian influences. Roman Catholic traditions come from the Spanish, but some people in the Andes still practice ancient religious customs.

> **Which country has three official languages?**
> _____

ECUADOR TODAY

Ecuador has faced recent instability. Widespread poverty is a constant threat to a stable government in this country. Although Ecuador is a democracy, it has not had a stable or popular government for a long time. Ecuador has three economic regions. Most of the agriculture and industry is found along the coastal plain region. The Andes region, where the capital, **Quito**, is located, is poor. Tourism is a major industry there. The third region, the Amazon basin, produces Ecuador's major export, oil.

> **Underline the region of Ecuador that has tourism as a major industry.**

BOLIVIA TODAY

After many years of military rule, Bolivia is now a democracy. The nation has two capitals. The supreme court meets in Sucre. The congress meets in **La Paz**, the highest capital city in the world. Bolivia is the poorest country in South America, although it does have resources such as metals and natural gas.

> **What are Bolivia's two capitals?**
> _____
> _____

PERU TODAY

Peru is the largest and most populous country in Pacific South America. Today it is making some progress against political violence and poverty. Its capital, **Lima**, is the region's largest city. Most poor people build themselves homes on the outskirts of Lima. These settlements are called "young towns." In the 1980s and 1990s, a terrorist group called the Shining Path used violence to oppose the government. After arresting the leaders, the government of Peru has made progress in fighting political violence and poverty. Peru has mineral deposits near the coast, and hydroelectric projects provide energy.

> **What group used violence to oppose the government of Peru?**
>
> _____
>
> _____
>
> _____

CHILE TODAY

Like Peru, Chile has ended a long, violent period. Chile now has a stable government and a growing economy. In the 1970s Chile's elected president was overthrown in a U.S.-backed military **coup**. The military leaders later imprisoned or killed thousands of their political opponents. In the late 1980s, Chileans restored democracy. The economy is now the strongest in the region and poverty rates have decreased. About one-third of Chileans live in central Chile. The capital, **Santiago**, is in this region. This area has a Mediterranean climate good for crops such as grapes used for making wine. Besides farming, fishing, and forestry, Chile's industries include copper mining, which accounts for one-third of Chile's exports. A massive earthquake in 2010 caused major damage in Chile.

> **Underline Chile's industries.**

Guided Reading Workbook

CHALLENGE ACTIVITY

Critical Thinking: Compare and Contrast You are
a recent arrival to a "young town" in Lima. Write
a letter to a friend in another country about Lima
and your home.

DIRECTIONS Read each sentence and fill in the blank with the
word in the word pair that best completes the sentence.

1. The Spanish appointed _____ to govern its colonies.
   (**Creoles/viceroys**)

2. _____ is the highest capital city in the world. (**La Paz/Quito**)

3. The main leaders in the region's revolt against Spanish rule were
   _____. (**Creoles/Callao**)

4. Chile's capital city, _____, has a mild Mediterranean
   climate. (**Santiago/Valparaíso**)

coup	Creoles	La Paz
Lima	Quito	Santiago
viceroy		

DIRECTIONS Answer each question by writing a sentence that
contains at least one term from the word bank.

5. Where does Bolivia's congress meet?

   _____

   _____

6. How would you describe Ecuador's capital?

   _____

   _____

7. What happened to the president of Chile in the 1970s?

   _____

   _____

Europe before the 1700s

MAIN IDEAS

1. Scientists study the remains of early humans to learn about prehistory.
2. Early humans moved out of Africa and migrated all over the world.
3. People adapted to new environments by making clothing and new types of tools.
4. The first farmers learned to grow plants and raise animals in the New Stone Age.
5. Farming changed societies and the way people lived.

Key Terms and Places

prehistory time before there was writing

tool handheld object that has been modified to help a person accomplish a task

Paleolithic Era first part of the Stone Age

society community of people who share a common culture

hunter-gatherers people who hunt animals and gather wild plants, seeds, fruits, and nuts to survive

migrate move to a new place

ice ages long periods of freezing weather

land bridge strip of land connecting two continents

Mesolithic Era Middle Stone Age

Neolithic Era New Stone Age

domestication process of changing plants or animals to make them more useful to humans

agriculture farming

megaliths huge stones used as monuments or as the sites for religious gatherings

Lesson Summary
PREHISTORIC HUMANS

Prehistory refers to the time before written history. Historians use the work of archaeologists and anthropologists to study prehistory. The first humans and their ancestors lived during an era

How do historians study prehistory?
_____
_____
_____

called the Stone Age. The Stone Age is divided into three periods based on the kinds of **tools** used at the time. The first part of the Stone Age is called the **Paleolithic Era**, or Old Stone Age. During this time people made tools of stone, particularly flint. Flint is easy to shape, and tools made from it can be very sharp. Attaching wooden handles to tools made them more useful.

As early humans developed tools and new hunting techniques, they formed societies. Each **society** developed a culture with language, religion, and art. The early humans of the Stone Age were **hunter-gatherers**. The most important development of early Stone Age culture was language. People also created art by carving stone, ivory, or bone, and by painting images on cave walls. Many scientists think that the first human religions developed during the Stone Age.

> Underline the sentence that lists parts of a culture.

PEOPLE MOVE OUT OF AFRICA

During the Old Stone Age, climate patterns around the world changed, causing people to **migrate**, or move to new places. Many places around the world experienced long periods of freezing weather called **ice ages**. During the ice ages, huge sheets of ice covered much of the earth's land. Scientists think that during the ice ages, the ocean level dropped and exposed a **land bridge** between Asia and North America. Land bridges allowed Stone Age peoples to migrate around the world. Humans migrated from Africa to Asia, Europe, and North America.

> How do scientists think people moved from Asia to North America during the ice ages?
> _____
> _____

PEOPLE ADAPT TO NEW ENVIRONMENTS

As early people moved to new lands, they found environments very different from those in East Africa. Many places were much colder and had new plants and animals. Early people had to adapt to these different environments. They learned to make clothing of animal skins and to

> How did early people adapt to different environments?
> _____
> _____
> _____
> _____

make shelters and houses. They also adapted with new tools, which were smaller and more complex than tools from the Old Stone Age. This was the **Mesolithic Era**, or the Middle Stone Age.

THE FIRST FARMERS

The Middle Stone Age was followed by the **Neolithic Era**, or New Stone Age. During the New Stone Age, people learned to polish stones to make tools like saws and drills. People also learned how to make fire. Before, they could only use fire that had been started by natural causes such as lightning. However, the biggest changes came in how people produced food. People learned to plant seed and grow crops. They also began keeping goats for milk, food, and wool, and larger animals to carry or pull loads. The **domestication** of plants and animals led to the development of **agriculture**, or farming. For the first time, people could produce their own food. This changed human society forever.

> Underline the sentence that explains how domestication related to farming.

FARMING CHANGES SOCIETIES

Domestication of plants and animals allowed people to look beyond survival. They also began to build permanent settlements rather than moving from place to place. They grew enough food to have a surplus which they could trade. Societies became more wealthy, and they began to divide people into classes based on wealth. People gathered to perform religious ceremonies. Some put up **megaliths** and honored gods and goddesses of air, water, fire, earth, and animals.

> How did a surplus of food change society?
>
> _____
>
> _____
>
> _____
>
> _____

CHALLENGE ACTIVITY

Critical Thinking: Explain Write a paragraph explaining how the ability to use fire changed life in the Neolithic Era. In what ways did life change?

agriculture	domestication	hunger-gatherers
Mesolithic Era	land bridge	megaliths
Paleolithic Era	migrate	Neolithic Era
tool	prehistory	society

DIRECTIONS On the line provided before each statement, write **T** if the statement is true and **F** if the statement is false. If the statement is false, write the correct term from the word bank on the line after each sentence that would make the sentence a true statement.

_____ 1. Historians rely on anthropologists and archaeologists to study <u>history</u>.

_____

_____ 2. Scientists believe that a land bridge formed between Asia and North America during the <u>Neolithic Era</u>.

_____

_____ 3. The <u>domestication</u> of plants and animals led to the development of farming.

_____

_____ 4. People learned to make polished stone saws and drills during the <u>Mesolithic Era</u>.

_____

_____ 5. During the ice ages, people began to <u>migrate</u> around the world.

_____

DIRECTIONS Answer each question by writing a sentence that contains at least two words from the word bank.

6. How did changing climate patterns change the lives of people?

_____

_____

7. How did developing plants and animals for use change life for people?

_____

_____

Europe before the 1700s

MAIN IDEAS
1. Early Greek culture saw the rise of the city-state and the creation of colonies.
2. The golden age of Greece saw advances in government, art, and philosophy.
3. Alexander the Great formed a huge empire and spread Greek culture into new areas.

Key Terms and Places

city-states political units made up of a city and all the surrounding lands

golden age period in a society's history marked by great achievements

Athens city-state in eastern Greece

Sparta rival city-state to Athens

Hellenistic Greek-like

Lesson Summary
EARLY GREEK CULTURE

To protect against invaders, early Greeks joined together. Over time, they developed into **city-states**, political units made up of a city and its surrounding lands. In time, some city-states formed colonies, or new cities—and Greek culture spread.

> **What was an effect of city-states forming new colonies?**
>
> _____
>
> _____

THE GOLDEN AGE OF GREECE

Greece is famous for its many contributions to world culture, especially during a period of great achievements called the **golden age**. Greece's golden age took place between 500 and 300 BC, after **Athens** and other city-states defeated a powerful Persian army around 500 BC. The defeat of the Persians increased the confidence of the Greeks, and they began to make many advances in art, writing, and thinking.

Athens became the cultural center of Greece during the golden age. Leaders such as Pericles supported the arts and other great works. But these leaders did not rule Athens. The city

> **Briefly define "golden age."**
>
> _____
>
> _____

> **Underline the sentence that explains how the defeat of the Persians contributed to the rise of Greece's golden age.**

became the world's first democracy. Power was in the hands of the people, who voted in an assembly, which made the laws.

Many accomplishments in art, architecture, literature, philosophy, and science took place during Greece's golden age. Among the earliest Greek writings are two epic poems by Homer. Drama, or plays, became an important part of Greek literature. Greek philosophers such as Socrates, Plato, and Aristotle continue to shape how we think today.

Greece's golden age came to an end when Athens and its rival **Sparta** went to war. Sparta had a strong army and was jealous of Athens's influence in Greece. The war raged for years, with other city-states joining in. Sparta finally won, but Greece overall had been weakened. It lay open to a foreign conqueror to take over.

Underline the areas of accomplishment during the golden age.

THE EMPIRE OF ALEXANDER

That conqueror was Alexander the Great, who took over Greece in the 330s BC. He conquered not only Greece, but also huge areas of the rest of the world from Greece to India and most of central Asia. He dreamed of conquering more territory, but his tired and homesick troops refused to continue. Alexander died on his return home at the age of 33.

Alexander wanted to spread Greek culture throughout his empire. He urged Greek people to move to new cities. Many Greeks did move. Greek culture then blended with other cultures. These blended cultures are referred to as **Hellenistic**, or Greek-like.

Do you think Alexander could have taken over Greece if Sparta and Athens had not gone to war? Why or why not?
_____
_____
_____

What was Alexander's attitude toward Greek culture?
_____
_____

CHALLENGE ACTIVITY

Critical Thinking: Analyze Write a brief article describing Athens from the viewpoint of a writer in Greece's golden age. In your article, include information about the many accomplishments during Greece's golden age.

Athens	city-states	colonies	empire
golden age	Hellenistic	Sparta	

DIRECTIONS On the line provided before each statement, write **T** if the statement is true and **F** if the statement is false. If the statement is false, write the correct term from the word bank on the line after each sentence to make the sentence a true statement.

_____ 1. <u>City-states</u> are political units made up of a city and all the surrounding lands.

_____

_____ 2. A period in a society's history marked by great achievements is called a/an <u>empire</u>.

_____

_____ 3. <u>Sparta</u> was a city-state in eastern Greece that led the fight against the invading Persians around 500 BC.

_____

_____ 4. A Greek-like blended culture is also called <u>Sparta</u>.

_____

_____ 5. Greece was weakened by a war between <u>Alexander the Great</u> and Athens.

_____

Europe before the 1700s

MAIN IDEAS
1. The Roman Republic was governed by elected leaders.
2. The Roman Empire was a time of great achievements.
3. The spread of Christianity began during the empire.
4. Various factors helped bring about the decline of Rome.

Key Terms and Places

Rome city in Italy

republic type of government in which people elect leaders to make laws for them

Senate council of rich and powerful Romans who helped run the city

citizens people who could take part in the Roman government

Carthage city in North Africa

empire land that includes many different peoples and lands under one rule

aqueducts channels used to carry water over long distances

Lesson Summary
THE ROMAN REPUBLIC

Rome began as a small city in Italy. It was ruled by a series of kings, some of whom were cruel rulers. Over time the Romans formed a **republic**, in which elected leaders made all government decisions. The leaders worked with the **Senate**, a group of powerful men. **Citizens** voted and ran for office.

Before long, Rome began to expand its territory. It took over much of the Mediterranean world, including the city of **Carthage** in North Africa. A general named Julius Caesar conquered many new lands. Afraid of his power, a group of senators killed him in 44 BC.

What is a republic?
_____
_____
_____
_____

THE ROMAN EMPIRE

Caesar's adopted son Octavian became Rome's first emperor, ruling a huge **empire**. This far-flung land contained many different people. Octavian was also called Augustus, or "honored one," because of his many accomplishments. Augustus

Circle the name of Rome's first emperor.

conquered many new lands. He built monuments and roads.

The Romans had a long period of peace and achievement called the Pax Romana. Their many building projects included **aqueducts**, roads, and bridges. The Romans also wrote literature and built a legal system that has had worldwide influence. The founders of the United States used the Roman government as a model.

> In what way does the Roman government affect the United States today?
>
> _____
> _____
> _____
> _____

THE SPREAD OF CHRISTIANITY

Christianity first appeared in the Roman Empire. The religion was based on the teachings of Jesus of Nazareth. Jesus' followers preached throughout the Roman world. For many years, Rome tried unsuccessfully to stop the spread of Christianity. Then in the 300s an emperor named Constantine became a Christian. Christianity soon became Rome's official religion. By the end of the 300s it had become a powerful force in the Roman world.

> Underline the name of the Roman emperor who converted to Christianity.

THE DECLINE OF ROME

Rome's decline had several causes. A number of bad emperors ignored their duties and the needs of the Roman people. Military leaders tried to take over, but many of them were poor rulers as well. The empire also became too large to control.

The emperor Constantine created a new capital in a central location. But this change was not enough. The empire, weakened by its internal problems, was vulnerable to invaders the Romans called barbarians. In 476 they attacked Rome and removed its emperor. The Roman Empire was no more.

> Why is the year 476 considered the end of the Roman Empire?
>
> _____
> _____
> _____
> _____

Lesson 3, *continued*

CHALLENGE ACTIVITY

Critical Thinking: Analyze Write a letter from a
Roman citizen to either Constantine or Augustus,
asking him to take action to improve the Roman
Empire. Include reasons why this action is
needed, based on details in the section.

DIRECTIONS Read each sentence and fill in the blank with the
word in the word pair that best completes the sentence.

1. The city of _____ is thought to have been set up in
   753 BC by a group called the Latins. (**Rome/Carthage**)

2. The _____ was made up of rich and powerful
   Romans who helped run the city. (**Pax Romana/Senate**)

3. _____ were people who could take part in Rome's
   government. (**Citizens/Aqueducts**)

4. A _____ is a form of government that has the people
   vote for leaders to make the laws. (**Senate/republic**)

5. Under Octavian's leadership, Rome became a/an _____, a
   land that included many different peoples under one rule. (**republic/empire**)

6. In addition to roads and bridges, Roman engineers built
   _____, channels used to carry water over long
   distances. (**aqueducts/Pax Romana**)

7. The long period of peace and achievement that Rome experienced is called
   the _____. (**Pax Romana/Colosseum**)

aqueducts	Carthage	citizens	Colosseum
empire	facilitate	Pax Romana	Republic
Rome	Senate		

DIRECTIONS Choose five of the words from the word bank. On a
separate sheet of paper, use these words to write a poem or short
story that relates to the lesson.

Europe before the 1700s

MAIN IDEAS
1. Eastern emperors ruled from Constantinople and tried but failed to reunite the whole Roman Empire.
2. The people of the eastern empire created a new society that was very different from society in the west.
3. Byzantine Christianity was different from religion in the west.

Key Terms and Places

Constantinople eastern capital of the Roman Empire

Byzantine Empire society that developed in the eastern Roman Empire after the west fell

mosaics pictures made with pieces of colored stone or glass

Lesson Summary
EMPERORS RULE FROM CONSTANTINOPLE

The capital of the eastern Roman Empire was **Constantinople**. The city was located between two seas. It controlled trade between Asia and Europe. After the fall of Rome in 476, this city was the center of Roman power.

The emperor Justinian ruled from 527 to 565. He tried to conquer lands to reunite the old Roman Empire. Justinian made other changes as well. He simplified Roman laws and organized them into a legal system called Justinian's Code. The code helped guarantee fairer treatment for all.

Justinian had many successes, but he also made enemies. These enemies tried to overthrow him in 532. His wife Theodora convinced Justinian to stay in Constantinople and fight. With her advice, he found a way to end the riots.

The eastern empire began to decline after Justinian died. Invaders took away all the land he had gained. Nearly 900 years after Justinian died, the eastern Roman Empire finally ended. In 1453 Ottoman Turks captured Constantinople. With

What was Justinian's Code?
_____
_____

Circle the name of Justinian's wife.

Underline the sentence that explains when and why the Roman Empire ended.

this defeat the 1,000-year history of the eastern Roman Empire came to an end.

A NEW SOCIETY

After Justinian's death, non-Roman influences took hold throughout the empire. Many people spoke Greek, and scholars studied Greek philosophy. A new society developed. This society is called the **Byzantine Empire**. The Byzantines interacted with many groups, largely because of trade.

The eastern empire was different from the western empire in another way. Byzantine emperors had more power than western emperors did. They were the heads of the church as well as political rulers. The leaders of the church in the west were bishops and popes. The western emperors had only political power.

> What were two ways that the Byzantine Empire was different from the western empire?
>
> _____
>
> _____
>
> _____
>
> _____

BYZANTINE CHRISTIANITY

Christianity was central to the lives of nearly all Byzantines. Artists created beautiful works of religious art. Many Byzantine artists made **mosaics**. These were pictures made with pieces of colored stone or glass. Some were made of gold, silver, and jewels. Magnificent churches also were built.

Over time, eastern and western Christianity became very different. People had different ideas about how to interpret and practice their religion. By the 1000s the church split in two. Eastern Christians formed the Orthodox Church.

> Underline the description of mosaics.

CHALLENGE ACTIVITY

Critical Thinking: Compare and Contrast Create a Venn diagram illustrating the similarities and differences between the eastern and western empires. Conduct library or Internet research to find interesting details for your diagram.

Name _____ Class _____ Date _____

| Byzantine Empire | Constantinople | Hagia Sofia |
| Justinian | mosaics | Theodora |

DIRECTIONS Answer each question by writing a sentence that contains at least one word from the word bank.

1. What city was the capital of the eastern Roman Empire? What was important about this city?

_____

_____

_____

2. Who is considered the last Roman emperor of the eastern empire? What changes occurred after his death?

_____

_____

_____

3. What new society developed in the eastern Roman Empire after the fall of the Roman Empire in the west? Name two ways this new society was different from the Roman Empire in the west.

_____

_____

_____

_____

4. What kind of religious art was popular with Byzantine artists? Describe this type of art.

_____

_____

_____

Europe before the 1700s

MAIN IDEAS
1. The Christian Church influenced nearly every aspect of society in the Middle Ages.
2. Complicated political and economic systems governed life in the Middle Ages.
3. The period after 1000 was a time of great changes in medieval society.

Key Terms and Places

Middle Ages period of history between ancient and modern times that lasted from about 500 until about 1500

pope head of the Roman Catholic Church

Crusade religious war

Holy Land region in which Jesus had lived

Gothic architecture style known for its high pointed ceilings, tall towers, and stained glass windows

feudal system system of exchanging land for military service

manor large estate owned by a noble or a knight

nation-state country united under a single strong government

Lesson Summary

THE CHRISTIAN CHURCH AND SOCIETY

Europe broke into many small kingdoms. The period from about 500 until about 1500 is called the **Middle Ages**. During this time, no one leader could unify Europe, but Christianity tied most Europeans together. As a result, the Christian Church gained influence, and church leaders became powerful.

The **pope** was the head of the Roman Catholic Church. Pope Urban II started a religious war called a **Crusade**. He wanted Europeans to take over the **Holy Land**, where Jesus had lived. It was then ruled by Muslims. The Crusaders failed. However, they brought back new foods, goods, and ideas. Trade between Europe and Asia increased.

> Circle the dates when the Middle Ages took place.

> Who was the leader of the Roman Catholic Church?
> _____

The church had a major influence on art and architecture. Many churches built during this period are examples of **Gothic architecture**. Most people's lives centered around their local church.

LIFE IN THE MIDDLE AGES

Religion was not the only influence on people's lives. Two other major influences were the **feudal system** and the **manor** system.

The feudal system was mainly a relationship between nobles and knights. The nobles gave land to knights. In turn, the knights promised to help defend their lands and the king.

> **Who participated in the feudal system? In the manor system?**
> _____
> _____
> _____

The manor system was a relationship between the owner of the manor and the workers. The owner provided workers with a place to live and a piece of land on which to grow their own food. In exchange, the workers farmed the owner's land.

CHANGES IN MEDIEVAL SOCIETY

France's William the Conqueror invaded England in 1066. He became king and built England's first strong government. In 1215, however, King John of England lost some of his power. A group of nobles drew up a document called Magna Carta, which limited the monarch's power. It gave the nobles power to advise the king.

> **How did Magna Carta affect King John?**
> _____

In 1347 a disease called the Black Death swept through Europe. It killed about a third of the population. The plague caused a labor shortage. As a result, people could demand higher wages.

In 1337 the Hundred Years' War broke out between England and France. The French won, and kings began working to end the feudal system and gain more power. France became a nation-state, a country united under a single government. Other **nation-states** arose around Europe, and the Middle Ages came to an end.

> **What is one negative and one positive outcome of the Black Death?**
> _____
> _____
> _____
> _____
> _____
> _____

CHALLENGE ACTIVITY

Critical Thinking: Make Generalizations Draw up a document like Magna Carta that includes your ideas of the basic rights for common people as well as limits on the power of rulers.

DIRECTIONS Read each sentence and fill in the blank with the word in the word pair that best completes the sentence.

1. The _____ is the time period between ancient and modern times, which lasted from about 500 to 1500. (**Middle Ages/Magna Carta**)

2. The head of the Roman Catholic Church in the Middle Ages was called the _____. (**manor/pope**)

3. A religious war is called a _____. (**Crusade/Holy Land**)

4. The pope wanted Europeans to take over the _____, the region where Jesus had lived. (**Crusade/Holy Land**)

5. Many churches built in the Middle Ages are examples of _____, a style known for its high pointed ceilings, tall towers, and stained glass windows. (**feudal system/Gothic architecture**)

6. The system of trading land for military service was called the _____. (**feudal system/manor system**)

7. A _____ was a large estate owned by a noble or knight. (**peasant/manor**)

8. A _____ was a country that was united under a single strong government. (**Holy Land/nation-state**)

Crusade	feudal system	Gothic architecture	Holy Land
Magna Carta	manor	Middle Ages	nation-state
peasant	pope	serf	

DIRECTIONS What would your life be like if you lived in the Middle Ages? On a separate sheet of paper, write a letter to a friend and describe what it's like to live in the Middle Ages, using five of the words in the word bank.

Europe before the 1700s

MAIN IDEAS
1. The Renaissance was a period of new learning, new ideas, and new advances in art, literature, and science.
2. The Reformation changed the religious map of Europe.

Key Terms and Places

Renaissance period of creativity and new ideas that swept Europe from about 1350 through the 1500s

Florence Italian city that became rich through trade during and after the Crusades

Venice Italian city that became rich through trade during and after the Crusades

humanism new way of thinking and learning that emphasized the abilities and accomplishments of human beings

Reformation religious reform movement that began with complaints about problems within the Catholic Church

Protestants Christians who split from the Catholic Church over religious issues

Catholic Reformation series of reforms launched by Catholic Church officials

Lesson Summary
THE RENAISSANCE

The **Renaissance** started in Italy in such cities as **Florence** and **Venice**. These cities became rich through trade. As goods from Asia moved through these cities, Italians became curious about the larger world. At this same time, scholars from other parts of the world came to Italy bringing books written by ancient Greeks and Romans. Interest in Greece and Rome grew. People studied subjects such as history, poetry, and grammar which had been taught in Greek and Roman schools. These subjects are known as the humanities. Increased study of the humanities led to **humanism**—an idea that people are capable of great achievements.

> Circle the name of the country where the Renaissance began.

> Underline three developments that led to the Renaissance.

Renaissance artists developed new painting techniques such as perspective, which made their art look more realistic. The artists Michelangelo and Leonardo da Vinci showed their belief in humanism by making the people in their paintings look like unique individuals. William Shakespeare's plays looked closely at human nature and behavior.

> **Circle the names of three Renaissance artists and writers.**

Reading about Greek and Roman scientific advances inspired Europeans to study math, astronomy, and other sciences. Some used their new knowledge to create new inventions. Johannes Gutenberg's invention, the movable-type printing press, printed books quickly and cheaply. It spread Renaissance ideas to all parts of Europe.

> **What effect did Gutenberg's printing press have on the Renaissance?**
>
> _____
>
> _____
>
> _____

THE REFORMATION

The **Reformation**, a religious reform movement, began in Germany. Many people there felt that Catholic Church officials cared more about power than their religious duties. Martin Luther, a German monk, was one of the first people to protest against the church. In 1517 he nailed a list of complaints on a church door in Wittenberg. Angry church officials expelled him from the church. Luther's followers became the first **Protestants**, splitting off from the Catholic Church to form a separate church. Other reformers created their own churches. By 1600 many Europeans had become Protestants.

> **Underline the sentence that tells how Luther made his protest.**

In response, Catholic Church leaders began a series of reforms, called the **Catholic Reformation**. They asked churches to focus more on religious matters. They tried to make church teachings easier to understand. Priests and teachers went to Asia, Africa, and other lands to spread Catholic teachings. After the Reformation, religious wars broke out in Europe between Catholics and Protestants. These

religious wars led to many changes in Europe.
People began to rely less on church leaders and
look to science for answers.

CHALLENGE ACTIVITY

Critical Thinking: Analyze What events prompted
Catholic leaders to begin the Catholic
Reformation?

Catholic Reformation	Florence	humanism
perspective	Protestants	Reformation
Renaissance	Venice	Wittenberg

DIRECTIONS On the line provided before each statement, write **T** if
a statement is true and **F** if a statement is false. If the statement is
false, write the term from the word bank that would make the
statement correct on the line after each sentence.

_____ 1. Lasting from about 1350 to 1500, the <u>Reformation</u> was a period of
great creativity in Europe.

_____

_____ 2. People who followed Martin Luther in forming their own religion
became the first <u>Protestants</u>.

_____

_____ 3. The technique of <u>humanism</u> enabled artists to show a realistic three-
dimensional scene on a flat surface.

_____

_____ 4. Italian cities such as Florence and <u>Wittenberg</u> became rich through
trade.

_____

_____ 5. <u>Catholic Reformation</u> emphasized the abilities and accomplishments
of human beings.

_____

DIRECTIONS On a separate sheet of paper, write
a story or poem that relates to the lesson. Include
five words from the word bank.

History of Modern Europe

MAIN IDEAS
1. During the Scientific Revolution, discoveries and inventions expanded knowledge and changed life in Europe.
2. In the 1400s and 1500s, Europeans led voyages of discovery and exploration.
3. As Europeans discovered new lands, they created colonies and new empires all over the world.

Key Terms and Places

Scientific Revolution series of events that led to the birth of modern science

New World term used by Europeans to describe the Americas after the voyages of Christopher Columbus

circumnavigate travel all the way around Earth

Columbian Exchange plants, animals, and ideas are exchanged between the New World and the Old World

Lesson Summary
THE SCIENTIFIC REVOLUTION

Before the 1500s most educated people depended on authorities such as ancient Greek writers and church officials for information. During the **Scientific Revolution**, people began to believe that what they observed was more important than what they were told. They developed the scientific method to make logical explanations for how the world worked, based on what they observed. This focus on observation marked the start of modern science.

Many Europeans feared the spread of scientific ideas. Church officials opposed many ideas because they went against church teachings. For example, the church taught that the sun circled Earth. From observations using telescopes, scientists now thought that Earth circled the sun. In 1632 church officials arrested Italian scientist Galileo for publishing a book that supported this view. However, science still developed rapidly.

> Underline the sentence that explains how educated people learned about the world before the Scientific Revolution.

> Why did church officials fear the spread of many scientific ideas?
>
> _____
>
> _____

New discoveries occurred in astronomy, biology, physics, and other fields. New inventions included the telescope, microscope, and thermometer. Isaac Newton made one of the most important discoveries—explaining how gravity works.

THE VOYAGES OF DISCOVERY

With improved devices, such as the compass, astrolabe, and better ships, Europeans made longer, safer sea voyages. They found new routes to distant places. Europeans had many reasons for exploring. Some were curious about the world; some wanted riches, fame, or adventure; and others hoped to spread Christianity. Prince Henry of Portugal sought new trade routes to Asia. After many other voyages, Portuguese explorer Vasco da Gama succeeded in finding a water route to Asia.

The voyages of Christopher Columbus, paid for by Queen Isabella of Spain, were the most significant. His explorations of the **New World** led other European countries to explore this new land, too. Ferdinand Magellan was the first person to attempt to **circumnavigate**, or sail completely around, the world. He was killed, but his crew completed the voyage. Others followed. Voyages of discovery added greatly to European wealth—and people's knowledge of the world.

NEW EMPIRES

The Spanish were the first Europeans to build colonies in the Americas. Their use of steel swords, firearms, and horses helped them conquer and destroy the Aztec and Inca Empires. Deadly diseases carried by the Spanish also killed many Native Americans. The gold the Spanish found in the Americas made Spain the richest country in Europe. Other European nations also founded colonies in the Americas. In many places

> Circle the three advances that helped make the voyages of discovery possible.

> List three explorers and where they explored.

> What effect did European explorers and colonists have on Native Americans?

they forced out Native Americans. European nations grew rich from trade in wood, fur, and other natural resources.

THE COLUMBIAN EXCHANGE

As Europeans continued to interact with new lands and people, they unexpectedly created a new effect called the **Columbian Exchange**, an exchange of plants, animals, and ideas between the New World and the Old World. As Europeans brought seeds to plant in the Americas, they provided new crops not seen before. They also brought animals, such as horses, and introduced their ideas, religions, language, and technology to the places they conquered. The Europeans also found plants and animals they had never seen before. They took these things back to Europe as well as to Africa and Asia. This exchange of plants changed the eating habits of people around the world.

> **What was the effect created by European explorers between Europe and the Americas?**
>
> _____
>
> _____

CHALLENGE ACTIVITY

Critical Thinking: Draw Conclusions Write a paragraph explaining three results of European explorations.

DIRECTIONS Read each sentence and fill in the blank with the word in the word pair that best completes the sentence.

1. In 1632 _____ was arrested for writing that Earth orbited the sun. (**Sir Isaac Newton/Galileo**)

2. The _____ led to the birth of modern science. (**Scientific Revolution/astrolabe**)

3. Without the support of _____, the voyage of Columbus might not have taken place. (**Queen Isabella/Sir Isaac Newton**)

4. In 1498 _____ sailed around the southern tip of Africa and on to Asia. (**Christopher Columbus/Vasco da Gama**)

5. _____ made important observations about the force of gravity. (**Sir Isaac Newton/Galileo**)

DIRECTIONS Write a word or phrase that has the same meaning as the term given.

6. New World _____

7. circumnavigate _____

8. Columbian Exchange _____

_____

9. Scientific Revolution _____

Guided Reading Workbook

History of Modern Europe

Lesson 2

MAIN IDEAS
1. During the Enlightenment, new ideas about government took hold in Europe.
2. The 1600s and 1700s were an Age of Revolution in Europe.
3. Napoleon Bonaparte conquered much of Europe after the French Revolution.

Key Terms

Enlightenment period in the 1600s and 1700s when the use of reason shaped European ideas about society and politics, also known as the Age of Reason

English Bill of Rights 1689 document listing rights of Parliament and the English people

Magna Carta document limiting the power of the English ruler and protecting some rights of the people

Declaration of Independence document signed in 1776 that declared the American colonies' independence from Britain

Declaration of the Rights of Man and of the Citizen French constitution that guaranteed some rights of French citizens and made taxes fairer

Reign of Terror period of great violence during the French Revolution

Lesson Summary
THE ENLIGHTENMENT

During the **Enlightenment** many people questioned common ideas about politics and government. Most of Europe was ruled by kings and queens, also called monarchs. Many monarchs believed God gave them the right to rule as they chose. This belief was called rule by divine right.

Enlightenment thinkers disagreed. John Locke saw government as a contract, or binding legal agreement, between a ruler and the people. A ruler's job was to protect people's rights. If a ruler did not do this, people had the right to change rulers. Jean-Jacques Rousseau also felt government's purpose was to protect people's freedoms. Such ideas inspired revolutions and political change.

> Underline the sentence that explains what rule by divine right is.

> Circle the names of two Enlightenment thinkers who had new ideas about the rights of citizens and the role of government.

THE AGE OF REVOLUTION

In the 1600s, England's rulers fought with Parliament for power. As a result, in 1689 Parliament passed the **English Bill of Rights** and made the king agree to honor **Magna Carta**. These steps limited the monarch's power and gave more rights to Parliament and the English people.

Enlightenment ideas spread to Britain's North American colonies. There, colonial leaders claimed Britain had denied their rights—and started the American Revolution. In July 1776 Americans signed the **Declaration of Independence**, declaring the American colonies' independence.

The American victory inspired the French people to fight for their rights. Members of the Third Estate, France's largest and poorest social class, demanded a part in government. They formed the National Assembly and demanded that the king limit his powers. When he refused, the French Revolution began. The National Assembly then issued the **Declaration of the Rights of Man and of the Citizen**, a new constitution for France.

France's revolutionary leaders ended the monarchy, but soon after the **Reign of Terror** began. It was a very violent time. After it ended, a strong leader rose to power.

> How did the English Bill of Rights and Magna Carta limit the monarch's power?
>
> _____
>
> _____
>
> _____

> Circle the names of two documents in addition to the English Bill of Rights that changed how rulers governed and that gave citizens more rights.

NAPOLEON BONAPARTE

In 1799 Napoleon Bonaparte took control of France. He conquered most of Europe and built a French empire. Napoleon created a fairer legal system, called the Napoleonic Code, but he was a harsh ruler. Napoleon's armies were defeated in 1814 and 1815. Soon after, European leaders redrew the map of Europe to prevent any other country from becoming too powerful.

> List two of Napoleon's achievements.
>
> _____
>
> _____
>
> _____
>
> _____
>
> _____

CHALLENGE ACTIVITY

Critical Thinking: Draw Conclusions In the Age
of Revolution, were ideas or armies more
important? Give support for your answer.

Declaration of Independence	Declaration of the Rights of Man and of the Citizen
English Bill of Rights	Enlightenment
Magna Carta	Reign of Terror

DIRECTIONS Answer each question by writing a sentence that
contains at least one term from the word bank.

1. How did England's Parliament limit the monarchy's power?

_____

_____

2. What peaceful steps did France take to guarantee its people more freedoms?

_____

_____

3. What effect did Enlightenment ideas have on the British colonies in North America?

_____

_____

4. What period came right after the French Revolution? Why was it called this?

_____

_____

5. What was the Age of Reason?

_____

_____

History of Modern Europe

MAIN IDEAS
1. Britain's large labor force, raw materials, and money to invest led to the start of the Industrial Revolution.
2. Industrial growth began in Great Britain and then spread to other parts of Europe.
3. The Industrial Revolution led to both positive and negative changes in society.

Key Terms

Industrial Revolution period of rapid growth in machine-made goods

textiles cloth products

capitalism economic system in which individuals own most businesses and resources, and people invest money in hopes of making a profit

suffragettes women who campaigned for the right to vote

Lesson Summary
START OF THE INDUSTRIAL REVOLUTION

Changes in agriculture helped prepare Britain for industrial growth. Rich farmers bought land and created larger, more efficient farms. At the same time, Europe's population grew, creating a need for more food. To meet this need, farmers tried new farming methods and invented new machines.

> Underline the sentence that tells why farmers needed to grow more food.

These improved methods and inventions helped farmers grow more crops, but with fewer workers. As a result, many small farmers and farm workers lost their farms and jobs—and moved to the cities.

In Britain, all these changes sparked the **Industrial Revolution**. By the 1700s, Britain had labor, natural resources, and money to invest—all the resources needed for industry to grow. Demand for manufactured goods soon grew. People looked for ways to make these goods even faster.

> Circle three resources needed for industrial growth.

INDUSTRIAL GROWTH

The **textile** industry, which made cloth products, developed first. In the early 1700s, cloth was made by hand. This began to change in 1769 when Richard Arkwright invented a water-powered spinning machine. Other new machines enabled workers to make large amounts of cloth quickly. As a result, the price of cloth fell. Soon workers were using machines to make other kinds of goods faster and cheaper.

Most early machines relied on water power. Factories, the buildings that housed the machines, had to be built near rivers. In the 1760s James Watt built the first modern steam engine. Factories could now be set up in cities. In 1855 Henry Bessemer invented a new way to make steel, and the steel industry grew. Transportation became faster as steam engines powered boats and trains. Advancements in communication and transportation helped spread ideas and culture more quickly.

Industrial growth changed how people worked. Many people—including children and young women—worked in unsafe factories. They worked long hours, usually for poor wages. However, by the late 1800s, the Industrial Revolution had spread. Industrial growth resulted in a new economic system—**capitalism**, in which individuals own most businesses and resources.

> Circle the industry that developed first. Then underline the invention that helped it grow fast.

> Why do you think the price of cloth fell as workers made more cloth?
> _____
> _____
> _____

> Explain why you think the Industrial Revolution led to a new economic system.
> _____
> _____
> _____

CHANGES IN SOCIETY

The Industrial Revolution made life better for some, but worse for others. Manufactured goods became cheaper. New inventions made life easier. More people joined the middle class. Meanwhile, cities grew, becoming dirty, noisy, and crowded. Workers often remained poor, living in unsafe apartments where diseases spread. Reformers worked to improve society, pushing for safer

> Underline the sentences that explain how people's lives improved as a result of the Industrial Revolution.

working conditions, higher wages, and cleaner
cities. Some women, called **suffragettes**, pressed
for the right to vote.

CHALLENGE ACTIVITY

Critical Thinking: Draw Conclusions Did the
benefits of the Industrial Revolution outweigh
the problems it caused? Write a paragraph to
explain your reasons.

DIRECTIONS Look at each set of four terms following each number. On the line provided, write the letter of the term that does not relate to the others.

_____ 1. a. voting
     b. suffragette
     c. guillotine
     d. women

_____ 2. a. Henry Bessemer
     b. textiles
     c. cloth
     d. spinning machine

_____ 3. a. capitalism
     b. profit
     c. investment
     d. military

_____ 4. a. inventions
     b. machines
     c. literature
     d. technology

_____ 5. a. steam power
     b. iron
     c. profit
     d. steel

DIRECTIONS Write three words or phrases that describe each term.

6. capitalism _____

_____

7. textiles _____

_____

8. suffragette _____

_____

9. Industrial Revolution _____

_____

History of Modern Europe

Lesson 4

MAIN IDEAS
1. Rivalries in Europe led to the outbreak of World War I.
2. After a long, devastating war, the Allies claimed victory.
3. The war's end brought great political and territorial changes to Europe.

Key Terms

nationalism devotion and loyalty to one's country

imperialism European nations' quest for colonies in Africa and Asia

alliance agreement between countries

trench warfare style of fighting in which each side fights from deep ditches, or trenches, dug into the ground

Treaty of Versailles final peace settlement of World War I

communism political system in which the government owns and controls all aspects of life in a country

Lesson Summary
THE OUTBREAK OF WAR

In the 1800s many people who were ruled by empires wanted to form their own nations. As **nationalism**—devotion and loyalty to one's country—became more common, tensions grew. **Imperialism** also helped set the stage for war. As European countries competed for overseas empires, their rivalry and mistrust deepened. In 1882 Italy, Germany, and Austria-Hungary formed the Triple Alliance. This **alliance** was an agreement to fight together if any of the three was attacked. Britain, Russia, and France also formed an alliance, the Triple Entente. By the 1900s many countries were preparing for war by building up their armies and stockpiling weapons. Germany and Great Britain built strong navies and powerful new battleships.

One source of tension was Bosnia and Herzegovina, a province of Austria-Hungary that neighboring Serbia wanted to control. On June 28,

> Underline the sentence that explains what an alliance is.

> When was Archduke Franz Ferdinand killed?
>
> _____

Guided Reading Workbook

1914, Archduke Franz Ferdinand of Austria-Hungary was assassinated by a Serbian gunman. Faced with war, Serbia turned to Russia for help. The alliance system split Europe into warring sides.

WAR AND VICTORY

Germany attacked the Allies (France, Great Britain, Serbia, and Russia), sending its army into Belgium and France. Russia attacked the Central Powers (Germany and Austria-Hungary) from the east. The two sides quickly prepared for **trench warfare** by digging hundreds of miles of trenches, which were easy to defend but hard to attack. Millions of soldiers died in the trenches, but neither side could win the war. New weapons, such as machine guns, poison gas, and tanks, were designed to gain an advantage on the battlefield.

> Circle the names of two countries that were part of the Central Powers.

In 1917 German U-boats attacked American ships that were helping Britain. The United States entered the war, strengthening the Allies. Around the same time, Russia pulled out of the war. Germany renewed its attack on the Allies. However, this last effort failed, and the Central Powers surrendered in 1918.

> Why did the United States enter the war?
> _____
> _____
> _____

THE WAR'S END

World War I, in which over 8.5 million soldiers died, changed Europe forever. American president Woodrow Wilson wanted a just peace after the war, but the **Treaty of Versailles** blamed Germany alone. The Germans were forced to slash the size of their army, give up overseas colonies, and pay billions of dollars for damages. The German empire gave way to a fragile republic. In Russia, a revolution had established a Communist government. **Communism** is a political system in which the government owns and controls every aspect of life. Austria and Hungary became separate countries, Poland and

> Where was the first Communist government established?
> _____

Czechoslovakia gained independence, Yugoslavia
was formed, and Finland, Latvia, Lithuania, and
Estonia broke away from Russia.

CHALLENGE ACTIVITY

Critical Thinking: Draw Inferences Write a
sentence explaining why machine guns and trench
warfare were such a deadly combination.

alliance	Allies	Central Powers	communism
nationalism	Treaty of Versailles	trench warfare	imperialism

DIRECTIONS Answer each question by writing a sentence that
contains at least one term from the word bank.

1. What led to the tension that sparked World War I?

   _____

   _____

2. What countries fought each other in World War I?

   _____

   _____

   _____

3. How did the new kind of fighting seen in World War I affect the soldiers?

   _____

   _____

4. What did the final peace settlement of World War I demand of Germany?

   _____

   _____

   _____

5. How did World War I change the way some European countries were governed?

_____

_____

DIRECTIONS Imagine that you are a newspaper reporter visiting Europe during World War I. On a separate sheet of paper, write a short article that explains what you have learned about the war and the fighting. Include at least five terms from the word bank.

_____

_____

History of Modern Europe

MAIN IDEAS

1. Economic and political problems troubled Europe in the years after World War I.
2. World War II broke out when Germany invaded Poland.
3. Nazi Germany targeted the Jews during the Holocaust.
4. Allied victories in Europe and Japan brought the end of World War II.

Key Terms

Great Depression global economic crisis in the 1930s

dictator ruler who has total control

Axis Powers alliance among Germany, Italy, and Japan

Allies France, Great Britain, and other countries that opposed the Axis

Holocaust attempt by the Nazi government during World War II to eliminate Europe's Jews

Lesson Summary

PROBLEMS TROUBLE EUROPE

With its economy booming after World War I, the United States provided loans to help Europe rebuild. But the U.S. stock market crashed in 1929, starting a global economic crisis, the **Great Depression**. Without United States funds, banks failed in Europe, and many people lost their jobs.

People blamed their leaders for the hard times. In some countries, **dictators** gained power by making false promises. In the 1920s Benito Mussolini spoke of bringing back the glory of the Roman Empire to Italy. Instead he took away people's rights. In Russia in 1924, Joseph Stalin became dictator and oppressed the people, using secret police to spy on them. Promising to restore Germany's military and economic strength, Adolf Hitler rose to power in 1933. Once in power, he outlawed all political parties except the Nazi Party. He also discriminated against Jews and other groups he believed to be inferior.

> **What caused many Europeans to lose their jobs after 1929?**
>
> _____
>
> _____
>
> _____

> **Underline the sentence that tells Adolf Hitler's actions when he first took power.**

Lesson 5, *continued*

WAR BREAKS OUT

No one moved to stop Mussolini when he invaded Ethiopia in 1935. Meanwhile, Hitler added Austria to the German empire in 1938 and Czechoslovakia in 1939. When Hitler invaded Poland in 1939, France and Britain declared war on Germany, beginning World War II. Germany, Italy, and Japan formed the **Axis Powers**. They were opposed by the **Allies**—France, Great Britain, and others. The Axis won most of the early battles and soon defeated France. Britain withstood intense bombing and did not surrender. The German army then turned toward Eastern Europe and the Soviet Union. Italy invaded North Africa. In 1941 Japan attacked the United States at Pearl Harbor, Hawaii.

> Underline the countries that Mussolini and Hitler invaded.

> Who won most of the early battles in World War II?
> _____

THE HOLOCAUST

The **Holocaust** was the Nazi Party's plan to eliminate people they believed were inferior, especially the Jews. By 1942 the Nazis had put millions of Jews in concentration camps, such as Auschwitz in Poland. Some Jews tried to hide, escape, or fight back. In the end, however, the Nazis killed about two-thirds of Europe's Jews and several million non-Jews.

END OF THE WAR

In 1943 the Allies won key battles. On D-Day in 1944, they invaded Normandy, France, and paved the way for an advance toward Germany. The war ended in 1945 soon after the U.S. dropped an atomic bomb on Japan. The war took the lives of more than 50 million people and led to the formation of the United Nations. The United States helped many countries rebuild. However, the United States and the Soviet Union soon became rivals for power.

> Circle the names of the countries that became rivals for power after World War II.

CHALLENGE ACTIVITY

Critical Thinking: Sequence Make a timeline
showing the main events leading up to
Germany's invasion of Poland in 1939.

DIRECTIONS On the line provided before each statement, write **T** if
the statement is true and **F** if the statement is false. If the statement
is false, write the term that makes the sentence a true statement on
the line after each sentence.

_____ 1. The two alliances fighting in World War II were the Allies and the
Nazi Powers.

_____

_____ 2. The Great Depression was triggered by the stock market crash in 1929.

_____

_____ 3. Benito Mussolini was Italy's first Communist.

_____

_____ 4. During the Holocaust, the Nazi government tried to wipe out
Europe's Jews.

_____

_____ 5. Joseph Stalin was the Communist leader of the Soviet Union.

_____

_____ 6. A major victory for the Axis Powers occurred in the D-Day invasion
on the beaches of Normandy, France.

_____

Allies	Axis Powers	dictator
Great Depression	Holocaust	Nazi

DIRECTIONS Look up three of the vocabulary terms in the word
bank. On a separate sheet of paper, write the dictionary definition
of the word that is closest to the definition used in your textbook.

_____

History of Modern Europe

MAIN IDEAS
1. The Cold War divided Europe between democratic and Communist nations.
2. Many Eastern European countries changed boundaries and forms of government at the end of the Cold War.
3. European cooperation has brought economic and political change to Europe.

Key Terms

superpowers strong and influential countries

Cold War period of tense rivalry between the United States and the Soviet Union

arms race competition between countries to build superior weapons

common market group of nations that cooperate to make trade among members easier

European Union (EU) organization that promotes political and economic cooperation in Europe

refugee someone forced to flee his or her own country because of persecution, war, or violence

asylum protection given by a government to someone who has left another country in order to escape being harmed

migrant person who goes from one place to another, especially to find work

Lesson Summary
THE COLD WAR

After World War II, the two **superpowers**—the United States and the Soviet Union—distrusted each other. This led to the **Cold War**, a period of tense rivalry between these two countries. The Soviet Union stood for communism, and the United States stood for democracy and free enterprise.

The United States and several Western nations formed an alliance called the North Atlantic Treaty Organization (NATO). The Soviet Union and most Eastern European countries were allies under the Warsaw Pact. The two sides used the threat of nuclear war to defend themselves.

> Underline the sentence that defines the Cold War.

> Which alliance did most Eastern European countries join after World War II?
>
> _____

Germany was split into East Germany and West Germany. Communist leaders built the Berlin Wall to prevent East Germans from fleeing to the West. Western countries were more successful economically than Communist Eastern Europe. People in the East suffered from shortages of money, food, clothing, and cars.

THE END OF THE COLD WAR

By the 1980s the **arms race**—a competition to build superior weapons—between the Soviet Union and the U.S. was damaging the Soviet economy. To solve the problem, Soviet leader Mikhail Gorbachev made changes. He reduced government control of the economy and held democratic elections.

These policies helped inspire change throughout Eastern Europe. Poland and Czechoslovakia threw off Communist rule. The Berlin Wall came down in 1989. East and West Germany reunited to form a single country again in 1990. In December 1991 the Soviet Union broke up.

Ukraine, Lithuania, and Belarus became independent countries. In 1993 Czechoslovakia split peacefully into the Czech Republic and Slovakia. However, ethnic conflict in Yugoslavia caused much violence. By 1994 Yugoslavia had split into five countries—Bosnia and Herzegovina, Croatia, Macedonia, Slovenia, and Serbia and Montenegro.

In what year did the Soviet Union break up?
_____

Underline the five countries that were created when Yugoslavia split.

EUROPEAN COOPERATION

After two deadly wars, many Europeans thought a sense of community would make more wars less likely. In the 1950s West Germany, Luxembourg, Italy, Belgium, France, and the Netherlands moved toward unity with a **common market**, a single economic unit to improve trade among members. Today, 28 countries make up

Guided Reading Workbook

the **European Union (EU)**. Many use a common currency, the euro. The European Union deals with issues such as environment, trade, and migration. Their governing body has executive, legislative, and judicial branches. Representatives are selected from all member nations. The EU has helped unify Europe, and other countries hope to join in the future.

The EU has experienced some turmoil in recent times because some members disagree with specific policies. For example, civil wars in other countries such as Syria have created a **refugee** crisis. Many refugees flee their home countries seeking **asylum**, or protection, in Europe to start new lives. Others, called **migrants**, have fled violence and poverty in Africa, the Middle East, and other regions. European countries struggled to figure out what to do with their new arrivals. This crisis caused divisions in the EU about how to best resettle so many people. These divisions created a new spirit of nationalism in Europe. As a result, the United Kingdom voted to leave the European Union in June 2016. This is the first time a member country has decided to leave the EU.

> Circle the issues that concern the European Union.

> Circle the word that helps to define the meaning of *asylum*.

CHALLENGE ACTIVITY

Critical Thinking: Cause and Effect Write a sentence that explains how the establishment of the European Union might make wars in Europe less likely in the future.

DIRECTIONS Read each sentence and fill in the blank with the word in the word pair that best completes the sentence.

1. The United States and the Soviet Union were rivals in the

   _____. (**Cold War/European Union**)

2. The _____ of East and West Germany came in 1989 when the Berlin Wall was torn down. (**common market/reunification**)

3. After the Cold War, _____ led to the breakup of Yugoslavia. (**superpowers/ethnic tensions**)

4. Belgium, France, Italy, Luxembourg, the Netherlands, and West Germany were the first countries to form a common market, which is now known as

   the _____. (**superpowers/European Union**)

5. The high costs of the _____ hurt the Soviet economy. (**arms race/Berlin Wall**)

6. The crisis in Syria has created many _____ seeking asylum. (**migrants/refugees**)

arms race	asylum	Berlin Wall
Cold War	common market	ethnic tensions
European Union (EU)	migrant	refugee
reunification	superpowers	

DIRECTIONS Choose five of the vocabulary words from the word bank. On a separate sheet of paper, use these terms to write a summary of what you learned in the lesson.

_____

_____

_____

Southern Europe

MAIN IDEAS
1. Southern Europe's physical features include rugged mountains and narrow coastal plains.
2. The region's climate and resources support such industries as agriculture, fishing, and tourism.

Key Terms and Places

Mediterranean Sea sea that borders Southern Europe

Pyrenees mountain range separating Spain and France

Apennines mountain range running along the whole Italian Peninsula

Alps Europe's highest mountains, some of which are located in northern Italy

Mediterranean climate type of climate found across Southern Europe, with warm, sunny days and mild nights for most of the year

Lesson Summary
PHYSICAL FEATURES

Southern Europe is composed of three peninsulas—the Iberian, the Italian, and the Balkan—and some large islands. All of the peninsulas have coastlines on the **Mediterranean Sea**.

These peninsulas are largely covered with rugged mountains. The land is so rugged that farming and travel in Southern Europe can be difficult. The **Pyrenees** form a boundary between Spain and France. The **Apennines** run along the Italian Peninsula. The **Alps**—Europe's highest mountains—are in the north. The Pindus Mountains cover much of Greece. The region also has coastal plains and river valleys, where most of the farming is done and where most of the people live. Crete, which is south of Greece, and Sicily, at the southern tip of Italy, are two of the larger islands in the region. Many of the region's islands are the peaks of undersea mountains.

> **What are the three peninsulas of Southern Europe?**
>
> _____
> _____
> _____

> **Circle the four mountain ranges in Southern Europe.**

Guided Reading Workbook

In addition to the Mediterranean Sea, the Adriatic, Aegean, and Ionian seas are important to Southern Europe. They give the people food and an easy way to travel around the region. The Po and the Tagus are two important rivers in Southern Europe. The Po flows across northern Italy. The Tagus, the region's longest river, flows across the Iberian Peninsula.

> **Circle the names of the four seas in Southern Europe.**

CLIMATE AND RESOURCES

The climate in Southern Europe is called a **Mediterranean climate**. The climate is warm and sunny in the summer and mild and rainy in the winter. Southern Europe's climate is one of its most valuable resources. It supports the growing of many crops, including citrus fruits, grapes, olives, and wheat. It also attracts millions of tourists each year.

> **What are the characteristics of a Mediterranean climate?**
>
> _____
>
> _____
>
> _____

The seas are another important resource in Southern Europe. Many of the region's cities are ports, shipping goods all over the world. In addition, the seas support profitable fishing industries.

> **Underline two ways in which the seas are a key resource in Southern Europe.**

CHALLENGE ACTIVITY

Critical Thinking: Analyze Write a paragraph explaining how Southern Europe's climate supports the region's economy.

| Alps | Apennines | Mediterranean climate |
| Mediterranean Sea | plains | Pyrenees |

DIRECTIONS On the line provided before each statement, write **T** if a statement is true and **F** if a statement is false. If the statement is false, write the term from the word bank that would make the statement true on the line after each sentence.

_____ 1. The <u>Alps</u> form a boundary between Spain and France.

_____

_____ 2. Islands and <u>peninsulas</u> form the region of Southern Europe.

_____

_____ 3. The <u>Apennines</u> are Europe's highest mountain range.

_____

_____ 4. The countries of Southern Europe all share a common location on the <u>Adriatic Sea</u>.

_____

_____ 5. The <u>Pyrenees</u> run along the Italian Peninsula.

_____

DIRECTIONS Read each sentence and fill in the blank with the word in the word pair that best completes the sentence.

6. Many of Southern Europe's islands are formed by _____.

   (undersea mountains/plains)

7. The _____ is ideal for growing a variety of crops.

   (Mediterranean Sea/Mediterranean climate)

Name _____ Class _____ Date_____

Southern Europe

MAIN IDEAS
1. Early in its history, Greece was the home of a great civilization, but it was later ruled by foreign powers.
2. The Greek language, the Orthodox Church, and varied customs have helped shape Greece's culture.
3. In Greece today, many people are looking for new economic opportunities.
4. Italian history can be divided into three periods: ancient Rome, the Renaissance, and unified Italy.
5. Religion and local traditions have helped shape Italy's culture.
6. Italy today has two distinct economic regions—northern Italy and southern Italy.

Key Terms and Places

Orthodox Church branch of Christianity that dates to the Byzantine Empire

Christianity major world religion based on the life and teachings of Jesus of Nazareth

Athens Greece's capital and largest city

Catholicism largest branch of Christianity

pope spiritual head of the Roman Catholic Church

Vatican City independent state within the city of Rome

Sicily island at Italy's southern tip

Naples largest city in southern Italy and an important port

Milan major industrial city in northern Italy and a fashion center

Rome capital of Italy

Lesson Summary
GREECE'S HISTORY

Ancient Greeks are known for their beautiful art, new forms of history and drama, and advances in geometry. They developed a system of reason that is the basis for modern science, and they created democracy. In the 300s BC Greece was conquered by Alexander the Great and was later ruled by the Romans and the Ottoman Turks. In the 1800s Greece became a monarchy. A military dictatorship ruled from 1967 to 1974. More recently, Greece has returned to democracy.

Name two achievements of ancient Greece.
_____
_____
_____
_____
_____
_____
_____

GREECE'S CULTURE

The Greek people today speak a form of the same language spoken by their ancestors. Nearly everyone in Greece is a member of the **Orthodox Church**, a branch of **Christianity** dating from the Byzantine Empire. Religion is important to the Greek people, and religious holidays are popular times for celebration and family gatherings. For centuries, the family has been central to Greek culture, and today it remains the cornerstone of Greek society.

> What is the cornerstone of Greek society?
> _____

GREECE TODAY

About three-fifths of all people in Greece live in cities. **Athens** is the largest city in Greece and is its capital. The city's industry has produced air pollution that damages the ancient ruins and endangers people's health. People in rural areas live much like they did in the past. They grow crops, raise sheep and goats, and socialize in the village square. Greece's economic growth lags behind most other European nations. Greece is a leading country in the shipping industry, with one of the largest shipping fleets in the world. Another profitable industry is tourism.

> Underline two important industries in Greece.

ITALY'S HISTORY

Ancient Rome grew into an empire that stretched from Britain to the Persian Gulf. Ancient Rome's achievements in art, architecture, literature, law, and government still influence the world today. When the Roman Empire collapsed in the AD 400s, cities in Italy formed their own states. Many cities became centers of trade. Wealthy Italian merchants helped bring about the Renaissance through their support of the work of artists and architects. In the mid-1800s a rise in nationalism led to Italian unification in 1861. In the 1920s Italy became a dictatorship under Benito Mussolini. This lasted until Italy's defeat in

> Underline five areas in which the achievements of ancient Rome still influence the world today.

Guided Reading Workbook

World War II, after which Italy became a
democracy.

ITALY'S CULTURE

Catholicism has historically been the strongest
influence on Italian culture. The **pope** heads the
government of **Vatican City** and the Roman
Catholic Church. Religious holidays and festivals
are major events. Local traditions and regional
geography have also influenced Italian culture.
Italian food varies widely from region to region.
Italians have long been trendsetters in
contemporary art forms, including painting,
composing, fashion, and film.

> **Underline three influences
> on Italian culture.**

ITALY TODAY

Southern Italy is poorer than northern Italy. It
has less industry and relies on agriculture and
tourism for its survival. Farming is especially
important in **Sicily**. **Naples** is a busy port and an
industrial center. Northern Italy has a strong
economy, including major industrial centers, the
most productive farmland, and the most popular
tourist destinations. **Milan** is an industrial center
and a worldwide center for fashion design. Turin
and Genoa are also industrial centers. Florence,
Pisa, and Venice are popular tourist destinations.
Rome, Italy's capital, is located between northern
Italy and southern Italy.

> **Why is the economy of
> northern Italy strong?**
>
> _____
>
> _____
>
> _____

CHALLENGE ACTIVITY

Critical Thinking: Synthesize Write a sentence to explain how religion and family work together to form a central part of Greek culture.

Athens	Catholicism	Christianity
Milan	Naples	Orthodox Church
pope	Rome	Sicily
Vatican City		

DIRECTIONS Read each sentence and fill in the blank with the word from the word bank that best completes the sentence.

1. Greece's capital and largest city, _____ , has a serious air pollution problem.

2. Most people in Greece are members of the _____ .

3. The pope heads the government of _____ , an independent state located within Rome.

4. The _____ is the head of the Roman Catholic Church.

5. The city of _____ in northern Italy is a worldwide center for fashion design.

DIRECTIONS Choose five words from the word bank. On a separate sheet of paper, use these words to write a poem, story, or letter that relates to the lesson.

_____

_____

Southern Europe

Lesson 3

MAIN IDEAS
1. Over the centuries, Spain and Portugal have been part of many large and powerful empires.
2. The cultures of Spain and Portugal reflect their long histories.
3. Having been both rich and poor in the past, Spain and Portugal today have struggling economies.

Key Terms and Places

Iberia westernmost peninsula in Europe

parliamentary monarchy form of government in which a king rules with the help of an elected parliament

Madrid capital of Spain

Barcelona center of industry, culture, and tourism in Spain

Lisbon large city in Portugal and important industrial center

Lesson Summary
HISTORY

Spain and Portugal lie on the Iberian Peninsula, or **Iberia**. Both countries have been part of large, powerful empires. Coastal areas of what is now Spain were first ruled by Phoenicians from the eastern Mediterranean. Later the Greeks established colonies there. A few centuries later, Iberia became part of the Roman Empire. After the fall of Rome, Iberia was conquered by the Moors—Muslims from North Africa. For about 600 years, much of the Iberian Peninsula was under Muslim rule.

Eventually the Christian kingdoms of Spain and Portugal banded together to drive out the Muslims and other non-Christians. Both countries went on to establish empires of their own in the Americas, Africa, and Asia. Both countries became rich and powerful until most of their colonies broke away and became independent in the 1800s and 1900s.

What foreign powers have ruled Spain and Portugal?

_____

_____

Where did Spain and Portugal establish colonies?

_____

_____

Guided Reading Workbook

CULTURE

Many dialects of Spanish and Portuguese are spoken in Iberia. Catalan, which is similar to Spanish, is spoken in eastern Spain. Galician, which is more closely related to Portuguese, is spoken in northwest Spain. The Basques of the Pyrenees have their own language and customs. For this reason, many Basques want independence from Spain. In both Spain and Portugal, the people are mainly Roman Catholic.

Music is important to both countries. The Portuguese are famous for sad folk songs called fados. The Spanish are known for a style of song and dance called flamenco. Much of the peninsula's art and architecture reflect its Muslim past. The round arches and elaborate tilework on many buildings were influenced by Muslim design.

> Circle the group in Spain that has its own language and customs.

> What Muslim influences can be seen on buildings in Iberia?
>
> _____
>
> _____

SPAIN AND PORTUGAL TODAY

When other countries started building industrial economies, Spain and Portugal relied on the wealth from their colonies. When their colonies broke away, the income they had depended on was lost. Despite recent economic growth and strong industries such as tourism, their economies are struggling.

Spain is governed by a **parliamentary monarchy**—a king rules with the help of an elected parliament. **Madrid**—the capital—and **Barcelona** are centers of industry, culture, and tourism.

Portugal is a republic whose leaders are elected. The economy is based on industries in **Lisbon** and other large cities. In rural areas, farmers grow many crops but are most famous for grapes and cork.

> Underline the definition of a parliamentary monarchy.

Guided Reading Workbook

CHALLENGE ACTIVITY
Critical Thinking: Compare and Contrast
Compare and contrast Spain and Portugal. Then
explain which country you would prefer to visit.

Barcelona	Iberia	Lisbon
Madrid	parliamentary monarchy	

DIRECTIONS Answer each question by writing a sentence that
contains at least one word from the word bank.

1. Describe the geographic setting of Spain and Portugal.

_____

_____

2. How are Spain and Portugal governed today?

_____

_____

3. Where are the centers of industry, tourism, and culture in Spain?

_____

4. Where are the industries of Portugal based?

_____

DIRECTIONS Look at each set of terms. On the line provided, write
the letter of the term that does not relate to the others.

_____ 5. a. Basque   b. Catalan   c. Galician   d. Lisbon

_____ 6. a. Muslim   b. Greek   c. Roman   d. Portuguese

Western Europe

Lesson 1

MAIN IDEAS
1. West-Central Europe includes many types of physical features and a mild climate that supports agriculture, energy production, and tourism.
2. Northern Europe contains low mountains, jagged coastlines, a variety of natural resources, and a range of climates.

Key Terms and Places

Northern European Plain broad coastal plain that stretches from the Atlantic coast into Eastern Europe

North Sea large body of water to the north of the region

English Channel narrow waterway to the north of the region that separates West-Central Europe from the United Kingdom

Danube River one of the major rivers of the region

Rhine River one of the major rivers of the region

navigable river river that is deep and wide enough for ships to use

North Atlantic Drift ocean current that brings warm, moist air across the Atlantic Ocean

British Isles group of islands located across the English Channel from the rest of Europe

Scandinavia region of islands and peninsulas in far northern Europe

fjord narrow inlet of the sea set between high, rocky cliffs

geothermal energy energy from the heat of Earth's interior

Lesson Summary
WEST-CENTRAL EUROPE

West-Central Europe has plains, uplands, and mountains. Most of the **Northern European Plain** is flat or rolling. The plain has the region's best farmland and largest cities. The Central Uplands are in the middle of the region. This area has many rounded hills, small plateaus, and valleys. Coal fields have helped to make it a major mining and industrial area. The area is mostly too rocky for farming.

> Circle the three major landform types in West-Central Europe.

The Alps and Pyrenees form the alpine mountain system. The Alps are the highest mountains in Europe. The **North Sea** and the **English Channel** lie to the north. The **Danube River** and the **Rhine River** are important waterways for trade and travel. The region has several **navigable rivers**. These rivers and a system of canals link the region's interior to the seas.

A warm ocean current, the **North Atlantic Drift**, brings warm, moist air across the Atlantic Ocean and creates a marine west coast climate in most of West-Central Europe. Summers are mild, but winters can be cold. In the Alps and other higher elevation areas, the climate is colder and wetter. The mild Mediterranean climate of southern France is a valuable resource. Farmers in this region grow grapes, grains, and vegetables. In the Alps and the uplands, farmers raise livestock. Energy resources are not evenly divided. France has iron ore and coal. Germany has coal, and the Netherlands has natural gas. Fast-flowing alpine rivers provide hydroelectric power. Even so, many countries have to import fuel. The beauty of the Alps is an important resource for tourism.

| Circle the names of two important rivers in the region. |

| Circle the energy resources of France. Underline the energy resources of Germany and the Netherlands. |

NORTHERN EUROPE

Northern Europe consists of two regions: the **British Isles** and **Scandinavia**. Iceland, to the west, is often considered part of Scandinavia. Fewer people live in the northern portion of the region, where rocky hills and low mountains make farming difficult. Farmland and plains stretch across the southern part of the region. Glaciers once covered Northern Europe, creating **fjords** along portions of the coastline and carving lakes in the interior.

Northern Europe's primary resources are its energy resources, forests and soils, and surrounding seas. Energy resources include oil

| What two features were created by glaciers? _____ _____ |

| Underline the energy resources of Northern Europe. |

and natural gas from North Sea deposits. Hydroelectric energy is produced by the many lakes and rivers. Iceland's hot springs produce **geothermal energy**, or energy from the heat of Earth's interior. Forests in Norway, Sweden, and Finland provide timber. Fertile farmland in southern portions of the region produce crops such as wheat and potatoes. The seas and oceans that surround the region have provided fish to the people of Northern Europe for centuries.

Although much of the region is close to the Arctic Circle, the climate is surprisingly mild because of the North Atlantic Drift. Denmark, the British Isles, and western Norway have a marine west coast climate. Although they have snow and frosts, the ports are not frozen for much of the winter. Central Norway, Sweden, and southern Finland have a humid continental climate. Subarctic regions in northern Scandinavia experience long, cold winters and short summers. Iceland's tundra and ice cap climates produce extremely cold temperatures year round. Not surprisingly, most people in Northern Europe live in urban areas and few live in the far north.

> **Why is the climate mild in much of Northern Europe?**
> _____
> _____
> _____

CHALLENGE ACTIVITY

Critical Thinking: Evaluate How have landforms and bodies of water affected activities in the region? Give support for your answer.

DIRECTIONS Read each sentence and fill in the blank with the word in the word pair that best completes each sentence.

1. West-Central Europe's best farmland and largest cities are found on the _____. (**Northern European Plain/North Sea**)

2. The two most important rivers in West-Central Europe are the Rhine River and the _____. (**North Atlantic Drift/Danube River**)

3. West-Central Europe's _____ link the region's interior to the oceans. (**fjords/navigable rivers**)

4. Northern Europe is made up of the British Isles and _____. (**Scandinavia/Northern European Plain**)

5. Oil and natural gas deposits are found in the _____. (**North Sea/English Channel**)

6. Northern Europe experiences a mild climate due to the _____. (**geothermal energy/North Atlantic Drift**)

7. Energy produced from the heat of Earth's interior is called _____. (**geothermal energy/hydroelectric energy**)

British Isles	Danube River
English Channel	fjord
geothermal energy	navigable rivers
North Atlantic Drift	North Sea
Northern European Plain	Rhine River
Scandinavia	

DIRECTIONS Answer each question by writing a sentence that contains at least two words from the word bank.

8. Why are West-Central Europe's rivers important?

_____

_____

9. What are some of Northern Europe's energy resources?

_____

_____

Western Europe

MAIN IDEAS
1. During its history, France has been a kingdom, empire, colonial power, and republic.
2. The culture of France has contributed to the world's arts and ideas.
3. France today is a farming and manufacturing center.
4. The Benelux Countries have strong economies and high standards of living.

Key Terms and Places

Paris capital and largest city in France

Amsterdam capital of the Netherlands

The Hague seat of government in the Netherlands

Brussels capital of Belgium, headquarters of many international organizations

cosmopolitan characterized by many foreign influences

Lesson Summary
HISTORY OF FRANCE

In ancient times, Celtic people from eastern Europe settled in what is now France. Later, this land was conquered by the Romans and Franks. The Franks' ruler, Charlemagne, built a large empire and was crowned emperor of the Romans by the pope in 800. Later, the Normans claimed northwestern France. They became kings of England and ruled part of France until they were driven out by the French. During the 1500s to 1700s, France became a colonial power with colonies in Asia, Africa, and the Americas.

In 1789 the French people overthrew their king in the French Revolution. Napoleon Bonaparte took power and conquered most of Europe, creating a vast empire. This ended in 1815 when European powers defeated his armies. During World Wars I and II, Germany invaded France. In the 1950s and 1960s, many French colonies declared independence. France is now a democratic republic.

> **Circle the names of three groups that ruled France during its early history.**

> **Underline the sentences that tell how Napoleon Bonaparte affected French history.**

Guided Reading Workbook

THE CULTURE OF FRANCE

The French share a common heritage. Most speak French and are Catholic. Recently, France has become more diverse due to immigration. The French share a love of good food and company. The French have made major contributions to the arts and ideas—including impressionism, Gothic cathedrals, and Enlightenment ideas about government.

> Underline the sentences that describe the ways the French are alike.

FRANCE TODAY

France is Western Europe's largest country. **Paris** is a center of business, finance, learning, and culture. France has a strong economy and is the EU's top agricultural producer. Major crops include wheat and grapes, but tourism and the export of goods such as perfumes and wines are also vital to the economy.

THE BENELUX COUNTRIES

Belgium, the Netherlands, and Luxembourg are the Benelux Countries. Their location has led to invasions but has also promoted trade. All are densely populated, lie at low elevations between larger, stronger countries, and have strong economies and democratic governments. North Sea harbors have made the Netherlands a center for trade. Major cities include Rotterdam, **Amsterdam**, and **The Hague**. About 25 percent of the Netherlands lies below sea level. **Brussels**, Belgium, is a **cosmopolitan** city with many international organizations. The country is known for cheese, chocolate, cocoa, and lace. Luxembourg's economy is based on banking and steel and chemical production.

> Circle the names of the three Benelux Countries.

> Underline the sentence that tells how the Benelux Countries are alike.

CHALLENGE ACTIVITY

Critical Thinking: Draw Conclusions Write a
sentence that explains how the location of the
Benelux Countries has both helped and hurt
them.

DIRECTIONS Read each sentence and fill in the blank with the
word in the word pair that best completes the sentence.

1. Also known as the City of Lights, _____ is the capital of France.
   (Brussels/Paris)

2. The seat of government in the Netherlands is _____. **(Amsterdam/
   The Hague)**

3. Brussels, the capital of Belgium, is considered a _____ city because
   of its many foreign influences. **(cosmopolitan/sprawling)**

4. _____ is the capital of the Netherlands. **(Amsterdam/The Hague)**

DIRECTIONS Write a word or short phrase that has the same
meaning as the term given.

5. The Hague _____

6. Brussels _____

7. Benelux _____

Western Europe

MAIN IDEAS
1. After a history of division and two world wars, Germany is now a unified country.
2. German culture, known for its contributions to music, literature, and science, is growing more diverse.
3. Germany today has Europe's largest economy, but eastern Germany faces challenges.
4. The Alpine Countries reflect German culture and have strong economies based on tourism and services.

Key Terms and Places

Berlin capital of Germany

Protestant those who protested against the Catholic Church

chancellor prime minister elected by Parliament who runs the government

Vienna Austria's capital and largest city

cantons districts of Switzerland's federal republic

neutral not taking sides in international conflict

Bern capital of Switzerland

Lesson Summary

HISTORY OF GERMANY

The land that is now Germany was a loose association of small states for hundreds of years. In 1871 Prussia united them to create Germany, which grew into a world power. After World War I, the German economy suffered and Adolf Hitler came to power. After its defeat in World War II, Germany was divided into democratic West Germany and Communist East Germany. **Berlin** was also divided. The Berlin Wall was built to stop East Germans from escaping to West Germany. In 1989 democracy movements swept Eastern Europe and communism collapsed. In 1990 East and West Germany were reunited.

Why did Communist leaders build the Berlin Wall?
_____
_____
_____

What events helped East and West Germany reunite?
_____
_____
_____
_____

CULTURE OF GERMANY

Most people in Germany are ethnic Germans who speak German. Immigrants are making Germany more multicultural. Most people are either **Protestant** or Catholic. Germans have made important contributions to classical music, literature, chemistry, engineering, and medicine.

> **Most Germans belong to one or the other of which two religious groups?**
>
> _____
>
> _____

GERMANY TODAY

Germany is a leading European power. It is a federal republic governed by a parliament and a **chancellor**. It is Europe's largest economy, exporting many products, including cars. Germany's economy is based mainly on industries such as chemicals, engineering, and steel, but agriculture is also important. Acid rain from industry and vehicle exhaust has damaged trees and soil in Germany.

> **What economic activities have made Germany Europe's largest economy?**
>
> _____
>
> _____
>
> _____
>
> _____
>
> _____

THE ALPINE COUNTRIES

The Alpine Countries are Austria and Switzerland. They share much in common. Both were once part of the Holy Roman Empire, are landlocked, influenced by German culture, and prosperous. Austria was the center of the powerful Habsburg Empire that ruled much of Europe. Today, Austria is a modern, industrialized nation. **Vienna** is a center of music and fine arts. Austria has a strong economy with little unemployment. Service industries and tourism are important.

> **Underline the sentence that explains what the Alpine Countries have in common.**

> **List two important industries in the Alpine Countries.**
>
> _____
>
> _____

Switzerland has been independent since the 1600s. It is a federal republic made up of 26 **cantons**. It is **neutral** and not a member of the EU or NATO. The Swiss speak several languages, including German and French. The capital, **Bern**, is centrally located. Switzerland is known for tourism and for its banks, watches, chocolate, and cheese.

CHALLENGE ACTIVITY

Critical Thinking: Draw Inferences What are some factors that have contributed to the prosperity of the Alpine Countries?

DIRECTIONS Read each sentence and fill in the blank with the word in the word pair that best completes the sentence.

1. _____ is the capital of

   Germany. (**Vienna/Berlin**)

2. In Germany, a parliament elects a

   _____, or prime minister, who runs the

   government. (**canton/chancellor**)

3. Switzerland is made up of 26 districts called _____.

   (**cantons/chancellors**)

4. _____ is the capital of Austria and also its largest city.

   (**Berlin/Vienna**)

5. The capital of Switzerland, _____, is centrally located

   between the country's German- and French-speaking regions. (**Bern/Vienna**)

Berlin	Bern	cantons	chancellor
neutral	Protestant	Vienna	

DIRECTIONS Choose five terms from the word bank. Use these terms to write a summary of what you learned in this lesson.

_____

_____

_____

_____

_____

Western Europe

MAIN IDEAS

1. Invaders and a global empire have shaped the history of the British Isles.
2. British culture, such as government and music, has influenced much of the world.
3. Efforts to bring peace to Northern Ireland and maintain strong economies are important issues in the British Isles today.

Key Terms and Places

constitutional monarchy type of democracy in which a king or queen serves as head of state, but a legislature makes the laws

Magna Carta document that limited the powers of kings and required everyone to obey the law

disarm give up all weapons

London capital of the United Kingdom

Dublin capital of the Republic of Ireland

Lesson Summary
HISTORY

The Republic of Ireland and the United Kingdom make up the British Isles. The United Kingdom consists of England, Scotland, Wales, and Northern Ireland.

> **What two countries make up the British Isles?**
>
> _____
>
> _____

The Celts were early settlers of the British Isles. Later, Romans, Angles, Saxons, Vikings, and Normans invaded Britain. Over time, England grew in strength, and by the 1500s it had become a world power. England eventually formed the United Kingdom with Wales, Scotland, and Ireland. It developed a strong economy thanks to the Industrial Revolution and its colonies abroad.

> **Underline the sentence that lists the countries that formed the United Kingdom.**

The British Empire stretched around the world by 1900 but later declined. The Republic of Ireland won its independence, and by the mid-1900s Britain had given up most of its colonies.

Lesson 4, *continued*

CULTURE

The United Kingdom is a **constitutional monarchy**. England first limited the power of monarchs during the Middle Ages in a document called **Magna Carta**. This document influenced the governments of many countries. Ireland's president serves as head of state, but a prime minister and Parliament run the government.

The people of the British Isles share many cultural traits, but each region is also unique. The people of Ireland and Scotland keep many traditions alive, and immigrants from all over the world add new traits to the culture of the British Isles.

British popular culture has influenced people around the world. British literature and music are well known, and the English language is used in many countries.

> **In what ways are the governments of the United Kingdom and Ireland similar and different?**
>
> _____
> _____
> _____
> _____
> _____
> _____

> **Underline the sentence that describes how British popular culture has influenced other people.**

BRITISH ISLES TODAY

Efforts to maintain a powerful economy, the United Kingdom's relationship with the EU, and challenges to peace in Northern Ireland are key issues facing the British Isles today. In 2016 citizens of the UK voted to exit the EU, a departure nicknamed Brexit. In Northern Ireland, many Catholics feel they have not been treated fairly by Protestants. Some hope to unite with the Republic of Ireland. In the late 1990s peace talks led to the creation of a national assembly in Northern Ireland. However, some groups refused to **disarm**, delaying the peace process.

Maintaining powerful economies in the British Isles is a key issue today. **London** is a center for world trade, and the country has reserves of oil and natural gas in the North Sea. **Dublin** has attracted new industries like computers and electronics.

> **What three key issues face the British Isles today?**
>
> _____
> _____
> _____
> _____
> _____
> _____
> _____

CHALLENGE ACTIVITY
Critical Thinking: Identify Cause and Effect
Explain the factors that caused the development
of a strong economy in the United Kingdom
following its formation. Then explain two effects
of the decline of the British Empire.

_____

_____

_____

_____

DIRECTIONS Read each sentence and fill in the blank with the
word in the word pair that best completes the sentence.

1. Many Catholics in Northern Ireland hope to unite with

   _____. **(the Republic of Ireland/Wales)**

2. The capital of the United Kingdom is _____.
   (London/Dublin)

3. The nickname for the United Kingdom's departure from the EU is

   _____. **(Magna Carta/Brexit)**

4. A _____ is a government that has a monarch but a
   legislative body that makes the laws. **(Magna Carta/constitutional monarchy)**

DIRECTIONS Write three words or phrases that describe the term.

5. disarm _____

   _____

6. London _____

7. Dublin _____

   _____

8. Magna Carta _____

   _____

Western Europe

> **MAIN IDEAS**
> 1. The history of Scandinavia dates back to the time of the Vikings.
> 2. Scandinavia today is known for its peaceful and prosperous countries.

Key Terms and Places

Vikings Scandinavian warriors who raided Europe in the early Middle Ages

Stockholm Sweden's capital and largest city

uninhabitable not able to support human settlement

Oslo the capital of Norway

Helsinki Finland's capital and largest city

geysers springs that shoot hot water and steam into the air

Lesson Summary

HISTORY

Vikings were Scandinavian warriors who raided Europe during the early Middle Ages. They were greatly feared and conquered the British Isles, Finland, and parts of France, Germany, and Russia.

Vikings were excellent sailors. They were the first Europeans to settle in Iceland and Greenland and the first Europeans to reach North America. They stopped raiding in the 1100s and focused on strengthening their kingdoms. Norway, Sweden, and Denmark competed for control of the region, and by the late 1300s Denmark ruled all the Scandinavian Kingdoms and territories. Sweden eventually broke away, taking Finland, and later Norway, with it. Norway, Finland, and Iceland became independent countries during the 1900s. Greenland remains part of Denmark as a self-ruling territory.

> **Underline the sentence that explains the areas that Vikings explored.**

> **Which three countries did not become independent until the 1900s?**
>
> _____
>
> _____
>
> _____

SCANDINAVIA TODAY

Scandinavians today have much in common, including similar political views, languages, and religions. They enjoy high standards of living, are well-educated, and get free health care. The countries have strong economies and large cities.

Sweden has the largest area and population. Most people live in large towns and cities in the south. **Stockholm** is Sweden's capital and largest city. Often called a floating city, it is built on 14 islands and part of the mainland. Although neutral, Sweden does play an active role in the UN and the EU.

Denmark is Scandinavia's smallest and most densely populated country. Its economy relies on farming and modern industries. Greenland is mostly covered with ice and **uninhabitable**. Most Greenlanders live on the southwest coast and rely heavily on Denmark for imports and economic aid.

Norway has one of the longest coastlines in the world. **Oslo** is Norway's capital, a leading seaport and industrial center. Oil and natural gas provide Norway with the highest per capita GDP in the region; however, oil fields in the North Sea are expected to run out during the next century. Norway's citizens have voted not to join the EU.

Finland relies on trade, and it exports paper and other forest products. Shipbuilding and electronics are also important. **Helsinki** is its capital and largest city.

Iceland has fertile farmland and rich fishing grounds. Tourists come to see its volcanoes, glaciers, and **geysers**. Geothermal energy heats many buildings.

> Underline the sentence that lists traits Scandinavians have in common.

> What is the largest country in area? What is the smallest?
>
> _____
>
> _____

> Why are tourists attracted to Iceland?
>
> _____
>
> _____

CHALLENGE ACTIVITY

Critical Thinking: Make Inferences How do you think Norway might change if oil fields run out during the next century? Write a short paragraph to explain your answer.

geysers	Helsinki	Oslo
Stockholm	uninhabitable	Vikings

DIRECTIONS Answer each question by writing a sentence that contains at least one word from the word bank.

1. How were longships used by Scandinavian warriors?

   _____

2. Why do most people in Greenland live on the southwest coast?

   _____

   _____

3. What is Norway's capital like?

   _____

4. How are many homes in Iceland heated?

   _____

5. What city in Scandinavia is often called a floating city and why?

   _____

Eastern Europe

MAIN IDEAS
1. The physical features of Eastern Europe include wide open plains, rugged mountain ranges, and many rivers.
2. The climate and vegetation of Eastern Europe differ widely in the north and the south.

Key Terms and Places

Carpathians low mountain range stretching from the Alps to the Black Sea area

Balkan Peninsula one of the largest peninsulas in Europe; extends into the Mediterranean

Chernobyl nuclear power plant in Ukraine

Lesson Summary
PHYSICAL FEATURES

The landforms of Eastern Europe stretch across the region in broad bands of plains and mountains. The Northern European Plain covers most of Northern Europe. South of this plain is a low mountain range called the **Carpathians**. It extends from the Alps to the Black Sea area. South and west of the Carpathians is another large plain, the Great Hungarian Plain, located mostly in Hungary. South of this plain are the Dinaric Alps and Balkan Mountains. These mountain ranges cover most of the **Balkan Peninsula**, one of Europe's largest peninsulas. It extends into the Mediterranean Sea.

Eastern Europe has many water bodies that are important routes for transportation and trade. The Adriatic Sea lies to the southwest. The Black Sea is east of the region. The Baltic Sea is in the far north. Some parts of the Baltic freeze over in winter, reducing its usefulness.

The rivers that flow through Eastern Europe are also important for trade and transportation,

> Circle three mountain ranges in Eastern Europe.

> List two reasons that rivers are important to the economy of Eastern Europe.
> _____
> _____

especially the Danube River. The Danube begins in Germany and crosses nine countries before it empties into the Black Sea. This river is very important to Eastern Europe's economy. Some of the region's largest cities are along its banks. Dams on the river provide electricity for the region. This river has become very polluted from heavy use.

Why is the Danube so polluted? _____

CLIMATE AND VEGETATION

Types of climates and vegetation in Eastern Europe vary widely. The shores of the Baltic Sea in the far north have the coldest climate, with long, harsh winters. The area does not get much rain but is often foggy. Its cold, damp climate allows huge forests to grow.

Underline the descriptions of climate found in the Baltic region.

The interior plains have a much milder climate than the Baltic region. Winters can be very cold, but summers are mild. The western parts of the interior plains get more rain than the eastern parts. Because of its varied climate, there are many types of vegetation. Forests cover much of the north, and grassy plains lie in the south.

In 1986 Eastern Europe's forests were damaged by a major nuclear accident at **Chernobyl** in Ukraine. An explosion released huge amounts of radiation into the air that poisoned forests and ruined soil across the region.

The Balkan coast along the Adriatic Sea has a Mediterranean climate, with warm summers and mild winters. Its beaches attract tourists. The area does not get much rain, so there are not many forests. The land is covered by shrubs and trees that do not need much water.

Why is the vegetation along the Balkan coast different from the vegetation of the Baltic region? _____ _____ _____ _____ _____

CHALLENGE ACTIVITY

Critical Thinking: Analyze Information How has climate affected the vegetation in Eastern Europe? Explain your answer in a brief paragraph.

| Adriatic Sea | Balkan Mountains | Balkan Peninsula | Carpathians |
| Chernobyl | Danube River | function | radiation |

DIRECTIONS On the line provided before each statement, write **T** if a statement is true and **F** if a statement is false. If the statement is false, write the correct term from the word bank on the line after each sentence that makes the sentence a true statement.

_____ 1. The <u>Balkan Mountains</u> are a low mountain range that stretch in a long arc from the Alps to the Black Sea area.

_____

_____ 2. The Black Sea serves the same function as the <u>Carpathians</u>; they are both important trade routes.

_____

_____ 3. A nuclear explosion at the <u>Chernobyl</u> power plant released huge amounts of radiation into the air.

_____

_____ 4. The <u>Danube River</u> begins in Germany and flows through nine countries before emptying into the Black Sea.

_____

_____ 5. One of the largest landforms in Europe, the <u>Chernobyl</u> extends south into the Mediterranean Sea.

_____

Eastern Europe

> **MAIN IDEAS**
> 1. History ties Poland and the Baltic Republics together.
> 2. The cultures of Poland and the Baltic Republics differ in language and religion but share common customs.
> 3. Economic growth is a major issue in the region today.

Key Terms and Places

infrastructure set of resources—like roads, airports, and factories—that a country needs in order to support economic activities

Warsaw capital of Poland

Lesson Summary
HISTORY

The groups who settled around the Baltic Sea in ancient times developed into the Estonians, Latvians, Lithuanians, and Polish. Each group had its own language and culture, but in time they became connected by a shared history. By the Middle Ages, each had formed an independent kingdom. Lithuania and Poland were the largest and strongest. They ruled large parts of Eastern and Northern Europe. Latvia and Estonia were smaller, weaker, and often invaded.

In the 1900s two world wars greatly damaged the Baltic region. In World War I, millions died in Poland, and thousands more were killed in the Baltic countries. The region also suffered greatly during World War II. This war began when Germany invaded Poland. Millions more died. While fighting the Germans, troops from the Soviet Union invaded Poland and occupied Estonia, Latvia, and Lithuania.

After World War II ended, the Soviet Union took over much of Eastern Europe, making Estonia, Latvia, and Lithuania part of the Soviet Union. The Soviets also forced Poland to accept a Communist government. In 1989 Poland

> How did the Baltic Republics lose their independence after World War II?
>
> _____
> _____
> _____
> _____
> _____
> _____

Lesson 2, *continued*

rejected communism and elected new leaders. In 1991 the Baltic Republics broke away from the Soviet Union. They became independent countries again.

> **Underline the sentences that tell how the governments of the Baltic countries changed beginning in 1989.**

CULTURE

The Baltic countries differ from each other in languages and religion but are alike in other ways. Latvian and Lithuanian languages are similar, but Estonian is like Finnish, the language spoken in Finland. Polish is more like languages of countries farther south. Most Polish people and Lithuanians are Roman Catholics because they traded with Catholic countries. Latvians and Estonians are Lutherans because these countries were once ruled by Sweden, where most people are Lutherans.

These countries' people share many customs and practices. They eat similar foods and practice crafts such as ceramics, painting, and embroidery, a type of decorative sewing. They also enjoy music and dance.

THE REGION TODAY

The economies of Baltic countries suffered because of the long Soviet rule. The Soviets did not build a decent **infrastructure** to support the economy, so the Baltic countries could not produce as many goods as Western countries. Poland and the Baltic Republics are working hard to rebuild their economies. As a result, cities like **Warsaw**, Poland's capital, have become major industrial centers. To help their economies grow, many Baltic countries are trying to attract more tourism. Since the Soviet Union collapsed in 1991, cities like Warsaw and Krakow have attracted tourists with their rich culture, historic sites, and cool summer climates.

> **What economic problems did Soviet rule cause for Poland and the Baltic Republics?**
>
> _____
> _____
> _____
> _____
> _____
> _____

> **What new source of income have the Baltic countries found?**
>
> _____

Guided Reading Workbook

CHALLENGE ACTIVITY

Critical Thinking: Understand Effects Imagine
that you are a newly elected leader of a Baltic
country. Write a speech that tells what you will
do to improve the country's economy.

DIRECTIONS Read each sentence and fill in the
blank with the word in the word pair that best
completes the sentence.

1. The Soviets failed to build a strong

   _____, which has weakened

   the economies of the Baltic countries.

   (embroidery/infrastructure)

2. By the Middle Ages, the kingdoms of Lithuania

   and _____ were large and

   strong. **(Poland/Warsaw)**

3. _____ is the capital of Poland. **(Warsaw/Krakow)**

4. The _____ include(s) Latvia, Estonia, and Lithuania.

   (infrastructure/Baltic Republics)

5. _____ is a type of decorative sewing that is popular

   among people in the Baltic region. **(Krakow/Embroidery)**

Baltic Republics	embroidery	infrastructure
Krakow	Poland	Warsaw

DIRECTIONS Choose four of the terms from the word bank. On a
separate sheet of paper, use these words to write a short story that
relates to the lesson.

_____

_____

Eastern Europe

Lesson 3

MAIN IDEAS

1. The histories and cultures of inland Eastern Europe vary from country to country.

2. Most of inland Eastern Europe today has stable governments, strong economies, and influential cities.

Key Terms and Places

Prague capital of the Czech Republic

Kiev present-day city where the Rus built a settlement

Commonwealth of Independent States CIS, an international alliance that meets to discuss issues such as trade and immigration that affect former Soviet republics

Budapest capital of Hungary

Lesson Summary
HISTORY AND CULTURE

Inland Eastern Europe consists of the Czech Republic, Slovakia, Hungary, Ukraine, Belarus, and Moldova. The region is located on the Northern European and Hungarian plains. The area of the Czech Republic and Slovakia was settled by Slavs, people from Asia who moved into Europe by AD 1000. In time, more powerful countries like Austria conquered these Slavic kingdoms. After World War I, land was taken away from Austria to create the nation of Czechoslovakia. In 1993 Czechoslovakia split into the Czech Republic and Slovakia.

The Czech Republic and Slovakia are located near Western Europe, with which they have much in common. Many people are Roman Catholic. The architecture of **Prague** shows Western influences.

In the 900s Magyar people invaded what is now Hungary. The Magyars influenced Hungarian culture, especially the Hungarian

> **What group of people settled the area of the Czech Republic and Slovakia?**
>
> _____

> **Circle the country that land was taken away from to create Czechoslovakia.**

language. In fact, people in Hungary today still refer to themselves as Magyars.

Ukraine, Belarus, and Moldova were also settled by Slavs, who were then conquered by Vikings. In the 800s a group called the Rus built the settlement that is now **Kiev** in Ukraine. The rulers of Kiev created a huge empire that became part of Russia in the late 1700s. In 1922 Russia became the Soviet Union. Ukraine, Belarus, and Moldova became Soviet republics. After the breakup of the Soviet Union in 1991, these countries became independent. Russia has strongly influenced their cultures. Most people are Orthodox Christians, and the Ukrainian and Belarusian languages are written in the Cyrillic, or Russian, alphabet.

> Underline two ways the cultures of Ukraine, Belarus, and Moldova have been influenced by Russia.

INLAND EASTERN EUROPE TODAY

All inland Eastern European countries were once either part of the Soviet Union or run by Soviet-influenced Communist governments. People had few freedoms. The Soviets did a poor job of managing these economies. Since the collapse of the Soviet Union, Hungary, Slovakia, the Czech Republic, Ukraine, and Moldova have become republics. The people elect their leaders. Belarus also claims to be a republic, but it is really a dictatorship.

> How have the governments of the region changed since the collapse of the Soviet Union?
>
> _____
>
> _____

The people of Ukraine are divided about whether to have a closer connection to Western democracies or Russia. The eastern part has more in common with Russia, while western Ukraine is similar to Europe. In 2014 Russia took over the eastern part of Ukraine known as Crimea. Many governments do not accept Russia's claim to the area.

Countries of Eastern Europe belong to international organizations. Belarus, Ukraine, and Moldova belong to the **Commonwealth of Independent States**. Its members meet to talk about issues like trade and immigration. The Czech Republic, Slovakia, Romania, Bulgaria, and Hungary seek closer ties to the West and belong to the EU. Slovakia, Hungary, and Ukraine have become prosperous industrial centers.

The capital cities of the region are also economic and cultural centers. Prague, Kiev, and **Budapest** are especially important. They are the most prosperous cities in the region, home to important leaders, universities, and cultural sites. Tourists from around the world visit these cities.

> **Why have some Eastern European countries joined the EU?**
>
> _____
>
> _____

CHALLENGE ACTIVITY

Critical Thinking: Evaluate Write a paragraph that explains how the location of inland Eastern Europe has affected its culture and history.

Budapest	Commonwealth of Independent States	Kiev
Magyars	Prague	Slavs

DIRECTIONS Read each sentence and choose the correct term from the word bank to replace the underlined phrase. Write the term in the space provided and then define the term in your own words.

1. Belarus, Ukraine, and Moldova are members of this organization. _____

   _____

   Your definition: _____

   _____

2. This group of fierce invaders swept into Hungary and influenced the language there. _____

   Your definition: _____

3. This is the most prosperous and cultural city in the Czech Republic.

   _____

   Your definition: _____

4. The Rus established this city in the 800s, which still stands in Ukraine today.

   _____

   Your definition: _____

   _____

5. The Czech Republic and Slovakia were settled by this group of people.

   _____

   Your definition: _____

Eastern Europe

Lesson 4

> **MAIN IDEAS**
> 1. The history of the Balkan countries is one of conquest and conflict.
> 2. The cultures of the Balkan countries are shaped by the many ethnic groups who live there.
> 3. Civil wars and weak economies are major challenges to the region today.

Key Terms and Places

ethnocentrism belief that one's own culture or ethnic group is superior

ethnic cleansing effort to remove all members of a group from a country or region

Lesson Summary
HISTORY

The Balkan Peninsula has been ruled by many different groups. In ancient times, the Greeks founded colonies near the Black Sea. This area is now Bulgaria and Romania. Next, the Romans conquered most of the area between the Adriatic Sea and the Danube River. When the Roman Empire divided into west and east in the AD 300s, the Balkan Peninsula became part of the Byzantine Empire. Under Byzantine rule, many people became Orthodox Christians.

Over 1,000 years later, Muslim Ottoman Turks conquered the Byzantine Empire. Many people in the Balkans became Muslims. Ottoman rule lasted until the 1800s, when the people of the Balkans drove the Ottomans out. They then created their own kingdoms.

In the late 1800s the Austria-Hungarian Empire took over part of the peninsula. To protest the takeover, a man from Serbia shot the heir to the Austro-Hungarian throne. This event led to World War I. After the war, Europe's leaders combined many formerly independent countries into Yugoslavia. In the 1990s this

> Underline the names of groups or empires that ruled the Balkan Peninsula until the 1800s.

> Underline the sentences that explain the events that led to World War I.

country broke apart. Ethnic and religious conflict led to its collapse.

CULTURE

The Balkans are Europe's most diverse region. People practice different religions and speak many different languages. Most people are Christians. They are either Orthodox, Roman Catholic, or Protestant. Islam is also practiced. Albania is the only country in Europe that is mostly Muslim. Most people speak Slavic languages that are related to Russian. People in Romania speak a language that comes from Latin. Albanian is like no other language in the world, as is the language spoken by the Roma people.

> **What makes the Balkans Europe's most diverse region?**
> _____
> _____
> _____
> _____

THE BALKANS TODAY

Balkan countries were once run by Communist governments. Poor economic planning has hurt the economies of the region. It is still the poorest region in Europe today.

There are also serious problems between the different religious and ethnic groups. When Yugoslavia broke apart, the new countries that formed had violent conflicts. **Ethnocentrism**—the belief that one's own culture or ethnic group is superior—led to **ethnic cleansing**. Religious or ethnic groups used threats and violence against people from other cultures who would not leave. In 1995 troops from all over the world came to Bosnia and Herzegovina to help end the fighting.

Since 2008, ten countries share the Balkan Peninsula. Macedonia and Slovenia were the first to break away from Yugoslavia. When Croatia broke away, fighting started between ethnic Croats and Serbs. Peace did not return until many Serbs left Croatia. Bosnia and Herzegovina also had terrible ethnic fighting. Serbia, the largest country to emerge from the former

> **What caused the violence in the Balkans after Yugoslavia broke apart?**
> _____
> _____
> _____

> **What ended the fighting in Bosnia and Herzegovina?**
> _____
> _____
> _____

Yugoslavia, also saw terrible fighting. Both Montenegro and Kosovo separated from Serbia.

The Balkans includes three other countries. Albania and Romania are poor and have serious economic and political problems. Bulgaria has a strong economy based on industry and tourism.

CHALLENGE ACTIVITY

Critical Thinking: Predict Write a paragraph that explains how ethnic diversity could be an advantage for the Balkan countries in the future.

DIRECTIONS Look at each set of terms following each number. On the line provided, write the letter of the term that does not relate to the others.

_____ 1. a. Protestant   b. Orthodox   c. Catholic   d. Slavic

_____ 2. a. World War I   b. Serbia   c. Germanic   d. Austro-Hungarians

_____ 3. a. Albania   b. Hungary   c. Croatia   d. Slovenia

_____ 4. a. Macedonia   b. Yugoslavia   c. violence   d. ethnic cleansing

_____ 5. a. Balkans   b. Greeks   c. Romans   d. Ottomans

Albania	Balkans	ethnic cleansing
ethnocentrism	Hungary	Orthodox
Slavic	Soviet Union	Yugoslavia

DIRECTIONS Choose at least three of the terms from the word bank. On a separate sheet of paper, use these words to write a summary of what you learned in the lesson.

Russia and the Caucasus

Lesson 1

MAIN IDEAS

1. The physical features of Russia and the Caucasus include plains, mountains, and rivers.
2. Russia's cold climate contrasts sharply with the warmer Caucasus.
3. Russia has a wealth of natural resources, but many are hard to access.

Key Terms and Places

Ural Mountains mountain range where Europe and Asia meet

Caspian Sea world's largest inland sea; borders the Caucasus Mountains

Caucasus Mountains mountain range that covers much of the area between the Black Sea and the Caspian Sea

Moscow capital of Russia

Siberia vast region in Russia stretching from the Urals to the Pacific Ocean

Volga River longest river in Europe, located in western Russia

taiga forest of mainly evergreen trees covering much of Russia

Lesson Summary

PHYSICAL FEATURES

The continents of Asia and Europe meet in Russia's **Ural Mountains**. Together, Asia and Europe form the large landmass of Eurasia. A large part of Eurasia is Russia, the world's largest country.

The Caucasus is the area south of Russia between the Black Sea and the **Caspian Sea**. It is named for the **Caucasus Mountains**, and includes Georgia, Armenia, Azerbaijan, and parts of southern Russia. The area is mostly rugged upland.

Russia's landforms vary from west to east. The fertile Northern European Plain, Russia's heartland, extends across western Russia. Most Russians live in this area, and **Moscow**, Russia's capital, is located there. Going east, the plain rises to form the low Ural Mountains. The area between the Urals and the Pacific Ocean is **Siberia**.

> Which two continents meet in the Ural Mountains?
> _____
> _____

> Circle the names of the three countries that are found in the Caucasus.

> What is the capital of Russia?
> _____

The West Siberian Plain is a huge, flat, marshy area. It is one of the largest plains in the world. The rivers in this plain flow toward the Arctic Ocean. East of this plain is an upland called the Central Siberian Plateau. High mountain ranges run through southern and eastern Siberia.

Eastern Siberia is called the Russian Far East, which includes the Kamchatka Peninsula and several islands. This area is part of the Ring of Fire, known for its volcanoes and earthquakes. There are over 120 volcanoes, 20 of which are still active. South of the peninsula lie the Sakhalin islands seized from Japan after World War II. Japan still claims ownership of the Kuril islands.

> **What is the Ring of Fire?**
> _____
> _____
> _____

Some of the longest rivers in the world flow through the region. The **Volga River** is the longest river in Europe and the core of Russia's river network. It runs south to the Caspian Sea and is linked to the Don River and Baltic Sea by canals. Other rivers include the Ob, Yenisey, and Lena rivers, which flow northward to the Arctic Ocean. Many of Russia's rivers stay frozen for much of the year, which can slow shipping and trade.

> **What is the longest river in Europe?**
> _____

Russia also has some 200,000 lakes. Lake Baikal is the world's deepest lake. It is called the Jewel of Siberia, but logging and factories have polluted the water. Russians are trying to clean it.

In the Caucasus, lowlands lie between the Black Sea, the region's western border, and the Caspian Sea, the eastern border. The Black Sea is an important trade route because it links to the Mediterranean. The Caspian Sea is a saltwater lake—the largest inland sea in the world.

CLIMATE AND PLANT LIFE

Russia is cold because it lies far north, partly in the Arctic Circle. It has short summers and long, snowy winters. Most Russians live west of the

> **Underline the sentence that explains why Russia is so cold.**

Guided Reading Workbook

Urals, where the climate is milder than the north and east.

Russia's northern coast is tundra, and most of the ground is permafrost, or permanently frozen soil. Only small plants like mosses grow. Areas closer to the Atlantic Ocean have more moisture than inland regions. South of the tundra is the vast **taiga**, a forest of mainly evergreen trees that covers half of Russia.

In the Caucasus, moist air from the Mediterranean Sea provides a warm and wet subtropical climate zone along the Black Sea. Tourists used to go to this area until ethnic conflict made it dangerous to travel there. It is cooler in the uplands. Azerbaijan is hot and dry. The Caucasus is one of the most biologically diverse regions on Earth. The climate and soil are good for farming, and the mountains are home to impressive forests and wildflowers.

What causes the subtropical climate in parts of the Caucasus?
_____
_____

NATURAL RESOURCES

Russia has a wealth of natural resources, including timber, metals, precious gems, and rich soils for farming. Energy resources, such as oil, natural gas, and coal, are among its largest exports. These resources have been poorly managed, however. Many resources near populated areas are gone, and it is hard to reach resources in more remote areas like Siberia.

What energy resources are important exports for Russia?
_____
_____
_____

CHALLENGE ACTIVITY

Critical Thinking: Make Generalizations Based on what you have read so far, write a short paragraph about what it might be like to live in Russia.

DIRECTIONS Read each sentence and fill in the blank with the word
in the word pair that best completes the sentence.

1. It is in the _____ that the continents of Europe and Asia

   meet. (**Caucasus Mountains/Ural Mountains**)

2. The _____ provides an important transportation route

   through Russia. (**Black Sea/Volga River**)

3. The _____ links the Caucasus to the Mediterranean.

   (**Caspian Sea/Black Sea**)

4. The Ring of Fire is located in eastern _____.

   (**Siberia/Moscow**)

5. The vast forest of evergreen trees that covers about half of Russia is called the

   _____. (**tundra/taiga**)

Black Sea	Caspian Sea	Caucasus Mountains
Moscow	Siberia	taiga
tundra	Ural Mountains	Volga River

DIRECTIONS Choose four of the terms from the word bank. On a
separate sheet of paper, use these words to write a story or poem
that relates to the lesson.

Russia and the Caucasus

Lesson 2

MAIN IDEAS

1. The Russian Empire grew under powerful leaders, but unrest and war led to its end.
2. The Soviet Union emerged as a Communist superpower with rigid government control.
3. Russia's history and diversity have influenced its culture.
4. The Russian Federation is working to develop democracy and a market economy.
5. Russia's physical geography, cities, and economy define its many culture regions.
6. Russia faces a number of serious challenges.

Key Terms and Places

Kiev early center of Russia, now the capital of Ukraine

Cyrillic form of the Greek alphabet

czar emperor

Bolsheviks Communist group that seized power during the Russian Revolution

gulags Soviet labor camps

dachas Russian country houses

St. Petersburg city founded by Peter the Great and styled after those of Western Europe

smelters factories that produce metal ores

Trans-Siberian Railway longest single rail line in the world, running from Moscow to Vladivostok on the east coast

Chechnya Russian republic in the Caucasus Mountains, an area of ethnic conflict

Lesson Summary
THE RUSSIAN EMPIRE

The Slavs came from Asia and settled in the area of what is now Ukraine and western Russia. In the AD 800s, Viking traders from Scandinavia, called Rus, invaded the Slavs. They created the first Russian state of Kievan, which centered around the city of **Kiev**. Kiev is now the capital of Ukraine.

Guided Reading Workbook

Over time, missionaries introduced Orthodox Christianity and **Cyrillic**, a form of the Greek alphabet that Russians still use today. This alphabet is one of the differences between Russian and European languages, which developed from Latin.

In the 1200s Mongol invaders called Tatars conquered Kiev. Local Russian princes ruled several states under the Mongols. Muscovy became the strongest state, with Moscow its main city. After about 200 years, Muscovy's prince Ivan III seized control from the Mongols. Then in the 1540s, his grandson Ivan IV crowned himself **czar**, or emperor. He had total power and became known as Ivan the Terrible because he was a cruel and savage ruler.

Muscovy developed into the country of Russia. Peter the Great and then Catherine the Great ruled as czars, building Russia into a huge empire and world power. Under their rule, east-to-west trade along the Silk Road increased. Spices, teas, cotton, silk, and more came from as far away as India and the Ottoman Empire. These trade routes also spread disease.

By the nineteenth century, a north–south "Cotton Road" brought cotton to Russia from India, Egypt, South Asia, and the United States. Russian industrialists used it to create thriving textile mills during the Industrial Revolution. Yet, Russia remained mostly a country of poor farmers, while the czars and nobles had most of the wealth.

In the early 1900s the Russian people began demanding improvements. Unrest, World War I, and other problems weakened the Russian empire. In 1917 the czar lost support and was forced to give up the throne. The **Bolsheviks**, a Russian Communist group, seized power in the Russian Revolution. They killed the czar and his family. Bolshevik leaders formed the Union

What is Cyrillic?

_____

_____

_____

Circle the names of two czars who built Russia into a world power.

Underline the sentence that explains why the Russian people began demanding improvements.

Who were the Bolsheviks?

_____

_____

_____

Guided Reading Workbook

of Soviet Socialist Republics (USSR), or the
Soviet Union, in 1922.

THE SOVIET UNION

The Soviet Union became a Communist country,
led by Vladimir Lenin. After Lenin's death in
1924, Joseph Stalin ruled as a brutal dictator. He
set up a command economy, where the
government owns all businesses and farms and
makes all economic decisions. It strictly
controlled its people. Anyone who spoke out
against the government was jailed, exiled, or
killed. Millions of people were sent to **gulags**,
harsh Soviet labor camps often located in Siberia.

During World War II, the Soviet Union sided
with the Allies. Millions of Soviet citizens died.
After the war, Stalin built a protective buffer
around the Soviet Union to prevent invasion. He
did this by setting up Communist governments in
Eastern Europe. The United States saw this as a
threat. This created the Cold War, a period of
tense rivalry between the two countries, where
they competed to develop powerful weapons.

The Soviet Union grew weak in the 1980s, in
part because of its economy. Under its leader,
Mikhail Gorbachev, the country began to loosen
government control. The Soviet republics began
to push for independence, leading to the collapse
of the Soviet Union in 1991. It broke into 15
independent countries, including Russia.

RUSSIA'S CULTURE TODAY

More than 140 million people live in Russia.
Most are ethnic Russians, or Slavs, but Russia
also has many other ethnic groups. The Soviet
government had opposed religion and it
controlled culture. Today, the main faith is
Russian Orthodox Christian, but other religions
are practiced. The country celebrates a variety of
traditional holidays. Russia has made many

What is a command economy?
_____
_____
_____
_____

What did Stalin do to create a protective buffer around the Soviet Union?
_____
_____
_____

How many people live in Russia today?
_____

contributions to the arts and sciences, especially in ballet and space research.

THE RUSSIAN FEDERATION TODAY

When the Soviet Union broke apart, Russia had to create a new government. The Russian Federation is a federal republic, which divides power between national and local governments. Voters elect a president, who then appoints a prime minister. The Federal Assembly makes the country's laws. It is similar to the parliamentary system of the UK.

> **Underline the sentence that explains how the Russian Federation divides power.**

Russians have more freedom today as the country moves toward democracy. However, there are still problems of government corruption that have slowed progress. The country is also moving to a market economy based on free trade and competition. Many businesses and farms are now privately owned. Russia produces and exports oil, natural gas, timber, metals, chemicals, and crops like grains. Heavy, light, and service industries are all important parts of the economy.

> **What is a market economy?**
>
> _____
>
> _____
>
> _____

About 75 percent of Russians live in cities, where there is a large range of consumer goods, restaurants, and stores. Some Russians have become very wealthy and own **dachas** in the country, but the average person still has a low standard of living.

CULTURE REGIONS

Four western culture regions—Moscow, St. Petersburg, Volga River, and Ural Mountains areas—make up Russia's heartland. These regions are home to the vast majority of Russia's people.

> **Circle the four western culture regions of Russia.**

Moscow is Russia's capital and largest city. The Kremlin holds Russia's government offices, as well as beautiful palaces and gold-domed churches. Moscow is a huge industrial region.

St. Petersburg was founded by Peter the Great and styled after cities of Western Europe. It was Russia's capital for some 200 years. Its location on the Gulf of Finland has made the city an important trade center.

The Volga River of the Volga region is a major shipping route and source of hydroelectric power. Factories here process oil and gas. The Caspian Sea provides black caviar.

The Urals region is an important mining area. Factories called **smelters** process metal ores, copper, and iron.

Siberia, another of Russia's culture regions, is east of the Urals. Winters there are long and severe. Siberia has many natural resources, but accessing them is difficult. Lumber, mining, and oil production are the most important industries. There are few towns in this region, and most follow the route of the **Trans-Siberian Railway**, the longest single rail line in the world.

Siberia's coastal areas and islands along the Pacific Ocean are known as the Russian Far East. This culture region's resources include timber, rich soils, oil, minerals, and fishing. Vladivostock is the region's main seaport.

RUSSIA'S CHALLENGES

Since 1991 Russia has made great progress, but the change to a market economy has caused prices and unemployment to rise. Also, the gap between rich and poor has widened. Other problems are a falling population and serious pollution, which has harmed Russia's environment. The country has not protected its natural resources, causing further damage to the environment.

There is also ongoing tension between Russia and its neighbors. In 2013 Russia took over the part of Ukraine called Crimea. Ukraine considers this a violation of international law.

> Where is St. Petersburg located?
> _____
> _____

> What is notable about the Trans-Siberian Railway?
> _____
> _____

> Circle two problems that are causing harm to Russia's environment.

Lesson 2, *continued*

Russia also faces ethnic conflicts with the
Russian republic of **Chechnya**, a Muslim area.
Some people want independence, and this has led
to fighting and terrorism in the region.

CHALLENGE ACTIVITY

Critical Thinking: Draw Inferences Based on what
you have learned about each region, which area
do you think holds the most potential
economically for Russia? Why?

DIRECTIONS Look at each set of four terms. On the line provided,
write the letter of the term that does not relate to the others.

_____ 1. a. market economy b. Stalin c. Siberia d. gulags

_____ 2. a. Cold War b. weapons c. Bolsheviks d. arms race

_____ 3. a. communism b. Cold War c. Soviet Union d. czar

_____ 4. a. Vikings b. Siberia c. Kiev d. Rus

_____ 5. a. St. Petersburg b. Moscow c. Volga River d. Chechnya

Bolsheviks	Chechnya	Cold War
communism	czar	gulags
market economy	Siberia	St. Petersburg

DIRECTIONS Choose five of the terms from the word bank. On a
separate sheet of paper, use these words to write a summary of what
you learned in the lesson.

Russia and the Caucasus

MAIN IDEAS
1. Many groups have ruled and influenced the Caucasus during its long history.
2. Today, the Caucasus republics are working to improve their economies but struggle with ethnic unrest and conflict.

Key Terms and Places

Tbilisi capital of Georgia

Yerevan capital of Armenia

Baku capital of Azerbaijan, center of a large oil-refining industry

Lesson Summary
HISTORY

The Caucasus lies in the Caucasus Mountains between the Black Sea and the Caspian Sea, where Europe blends with Asia. The region reflects a range of cultural influences and at one time or another has been ruled or invaded by Persians, Greeks, Romans, Arabs, Turks, Mongols, and Russians.

In the early 1800s Russia took over much of the Caucasus, but the Ottoman Turks held western Armenia. Before and during World War I, Armenians were targets of ethnic cleansing by the Turks. Hundreds of thousands were removed by force or killed. After the war, Armenia, Azerbaijan, and Georgia gained independence, but by the early 1920s they became part of the Soviet Union. They regained independence when the Soviet Union fell in 1991.

> **Which groups have ruled or invaded the Caucasus?**
> _____
> _____
> _____

> **What happened to the Caucasus countries in the early 1920s?**
> _____
> _____

THE CAUCASUS TODAY

Although the region has a long history, the Caucasus countries have had to create new governments and economies. Progress has been slowed by ethnic unrest and conflicts. The countries have similar governments. An elected president governs each nation, and an appointed

> **Circle the reasons for the slow progress of the Caucasus countries.**

Guided Reading Workbook

prime minister runs each government. An elected parliament, or legislature, makes the laws.

Georgia is located in the Caucasus Mountains, east of the Black Sea. **Tbilisi** is the capital. About 70 percent of the people are ethnic Georgians and belong to the Georgian Orthodox Church. Georgian is the official language, with its own alphabet, but many other languages are spoken.

Georgia has struggled with unrest and civil war since independence. Georgians peacefully forced out their president in 2003. However, ethnic groups in northern Georgia continue to fight for independence from the rest of the country. Georgia's unrest has hurt its economy, but it is helped by international aid. The country's economy is based on services and farming. Other industries include steel, mining, wine, and tourism in Black Sea resorts.

Why is there unrest in northern Georgia?
_____
_____
_____

Armenia is a small, landlocked country south of Georgia. **Yerevan** is the capital. Most of the people are Armenian and belong to the Armenian Orthodox Church.

Armenia fought a war with Azerbaijan in the early 1990s. Armenia took over an area of Azerbaijan where most people were ethnic Armenian. Although there was a cease-fire in 1994, the area is still controlled by Armenian forces. The conflict remains unsettled and has hurt Armenia's economy, but international aid is helping. Diamond processing is now a growing industry.

Underline the sentence that explains why Armenia and Azerbaijan got into a war.

Azerbaijan is east of Armenia and borders the Caspian Sea. The Azeri make up 90 percent of the population, and the country is mostly Muslim. Oil, found along the Caspian Sea, is the most important part of the economy. **Baku**, the capital, is the center of this industry, which has led to strong economic growth. Problems include corruption, poverty, and refugees as a result of the conflict with Armenia.

What is the most important part of Azerbaijan's economy?
_____

CHALLENGE ACTIVITY

Critical Thinking: Compare and Contrast Describe
the similarities and differences between the
Caucasus countries.

DIRECTIONS Write three words or phrases that describe each term.

1. Caspian Sea _____

2. Baku _____

DIRECTIONS Read each sentence and fill in the blank with the
word in the word pair that best completes the sentence.

3. The capital of Armenia is _____. (**Baku/Yerevan**)

4. _____ is the capital of Georgia. (**Yerevan/Tbilisi**)

5. Oil is the most important part of _____'s economy.
   (**Tbilisi/Azerbaijan**)

6. Georgia, Armenia, and Azerbaijan all lie south of the _____.
   (**Black Sea/Caucasus Mountains**)

7. The Armenians were targets of _____.
   (**ethnic cleansing/Yerevan**)

Early Civilizations of the Fertile Crescent and the Nile Valley

Lesson 1

MAIN IDEAS
1. The rivers of Southwest Asia supported the growth of civilization.
2. New farming techniques led to the growth of cities.

Key Terms and Places

Fertile Crescent large arc of rich farmland extending from the Persian Gulf to the Mediterranean Sea

silt fertile mix of rich soil and small rocks

civilization organized society within a specific area

irrigation way of supplying water to an area of land

canals human-made waterways

surplus more of something than is needed

division of labor arrangement in which people specialize in specific tasks

Lesson Summary
RIVERS SUPPORT THE GROWTH OF CIVILIZATION

Early people settled where crops would grow. Crops usually grew well near rivers, where water was available and regular floods made the soil rich.

Mesopotamia was located in Southwest Asia between the Tigris and Euphrates rivers. The region is known as the **Fertile Crescent**. Hunter-gatherer groups first settled in Mesopotamia more than 12,000 years ago. Over time, these people learned how to grow food from seeds. Part of the year they would settle in one area to grow food, and the rest of the year they would hunt and gather in other areas.

Eventually, they created tools to help them farm, which made them better at growing food. They no longer needed to leave the area to find food. They began building permanent settlements where they could raise crops. The change from looking for food to staying in one place and

> Mesopotamia means "between the rivers" in Greek. Which two rivers does the name refer to?
>
> _____
>
> _____

> Underline the sentences that explain why the Mesopotamian people stopped hunting and gathering and settled in one place.

growing food is so important it is called the
Neolithic Revolution.

Farm settlements formed in Mesopotamia as
early as 7000 BC. Every year, floods on the rivers
brought **silt**. The fertile silt made the land ideal
for farming. Farmers grew wheat, barley, and
other grains. Livestock, birds, and fish were also
sources of food.

Plentiful food led to population growth and
villages formed. Eventually, these early villages
developed into the world's first **civilization**.
Civilizations usually have certain features, such
as large cities with different types of people.
They have culture like writing, education, art,
and architecture. Governments with leaders and
laws help civilizations develop. The governments
make economic decisions that can improve
people's lives.

Why is silt important?
_____
_____
_____

Circle four features of a civilization.

FARMING AND CITIES

Early farmers faced the challenge of learning
how to control the flow of river water to their
fields in both rainy and dry seasons. Flooding
destroyed crops, killed livestock, and washed
away homes. When water levels were too low,
crops dried up.

To solve their problems, Mesopotamians used
irrigation. They dug out large storage basins to
catch rainwater. Then they dug **canals** that
connected these basins to a network of ditches.
These ditches brought water to the fields. To
protect the fields from flooding, farmers built up
riverbanks. This held back floodwaters even when
river levels were high.

Irrigation increased the amount of food
farmers could grow and gave them water to graze
cattle and sheep. This provided a variety of foods
and led to a food **surplus**. Fewer people needed to
farm, and they started doing other jobs.

Underline the sentence that lists some of the problems caused by flooding.

How did Mesopotamians move water from storage basins to irrigation ditches?
_____

For the first time, people became crafters, religious leaders, and government workers. A **division of labor** developed, where specialized workers could work on different parts of large projects. This helped society accomplish more, but it also required order. So Mesopotamians created structure and rules through laws and government.

Mesopotamian settlements grew in size and complexity between 4000 and 3000 BC. Most people continued to work in farming jobs. However, cities became important places. People traded goods in cities. Cities became the political, religious, cultural, and economic centers of Mesopotamian civilization.

> **Why were cities important to Mesopotamian civilization?**
>
> _____
> _____
> _____

CHALLENGE ACTIVITY

Critical Thinking: Draw Inferences Use information from this lesson to list six jobs Mesopotamians might have had.

DIRECTIONS Write a word or phrase that has the same meaning as the term given.

1. surplus _____

_____

2. irrigation _____

_____

3. division of labor _____

_____

4. Fertile Crescent _____

_____

5. silt _____

_____

6. canal _____

_____

DIRECTIONS Look at each set of three terms following each number. On the line provided, write the letter of the term that does not relate to the others.

_____ 7. a. irrigation
        b. crafter
        c. canal

_____ 8. a. surplus
        b. division of labor
        c. Fertile Crescent

_____ 9. a. hunter-gatherer
        b. Mesopotamia
        c. Fertile Crescent

Early Civilizations of the Fertile Crescent and the Nile Valley

Lesson 2

MAIN IDEAS
1. The Sumerians created the world's first advanced society.
2. Religion played a major role in Sumerian society.
3. The Sumerians invented the world's first writing system.
4. Advances and inventions changed Sumerians' lives.
5. Many types of art developed in Sumer.

Key Terms and Places

Sumer area of Mesopotamia where the world's first civilization was developed

city-state political unit consisting of a city and the surrounding countryside

empire land with different territories and people under a single rule

polytheism worship of many gods

priests people who performed religious ceremonies

social hierarchy division of society by rank or class

cuneiform Sumerian system of writing, which used symbols to represent basic parts of words

pictographs picture symbols that represented objects such as trees or animals

scribe writer

epics long poems that tell the story of a hero

architecture the science of building

ziggurat pyramid-shaped temple tower

Lesson Summary
AN ADVANCED SOCIETY

In southern Mesopotamia in about 3000 BC, people known as the Sumerians (soo-MER-ee-unz) developed the world's first advanced civilization. Most people in **Sumer** (SOO-muhr) lived in rural areas, but the centers of Sumerian society were the urban areas. These cities grew into political units called **city-states**, which contained the central city and its surrounding countryside. City-states built strong armies so they could gain more farmland and control larger areas. Over time, individual city-states gained and lost power.

> **When and where did the Sumerian society begin?**
> _____
> _____

Lesson 2, *continued*

Another society called the Akkadians developed along the Tigris and Euphrates rivers, north of Sumer. They lived in peace with the Sumerians until the 2300s BC. The Akkadian leader Sargon wanted to extend his territory. He built a large permanent army and defeated all the city-states of Sumer as well as all of northern Mesopotamia. With these conquests, Sargon established the world's first **empire**. It stretched from the Persian Gulf to the Mediterranean Sea. The Akkadian empire lasted about 150 years. After its downfall, the Sumerians once again became the most powerful civilization in the region.

> **Who established the world's first empire?**
> _____

RELIGION SHAPES SOCIETY

Religion played an important role in nearly every aspect of Sumerian public and private life. Sumerians practiced **polytheism**, the worship of many gods. Each city-state considered one god to be its special protector. Sumerians believed their gods had enormous powers. Gods could bring a good harvest or a disastrous flood. They could bring illness, or they could bring good health and wealth. The Sumerians believed success in every area of life depended on pleasing the gods. People relied on **priests** to help them gain the gods' favor. Priests had great status. They interpreted the wishes of the gods and made offerings to them.

> **Why did Sumerians try to please the gods?**
> _____
> _____
> _____
> _____

A **social hierarchy** developed in Sumerian city-states. Kings were at the top. They claimed they had been chosen by gods to rule. Below kings were priests and nobles. The middle ranks included skilled craftspeople, merchants, and traders. Farmers and laborers made up the large working class. Slaves were at the bottom of the social order. Although the role of most women was limited to the home and raising children, some upper-class women were educated and even became priestesses.

> **Underline the sentence that explains the role of priests in Sumerian society.**

> **Circle the two groups that formed the Sumerian upper classes.**

INVENTION OF WRITING

The Sumerians made one of the greatest cultural advances in history. They developed **cuneiform** (kyoo-NEE-uh-fohrm), the world's first system of writing. But Sumerians did not have pencils, pens, or paper. Instead, they used sharp reeds, called styluses, to make wedge-shaped symbols on clay tablets. Before cuneiform, written communication used **pictographs**, picture symbols that represented objects. Cuneiform was able to use a variety of symbols that could be combined into one word and express complex ideas and not just objects.

Sumerians first used cuneiform to keep business records, and they would hire a **scribe** to keep track of traded items. They also kept records for the government and temples. Becoming a scribe was a way to move up in social class. Writing was taught in schools. In time, scribes wrote works on law, grammar, and mathematics. Sumerians also wrote stories, proverbs, songs, poems to celebrate military victories, and long poems called **epics**.

ADVANCES AND INVENTIONS

The Sumerians were the first to build wheeled vehicles like carts and wagons. They invented the potter's wheel, a device that spins wet clay as a craftsperson shapes it into bowls. They invented the ox-drawn plow to prepare hard soil for planting, which greatly improved farm production. They built sewers under city streets. They learned to use bronze to make strong tools and weapons, and even invented a clock.

Sumerians developed a math system based on the number 60. From this, they were able to

> Write the name of the world's first system of writing.
>
> _____

> Why were scribes important?
>
> _____
>
> _____

> Which Sumerian invention greatly improved farm production?
>
> _____

Guided Reading Workbook

calculate areas of rectangles and triangles and
they divided a year into 12 months. They named
thousands of animals, plants, and minerals, and
used them to produce healing drugs.

THE ARTS OF SUMER

Sumerian ruins reveal great skill in art and
architecture. Most Sumerian rulers lived in large
palaces. Rich Sumerians had two-story homes,
though most people lived in one-story houses
with rooms arranged around a small courtyard.
Their homes were built of bricks, made from the
dried clay of riverbanks. A pyramid-shaped
temple called a **ziggurat** rose high above each city.

Sumerian artists made sculpture and jewelry.
Sculptors created statues of gods for the temples
and made small objects of ivory or rare woods.
Jewelers worked with imported gold, silver, and
gems. Earrings and other items found in the
region show that Sumerian jewelers knew
advanced methods for putting gold pieces
together.

The Sumerians also developed a special art
form called the cylinder seal. The cylinder seal
was a small stone cylinder that was engraved with
designs and could be rolled over wet clay to
decorate objects or to "sign" documents.

Music played an important role in Sumerian
society. Musicians played reed pipes, drums,
tambourines, and stringed instruments called
lyres. People sang songs and hymns to gods and
kings. Music and dance provided entertainment
in marketplaces and homes.

> Underline the text that
> describes the houses most
> Sumerians lived in.

> What was a cylinder seal
> used for?
> _____
> _____

CHALLENGE ACTIVITY

Critical Thinking: Analyze Information Make
a chart or table to show the social hierarchy
of Sumer.

DIRECTIONS On the line provided before each statement, write **T** if
a statement is true and **F** if a statement is false. If the statement is
false, write the correct term on the line after each sentence to make
the sentence a true statement.

_____ 1. Land with different territories and peoples under a single rule is called
a <u>city-state</u>.

_____

_____ 2. A <u>ziggurat</u> would be hired to keep track of the items people traded.

_____

_____ 3. Kings in <u>Sargon</u> believed the gods had chosen them to rule the people.

_____

_____ 4. <u>Empires</u> consist of a cities, which are the political centers, and the
surrounding countryside.

_____

_____ 5. An <u>epic</u> is a long poem that tells a story of a hero.

_____

_____ 6. People relied on <u>priests</u> to help them gain the gods' favor.

_____

Guided Reading Workbook

DIRECTIONS Read each sentence and fill in the blank with the word in the word pair that best completes the sentence.

7. A _____ is a division of society by rank or class. (**city-state/social hierarchy**)

8. A pyramid-shaped tower that rose above each Sumerian city was called a _____. (**Sumer/ziggurat**)

9. The Sumerians developed the world's first system of writing called _____. (**cuneiform/pictograph**)

10. The practice of worshiping many gods is called _____. (**polytheism/social hierarchy**)

11. The _____ was the earliest form of written communication. (**pictograph/scribe**)

Early Civilizations of the Fertile Crescent and the Nile Valley

Lesson 3

> **MAIN IDEAS**
> 1. The Babylonians conquered Mesopotamia and created a code of law.
> 2. Invasions of Mesopotamia changed the region's culture.
> 3. The Phoenicians built a trading society in the eastern Mediterranean region.

Key Terms and Places

Babylon important Mesopotamian city-state near present-day Baghdad

Hammurabi's Code earliest known written collection of laws, comprising 282 laws that dealt with almost every part of life

chariot wheeled, horse-drawn battle cart

alphabet set of letters that can be combined to form written words

Lesson Summary
THE BABYLONIANS CONQUER MESOPOTAMIA

By 1800 BC a powerful city-state called **Babylon** had developed on the Euphrates River. Babylon was originally a Sumerian city. In 1792 BC Babylon's greatest monarch, Hammurabi, became king. He was a brilliant warrior and eventually conquered all of Mesopotamia. This new empire was called the Babylonian Empire. Babylon was its capital city and the major city in Mesopotamia.

During his 42-year reign, Hammurabi oversaw many building and irrigation projects, improved the tax collection system, and brought wealth through increased trade. He is most famous, however, for **Hammurabi's Code**, the earliest known written collection of laws. It contained laws on everything from trade, loans, and theft to injury, marriage, and murder. Some of its ideas are still found in laws today. The code was important not only for how thorough it was, but also because it was written down for all to see. After Hammurabi's death, Babylonian power declined and the empire came to an end.

> On what river was the city of Babylon located?
>
> _____

> What is Hammurabi's Code?
>
> _____
> _____
> _____

INVASIONS OF MESOPOTAMIA

Several other civilizations developed in and around the Fertile Crescent. Their armies battled each other for Mesopotamia's fertile land, and control of the region passed from one empire to another. The Hittites of Asia Minor captured Babylon in 1595 BC, using strong iron weapons and swift **chariots** on the battlefield. Hittite rule did not last long. Their king was killed by an assassin, creating chaos in the kingdom. The Kassites invaded from the north. They captured Babylon and ruled for almost 400 years.

> Circle the two inventions that helped the Hittites conquer Babylon.

The Assyrians came from northern Mesopotamia and briefly gained control of Babylon in the 1200s BC. They were soon overrun by invaders. However, 300 years later, they began to conquer all of the Fertile Crescent and went as far as Asia Minor and Egypt. The Assyrians had a strong army and were fierce in battle. Anyone who resisted them was killed or harshly punished. They ruled from Nineveh, their own capital city, and demanded taxes across the empire. This required the Assyrians to use local leaders, who governed a small area, collected taxes, enforced laws, and raised troops. The Assyrians also built roads to link distant parts of the empire.

> How did the Assyrians rule their large empire from Nineveh?
>
> _____
> _____
> _____
> _____

In 612 BC the Chaldeans, a group from the Syrian Desert, conquered the Assyrians and set up their own empire. Nebuchadnezzar (neb-uh-kuhd-NEZ-uhr), the most famous Chaldean king, rebuilt Babylon into a beautiful city. According to legend, his grand palace featured the famous Hanging Gardens. The Chaldeans admired Sumerian culture and made notable advances in astronomy and mathematics.

> Which older Mesopotamian culture did the Chaldeans admire and study?
>
> _____

THE PHOENICIANS

Phoenicia was a wealthy trading society, located at the western end of the Fertile Crescent along the

Guided Reading Workbook

Lesson 3, *continued*

Mediterranean Sea. Mountains bordered the regions to the north and east. The Phoenicians were mostly urban people. Their chief cities were Tyre, Sidon, and Byblos, port cities that still exist today in the country of Lebanon on the Mediterranean Sea. Phoenicia had few resources other than cedar trees. This wood was a valuable trade item. Since an overland trade route was blocked by mountains, Phoenicians used the sea for trade.

Tyre became one of the best harbors in the world. Fleets of fast Phoenician trading ships sailed throughout the Mediterranean and even as far as the Atlantic Ocean. The Phoenicians built new cities, like Carthage, along their trade routes. They became wealthy by trading cedar wood, silverwork, ivory carvings, glass, and slaves. Purple dye made from shellfish was one of the Phoenicians' most important products. They dyed cloth purple, and it became very popular with rich people around the Mediterranean.

The Phoenicians' most lasting achievement, however, was developing one of the first **alphabets**. It made writing much easier and had a huge impact on the ancient world. The alphabet we use today is based on the Phoenicians'.

CHALLENGE ACTIVITY

Critical Thinking: Sequence Make a timeline with approximate dates showing the various empires and invasions that characterized the history of Mesopotamia up to the time of the Chaldeans.

> On what body of water were Tyre, Sidon, and Byblos located?
> _____
> _____

> Underline the sentence that explains why the Phoenician alphabet had such a lasting effect.

Guided Reading Workbook

DIRECTIONS Read each sentence and fill in the blank with the word in the word pair that best completes the sentence.

1. Nebuchadnezzar was a famous Chaldean king who rebuilt battle-damaged _____ into a beautiful city and whose palace was famous for the Hanging Gardens. (**Phoenicia/Babylon**)

2. A set of letters that can be combined together to form words, or a(n) _____, was developed by the Phoenicians. (**alphabet/chariot**)

3. _____ was a land with few resources other than cedar trees. (**Babylon/Phoenicia**)

4. The Hittites skillfully used the _____, a wheeled, horse-drawn battle cart, to move quickly around the battlefield and fire arrows at their enemy. (**chariot/alphabet**)

5. _____ was a set of laws that dealt with almost every part of daily life and was written down for all to see. (**The alphabet/Hammurabi's Code**)

Early Civilizations of the Fertile Crescent and the Nile Valley

Lesson 4

MAIN IDEAS

1. Egypt was called the gift of the Nile because the Nile River was so important.
2. Civilization developed after people began farming along the Nile River.
3. Strong kings unified all of ancient Egypt.
4. Life in the Old Kingdom was influenced by pharaohs, roles in society, and trade.
5. Religion shaped Egyptian life.
6. The pyramids were built as tombs for Egypt's pharaohs.

Key Terms and Places

Nile River important river in Egypt

Upper Egypt southern part of Egypt, located upriver in relation to the Nile's flow

Lower Egypt northern part of Egypt, located downriver in relation to the Nile's flow

cataracts river rapids

delta triangle-shaped area of land made from soil deposited by a river

pharaoh ruler of ancient Egypt, literally means "great house"

dynasty series of rulers from the same family

Old Kingdom period in Egyptian history that lasted from about 2700 to 2200 BC

theocracy government ruled by religious authorities

nobles people from rich and powerful families

afterlife life after death, a widely held ancient Egyptian belief

mummies specially treated bodies wrapped in cloth

pyramids huge stone tombs with four triangle-shaped walls that meet at a top point

engineering application of scientific knowledge for practical purposes

Lesson Summary
THE GIFT OF THE NILE

The existence of Egypt was based solely around the **Nile River**, the world's longest river. The Nile carries water from central Africa north through a

Why is Egypt called the gift of the Nile?
_____
_____
_____

Lesson 4, *continued*

vast stretch of desert land to the Mediterranean Sea. The river was so important that Egypt was called the gift of the Nile.

Ancient Egypt developed along a 750-mile stretch of the Nile and included two regions— **Upper Egypt** and **Lower Egypt**. Upper Egypt was the southern region, upriver in relation to the Nile's flow. Lower Egypt was the northern region and was located downriver.

Cataracts, or rapids, marked the southern border of Upper Egypt. In Lower Egypt, the Nile divided into several branches that flowed into the Mediterranean. The branches formed a triangle-shaped **delta**, where soil was deposited by the river. It was a swampy area. Most of Egypt's fertile farmland was in the Nile delta.

Where was most of Egypt's farmland located?
_____

Most of Egypt was desert, but rainfall to the south of Egypt would cause the Nile to flood. Almost every year, it would flood Upper Egypt in midsummer and Lower Egypt in the fall. This coated the land around the Nile with rich silt, which made the soil ideal for farming. For Egyptians, the regular floods were a life-giving miracle.

Why were yearly floods so important for Egyptians?
_____
_____
_____

CIVILIZATION DEVELOPS IN EGYPT

Hunter-gatherers first moved to the Nile valley around 12,000 years ago and found plenty of plants, animals, and fish to eat. In time, these people learned how to farm. By 4500 BC farmers were living in villages and growing wheat and barley. They developed an irrigation system to carry water to the fields. Eventually, they were able to raise an abundance of food, including grains, fruits and vegetables, cattle, and sheep. They could also catch geese, ducks, and fish.

What does an irrigation system do?
_____
_____

Egypt was protected from invaders by its harsh deserts, the Mediterranean Sea, and the Red Sea. Cataracts made it difficult to sail on the Nile from the south. This helped the villages of Egypt

Circle the four natural barriers that protected Egypt from invaders.

Lesson 4, *continued*

grow. By 3200 BC the villages had organized into two kingdoms with their own rulers. Lower Egypt's capital was Pe, located in the Nile delta. The capital of Upper Egypt was Nekhen, located on the Nile's west bank. For centuries, Egypt was divided into two lands.

KINGS UNIFY EGYPT

According to legend, Menes (MEE-neez), the king of Upper Egypt, invaded Lower Egypt around 3100 BC. He married a princess there in order to unite the two kingdoms under his rule. Menes was the first **pharaoh**, which means ruler of a "great house." He also started the first Egyptian **dynasty**, or series of rulers from the same family. He built a new capital city, Memphis, near where Lower Egypt met Upper Egypt. For centuries, it was the political and cultural center of Egypt. Menes's dynasty, called the First Dynasty, ruled for nearly 200 years. Eventually, rivals challenged the First Dynasty for power and took over Egypt, starting the Second Dynasty.

What is a dynasty?
_____
_____

THE OLD KINGDOM

Around 2700 BC the Third Dynasty began a period in Egyptian history known as the **Old Kingdom**. During the next 500 years, the Egyptians developed a political system based on the belief that the pharaoh was both a king and a god. A government ruled by religious authorities is called a **theocracy**.

Underline the sentence that defines theocracy.

Although the pharaoh had absolute power over the lands and people, it came with many responsibilities. He was also held personally responsible if anything went wrong. He was blamed if crops did not grow or if there was disease. He was expected to make trade profitable and prevent war.

As the population of Egypt grew, social classes developed. At the top was the pharaoh, with priests and key government officials making up the upper class. Many of these people were rich and powerful **nobles**. The middle class included lesser government officials, scribes, and rich craftspeople. Most people, including farmers, belonged to the lower class. Farmers were often used by the pharaoh as labor when they did not work the fields. There were also servants and slaves for labor.

Trade also developed during the Old Kingdom. Merchants traveled south along the Nile to Nubia to acquire gold, copper, ivory, slaves, and stone. They also traded with Syria for wood. As society grew more complex, it also became more disciplined, organized, and highly religious.

> Circle two countries that Egypt traded with.

RELIGION AND EGYPTIAN LIFE

The Egyptians practiced polytheism, or the worship of many gods. During the Old Kingdom, everyone was expected to worship the same gods, though the type of worship might be different from place to place. Egyptians built temples all over the kingdom. They collected payments from both worshipers and the government, and the wealth made them powerful.

> What is *polytheism*?
> _____
> _____

Over time, certain cities became centers of worship for particular gods. In Memphis, for example, people prayed to Ptah, the creator of the world. There were, however, many other gods. Egyptians had a god for nearly everything, including the sun, sky, and Earth.

Much of Egyptians' religion focused on the **afterlife**. They believed the afterlife was a happy place. Each person had a *ka* (KAH), a spirit or life force, that left the body after death. However, it remained linked to the body and could not leave the burial site. It had to eat, sleep, and be entertained like a living person. To fulfill the *ka*'s needs, tombs were filled with furniture, clothing, tools, jewelry, weapons, and even food and drink.

If the body decayed, the *ka* could not recognize it, which would break the link between body and spirit. So the Egyptians developed a method called embalming to preserve bodies. The bodies were preserved as **mummies**, specially treated bodies wrapped in cloth.

Embalming preserved a body for many years, but it was a complex process that took weeks to complete. The organs were all removed from the body and stored in special jars. The body was then dried out and wrapped in cloths and bandages, often with special charms. Once wrapped, the mummy was placed in a coffin called a sarcophagus. Only royalty and people of wealth and power could afford to be buried as mummies. Poor families buried their dead in shallow graves in the desert, which preserved the bodies naturally.

THE PYRAMIDS

Egyptians believed burial sites were very important. Starting in the Old Kingdom, they built **pyramids** to bury their dead rulers. Pyramids are huge stone structures with a burial chamber deep inside. The largest, the Great Pyramid of Khufu, stands 481 feet (147 m) high.

Many pyramids are still standing today and are amazing examples of Egyptian **engineering**. Historians still are not certain how ancient Egyptians moved the massive stones they needed to build them. A pyramid probably took tens of thousands of workers to build. These workers were paid in grain by the government.

Egyptians believed the pharaoh controlled everyone's afterlife, so they wanted to make his spirit happy with a spectacular pyramid. Pointing to the sky above, the pyramid symbolized the pharaoh's journey to the afterlife. There were often magical spells and hymns on the tomb to keep the pharaoh safe.

Why did Egyptians want to preserve bodies by embalming?

_____

What class of people had themselves embalmed as mummies?

_____

What question are historians still trying to solve about the pyramids?

_____

Underline the sentence that explains the pointed shape of pyramids.

CHALLENGE ACTIVITY

Critical Thinking: Draw Inferences Think about the way in which Egyptians viewed the pharaoh. Then think about how we view our U.S. presidents. In what ways are these views similar? In what ways are they different? Write a one-page essay considering whether people would accept a god-king pharaoh today.

DIRECTIONS Write a word or phrase that has the same meaning as the term given.

1. Lower Egypt _____

2. dynasty _____

3. afterlife _____

4. pharaoh _____

5. delta _____

6. Nile River _____

7. pyramid _____

DIRECTIONS Look at each set of three vocabulary terms following each number. On the line provided, write the letter of the term that does not relate to the others.

_____ 8. a. cataract
        b. pharaoh
        c. Nile River

_____ 9. a. delta
        b. dynasty
        c. pharaoh

_____ 10. a. engineering
        b. Upper Egypt
        c. pyramid

_____ 11. a. mummies
        b. theocracy
        c. afterlife

Early Civilizations of the Fertile Crescent and the Nile Valley

Lesson 5

MAIN IDEAS

1. The Middle Kingdom was a period of stable government between periods of disorder.
2. The New Kingdom was the peak of Egyptian trade and military power, but its greatness did not last.
3. Work and daily life differed among Egypt's social classes.
4. Egyptian writing used symbols called hieroglyphics.
5. Egypt's temples and tombs were lavishly decorated.

Key Terms and Places

Middle Kingdom period of stability and order in ancient Egypt between about 2050 and 1750 BC

New Kingdom height of Egypt's power and glory, between 1550 and 1050 BC

Kush kingdom south of Egypt

trade routes paths followed by traders

hieroglyphics Egyptian writing system, one of the world's first, which used symbols

papyrus long-lasting, paper-like substance made from reeds

Rosetta Stone stone slab discovered in 1799 that was inscribed with hieroglyphics and their Greek meanings

sphinxes imaginary creatures with the bodies of lions and the heads of other animals or humans

obelisk tall, four-sided pillar that is pointed on top

Lesson Summary
THE MIDDLE KINGDOM

Building pyramids cost a lot of money. By the end of the Old Kingdom, pharoahs could not collect enough taxes to pay for their expenses. Ambitious government officials managed to take power from the pharoahs. These nobles ruled most of Egypt for nearly 160 years, and there was no central ruler.

Finally, a powerful pharaoh regained control of Egypt around 2050 BC and started a peaceful period of rule. This era was called the **Middle**

> Underline the text that explains why the Old Kingdom came to an end.

Guided Reading Workbook

Kingdom. It lasted until around 1750 BC when Lower Egypt was conquered by the Hyksos, a people from Southwest Asia. The Hyksos ruled as pharoahs for 200 years until Ahmose of Thebes drove them out in the mid-1500s BC.

> Who were the raiders who ended the Middle Kingdom, and where were they from?
> _____
> _____

THE NEW KINGDOM

Ahmose declared himself king of all Egypt and started the eighteenth dynasty. It was the beginning of the **New Kingdom**, when Egypt reached its height of power and glory.

To prevent invasions like those of the Hyksos, Egypt took control of possible invasion routes. It first took over the Hyksos homeland, then continued north to Syria and as far as the eastern Mediterranean. Next was the kingdom of **Kush**, in Nubia, south of Egypt. By the 1400s BC Egypt was the leading military power in the region. Its empire extended from the Euphrates River to southern Nubia.

> Which direction would you go from Egypt to reach Nubia?
> _____

Military conquests also made Egypt rich. Conquered kingdoms like Kush sent yearly payments of gold, jewels, and animal skins. Nearby kingdoms like Assyria, Babylon, and the Hittites sent expensive gifts to make sure they had good relations with Egypt. The large empire also expanded Egyptian trade. Profitable **trade routes** were created to distant lands with valuable resources. One ruler in particular, Queen Hatshepsut, was active in sending traders to new lands. She and later pharaohs used the money from trade to create more monuments and temples.

> What are two reasons Egypt expanded its trade?
> _____
> _____
> _____

Despite its power, Egypt was threatened by the Hittites from Asia Minor. Pharaoh Ramses the Great fought them fiercely for years, but neither side could defeat the other. Finally, in 1275 BC, both sides signed the Treaty of Kadesh, which historians consider the first peace treaty.

> Why did the Egyptians and Hittites sign a peace treaty?
> _____
> _____

Soon after Ramses died, strong warriors called the Sea People crushed the Hittites and destroyed cities in Southwest Asia. The Egyptians fought them for over 50 years before turning them back. Egypt survived but fell into a period of violence and disorder. The New Kingdom and its empire ended. Egypt would never regain its power.

WORK AND DAILY LIFE

During the Middle and New Kingdoms, Egypt's population continued to grow and become more complex. People took on different trades, which were usually passed on from fathers to sons within families. Professional and skilled workers like scribes, artisans, artists, and architects were honored and admired. These jobs required advanced skills, and many of these people worked for the government and temples.

> **Why would Egyptians want to be a scribe or artisan?**
>
> _____
>
> _____

Although trade was important to Egypt, only a small group of people were merchants and traders. Some traveled long distances, and soldiers, scribes, and laborers often went on the trade journeys. Soldiers became more important after the wars of the Middle Kingdom, when Egypt created a permanent army. The military allowed people a chance to improve their social status. They were also paid with land and treasure captured in a war.

> **How were soldiers paid?**
>
> _____
>
> _____

For farmers and peasants, who made up most of the population, life never changed. In addition to hard work on the land, they were required to give some of their crop as taxes to the pharaoh. They were also subjected to special labor duty at any time. Only slaves were beneath them in social status. There were few slaves in Egypt, and many were criminals or war prisoners. They had some rights and could earn their freedom.

Lesson 5, *continued*

Family life was important. Most families lived in their own homes. Men were expected to marry young and start families. Women were expected to focus on home and family. Some, though, served as priestesses, royal officials, or artisans. Egyptian women also had legal rights. They could own property, make contracts, and divorce their husbands. Children played games and hunted. Both boys and girls received some education. Schools taught morals, writing, math, and sports. At age 14, most boys entered their father's profession.

> **What legal rights did women have in the Middle and New Kingdoms?**
> _____
> _____
> _____

EGYPTIAN ACHIEVEMENTS

Egyptians invented one of the world's first writing systems, called **hieroglyphics** (hy-ruh-GLIH-fiks). It used more than 600 symbols, mostly pictures of objects. Each symbol represented one or more sounds in the Egyptian language. Hieroglyphics could be written horizontally or vertically, and from either right to left or left to right. This made them difficult to read.

> **Underline the sentence that explains why hieroglyphics were difficult to read.**

At first, hieroglyphics were carved in stone. Later, Egyptians learned how to make a type of paper called **papyrus**. It was made from reeds. Scribes could write on this with brushes and ink. Because papyrus did not decay, many ancient Egyptian texts still survive, including government records, historical records, science texts, medical manuals, and literary works such as *The Book of the Dead*. The discovery of the **Rosetta Stone** in 1799 provided the key to understanding Egyptian writing. The text on the stone slab was written in hieroglyphics and in Greek. Scholars could figure out the hieroglyphics from the Greek words.

> **What language helped scholars to understand the meaning of hieroglyphics on the Rosetta Stone?**
> _____

EGYPTIAN ARCHITECTURE AND ART

Egyptian architects are known not only for the pyramids but also for their magnificent temples.

Guided Reading Workbook

Lesson 5, *continued*

The temples were lavishly decorated with numerous statues and beautifully painted walls and pillars. **Sphinxes** and **obelisks** were usually found near the entrances to the temples.

Ancient Egyptians were masterful artists, and many of their greatest works are found in either the temples or the tombs of the pharaohs. Most Egyptians, however, never saw these paintings because only kings, priests, or other important people could enter these places.

Egyptian paintings depict a variety of subjects, from crowning kings to religious rituals to scenes from daily life. The paintings also have a particular style. People are drawn showing the sides of their heads and legs, but the fronts of their upper bodies and shoulders are shown straight on. The size of the figure depends on the person's importance in society. Pharaohs are huge and servants are small. In contrast, animals are drawn more realistically. The Egyptians were also skilled stone and metalworkers, creating beautiful statues and jewelry.

Much of what we know about Egyptian art and burial practices comes from the tomb of King Tutankhamen. His tomb was one of the few left untouched by thieves looking for valuables. The tomb was discovered in 1922, and it was filled with treasures.

Who were allowed to see ancient Egyptian sculptures and paintings?

_____

_____

_____

Why is King Tutankhamen's tomb so important for the study of Egyptian history?

_____

_____

_____

_____

CHALLENGE ACTIVITY

Critical Thinking: Interpret Using the library or an online resource, find a key for translating Egyptian hieroglyphics into English. Write a short message using hieroglyphics and trade with another student to see if you can read each other's messages. Give a copy of your message and the translation to your teacher.

hieroglyphics	King Tutankhamen	Kush
Middle Kingdom	New Kingdom	obelisk
papyrus	Queen Hatshepsut	Ramses the Great
Rosetta Stone	sphinxes	trade routes

DIRECTIONS Answer each question by writing a sentence that
contains at least one word from the word bank.

1. What Nubian kingdom sent yearly payments to the pharoahs?

   _____

   _____

2. During what kingdom did Egypt reach the height of its power and glory?

   _____

   _____

3. What discovery was the key needed to read ancient Egyptian writing?

   _____

   _____

4. Which pharaoh's tomb provided information about Egyptian burial practices
   and beliefs?

   _____

   _____

5. What is the name of the ancient Egyptian writing system?

   _____

   _____

6. What objects stand near the entrance of many Egyptian temples?

_____

_____

7. Which pharaoh signed the world's first peace treaty?

_____

_____

8. How did Egypt expand its empire?

_____

_____

_____

Early Civilizations of the Fertile Crescent and the Nile Valley

Lesson 6

MAIN IDEAS
1. Geography helped early Kush civilization develop in Nubia.
2. Kush and Egypt traded, but they also fought.
3. Later, Kush became a trading power with a unique culture.
4. Both internal and external factors led to the decline of Kush.

Key Terms and Places

Nubia region in northeast Africa where the kingdom of Kush developed

ebony type of dark, heavy wood

ivory white material taken from elephant tusks

Meroë economic center of Kush; last Kushite capital

trade network system of people in different lands who trade goods back and forth

merchants traders

exports items sent to other regions for trade

imports goods brought in from other regions

Lesson Summary
GEOGRAPHY AND EARLY KUSH

The kingdom of Kush developed south of Egypt along the Nile, in the region we now call **Nubia**. It was the first large kingdom in the interior of Africa. Every year, floods from the Nile provided a rich layer of fertile soil. Farmers planted grains and other crops. The area was also rich in minerals such as gold, copper, and stone. These resources contributed to the region's wealth.

Over time, some rich farmers became leaders of their villages. Around 2000 BC one of these leaders took control of other villages and made himself king of Kush. The kings of Kush ruled from their capital at Kerma (KAR-muh). The city was located on the Nile just south of a cataract, or stretch of rapids. Because the Nile's cataracts made parts of the river hard to pass through,

> **What valuable minerals were important to Kush's prosperity?**
> _____

> **Around what year did the first king of Kush appear?**
> _____

Lesson 6, *continued*

they were natural barriers to the powerful Egyptians in the north.

As time passed, Kushite society became more complex. In addition to farmers and herders, some people of Kush became priests or artisans.

> **How did the Nile's cataracts protect the Kush?**
> _____
> _____

KUSH AND EGYPT

Kush and Egypt were neighbors and trading partners. The Kushites sent gold, copper, and stone to Egypt, as well as prized materials such as dark **ebony** wood and **ivory** tusks from elephants. They also sent slaves to be servants or soldiers for the pharaoh.

Relations between Kush and Egypt were not always peaceful, however. As Kush grew rich and more powerful, the Egyptians feared Kush would attack them. Around 1500 BC Egyptian armies under the pharaoh Thutmose I invaded and conquered northern Nubia, including all of Kush. Thutmose destroyed the Kushite palace at Kerma. Kush remained an Egyptian territory for 450 years. During that time, Egypt influenced the language, culture, and religion of Kush.

> **Why did Egypt invade Kush?**
> _____
> _____

In the mid-1000s BC, when Egypt's New Kingdom was ending, Kushite leaders regained control. Kush once again became independent. By around 850 BC Kush was as strong as it had been before it was conquered by Egypt. During the 700s BC, under the king Kashta, Kush attacked Egypt. By 751 BC he had conquered Upper Egypt and established relations with Lower Egypt. After Kashta died, his son Piankhi (PYANG-kee) continued to attack Egypt. He believed the gods wanted him to rule all of Egypt. By the time he died in 716 BC, Piankhi had accomplished this task. His kingdom extended north from Kush's capital of Napata all the way to the Nile delta.

Piankhi's brother, Shabaka (SHAB-uh-kuh), declared himself pharaoh and began the

> **Underline the sentence that explains why Piankhi continued to attack Egypt after his father's death.**

Lesson 6, *continued*

Twenty-fifth, or Kushite, Dynasty in Egypt. Egyptian culture thrived during the Kushite Dynasty, which remained strong for about 40 years. In the 670s BC, however, Egypt was invaded by the Assyrians from Mesopotamia. The Assyrians' iron weapons were better than the Kushites' bronze weapons. The Kushites were driven completely out of Egypt in just ten years.

> **How were Assyrian weapons different from Kushite weapons?**
> _____
> _____
> _____

LATER KUSH

After they lost control of Egypt, the people of Kush devoted themselves to increasing agriculture and trade. They hoped to make their country rich again and succeeded within a few centuries. The new capital, **Meroë** (MER-oh-wee), was the economic center of Kush. Gold could be found nearby, as could forests of ebony and other wood. The area was also rich in iron ore, and the Kushites quickly developed an iron industry.

> **What industry helped make Kush a rich and successful kingdom again?**
> _____

Meroë was located on the Nile, and it became the center of a large **trade network**. The Kushites sent goods down the Nile to Egypt. From there, Egyptian and Greek **merchants** carried goods to ports on the Mediterranean and Red Seas and to southern Africa. These goods may have eventually reached India and perhaps China. Kush's **exports** included gold, pottery, iron tools, ivory, leopard skins, ostrich feathers, elephants, and slaves. **Imports** included jewelry and luxury items from Egypt, Asia, and lands along the Mediterranean.

> **What direction is "down the Nile"?**
> _____

Kushite merchants brought back customs from many cultures, but Egypt was the most obvious influence on Kush's culture during this period. However, many elements of Kushite culture were not borrowed from anywhere else. Although many Kushites worshiped Egyptian gods, they also worshiped their own gods. They also developed their own written language.

> **Circle two elements of Kushite culture that were unique to them.**

Women were expected to be active in their society. They worked alongside men in the fields, as well as raised children and performed household tasks. Many women fought during wars. Women could rise to positions of great authority, especially in religion. Some rulers made princesses in their families powerful priestesses. Some women were co-rulers with their husbands or sons. A few women, such as Queen Shanakhdakheto (shah-nahk-dah-KEE-toh), even ruled the empire alone and helped increase the strength and wealth of the kingdom.

> **How were the roles of Kushite women different from most other ancient civilizations?**
>
> _____
>
> _____
>
> _____
>
> _____

DECLINE AND DEFEAT

Kushite civilization centered at Meroë reached its height in the first century BC. However, after four centuries, it fell due to both external and internal factors. It is possible that farmers overgrazed cattle, so that the soil could no longer be farmed. Also, ironmakers probably used up the forests where they got wood to fire their iron furnaces. Kush could no longer produce enough weapons for its army or trade goods for its economy.

> **Underline the text that explains how the iron industry might have helped cause the fall of Kush.**

Trade routes started going around Kush to another powerful trading center, Aksum (AHK-soom). Aksum was located southeast of Kush on the Red Sea, where Ethiopia and Eritrea are today. As Kush declined, Aksum became the most powerful state in the region. About AD 350 the Aksumite leader King Ezana (AY-zah-nah) sent an invading army and conquered the once-powerful Kush. In the late 300s Aksum's rulers became Christian. The new religion reshaped Nubian culture, and Kush's influence disappeared.

> **Circle the name and kindgom of the ruler who eventually defeated Kush.**

Guided Reading Workbook

CHALLENGE ACTIVITY

Critical Thinking: Draw Conclusions Kush
invaded Egypt during the 700s. Why do you think
Kashta and his son Piankhi wanted to control
Egypt? What advantages would control of Egypt
give to Kush?

ebony	exports	imports	ivory
Kashta	Kerma	Kush	merchants
Meroë	Nubia	Piankhi	Shabaka
trade network			

DIRECTIONS On the line provided before each statement, write **T** if
a statement is true and **F** if a statement is false. If the statement is
false, write the correct term from the word bank on the line after
each sentence to make the sentence a true statement.

_____ 1. The Kushites sent <u>ivory</u>, a white material made from elephant tusks, to
Egypt.

_____

_____ 2. Kush received <u>imports</u> like jewelry and luxury items from Egypt and
Asia.

_____

_____ 3. <u>Exports</u> are goods brought in from other regions.

_____

_____ 4. The kingdom of <u>Kashta</u> was established in the region we now call
Nubia.

_____

_____ 5. <u>Meroë</u> was the last capital city of Kush and its economic center.

_____

_____ 6. <u>Shabaka</u> took control of the territory his brother Piankhi had
conquered.

_____

_____ 7. <u>Nubia</u> is a region in northeast Africa that lies on the Nile River south
of Egypt.

_____

_____ 8. <u>Kerma</u> was the son of Kashta, and he extended Kush's kingdom all
the way to the Nile delta.

_____

_____ 9. A <u>trade network</u> is a system of people, or merchants, in different lands
who trade goods back and forth.

_____

World Religions of Southwest Asia

Lesson 1

MAIN IDEAS

1. The Jews' early history began in Canaan and ended when the Romans forced them out of Israel.
2. Jewish beliefs in God, justice, and law anchor their society.
3. Jewish sacred texts describe the laws and principles of Judaism.
4. Traditions and holy days celebrate the history and religion of the Jewish people.

Key Terms and Places

Judaism Hebrews' religion

Canaan land where Abraham settled by the Mediterranean Sea

Exodus journey of the Hebrews out of Egypt, led by Moses

rabbis religious teachers of Judaism

monotheism belief in one and only one God

Torah most sacred text of Judaism

Lesson Summary
EARLY HISTORY

The Hebrews appeared in Southwest Asia sometime between 2000 and 1500 BC. Their religion was **Judaism**. Some of their early history was written by Hebrew scribes. These accounts became the Hebrew Bible. The Bible says that the Hebrews started with a man named Abraham. According to the Bible, God told Abraham to leave Mesopotamia and go to the land of **Canaan** on the Mediterranean Sea. God promised that Abraham's descendants would become a mighty nation.

Some of Abraham's descendants, the Israelites, lived in Canaan for many years. Later, a famine caused some to move to Egypt. They prospered there. Egypt's pharaoh feared that the Israelites would become too powerful, so he made them slaves. According to the Bible, a leader named Moses freed the Israelites and led them out of Egypt. During this long journey, called the

> Circle the name of the man who the Bible says is the first Hebrew.

> Why did some Israelites move to Egypt?
>
> _____
> _____

Exodus, God is said to have given Moses two stone tablets on a mountain called Sinai. A code of moral laws called the Ten Commandments was written on the tablets.

The Israelites reached Canaan, or Israel, but in the mid-1000s BC, invaders swept through the land. Strong kings like David and Solomon kept the country together and expanded its territory. It grew rich through trade, and Solomon built a great temple in Jerusalem.

Eventually, conflict split Israel into two kingdoms—Israel and Judah. The people of Judah became known as Jews. The two kingdoms lasted for a few centuries until they fell to invaders. When Judah fell in 586 BC, the Jews were sent from Jerusalem as slaves. When the invaders were conquered, some Jews returned home. Some moved to other places. This scattering of Jews outside of Israel and Judah is called the Diaspora.

The Jews ruled themselves for about 100 years, but then the Romans conquered them. The Jews rebelled and the Romans punished them. The great temple was destroyed. Many people were killed or enslaved, and thousands fled Jerusalem. Over the next centuries, Jews moved around the world, where they often faced discrimination from other religious groups.

After the temple was destroyed, roles in society changed. The role of a priest was no longer as important for religious practices. Instead, **rabbis,** or religious teachers, became more important as the Jews spread across the world. Even before the temple was destroyed, women could not become priests or rabbis. Men made most decisions. Women's husbands were chosen by the woman's father, and family property went to the eldest son.

> Who were the kings who saved Israel and made it rich?
> _____

> What is the Diaspora?
> _____
> _____
> _____

> Underline the sentence that explains why rabbis replaced priests as the most important religious figures.

JEWISH BELIEFS

No matter where they live, Jews base their society on Jewish beliefs. Their most important belief is that there is one, and only one, God. This is known as **monotheism.** Most ancient cultures worshipped many gods, so the Jews' belief set them apart. Also central to Jewish religion are the ideas of justice and righteousness. *Justice* means kindness and fairness toward all: to the poor, sick, and even strangers and criminals. *Righteousness* means doing what is right, even if others do not. Jews value righteousness over rituals.

Jews believe their religious laws were given to them by God. The most important laws are the Ten Commandments, which are still followed by many people today. The Jews also follow laws, called Mosaic laws, that guide their daily lives. These rules explain how people worship and even what foods they eat. Foods that are allowed and prepared according to these laws are called kosher.

| Underline the definition of *monotheism*. |

| What are the most important laws for the Jewish people? _____ |

JEWISH TEXTS

Judaism has several sacred texts. These contain the religion's basic laws and principles. The **Torah,** the first five books of the Hebrew Bible, is the most sacred text. It is central to Jewish religious services. The Hebrew Bible has two other parts besides the Torah. The second is the writing of Hebrew prophets, people who were believed to receive messages from God. The final part has poetry, songs, stories, lessons, and history. Many of these stories show the power of faith.

The Talmud is a collection of commentaries written by rabbis and scholars over the centuries. The commentaries explain the Torah and Jewish law. Most were written between AD 200 and 600.

| What are the three parts of the Hebrew Bible? _____ _____ _____ _____ |

Guided Reading Workbook

They are second only to the Hebrew Bible in importance.

TRADITIONS AND HOLY DAYS

The Jewish holiday Hanukkah falls in December. It honors a historical event. The Jews wanted to celebrate a victory that had convinced their rulers to let them keep their religion. According to legend, the Jews did not have enough lamp oil to celebrate at the temple. But somehow the oil they had, enough for one day, burned for eight days. So Jews today celebrate by lighting candles for eight days. More important is the holiday of Passover, celebrated in March or April. It honors the Exodus from Egypt. During this holiday, Jews eat a flat, unrisen bread called matzo.

> **Circle the type of bread eaten during Passover.**

The two most sacred Jewish holidays are called the High Holy Days. These take place in September or October. The first two days of celebration are Rosh Hashanah, which is the start of the new year in the Jewish calendar. Yom Kippur comes shortly after. It is the holiest day of the year for Jews. On this day, Jews ask God to forgive their sins. They pray and do not eat or drink. They reflect on the past year and resolve to improve.

> **What is the holiest day of the year for Jews?**
> _____

CHALLENGE ACTIVITY

Critical Thinking: Draw Conclusions Imagine you are helping to plan a museum of ancient Jewish history. Write a brief recommendation for three exhibits you would like to include.

Lesson 1, *continued*

DIRECTIONS Read each sentence and fill in the blank with the word in the word pair that best completes the sentence.

1. The Bible says Abraham moved from his home in Mesopotamia to the land of _____ on the Mediterranean Sea. (**Egypt/Canaan**)

2. The Hebrews' belief in one God is a type of religion known as _____. (**monotheism/Judaism**)

3. The long journey of the Israelites away from slavery in Egypt is known as the _____. (**Exodus/Torah**)

4. The most sacred text of the Hebrews, the _____, is made up of five books of the Bible. (**Judah/Torah**)

5. _____ is celebrated during the High Holy Days. (**Passover/Yom Kippur**)

DIRECTIONS Write a sentence or phrase that has the same meaning as the term given.

6. Israel _____

7. Passover _____

Guided Reading Workbook

Name _____ Class _____ Date_____

World Religions of Southwest Asia

MAIN IDEAS
1. The life and death of Jesus of Nazareth inspired a new religion called Christianity.
2. Christians believe that Jesus' acts and teachings focused on love and salvation.
3. Jesus' followers taught others about Jesus' life and teachings.
4. Christianity spread throughout the Roman Empire by 400.

Key Terms and Places

Messiah great leader the ancient Jews predicted would come to restore the greatness of Israel

Christianity religion based on Jesus' life and teachings

Bible holy book of Christianity

Bethlehem small town where Jesus was born

Resurrection Jesus' rise from the dead

disciples followers

saint person known and admired for his or her holiness

Lesson Summary
JESUS OF NAZARETH

Many people thought a Jewish teacher named Jesus was the **Messiah,** a leader who would bring back Israel's greatness. The life and teachings of Jesus of Nazareth are the basis of a religion called **Christianity.** Everything we know about Jesus' life comes from the **Bible,** the holy book of Christianity. The Christian Bible has two parts. The first is the Old Testament, which is mostly the same as the Hebrew Bible. The second is the New Testament. It tells about the life and teachings of Jesus and the early history of Christianity.

According to the Bible, Jesus was born in the town of **Bethlehem.** His mother was Mary. She was married to Joseph, a carpenter. But Christians believe that God was Jesus' real father.

> **What did people think the Messiah would do?**
>
> _____
>
> _____

> **What is the Old Testament?**
>
> _____

Guided Reading Workbook

By the time Jesus was about 30, he began to travel and teach.

Jesus had many followers, but his teachings challenged political and religious leaders. They arrested him while he was in Jerusalem around AD 30. Shortly after his arrest, the Romans tried and executed Jesus. He was nailed to a cross, which is called crucifixion. After he died, his followers buried him. According to the Bible, Jesus rose from the dead three days later. This event is known as the **Resurrection.** He then appeared to his **disciples,** or followers. He gave them instructions about how to pass on his teachings. Then he rose up to Heaven.

Early Christians believed that the Resurrection was a sign that Jesus was the Messiah and the son of God. They called him Jesus Christ from the Greek word for Messiah, *Christos.*

> **Why is the Resurrection so important?**
> _____
> _____
> _____
> _____
> _____

JESUS' ACTS AND TEACHINGS

During his life, Jesus traveled from village to village, spreading his message. Many people became followers after they saw him perform miracles. He also told many parables, or stories that taught lessons about how people should live. He explained complicated ideas in ways most people could understand. Jesus taught people to love God and love all people, two rules from the Torah. Jesus also taught about salvation, or the rescue of people from sin.

Since Jesus' death, people have interpreted his teachings in different ways. As a result, different denominations, or groups, of Christianity have developed.

> **Underline three of Jesus' major teachings.**

JESUS' FOLLOWERS

After Jesus' death, his followers continued to spread his teachings. The 12 disciples who knew him best were called the Apostles. One of them, Peter, traveled as far as Rome to teach people about Jesus. He is often thought of as the first leader of the Christian Church. The disciples Matthew, Mark, Luke, and John wrote accounts of Jesus' life and teachings. These accounts are called the Gospels. They are in the New Testament.

Probably the most important person involved in spreading Christianity was Paul of Tarsus. Christians regard Paul as a **saint.** A saint is a person known and admired for his or her holiness. Paul never met Jesus and at first opposed the Christians. According to the New Testament, one day he saw a blinding light and heard Jesus calling out to him. After that, he became a Christian and traveled around the Mediterranean teaching Christian beliefs. His work attracted so many people that Christianity began to break from its Jewish roots. It became a separate religion.

What are the Gospels?
_____
_____
_____
_____

Why do you think Paul is important to Christians?
_____
_____

THE SPREAD OF CHRISTIANITY

Christianity spread quickly in Roman communities. Some Roman leaders wanted to put an end to the new religion. They arrested and killed Christians who refused to worship the gods of Rome. By the 200s and 300s, some emperors feared Christians could cause unrest. They banned Christian worship.

Christians continued to meet in secret. This made it hard to have a single leader. Instead, local leaders called bishops led each Christian community. Christians looked to the bishops in large cities for guidance. Eventually, the bishop of Rome, or the pope, came to be viewed as the head of the whole Christian Church. Women had been leaders in early Christian communities, but they were not allowed to be bishops or popes as Christianity became more established.

Christianity continued to spread throughout Rome. Then the Roman emperor Constantine

What did the first bishops do?
_____
_____
_____

Circle the name for the bishop of Rome.

converted to Christianity. He lifted the bans
against the practice of the religion. Christianity
eventually spread from Rome all around the world.

CHALLENGE ACTIVITY

Critical Thinking: Understand Cause and Effect
Write a sentence that explains the effect
Constantine's conversion had on the spread of
Christianity.

Bethlehem	Bible	Christianity	crucifixion
disciples	Gospels	Messiah	miracles
New Testament	parables	Resurrection	saint

DIRECTIONS On the line provided before each statement, write a **T**
if the statement is true and **F** if the statement is false. If the
statement is false, write the correct term from the word bank on the
line after each sentence to make the sentence a true statement.

_____ 1. Many people believed that Jesus of Nazareth was the <u>Messiah</u>.

_____

_____ 2. According to the New Testament, Jesus performed <u>Gospels</u> that
convinced people to follow him.

_____

_____ 3. The New Testament says that Jesus appeared to his <u>parables</u> after the
Resurrection.

_____

_____ 4. Jesus' life and teachings form the basis of a religion called <u>Christianity</u>.

_____

DIRECTIONS Choose four of the words from the word bank. On a
separate sheet of paper, use these words to write a summary of what
you learned in the lesson.

World Religions of Southwest Asia

Lesson 3

MAIN IDEAS
1. Arabia is mostly a desert land, where two ways of life, nomadic and sedentary, developed.
2. A new religion called Islam, founded by the prophet Muhammad, spread throughout Arabia in the 600s.
3. The Qur'an guides Muslims' lives.
4. The Sunnah tells Muslims of important duties expected of them.
5. Islamic law is based on the Qur'an and the Sunnah.

Key Terms and Places

oasis wet, fertile area in a desert

Mecca birthplace of Muhammad

Islam religion based on messages Muhammad received from God

Muslim person who follows Islam

Qur'an holy book of Islam

Medina city that Muhammad and his followers moved to from Mecca in 622

mosque building for Muslim prayer

jihad literally means "to make an effort" or "to struggle"

Sunnah collection of actions or sayings by Muhammad

Five Pillars of Islam five acts of worship required of all Muslims

Lesson Summary

LIFE IN A DESERT LAND

Arabia lies in the southwest corner of Asia, near where Asia meets Africa and Europe. It is a mostly hot and dry desert, with scorching temperatures and little water. Water exists mainly in oases. An **oasis** is a wet, fertile area in a desert. Oases are key stops along Arabia's trade routes.

People developed two ways to live in the desert. Nomads moved from place to place. They lived in tents and raised goats, sheep, and camels. Tribes—groups of related nomads—traveled with their herds to find food and water for their animals. Tribe membership offered safety and prevented conflicts over grazing lands.

What three continents meet near Arabia?
_____
_____
_____

Why might a nomad prefer to travel in a tribe?
_____
_____
_____

Other Arabs led a settled life. They lived in oases where they could farm. Towns sprang up in oases along the trade routes. There, nomads could trade animal products for supplies. Merchants came in caravans to sell goods like spices, gold, and leather.

A NEW RELIGION

In early times, Arabs worshipped many gods. That changed when a man named Muhammad brought a new religion to Arabia. Most of what we know about him comes from religious writings. Muhammad was born in the city of **Mecca** around 570. As a child, he traveled with his uncle's caravans. As an adult, Muhammad managed a caravan business owned by his wife Khadijah.

> Circle the name of the city where Muhammad was born.

Trade made Mecca a rich city, but most of the wealth belonged to a few people. Muhammad was upset that rich people did not help the poor. He often went to a cave to pray and meditate on this problem. According to Islamic writings, when Muhammad was 40, an angel spoke to him. The angel told him the words of God. Muhammad was God's prophet, and he would tell God's messages to the world. These messages form the basis of the religion called **Islam,** which means "to submit to God" in Arabic. A follower of Islam is called a **Muslim.** The messages were collected in the **Qur'an** (kuh-RAN), the holy book of Islam.

> What problem troubled Muhammad?
>
> _____
> _____
> _____

In 613, Muhammad began to spread his message. He taught that there was only one God, Allah, which means "the God" in Arabic. Like Judaism and Christianity, Islam is monotheistic, believing in one God. However, their beliefs about God are not the same. Muhammad also taught that all people who believed in Allah should be like family. Like in families, people with money should help people who are less fortunate.

> What does Islam have in common with Judaism and Christianity?
>
> _____
> _____
> _____

Slowly, Muhammad got more followers. As Islam spread, Mecca's rulers grew worried. They planned to kill Muhammed. In 622 Muhammed and his followers moved to **Medina,** which means "the Prophet's city" in Arabic. His departure from Mecca is called the hegira, or journey. It is such an important event that Muslims made 622 the first year of the Islamic calendar.

Muhammad became a spiritual and political leader in Medina. His house became the first **mosque,** a building for worship and prayer. More Arab tribes began to accept Islam. After some years of fighting, the people of Mecca also became Muslim. By the time Muhammad died in 632, Islam was practiced by most people in Arabia. Over the centuries, it spread throughout the world.

What is the hegira?
_____
_____
_____

THE QUR´AN

After Muhammad died, his followers wrote down all his teachings to form the book known as the Qur´an. Muslims believe that the Qur´an is the exact word of God as it was told to Muhammad. The Qur´an says there is one God—Allah—and that Muhammad is his prophet. Muslims must obey Allah's commands, which they learned from Muhammad.

Underline the sentence that explains what Muslims believe about the words in the Qur´an.

Islam teaches that there is a definite beginning and end to the world. On that final day, Muslims believe, God will judge all people. Those who have obeyed God's orders will go to paradise. Those who have not obeyed God will be punished.

The Qur´an also gives rules that guide the everyday life of Muslims. These include rules about worship, moral behavior, social life, and what Muslims can eat and drink. For example, Muslims cannot eat pork or drink alcohol. Some rules are not stated directly in the Qur´an,

According to the Qur´an, what will happen at the end of the world?
_____
_____
_____
_____
_____

but Muslims still use it as a guide. Before
Muhammad, many Arabs owned slaves, but
many Muslims chose to free their slaves based on
the teachings of the Qur´an.

Women's rights were also described in the
Qur´an. Like other societies at that time, women
had fewer rights than men. However, they could
own property, earn money, and get an education.

Jihad (ji-HAHD) is an important subject in the
Qur´an. Jihad means "to make an effort" or
"to struggle." It refers to the internal struggle of
a Muslim trying to obey God and follow Islamic
beliefs. It can also mean the struggle to defend
the Muslim community or, historically, to convert
people to Islam. The word has also been
translated as "holy war."

> Circle the two meanings of jihad.

THE SUNNAH

Besides the Qur´an, Muslims also study the
hadith. This is the written record of
Muhammad's words and actions. It is the basis
for the **Sunnah** (SOOH-nuh). The Sunnah refers
to the way Muhammad lived, which is a model
for how Muslims should behave.

> What is the hadith?
> _____
> _____
> _____
> _____

The Sunnah explains five acts of worship
required of all Muslims. These are known as the
Five Pillars of Islam. The *first pillar* is a statement
of faith that Muslims must say at least once in
their lives: "There is no god but God, and
Muhammad is his prophet." The *second pillar*
says a Muslim must pray five times daily. The
third pillar is a yearly donation to charity. The
fourth pillar is fasting during the holy month of
Ramadan (RAH-muh-dahn). The Qur´an says
that this is the month that Muhammad first
received the word of God. During that month,
Muslims will not eat or drink anything between
dawn and dusk. This shows that God is more
important than one's own body. It also reminds
Muslims of people who struggle to get enough

> What is the fourth pillar, and why is it important to Muslims?
> _____
> _____
> _____
> _____
> _____
> _____

food. The *fifth pillar* is the hajj (HAJ), a
pilgrimage to Mecca. The Kaaba in Mecca is
Islam's most sacred place. Muslims must try to
go to Mecca at least once in their lifetime.

The Sunnah also preaches moral duties that
must be met in daily life, in business, and in
government. One rule says that it is bad to owe
someone money. There are also rules about
lending money and charging interest. This has
affected the economies of Muslim countries.
Many people would not use banks. Today,
banking is more common because of the global
economy.

> Underline the sentence that explains what parts of Muslim life are affected by the Sunnah.

ISLAMIC LAW

The Qur´an and the Sunnah form the basis of
Islamic law, or Shariah (shuh-REE-uh). Shariah
uses both Islamic sources and human reason to
judge a person's actions. Actions fall on a scale
ranging from required to accepted to disapproved
to forbidden. Shariah sets rewards for good
behavior and punishments for crimes. It also sets
limits on authority. It was the basis for law in
Muslim countries until modern times. Today,
most Islamic countries blend Islamic law with a
legal system much like that in the United States.

> Describe the system of laws used in most Islamic nations today.
>
> _____
>
> _____
>
> _____
>
> _____

CHALLENGE ACTIVITY

Critical Thinking: Draw Inferences Why might it
be helpful to have Five Pillars, or main duties, to
perform?

DIRECTIONS Write two words or phrases that describe the term.

1. Islam _____

   _____

2. Sunnah _____

   _____

   _____

3. Medina _____

   _____

4. Five Pillars of Islam _____

   _____

   _____

5. Muslim _____

   _____

6. Qur´an _____

   _____

7. jihad _____

   _____

8. Mecca _____

   _____

9. mosque _____

   _____

The Arabian Peninsula to Central Asia

Lesson 1

MAIN IDEAS
1. Major physical features of the Arabian Peninsula, Iraq, and Iran include desert plains and mountains, a dry climate with little vegetation, and valuable oil resources.
2. Central Asia is a landlocked region with rugged mountains, a harsh, dry climate with minimal vegetation, and valuable mineral and oil resources.

Key Terms and Places

Arabian Peninsula region that has the largest sand desert in the world

Persian Gulf body of water surrounded by the Arabian Peninsula, Iran, and Iraq

Tigris River river that flows across a low, flat plain in Iraq and joins the Euphrates River

Euphrates River river that flows across a low, flat plain in Iraq and joins the Tigris River

oasis wet, fertile area in a desert that forms where underground water bubbles to the surface

wadis dry streambeds

fossil water water that is not being replaced by rainfall

landlocked completely surrounded by land with no direct access to the ocean

Pamirs some of Central Asia's high mountains

Fergana Valley large fertile valley in the plains region of Central Asia

Aral Sea sea that is actually a large lake, which is shrinking due to irrigation

Kara-Kum desert in Turkmenistan

Kyzyl Kum desert in Uzbekistan and Kazakhstan

Lesson Summary
THE ARABIAN PENINSULA, IRAQ, AND IRAN

The region of the **Arabian Peninsula,** Iraq, and Iran is sometimes called the Middle East. It lies at the intersection of Africa, Asia, and Europe. The Arabian Peninsula has the largest sand desert in the world, but much of these dry, rugged countries are covered with bare rock or gravel. The **Persian Gulf** is at the center of the region.

What is this region sometimes called?

_____

Guided Reading Workbook

The region's main landforms are rivers, plains, plateaus, and mountains. Its two major rivers are the **Tigris** and **Euphrates** in Iraq. They join together before they reach the Persian Gulf. They are called exotic rivers because they start in wet regions and flow through dry areas. The rivers create a narrow fertile area, which was called Mesopotamia in ancient times.

The Arabian Peninsula has no permanent rivers. It is covered with vast dry plains in the east. These desert plains are covered with sand in the south and volcanic rock in the north. The landscape rises as the peninsula reaches the Red Sea. It becomes mountains and plateaus. The mountains of Yemen are the highest point.

Plateaus and mountains also cover most of Iran. Iran is one of the world's most mountainous countries. The Zagros Mountains are in the west. The Elburz Mountains and the Kopet-Dag lie in the north.

The region's desert climate can get very hot in the day and very cold at night. Southern Saudi Arabia has the world's largest sand desert, the Rub al Khali. Its name means "Empty Quarter" because it has so little life. In northern Saudi Arabia, there is another large desert called An Nafud. These deserts are among the driest places in the world.

Some areas with plateaus and mountains get rain or winter snow. They usually have semiarid steppe climates and may get more than 50 inches of rain a year. Trees grow in these areas. Plants may also grow in **oases** in the desert. At an oasis, underground water bubbles up to the surface. Most desert plants grow without much water. Their roots either go very deep or spread out very far to get as much water as they can.

> **What country has two exotic rivers flowing through it?**
>
> _____

> **Underline the sentence that explains where the highest point is on the Arabian Peninsula.**

> **Why is Rub al Khali called the Empty Quarter?**
>
> _____
>
> _____

Water is one of this region's two most valuable resources. But water is scarce. Some places in the desert have springs that give water. Wells also provide water. Some wells are dug into dry streambeds called **wadis.** Modern wells can go very deep underground to get **fossil water.** This is water that is not replaced by rain, so these wells will run dry over time.

Oil is the region's other important resource. This resource is plentiful. Oil has brought great wealth to the countries that have oil fields. Most oil fields are near the shores of the Persian Gulf. But oil cannot be replaced once it is taken. Too much drilling for oil now may cause economic problems in the future.

> **Circle the most important resources in this region.**

CENTRAL ASIA

Central Asia is in the middle of Asia. Its physical geography includes rugged terrain that has isolated the region. All the countries in this region are **landlocked.** That means they are surrounded by land, with no access to the ocean.

In the south, the high Hindu Kush mountains stretch through Afghanistan. In the east, Tajikistan and Kyrgyzstan are also very mountainous. High mountains, such as the **Pamirs,** have glaciers. Through history, the mountains have made communication and travel difficult.

> **What two factors make Central Asia isolated?**
> _____
> _____

From the mountains, the land slowly slopes down to the Caspian Sea in the west. Some land there is 95 feet (29 m) below sea level. Between the sea and mountains are plains and low plateaus. The fertile **Fergana Valley** is in the plains. It has been a center of farming for thousands of years. Two rivers flow through it: the Syr Darya and the Amu Darya. They flow from the eastern mountains into the **Aral Sea,** which is really a large lake. Lake Balkhash is also

> **Circle the name of the sea that is really a large lake.**

Guided Reading Workbook

an important lake. It has fresh water at one end and salty water at the other.

Most of Central Asia has a harsh, dry climate. Temperatures range from very cold to very hot, and there is not much rain. It is hard for plants to grow. The high eastern mountain peaks are cold, dry, and windy. Between these mountains and the Caspian Sea, there are two harsh deserts. **Kara-Kum** is in Turkmenistan, and **Kyzyl Kum** is in Uzbekistan and Kazakhstan. They have extremely high temperatures in the summer and limited rainfall. Yet both deserts have rivers crossing them, which lets some people live there. Only the far north of Central Asia has a milder climate.

What part of Central Asia has the mildest climate?
_____

Water is one of Central Asia's most valuable resources. The main water sources are the Syr Darya and Amu Darya rivers. They are used for irrigation and to supply power. But water is limited. This has led to conflicts between Uzbekistan and Turkmenistan over how to use it. Farmers use it mostly to irrigate cotton fields. However, cotton requires so much water that the rivers no longer have enough water to flow to the Aral Sea.

Why has use of water sources led to conflicts between countries?
_____
_____
_____

Uzbekistan, Kazakhstan, and Turkmenistan all have huge reserves of oil and natural gas. This could help their economies. However, oil and gas can only help the region if the countries can export it. There are no ocean ports to transport it, so they need to build and maintain pipelines. Rugged land and economic and political conflicts make this difficult. Some parts of Central Asia have minerals like gold, silver, copper, zinc, uranium, and lead. Kazakhstan also has large amounts of coal.

CHALLENGE ACTIVITY

Critical Thinking: Design Design an illustrated
poster using the term *Persian Gulf*. For each
letter, write a word containing that letter that tells
something about the region.

DIRECTIONS Read each sentence and fill in the blank with the
word in the word pair that best completes the sentence.

1. At the center of Iraq, Iran, and the Arabian Peninsula lies the
    _____. **(Persian Gulf/Tigris River)**

2. The _____ begins in a wet region and flows through a dry area.
    (Euphrates River/fossil water)

3. A well that uses _____ will eventually run dry. **(fossil water/oases)**

4. A _____ country cannot export oil easily. **(landlocked/Persian Gulf)**

5. One water resource for this region are wells dug into _____, or dry
    streambeds. **(fossil water/wadis)**

6. The _____ receives very little rainfall. **(Kara-Kum/Fergana Valley)**

7. Large glaciers can be found in the _____ . **(Kara-Kum/Pamirs)**

8. The _____ is a major farming area in Central Asia.
    (Aral Sea/Fergana Valley)

9. The _____ is actually a large lake. **(Aral Sea/Persian Gulf)**

Arabian Peninsula	Aral Sea	Euphrates River	Fergana Valley
fossil water	Kara-Kum	Kyzyl Kum	landlocked
oases	Pamirs	Persian Gulf	Tigris River
wadis			

DIRECTIONS Choose at least six terms from the word bank. On a
separate sheet of paper, write a summary of what you learned in the
lesson.

Guided Reading Workbook

MAIN IDEAS
1. Islamic culture and an economy greatly based on oil influence life in Saudi Arabia.
2. Most Arabian Peninsula countries other than Iraq and Iran are monarchies influenced by Islamic culture and oil resources.

Key Terms and Places

Islam religion founded by Muhammad around AD 622 in Arabia

Shia branch of Islam in which Muslims believe that true interpretations of Islamic teachings can only come from certain religious and political leaders

Sunni branch of Islam in which Muslims believe in the ability of the majority of the community to interpret Islamic teachings

OPEC Organization of Petroleum Exporting Countries, an international organization whose members work to influence the price of oil on world markets by controlling the supply

quota number or value limit on goods

Lesson Summary
SAUDI ARABIA

Saudi Arabia is the largest country on the Arabian Peninsula. It is a major center of religion and culture, and it has one of the region's strongest economies. Most Saudis speak Arabic. Their culture and customs are strongly influenced by **Islam.**

Islam began in Arabia, and it is based on the messages that Muslims believe Muhammad received from God around AD 622. The messages are written in the Qur´an. Most Saudis follow one of two branches of Islam. **Shia** Muslims believe that only certain imams— religious and political leaders—can interpret Islamic teaching. About 85–90 percent of Saudi Muslims are **Sunni.** They believe Islam can be interpreted by the community.

> **What is the main language in Saudi Arabia?**
> _____

> **What branch of Islam do most Saudis follow?**
> _____

Lesson 2, *continued*

Islam influences Saudi laws and customs in many ways. It teaches modesty, so traditional clothing is long and loose, covering the arms and legs. Women usually wear a black cloak and veil in public, though some wear Western-style clothing. Few go out in public without a husband or male relative with them. However, women can own and run businesses. In 2015 women were given the right to vote, and by June of 2018 they will be allowed to drive.

Saudi Arabia's government is a monarchy. The Saud family has ruled the country since 1932. Most government officials are relatives of the king. However, local officials are elected.

Oil is one of the most important influences on Saudi Arabia's economy and foreign policy. The country has almost one-fifth of the world's oil. It exports the most oil. This makes Saudi Arabia an important member of **OPEC,** the Organization of the Petroleum Exporting Countries.

OPEC has members from many countries. It controls the supply of oil, which affects the price of oil around the world. The organization places a **quota,** or limit, on each member nation. No OPEC member can produce and export more oil than the quota value it is allowed.

Money from oil has helped Saudi Arabia build roads, schools, hospitals, and universities. This has helped create a large middle class. Its people also have free health care and education. However, there are also challenges. There are few industries besides oil, which will run out one day. About one quarter of young Saudis are unemployed because there are not many opportunities for work.

Saudi Arabia has created programs to fight unemployment and encourage economic growth. It is trying to make it easier for people to start their own small businesses and to give support to entrepreneurs. It is also making changes to its

When were Saudi women first allowed to vote? _____

Why is Saudi Arabia such an important member of OPEC? _____ _____ _____

Underline the sentence that explains why Saudi Arabia may have economic problems in the future.

Why does Saudi Arabia need to find new ways to grow food? _____ _____ _____

Guided Reading Workbook

Lesson 2, *continued*

agricultural and water policies. Because it has few water resources, the country is studying new ways to grow enough food for its population without losing too much of its underground water.

OTHER COUNTRIES OF THE ARABIAN PENINSULA

There are six smaller countries in this region: Kuwait, Bahrain, Qatar, the United Arab Emirates (UAE), Oman, and Yemen. Like Saudi Arabia, they are all influenced by Islam. Most have monarchies and depend on oil.

Oil was discovered in Kuwait in the 1930s. It made the country very rich. In 1990 Iraq invaded Kuwait to gain control of Kuwaiti oil. This started the Persian Gulf War. The United States and other countries defeated Iraq, but the war destroyed many of Kuwait's oil fields.

Kuwait's government is a monarchy, but the country elected a legislature in 1992. Until 2005, only about 15 percent of Kuwait's men were allowed to vote. In 2005 women were given the right to vote.

Bahrain is a group of islands in the Persian Gulf. It has a powerful monarchy with a legislature. Oil made Bahrain wealthy. Most people there live in big, modern cities. In the 1990s the country began to run out of oil. Now banking and tourism are major industries.

Qatar is located on a small peninsula in the Persian Gulf. Its economy is based on oil and natural gas, which have made it rich. Qatar has a powerful monarch. However, in 2003 the people voted to approve a new constitution. It gave more power to elected officials.

The United Arab Emirates, or UAE, is seven tiny kingdoms. People there have a modern, comfortable lifestyle because of profits from oil and natural gas. It has more foreign workers than citizens because it has such a small population.

> List the six smaller countries on the Arabian Peninsula.
> _____
> _____
> _____
> _____
> _____
> _____

> Circle three ways besides oil that countries in this region are supporting their economies.

> Why does the UAE have more foreign workers than citizens?
> _____
> _____

Oman covers most of the southeastern part of the Arabian Peninsula. Though its economy is also based on oil, it is not as rich as Kuwait or the UAE. The government is trying to create new industries such as tourism and manufacturing.

Yemen is in the southwestern part of the Arabian Peninsula. Its government is elected, but it suffers from corruption. Oil was discovered in Yemen in the 1980s. Even though oil and coffee created income for the country, it is still the poorest on the Arabian Peninsula.

A civil war has caused many problems in the country. Forces loyal to the government are fighting rebel movements. Citizens cannot get the food and fuel they need. About two million people have either left their homes or fled the country. The United Nations is working to end the conflict.

> **What problems has the civil war caused Yemen's people?**
>
> _____
>
> _____
>
> _____
>
> _____

CHALLENGE ACTIVITY

Critical Thinking: Compare and Contrast Use a Venn diagram or a Features Chart to compare and contrast Saudi Arabia with at least two other countries of the Arabian Peninsula. Consider features such as religious influences, resources, governments, and economies.

Islam	monarchy	OPEC
quota	Shia	Sunni

DIRECTIONS Use a word from the word bank to fill in the blank in each sentence below.

1. The majority of Saudis are _____ Muslims.

2. A _____ is a number or value limit.

3. _____ Muslims believe that only imams can interpret Islamic teachings.

4. _____ is an international organization that controls the supply of oil to influence oil prices.

5. The government of most Arab Peninsula countries is a strong _____ .

6. The laws and customs of Saudi Arabia are based on the teachings of _____ .

The Arabian Peninsula to Central Asia

 MAIN IDEAS
1. Iraq's history includes rule by many conquerors and cultures. Its recent history includes wars.
2. Most of Iraq's people are Arab, and Iraqi culture includes the religion of Islam.
3. Iraq today must rebuild its government and economy, which have suffered from years of conflict.

Key Terms and Places

embargo limit on trade

Baghdad capital of Iraq

Lesson Summary
HISTORY

The world's first civilization was in Iraq, in the area called Mesopotamia. Throughout history, many cultures and empires conquered Mesopotamia, including the Sumerians, Persians, and Greeks. In the AD 600s, Arabs conquered the area and the people became Muslims. During World War I, Great Britain took control. Iraqi army officers overthrew British rule in the 1950s.

In 1968 the Ba'ath Party took power. The party's leader, Saddam Hussein, became president in 1979. He restricted the press and people's freedoms. He killed an unknown number of political enemies.

Saddam led Iraq into two wars. In 1980 Iraq invaded Iran. The Iran-Iraq War lasted until 1988. Many people died, and the economies of both countries were seriously damaged.

In 1990 Iraq invaded Kuwait. Western leaders worried that Iraq would control too much oil and that it had weapons of mass destruction. An alliance of countries led by the United States

> **What country controlled Iraq after World War I?**
> _____

> **Why was Saddam Hussein considered a harsh leader?**
> _____
> _____
> _____
> _____

Guided Reading Workbook

forced Iraq from Kuwait. This was called the
Persian Gulf War, and it lasted six weeks. After
the war, Saddam Hussein did not accept all the
terms of peace, so the United Nations placed an
embargo, or trade limit, on Iraq. This hurt the
economy.

Soon after, Shia Muslims and Kurds rebelled
against Saddam. He brutally put down these
uprisings. The UN forced Iraq to end all military
activity and sent inspectors to make sure Saddam
destroyed all weapons of mass destruction. Iraq
refused to cooperate.

The terrorist attacks on U.S. soil on September
11, 2001, led to more tension between the United
States and Iraq. In March 2003 the United States
invaded Iraq and defeated the Iraqi army in a few
weeks. Saddam Hussein went into hiding, and
Iraq's government fell. When he was found,
Saddam Hussein was arrested, tried, and
executed for his crimes.

PEOPLE AND CULTURE

Iraq has about 38 million people and is about the
size of California. Most Iraqis live in cities. They
belong to two major ethnic groups: Arabs and
Kurds. Arabs make up 75 to 80 percent of Iraq's
population. They speak Arabic, the country's
official language. The Kurds speak Kurdish as
well as Arabic. Kurds are mostly farmers and live
in a large region in the north of Iraq.

Most Iraqis are Muslim, and religion plays a
large role in their lives. The two branches of
Islam—Shia and Sunni—are practiced. About 60
to 65 percent of Iraqis are Shia Muslims and live
in the south. About one third are Sunni Muslims
and live in the north. Most Kurds identify as
Muslims, but they practice a variety of religions
and are known for their religious tolerance.

> **Why did the UN place an embargo on Iraq?**
> _____
> _____
> _____

> **When did the United States invade Iraq?**
> _____

> **Circle the names of Iraq's two ethnic groups.**

> **What branch of Islam is practiced by the majority of Iraqis?**
> _____

IRAQ TODAY

Today, Iraq is slowly recovering from war, though there is still fighting and violence. **Baghdad,** Iraq's capital of 6 million people, was badly damaged. People lost electricity and running water. After the war, the U.S. military and private companies helped to restore water and electricity and to rebuild homes, businesses, and schools.

In January 2005 the people of Iraq took part in democracy for the first time. Millions voted for members of the National Assembly. This group's main task was to write Iraq's new constitution. However, conflicts between groups made it difficult to have a stable government.

Iraq is trying to rebuild a strong economy. The country was once the world's second-largest oil exporter, but it is not clear if they can restore that level of oil production. Crops like barley, cotton, and rice are also important resources.

Iraq's future remains uncertain. Although there has been some progress building a new elected government, it remains weak and corrupt. Poverty is widespread and there are many refugees. A violent Sunni Muslim militant group called the Islamic State and the Levant (ISIL) has committed acts of terror across the globe and ethnic cleansing in Iraq. They want to create a state that supports an extreme form of Islam. U.S. military advisors returned to Iraq in 2014. However, the threat of ISIL and Iraq's weak government continue to be a challenge for the country and the rest of the world.

In 2015 the population of the city of Los Angeles was almost 4 million people. How does this compare to Baghdad's population?
_____
_____
_____

Underline the sentence that describes Iraq's important resources other than oil.

Name four reasons that Iraq is having trouble rebuilding.
_____
_____
_____
_____

Guided Reading Workbook

CHALLENGE ACTIVITY

Critical Thinking: Sequence On a separate piece of paper, create a timeline of events in Iraq since 1968.

DIRECTIONS Read each sentence and fill in the blank with the word in the word pair that best completes the sentence.

1. The United Nations placed an _____, or limit on trade, on Iraq after the 1991 war. (**embargo/alliance**)

2. _____ is Iraq's capital. (**Kurds/Baghdad**)

3. _____ led the invasion of Iran and Kuwait.
   (**Saddam Hussein/Kurds**)

4. The _____ are mostly farmers and live in northern Iraq. (**Kurds/ISIL**)

5. _____ commits terrorist acts and wants to create a state that supports an extreme form of Islam. (**Saddam Hussein/ISIL**)

alliance	Baghdad	embargo
ISIL	Kurds	Saddam Hussein

DIRECTIONS On a separate sheet of paper, use four terms from the word bank to write a summary of what you learned in the lesson.

The Arabian Peninsula to Central Asia

Lesson 4

> **MAIN IDEAS**
> 1. Iran's history includes great empires and an Islamic republic.
> 2. In Iran today, Islamic religious leaders restrict the rights of most Iranians.

Key Terms and Places

shah king

Esfahan capital of the Safavid Empire

revolution drastic change in a country's government and way of life

Tehran capital of Iran

theocracy government ruled by religious leaders

Lesson Summary

HISTORY

Iran today is an Islamic republic. In the 500s BC, it was part of the Persian Empire. Persia was a great center of art and learning. It was known for architecture as well as paintings, metalwork, and carpets. The capital, Persepolis, had walls and statues that glittered with gold, silver, and jewels. When Muslims conquered the region, they converted the Persians to Islam. But most people kept their Persian culture.

The great era of Arab Muslim expansion lasted until the 1100s. After that, three non-Arab Muslim empires took control of much of Europe, Asia, and Africa. These were the Ottoman, Safavid, and Mughal empires. The Safavid Empire began in 1501 when the leader Esma'il conquered Persia. Esma'il became the **shah,** or king. He made Shiism—Shia beliefs—the official religion. He tried to gain more lands and convert more Muslims to Shiism, but he was defeated by the Ottomans in 1514.

The Safavid Empire lasted until the mid-1700s. The culture blended both Persian and Muslim

> **Name and describe the capital of the Persian Empire.**
>
> _____
> _____
> _____
> _____

> **When did the Safavid Empire begin and when did it end?**
>
> _____
> _____

Guided Reading Workbook

traditions. Trade made the Safavids wealthy and they built glorious mosques in their capital **Esfahan.**

In 1921 the Persian title of shah was again taken. This time it was claimed by an Iranian military officer who took power. In 1941 his son took control. This shah was an ally of the United States and Britain. He tried to make Iran more modern, but his programs were not popular.

In 1978 Iranians began a **revolution.** By 1979 they overthrew the shah and set up an Islamic republic. This type of government follows strict Islamic law. Soon after the revolution began, Iran's relations with the United States broke down. A mob of students attacked the U.S. Embassy in **Tehran,** Iran's capital. Over 50 Americans were held hostage for a year, with the approval of Iran's government.

Underline the phrase that explains what an Islamic republic does.

IRAN TODAY

In Southwest Asia most people are Arabs and speak Arabic. In Iran, however, more than half the people are Persian. They speak Farsi, the Persian language.

Iran has one of Southwest Asia's largest populations. It has about 83 million people, and the average age is about 29. It is ethnically diverse. Along with Persians, there are Azeris, Lurs, Kurds, Arabs, and Turks. Most Iranians are Shia Muslim. About 5 to 10 percent are Sunni Muslim. Others practice Christianity, Judaism, and other religions.

How is Iranian culture different from other Southwest Asian cultures? _____ _____ _____

In addition to Islamic holy days, Iranians celebrate Nowruz, the Persian New Year. The culture centers on families, and Persian food is important at family gatherings. Meat is especially significant during holidays. It also is associated with upper-class meals, so it has social significance. However, raising animals for food is an environmental problem in a country where land and water use must be limited.

Iran's huge oil reserves have made it wealthy. The country is also known for its beautiful woven carpets. Agriculture is also important to the economy, employing about one-third of Iran's workforce. The younger population is finding jobs in a growing technology sector. Technology is considered a national priority, and many university graduates have science and engineering degrees. Entrepreneurs are also creating new businesses.

> **Circle three occupations that employ Iran's workforce.**

Iran's government is a **theocracy.** Its rulers, or *ayatollahs,* are religious leaders with unlimited power. The country also has an elected president and parliament. Iran's government has supported many hard-line policies, such as terrorism. In 1997, there were signs that it might adopt some democratic reforms that would improve Iran's economy and women's rights.

> **What is an *ayatollah*?**
> _____
> _____
> _____

In 2005 and 2009, however, Iranians elected a president who wanted Iranians to follow strict Islamic law. He lost supporters when his government was accused of corruption and mismanagement. A new president was elected in 2013.

Today, the United States and other nations are concerned about Iran's nuclear program as a threat to world security. The United Nations imposed sanctions, or penalties, on Iran. These were reduced by several countries when Iran confirmed that it had scaled back its nuclear activities.

> **What activity in Iran is causing concern for the United States and other nations?**
> _____

Guided Reading Workbook

CHALLENGE ACTIVITY

Critical Thinking: Analyze Information
Create a table about Saudi Arabia, Iraq, and
Iran. For each nation, list information about
religion, government, language, ethnic groups,
and economy. After you complete your chart,
write one or two sentences to summarize the
ways these nations are alike and different.

DIRECTIONS Write three words or phrases related to the term.

1. Nowruz _____

2. revolution _____

3. shah _____

4. Tehran _____

5. theocracy _____

6. Farsi _____

Farsi	Nowruz	revolution
Shah	Tehran	theocracy

DIRECTIONS Choose three of the words from the word bank. On a
separate sheet of paper, use the words to write a paragraph
about Iran.

The Arabian Peninsula to Central Asia

Lesson 5

MAIN IDEAS
1. Throughout history, many different groups have conquered Central Asia.
2. Many different ethnic groups and their traditions influence culture in Central Asia.
3. The countries of Central Asia are working to develop their economies and to improve political stability in the region.
4. The countries of Central Asia face issues and challenges related to the environment, the economy, and politics.

Key Terms and Places

Samarqand city along the Silk Road that grew rich from trade

nomads people who move often from place to place

yurt moveable round house made of wool-felt mats hung over a wood frame

Taliban radical Muslim group that arose in Afghanistan in the mid-1990s

Kabul capital of Afghanistan

dryland farming farming that relies on rainfall instead of irrigation

arable suitable for growing crops

Lesson Summary

HISTORY

For hundreds of years, traders and invaders crossed through Central Asia. They left lasting influences.

At one time, there were two major trade routes through Central Asia. One route went from Europe to India, through Afghanistan. The other route started around 100 BC. It went from Europe to China, through the rest of Central Asia. It was called the Silk Road because merchants traded European gold and wool for Chinese silk and spices. **Samarqand** and other cities on the Silk Road grew rich.

By 1500 Europeans stopped using these roads. They discovered they could sail to East Asia on the Indian Ocean. The region became isolated and poor.

Underline the reason that Europeans stopped using the Silk Road.

Guided Reading Workbook

The Silk Road brought many people into Central Asia. In AD 500 Turkic-speaking nomads came from northern Asia. In the 700s Arabs conquered the region. They brought their religion, Islam. The Mongols took over in the 1200s. When their empire fell, groups such as the Uzbeks, Kazaks, and Turkmen came in.

In the mid-1800s Russia conquered this region. Russians built railroads and increased oil and cotton production. But people began to resist Russia's rule. After the Soviets took power in Russia, they wanted to weaken resistance to their rule. So they divided Central Asia into republics. They encouraged ethnic Russians to move in. The Soviets also built huge irrigation projects for more cotton production. In 1991 the Soviet government collapsed. Central Asia's republics became independent countries.

Circle the dates that the Arabs and Mongols conquered Central Asia.

What happened to Central Asia's republics when the Soviet government collapsed in 1991?
_____
_____

CULTURE

The people who came through Central Asia brought new languages, religions, and ways of life. These mixed with traditional ways.

For centuries, Central Asians raised horses, cattle, goats, and sheep. Many lived as **nomads.** They moved their herds to different pastures in summer and winter. They also moved their houses. The Central Asian nomad's moveable house is called a **yurt.** It is an important symbol today, even though most people now live in permanent settlements. Even people in cities put up yurts for special events. Nomads, though, are still common in Kyrgyzstan.

Today, most of the region's ethnic groups are part of the larger Turkic group. There are ethnic Russians, also. Each group speaks its own language. Most countries have more than one official language. In some, Russian is still the

Lesson 5, *continued*

official language because of earlier Russian rule. The Russians also brought Cyrillic, their alphabet. Now most countries use the Latin alphabet, the one for writing English. However, Afghanistan uses its own alphabet for writing Pashto, one of its official languages.

The region's main religion is Islam, but there are also others. Some people are Russian Orthodox, a Christian religion. Today, many religious buildings that were closed by the Soviets have opened again.

CENTRAL ASIA TODAY

Central Asia is working to recover from a history of invasions and foreign rulers. The region is trying to build more stable governments and stronger economies.

In the 1980s Afghanistan fought a war with the Soviet Union that ended in 1989. It left the country in turmoil. In the mid-1990s, the **Taliban** took power. This was a radical Muslim group. It ruled most of the country, including **Kabul,** the capital. It based its laws on strict Islamic teachings. Women's lives were very limited, and even music and dancing were banned. Most people disagreed with the Taliban, but it stayed in power for many years.

On September 11, 2001, a terrorist group called al Qaeda attacked the United States. The group was based in Afghanistan and linked to the Taliban. As a result, U.S. and British forces attacked and toppled the Taliban government. Now people in Afghanistan have a constitution and can vote. Women have more freedom. However, the Taliban is trying to regain power and continues to cause problems.

Kazakhstan was the first part of Central Asia that Russia conquered. It still has many Russian influences. About one third of its people are ethnic Russian and many people speak both

---

Why do many people in Central Asian countries speak Russian?
_____
_____

What group ruled Afghanistan from the mid-1990s to 2001?
_____

Describe three changes that have happened in Afghanistan since the fall of the Taliban.
_____
_____
_____
_____

Guided Reading Workbook

Russian and Kazakh. Kazakhstan's economy suffered when the Soviet Union fell. But it is growing again because of oil reserves and a free market. The country is the richest in Central Asia. Kazakhstan also has a stable democratic government. People elect a president and parliament.

In Kyrgyzstan, clan membership is an important part of social, political, and economic life. Many people still follow nomadic traditions, though there are also many that farm. Farmers use both irrigation and **dryland farming,** which relies on rainfall. Farming is the most important industry in Kyrgyzstan, but it does not provide much income for the country. Tourism is helping to strengthen the economy. The government is also changing. In 2010, the president was overthrown. A new constitution was adopted and first-ever elections were held.

Tajikistan has many problems. In the 1990s rebels fought the Communist government. Some wanted democracy and some wanted Islamic law. In 1997 the groups ended the conflict. Now Tajikistan is a republic with an elected president. Years of war ruined the country's economy. Today, the economy relies on cotton farming. But progress is difficult because only about 7 percent of the land is **arable,** or suitable for growing crops.

Turkmenistan's president is elected for life by the country's parliament. He has all the power. He has made education, health, and technology reforms. The government supports Islamic principles, but tries to keep them separate from politics. Turkmenistan's economy is based on oil, gas, and cotton. About half the country is planted with cotton, even though it is a desert. This is possible because Turkmenistan has one of the longest irrigation channels in the world.

Uzbekistan has the largest population and cities in Central Asia. The United States criticizes

> **Circle the name of the industry that is strengthening Kyrgyzstan's economy.**

> **Why should Tajikistan look for other ways to support its economy?**
>
> _____
>
> _____

> **Why does Turkmenistan have such a long irrigation channel?**
>
> _____
>
> _____

Lesson 5, *continued*

the government because it restricts political freedom and human rights. Its elected president holds all the power. The government also controls the economy, which is based on oil, gold, and cotton. The economy is stable, but is growing very slowly.

ISSUES AND CHALLENGES

Central Asia faces challenges in three areas today: environment, economy, and politics.

The shrinking Aral Sea is a serious problem for Central Asia's environment. The seafloor is dry. Dust, salt, and pesticides blow out of it. Towns that relied on fishing are now miles from shore. Another problem is leftover radiation from Soviet nuclear testing. It causes people's health to suffer. Crop chemicals are also a threat. They have been used too much and ended up ruining farmlands.

Central Asia's economy relies on only one crop—cotton. Since there is little farmland, there are limited jobs. Oil and gas reserves may bring in more money one day. However, old equipment, lack of funds, and poor transportation slow development.

Central Asia does not have widespread political stability. In some countries, like Kyrgyszstan, people do not agree on the best kind of government. Often, these people turn to violence or terrorism, which threaten their own countries.

> Underline the main environmental challenges that Central Asian countries face.

CHALLENGE ACTIVITY

Critical Thinking: Analyze Information If you were asked to plan a meeting about protecting the environment in Central Asia, what topics would you put on the agenda? What topic would you want to spend the most time discussing?

Guided Reading Workbook

arable	Aral Sea	dryland farming	Kabul
nomads	Samarqand	Taliban	yurt

DIRECTIONS On the line provided before each statement, write **T** if the statement is true and **F** if the statement is false. If the statement is false, write the correct term from the word bank to make the sentence a true statement on the line after each sentence.

_____ 1. Yurts are people who move around often.

_____

_____ 2. A nomad is a movable, round house.

_____

_____ 3. The capital of Afghanistan is Kabul.

_____

_____ 4. The Samarqand took power after the Russians left Afghanistan.

_____

_____ 5. Only 7 percent of Tajikistan's land is dryland farming.

_____

_____ 6. Cotton farming is causing environmental problems to the Aral Sea.

_____

_____ 7. Agriculture is a poor industry for countries that do not have much arable land.

_____

_____ 8. The Taliban forced people to follow a strict interpretation of Islam.

_____

The Eastern Mediterranean

MAIN IDEAS

1. The Eastern Mediterranean's physical features include the Bosporus, the Dead Sea, rivers, mountains, deserts, and plains.
2. The region's climate is mostly dry with little vegetation.
3. Important natural resources in the Eastern Mediterranean include valuable minerals and the availability of water.

Key Terms and Places

Dardanelles body of water that connects the Sea of Marmara and the Mediterranean Sea; part of the narrow waterway that separates Europe and Asia

Bosporus body of water that connects the Black Sea and the Sea of Marmara; part of the narrow waterway that separates Europe and Asia

Sea of Marmara body of water that connects the Bosporus and the Dardanelles; part of the narrow waterway that separates Europe and Asia

Jordan River river that begins in Syria and flows south through Israel and Jordan, finally emptying into the Dead Sea

Dead Sea lowest point on any continent and the world's saltiest body of water

Syrian Desert desert of rock and gravel covering much of Syria and Jordan

Lesson Summary

PHYSICAL FEATURES

A narrow waterway separates Europe from Asia. It is made up of the **Dardanelles,** the **Bosporus,** and the **Sea of Marmara.** Ships travel through the waterway between the Black Sea and the Mediterranean Sea. The Bosporus splits Turkey. A small part of Turkey lies in Europe. The larger Asian part is called Anatolia.

The **Jordan River** flows from Syria, through Israel and Jordan, then empties into the **Dead Sea.** The Dead Sea is the world's saltiest lake. It lies below sea level and only bacteria can live in it.

Two mountain systems stretch east to west across Turkey. The Pontic Mountains lie in the north, and the Taurus Mountains lie in the south.

> **What three bodies of water separate Europe and Asia?**
> _____
> _____
> _____

> **Which two mountain systems stretch across Turkey?**
> _____
> _____

A narrow plain runs from Turkey into Syria. The Euphrates River flows south-east through this plain. Farther inland are hills, valleys, and plateaus. A rift valley extends into Syria all the way from Africa. Two mountain ridges run north to south. One runs from Syria through western Jordan. The other runs through Lebanon and Israel near the coast.

CLIMATE AND VEGETATION

The Eastern Mediterranean is a mostly dry region. However, there are important variations. Turkey's Black Sea coast and the Mediterranean coast to northern Israel have a Mediterranean climate. Turkey's interior has a steppe climate, but a small area in the northeast has a humid subtropical climate. Central Syria and lands farther south have a desert climate.

> Circle the four words and phrases that describe climates in the Eastern Mediterranean.

The driest areas are the deserts. The **Syrian Desert** covers much of Syria and Jordan. The Negev Desert lies in southern Israel. Only shrubs can grow in the deserts' high temperatures and dry conditions.

NATURAL RESOURCES

Because the region is so dry, water is a valuable resource. Many people are farmers. However, commercial farms can only grow crops where there is irrigation or rain. In drier areas, people do subsistence farming and herding.

The region has little oil, but it does have valuable minerals, including sulfur, mercury, and copper. Phosphates are produced in Syria, Jordan, and Israel. They are used to make fertilizers. The area also produces asphalt, the dark tarlike material used to pave streets.

> What mineral resources are found in the region?
> _____

CHALLENGE ACTIVITY

Critical Thinking: Draw Inferences: Based on what you have learned about the climates in the Eastern Mediterranean region, write an essay describing which location you think would be best for farming. What crops would you expect to grow well there?

Bosporus	Dardanelles	Dead Sea	Jordan River
Negev Desert	phosphates	Sea of Marmara	Syrian Desert

DIRECTIONS On the line provided before each statement, write **T** if a statement is true and **F** if a statement is false. If the statement is false, write the correct term from the word bank on the line after each sentence to make the sentence a true statement.

_____ 1. The Sea of Marmara, the Bosporus, and the <u>Negev</u> separate the European and Asian parts of Turkey.

_____

_____ 2. <u>Phosphates</u> are produced in Syria, Israel, and Jordan.

_____

_____ 3. The <u>Syrian Desert</u> lies below sea level.

_____

_____ 4. The <u>Bosporus</u> connects the Black Sea and the Sea of Marmara.

_____

_____ 5. The <u>Dardanelles</u> empties into the Dead Sea.

_____

DIRECTIONS Choose four terms from the word bank. On a separate piece of paper, use these words in a written summary of what you learned in the lesson.

The Eastern Mediterranean

Lesson 2

MAIN IDEAS
1. Turkey's history includes invasion by the Romans, rule by the Ottomans, and a 20th-century democracy.
2. Turkey's people are mostly ethnic Turks, and its culture is a mixture of modern and traditional.
3. Today, Turkey is a democratic nation seeking economic opportunities and considering European Union membership.

Key Terms and Places

Istanbul Turkey's largest city

janissaries slave boys converted to Islam and trained as soldiers

Ankara capital of Turkey

secular religion is kept separate from government

Lesson Summary
HISTORY

About 8,000 years ago, the area that is now Turkey was home to the world's earliest farming villages. The region was invaded for centuries. The ancient Greeks created the city of Byzantium, which is now the site of modern **Istanbul.** Romans captured Byzantium and changed the name to Constantinople. The city was an important trading port because it was at the crossroads between Europe and Asia. After the fall of Rome, Constantinople became the capital of the Byzantine Empire.

Seljuk Turks, a nomadic people from Central Asia, invaded the area in the AD 1000s. In the mid-1200s, Muslim Turkish warriors, known as the Ottomans, took territory from the Christian Byzantine Empire. The Ottomans had an army with fiercely loyal soldiers. Many of these were **janissaries,** Christian boys from conquered areas who converted to Islam. The army also had new weapons, including gunpowder.

> **What did the Romans rename Byzantium?**
> _____

> **Who were the Seljuk Turks?**
> _____
> _____
> _____
> _____

In 1453 the Ottoman Turks, led by Mehmed II "the Conqueror," captured Constantinople and defeated the Byzantine Empire. He changed the name of Constantinople to Istanbul and made it his capital. He also turned the great church Hagia Sophia into a mosque.

After Mehmed's death, other rulers, or sultans, continued to expand the empire. They conquered Asia Minor, Syria, Egypt, and the holy cities of Mecca and Medina. The Ottoman Empire reached its height under Suleyman I "the Magnificent." From 1520 to 1566, the Ottomans took control of the eastern Mediterranean and pushed into Europe.

> **Circle the names of two Ottoman rulers who greatly expanded the empire.**

The Ottoman Empire stayed powerful during the 1500s and 1600s. It controlled territory in northern Africa, southwestern Asia, and southeastern Europe through the 1800s. In the early 1900s, the Ottomans fought on the losing side of World War I. They lost most of their territory at the end of the war.

Military officers, led by Mustafa Kemal, took over the government after World War I. Mustafa Kemal later adopted the name Kemal Atatürk, which means Father of Turks. Atatürk created the democratic nation of Turkey and moved the capital to **Ankara** from Constantinople, which he officially renamed Istanbul.

> **Who was the leader of Turkey after World War I?**
> _____

Atatürk wanted to modernize Turkey to make it stronger. He adopted some elements of western culture. He also banned the wearing of certain traditional Turkish clothing like veils and the fez. Women were encouraged to vote, work, and hold office. He also replaced the Arabic alphabet with the Latin alphabet, and adopted the metric system.

> **Why did Atatürk make so many changes and laws?**
> _____
> _____
> _____
> _____

Guided Reading Workbook

PEOPLE AND CULTURE

Most of the people living in Turkey are ethnic Turks. Kurds are the largest minority. They make up 20 percent of the population.

Turkey's culture today reflects Kemal Atatürk's changes. He created a cultural split between the urban middle class and rural villagers. In general, middle-class lifestyle and attitude reflect middle-class Europeans. However, rural Turks are more traditional and reflect Islamic influences.

> **What is the largest minority living in Turkey today?**
> _____

TURKEY TODAY

Istanbul is Turkey's largest city, but the government meets in the capital of Ankara. Istanbul serves as an economic bridge to Europe as Turkey plans to join the European Union.

Turkey is a parliamentary republic. Its legislature is called the National Assembly. A president and prime minister share executive power. Although most of the people are Muslim, Turkey is a **secular** state. That means that the religion is kept separate from government. In recent years, Islamic political parties have tried to increase Islam's role in Turkish society.

> **Underline the sentence that explains why Istanbul is an important city for Turkey.**

Turkey has long sought membership into the European Union. Turkey's people and economy would benefit from increased trade with Europe if they join the European Union. Today's economy includes modern factories, subsistence farming, and craft making. The most important industries are textiles and clothing, cement, and electronics, as well as agriculture.

Turkey is also rich in natural resources, including oil, coal, and iron ore. Water is another valuable resource. Turkey has built dams to increase its water supply and provide power. However, some of these dams restrict water flow to other countries.

> **How would joining the European Union help Turkey's economy?**
> _____
>
> _____

CHALLENGE ACTIVITY

Critical Thinking: Draw Inferences Kemal Atatürk is the founder of modern Turkey. Do you think he had a greater influence on people living in cities or in the countryside? Explain your reasoning.

Ankara	Constantinople	European Union	Istanbul
janissaries	modernize	Ottoman Empire	secular

DIRECTIONS Answer each question by writing a sentence that contains at least one term from the word bank. You should use all the terms.

1. What role did Constantinople have in Turkey's past? What role does the city of Istanbul have now? _____

   _____

2. Describe some of the changes made by Kemal Atatürk. _____

   _____

3. Who controlled Turkey during the 1500s and 1600s? What happened to this power? _____

   _____

4. What were some of the key reasons the Ottoman Empire conquered so much territory? _____

   _____

5. What is Turkey's government like today? Where does Turkey's government meet? _____

   _____

The Eastern Mediterranean

Lesson 3

MAIN IDEAS
1. Israel's history includes the ancient Israelites and the creation of the State of Israel.
2. In Israel today, Jewish culture is a major part of daily life.
3. The Palestinian Territories are areas next to Israel—Gaza and the West Bank—controlled partly by Palestinian Arabs.

Key Terms and Places

Judaism religion of the Jewish people and the oldest monotheistic religion

Diaspora scattering of the Jewish population

Jerusalem capital of Israel

Zionism movement that called for Jews to reestablish a Jewish state in Palestine

kosher term used for food allowed under Jewish dietary laws

kibbutz large farm where people share everything in common

Gaza small, crowded piece of coastal land disputed over by Jews and Arabs

West Bank largely populated, rural piece of land disputed over by Jews and Arabs

Lesson Summary
HISTORY

Israel is often referred to as the Holy Land. It is home to sacred sites for three major religions: **Judaism,** Christianity, and Islam. Many events in the Jewish and Christian Bibles happened in Israel.

The Israelites established the kingdom of Israel about 1000 BC. In the 60s BC, the Romans conquered the region. They renamed it Palestine in AD 135. After several Jewish revolts, the Romans forced many Jews to leave the region and move to other lands. This was known as the **Diaspora.**

Arabs conquered Palestine in the mid-600s, but during the Crusades, it was invaded by Christians. The Crusaders captured the city of **Jerusalem** in 1099 but were eventually driven out.

> **Why is Israel often referred to as the Holy Land?**
> _____
> _____
> _____
> _____

> **When did Arabs conquer Palestine?**
> _____

Palestine was part of the Ottoman Empire until it came under British control after World War I.

In the late 1800s, European Jews began a movement called **Zionism.** It called for Jews to reestablish a Jewish state in their ancient homeland. Many thousands of Jews and Arabs moved to the region, then under British control. Arabs also moved there to counterbalance the number of Jews moving into the region. In 1947 the United Nations voted to divide the Palestine Mandate into Jewish and Arab states. Arab countries rejected this plan. The Jews accepted it and a year later created the State of Israel. Five Arab armies invaded Israel but were defeated. Many Palestinians then fled to neighboring Arab countries. Israel and Arab countries have fought several wars since, and disputes between the two sides continue today.

What is Zionism?
_____
_____
_____
_____

ISRAEL TODAY

Jews from all over the world have come to Israel, hoping to find peace and stability. Yet the country faces continual conflicts with neighboring countries. Despite this, Israel is a modern, democratic country. It has a prime minister and parliament. The country also has a strong military, in which most men and women serve for at least one year.

Why does Israel have such a strong military?
_____
_____
_____

Israel has a modern, diverse economy. It exports high-tech equipment and cut diamonds. Irrigation increases food production. Millions of visitors come to see the historic sites.

Most Israelis live in cities. Jerusalem, the capital, and Tel Aviv are Israel's largest cities. About 75 percent of Israel's population is Jewish. The rest of the population is mostly Arab. While most Arabs are Muslim, about a quarter are Christian. Both Hebrew and Arabic are official languages.

What percentage of Israel's population is Jewish?
_____

Jewish holidays and traditions are an important aspect of Israeli Jewish culture. Jewish religious laws address every aspect of daily life. Many Jews follow a **kosher** diet based on ancient dietary laws. Also, some Israeli Jews live in collective communities called kibbutzim. A **kibbutz** is a large farm where people share everything in common.

> **What is the special diet many Jews follow, and what is it based on?**
> _____
> _____

THE PALESTINIAN TERRITORIES

In 1967 Israel captured land from Egypt and Jordan—**Gaza,** the **West Bank,** and East Jerusalem. In the 1990s Israel agreed to give parts of these territories to the Palestinian Arabs who lived there. In return, the Palestinian leadership—the Palestinian Liberation Organization (PLO)—agreed to renounce terrorism and recognize Israel.

> **Which areas of land have been the sources of the greatest conflict between Arabs and Israelis?**
> _____
> _____

Gaza is a small, crowded coastal area where more than a million Palestinians live. There are few resources and unemployment is high. In 2005 Israelis transferred control of Gaza to the Palestinians.

The **West Bank** is much larger than Gaza and has a population of about 2.7 million. It has three large cities but is mostly rural. Its economy is mostly agricultural, relying on irrigation. Since Israel gained control of the area in 1967, hundreds of thousands of Israelis have moved there.

> **About how many Palestinians live in Gaza and the West Bank?**
> _____

Israel and Palestinians continue to dispute these territories. Peace agreements have tried to divide the lands fairly. However, terrorist attacks and conflicts over land are a great source of tension between the two groups. Jerusalem is also a center of tension between Jews, Arabs, and Christians. Both Israel and Palestinians claim Jerusalem as their capital.

In 2006 control of the territories was split between two opposing Palestinian political groups. Fatah governs the West Bank, and Hamas controls Gaza. Political tensions in the region remain high. There are still many acts of terrorism, and the future of the peace process is uncertain.

> **Circle the names of the two groups that govern the West Bank and Gaza.**

CHALLENGE ACTIVITY

Critical Thinking: Interpret In what areas of Israel do you think most Arabs live? Draw an outline map of Israel, locating major cities and the areas with the largest Arab populations.

Arabic	Diaspora	Gaza	Hebrew
Jerusalem	Judaism	kibbutz	kosher
Palestinian	West Bank	Zionism	

DIRECTIONS Read each sentence and fill in the blank with the term in the word bank that best completes the sentence.

1. Arabic and _____ are both official languages of Israel.

2. The movement that called Jewish people to reestablish a country in Palestine is called _____.

3. If you lived on a _____ you would work on the farm and share everything with other people.

4. Many Jews follow a _____ diet, which follows ancient dietary laws.

5. _____ is a disputed territory located on the coast of Israel.

6. _____ is a holy city to Jews, Christians, and Muslims.

7. Many Israelis have moved into the Palestinian territory of the _____.

8. The forced removal of Jewish people from Palestine by the Romans is called the _____.

The Eastern Mediterranean

MAIN IDEAS
1. Syria is an Arab country that has been ruled by a powerful family and recently torn by civil war.
2. Lebanon is recovering from civil war, and its people are divided by religion.
3. Jordan has few resources and is home to Bedouins and Palestinian refugees.

Key Terms and Places

Damascus capital of Syria

Beirut capital of Lebanon

Bedouins Arab-speaking nomads who mostly live in the deserts of Southwest Asia

Amman capital of Jordan

Lesson Summary
SYRIA

Syria, Lebanon, and Jordan all border Israel and have had conflicts with it. They have majority Arab populations and share a similar history, religion, and culture.

The capital of Syria, **Damascus,** is believed to be the oldest continuously inhabited city in the world. Syria became part of the Ottoman Empire in the 1500s. After World War I, France controlled Syria. Syria gained independence in the 1940s.

From 1971 to 2000, Syria was ruled by the dictator Hafiz al-Assad. He increased Syria's military to protect himself from political enemies and to match Israel's military strength. Assad's son, Bashar, was elected president after his father's death in 2000. In 2011 anti-government protesters challenged Bashar al-Assad's rule. Syria used brutal force to crush the protests. By 2012 Syria was divided by a civil war.

About 23 million people live in Syria. Almost 90 percent of the population is Arab. The remaining 10 percent include Kurds and Armenians.

> **Which country controlled Syria after World War I?**
> _____

> **What caused the civil war in Syria?**
> _____
> _____
> _____
> _____
> _____

About 74 percent of Syria's Muslims are Sunni, and the rest are smaller Islamic groups. Syria also has Christians and some small Jewish communities.

The civil war has drastically affected the population. By March 2017 over 386,000 Syrian people had died as a result of the fighting. More than 11 million have lost their homes, and almost 5 million refugees have left the country.

LEBANON

Lebanon is a small, mountainous country on the Mediterranean coast. Many ethnic minority groups settled in Lebanon during the Ottoman Empire. After World War I, it was controlled by France. Lebanon finally gained its independence in the 1940s.

> When did Lebanon gain its independence?
>
> _____

Most Lebanese people are Arab, but they are divided by religion. The main religions in Lebanon are Islam and Christianity. Both religions are divided into smaller groups. Muslims are divided into Sunni and Shia. Islam is Lebanon's majority religion.

> What are the two main religious groups in Lebanon?
>
> _____

After independence, Christians and Muslims shared political power. However, over time tensions mounted and civil war broke out. In the 1970s Muslims fought against Christians. Other countries, including Syria and Israel, got involved. Many people died and the capital, **Beirut,** was badly damaged.

> When did Lebanon's civil war take place?
>
> _____
>
> _____

Warfare lasted until 1990. After that, Syrian troops stayed in Lebanon. They were pressured to leave in 2005. However, border attacks from Lebanon against Israel led to fighting between those two countries.

JORDAN

The country of Jordan was created after World War I. Britain controlled the area until the 1940s, when the country gained full independence.

Guided Reading Workbook

Lesson 4, *continued*

Jordan had a small population until hundreds of thousands of Palestinians fled there from Israel. King Hussein ruled Jordan from 1952 to 1999. He enacted some democratic reforms in the 1990s.

Many people in Jordan are **Bedouins,** or Arab-speaking nomads who live mainly in the deserts. **Amman,** the capital, is Jordan's largest city. The country produces phosphates, cement, and potash. Farmers raise fruits and vegetables and livestock, though water shortages are always a serious concern. Tourism and banking are growing industries. Jordan depends on economic aid from oil-rich Arab nations and the United States.

What caused Jordan's population to grow?
_____
_____

Underline Jordan's two growing industries.

CHALLENGE ACTIVITY

Critical Thinking: Categorize Make a table with a column for each country in this section. List information about the people of each country in the appropriate column.

Guided Reading Workbook

DIRECTIONS Read each sentence and fill in the blank with the word in the word pair that best completes the sentence.

1. _____ is the capital of Syria and is thought to be the oldest continuously inhabited city in the world. (**Damascus/Beirut**)

2. Lebanon's _____ created a terrible conflict between the country's Muslims and Christians. (**Bashar al-Assad/civil war**)

3. A civil war started in Syria after anti-government protests challenged _____. (**Bedouins/Bashar al-Assad**)

4. _____, who mostly live in the deserts of Southwest Asia, are Arabic-speaking nomads. (**Bedouins/Amman**)

5. The capital of Jordan, _____, is also the country's largest city. (**Beirut/Amman**)

Amman	Bashar al-Assad	Bedouins
Beirut	civil war	Damascus

DIRECTIONS On a separate piece of paper, create a crossword puzzle using the words in the word bank. Use the definition or description of each term as a clue. If you wish, add other words from the lesson to create a bigger puzzle.

North Africa

MAIN IDEAS
1. Major physical features of North Africa include the Nile River, the Sahara, and the Atlas Mountains.
2. The climate of North Africa is hot and dry, and water is the region's most important resource.

Key Terms and Places

Sahara world's largest desert, covering most of North Africa

Nile River world's longest river, located in Egypt

silt finely ground fertile soil good for growing crops

Suez Canal strategic waterway connecting the Mediterranean and Red Seas

oasis wet, fertile area in a desert where a natural spring or well provides water

Atlas Mountains mountain range on the northwestern side of the Sahara

Lesson Summary
PHYSICAL FEATURES

Morocco, Algeria, Tunisia, Libya, and Egypt are the five countries of North Africa. All five countries have northern coastlines on the Mediterranean Sea. The largest desert in the world, the **Sahara,** covers most of North Africa.

The **Nile River,** the world's longest river, flows northward through the eastern Sahara. Near its end, the Nile becomes a large river delta that empties into the Mediterranean Sea. The river's water irrigates the farmland along its banks. In the past, flooding along the Nile left finely ground fertile soil, called **silt,** in the surrounding fields. Today, the Aswan High Dam controls flooding and prevents silt from being deposited in the nearby fields. Farmers must use fertilizer to aid the growth of crops.

East of the Nile River is the Sinai Peninsula, which is made up of rocky mountains and desert.

> **Name the five countries of North Africa.**
> _____
> _____

> **Describe the Nile River.**
> _____
> _____
> _____
> _____
> _____
> _____

The **Suez Canal,** a narrow waterway, connects the Mediterranean Sea with the Red Sea. Today large cargo ships carry oil and other goods through the canal.

The Sahara has a huge impact on all North Africa. It is made up of sand dunes, gravel plains, and rocky, barren mountains. Because of the Sahara's harsh environment, few people live there. Small settlements of farmers are located by **oases**—wet, fertile areas in the desert that are fed by natural springs. Oases provide a shady place to rest in the desert. The Ahaggar Mountains are located in central North Africa. The **Atlas Mountains** are in the northwestern part of North Africa.

> **Why would an oasis be valuable to someone traveling in the desert?**
> _____
> _____
> _____

CLIMATE AND RESOURCES

Most of North Africa has a desert climate. It is hot and dry during the day and cool or cold during the night. There is very little rain. Most of the northern coast west of Egypt has a Mediterranean climate. There it is hot and dry in the summer and cool and moist in the winter. Areas between the coast and the Sahara have a steppe climate.

> **What kind of climate covers most of North Africa?**
> _____

Important resources include oil and gas, particularly for Libya, Algeria, and Egypt. In Morocco, iron ore and minerals are important. Coal, oil, and natural gas are found in the Sahara.

CHALLENGE ACTIVITY

Critical Thinking: Evaluate Why do you think almost all of Egypt's population lives along the Nile River? Write a brief paragraph that explains your answer.

Aswan High Dam	Atlas Mountains	delta
Nile River	oasis	Sahara
silt	Sinai Mountains	Suez Canal

DIRECTIONS On the line provided before each statement, write **T** if a statement is true and **F** if a statement is false. If the statement is false, write the term from the word bank on the line provided below the sentence to make the sentence a true statement.

_____ 1. The <u>Aswan High Dam</u> connects the Mediterranean Sea with the Red Sea.

_____

_____ 2. The <u>Nile River</u> is the world's longest river.

_____

_____ 3. Annual floods along the northern Nile River have left fertile soil called <u>silt</u> in the surrounding fields.

_____

_____ 4. The <u>Atlas Mountains</u> are in the northwestern part of North Africa.

_____

_____ 5. In a desert such as the Sahara, the <u>delta</u> is a wet, fertile area where a natural spring, or well, provides water.

_____

DIRECTIONS Write three words or phrases that describe each term.

6. Sahara _____

7. Nile River _____

_____

8. silt _____

9. oasis _____

_____

10. Suez Canal _____

_____

North Africa

MAIN IDEAS
1. Egyptian civilization goes back thousands of years.
2. Many of Egypt's people are farmers and live along the Nile River.
3. Islam influences Egyptian culture and most people speak Arabic.

Key Terms and Places

Alexandria city in Egypt founded by Alexander the Great in 332 BC

Cairo Egypt's capital and largest city

Arab Spring massive protest that broke out in Egypt in 2011

Lesson Summary
HISTORY

Around 3200 BC people along the northern Nile united into a single Egyptian Kingdom. The ancient Egyptians participated in trade, developed a writing system, and built pyramids in which to bury their pharaohs, or kings. The pyramids were made of large blocks of stone that were probably rolled on logs to the Nile and then moved by barge to the building site. The Great Pyramid of Egypt took about 20 years to finish.

Hieroglyphics, pictures and symbols that stand for ideas and words, formed the basis for Egypt's first writing system. Each symbol stood for one or more sounds in the Egyptian language. Many writings recorded the achievements of pharaohs.

Invaders of North Africa included people from the eastern Mediterranean, Greeks, and Romans. Alexander the Great, the Macedonian king, founded the city of **Alexandria** in Egypt in 332 BC. It became an important port of trade and a great center of learning. Arab armies from Southwest Asia started invading North Africa in the AD 600s. They ruled most or all of North Africa until the 1800s, bringing the Arabic language and Islam to the region. Under Muslim

Where did ancient Egyptians bury their kings?
_____

What are hieroglyphics?
_____
_____
_____

Underline the sentences that state how long Arabs from Southwest Asia ruled North Africa.

Guided Reading Workbook

rule, Egyptian cities such as **Cairo** became major centers of learning, trade, and craft making.

EGYPT TODAY

Egypt is North Africa's most populous country. More than 85 million people live there.

In 2011, a massive protest known as **Arab Spring** broke out. This wave of uprisings shook North Africa and Southwest Asia. Egypt's military forced President Hosni Mubarak from power, ending 30 years of autocratic rule. Since an autocratic ruler has absolute power, people living under this type of regime do not have the power to vote or express their true thoughts on the government.

Egyptians elected Mohamed Morsi in 2012. Morsi had the support of the Muslim Brotherhood, a group that believes all aspects of society should be based on Islamic law. However, the Egyptian people were still divided and unhappy. This resulted in a massive protest for Morsi's resignation. In May 2014, former general Abdel Fattah el-Sisi was elected president.

Egypt is challenged by its limited resources. The only farmland is along the Nile River. Farmers use fertilizers to make the land productive. Still, Egypt must import much of its food.

The Suez Canal is an important part of Egypt's economy. It makes more than $5 billion a year in tolls. It is one of the world's busiest waterways.

Ninety-nine percent of Egyptians live in the Nile valley and delta. Cairo, Egypt's capital and largest city, is located in this Nile valley. Cairo's location at the southern end of the Nile delta helped the city grow to around 18 million people. Today Cairo is a mixture of modern buildings, historic mosques, and mud-brick houses.

Except for Cairo and Alexandria, Egypt's second-largest city, more than half of all

> How many Egyptians live in the Nile valley and delta?
>
> _____

Lesson 2, *continued*

Egyptians live in small villages and other rural areas. Farmers own very small plots of land along the Nile River.

CULTURES

Egypt shares much of its history and culture with other countries of North Africa. Egyptians, Berbers, and Bedouins make up almost all of Egypt's population. Most Egyptians and North Africans speak Arabic. About 90 percent of Egyptians are Muslims who practice the religion of Islam.

> **What religion do most Egyptians practice?**
>
> _____

Grains, vegetables, fruits, and nuts are common foods. Couscous, a pellet-like pasta made from wheat, is served steamed with vegetables or meat. Another favorite dish is *fuul*, made from fava beans. It is often served with hard-boiled eggs and bread.

Egypt observes two Revolution Day holidays. The one on January 25 celebrates the 2011 revolution, while the one on January 23 celebrates the 1962 revolution, when Egypt gained its independence from Britain.

There are two important religious holidays that Egyptians observe as well. The birthday of Muhammad, the prophet of Islam, is marked with lights, parades, and special sweets. Ramadan is a holy month during which Muslims fast.

North Africa is known for its beautiful architecture, wood carving, carpets, and hand-painted tiles. Egypt has produced important writers, including Egypt's Nobel Prize winner Naguib Mahfouz. Egypt also has a thriving film industry.

CHALLENGE ACTIVITY

Critical Thinking: Elaborate Imagine that you are traveling throughout Egypt. Write a letter to a friend at home that describes the people you meet and the places you visit.

Guided Reading Workbook

DIRECTIONS Look at each set of four terms. On the line provided, write the letter of the term that does not relate to the others.

_____ 1. a. pharaohs
          b. pyramids
          c. Egyptians
          d. Muslims

_____ 3. a. writing
          b. couscous
          c. hieroglyphics
          d. pictures

_____ 2. a. couscous
          b. fuul
          c. Cleopatra
          d. vegetables

_____ 4. a. trade
          b. Alexandria
          c. Morocco
          d. Cairo

Alexandria	Arab Spring	Cairo	couscous
fuul	hieroglyphics	pharaohs	Ramadan

DIRECTIONS Answer each question by writing a sentence that contains at least one word from the word bank.

5. What are two important religious holidays observed by Egyptians?

_____

6. What are some common foods served in Egypt?

_____

_____

7. Name two important trade cities found in Egypt.

_____

_____

_____

Name _____ Class _____ Date_____

MAIN IDEAS

1. In 2011 a pro-democracy movement called the Arab Spring brought change to North Africa.
2. The North African countries share a common history and culture, with most people following Islam.
3. People in the Maghreb countries of North Africa are mostly pastoral nomads or farmers, and oil is an important resource in the region.

Key Terms and Places

dictator someone who rules a country with complete power

Maghreb collective name for Western Libya, Tunisia, Algeria, and Morocco

souks large marketplaces

free port city in which almost no taxes are placed on goods sold there

Lesson Summary
THE ARAB SPRING

In 2011 a wave of pro-democracy uprisings called the Arab Spring shook North Africa and Southwest Asia. Protesters demanded the right to vote and the end of political corruption. Each country touched by the Arab Spring has had a different outcome. **Dictators,** rulers with complete power, were removed in Tunisia, Egypt, and Libya. Other protests were squashed by brute force.

> **What did the Arab Spring protesters want?**
>
> _____
> _____
> _____

SHARED HISTORY AND CULTURE

North Africa's long Mediterranean coastline opened it to invasion over the centuries from people from the eastern Mediterranean, Greeks, and Romans. Arab armies also invaded it from Southwest Asia. In the 1800s European countries began to take over the region. By 1912 Europeans had authority over all of North Africa. During World War II the region was a major battleground, but in the 1950s Libya, Morocco,

> **What countries began to take over the North African region in the 1800s?**
>
> _____

and Tunisia each won independence. Algeria did not win independence until 1962.

Most people in North Africa are of mixed Arab and Berber ancestry. The majority of North Africans speak Arabic, but some also speak French, Italian, and English.

Since most North Africans are Muslim, they observe holidays such as Muhammad's birthday and the holy month of Ramadan. Men like to gather in cafes where they can play chess or dominoes. Most North African women socialize only in their homes.

North Africa is famous for beautiful hand-woven carpets. These carpets are woven with bright colors and complex geometric patterns. Detailed hand-painted tilework is also a major art form in the region. North Africans also enjoy popular music based on singing and poetry. The musical scale there has many more notes than are common in Western music, which makes the tunes seem to wail or waver.

> Underline the sentence that lists the holidays often observed in North Africa.

COUNTRIES OF NORTH AFRICA

Western Libya, Tunisia, Algeria, and Morocco are known as the **Maghreb.** The Sahara covers most of this region. Oil is the most important resource, and agriculture is a major economic activity. Tourism is also important, especially in Tunisia and Morocco. Marketplaces called **souks** jam the narrow streets of many North African cities, such as the Casbah in Algiers, the capital of Algeria. There they sell spices, carpets, copper teapots, and other goods. Tangier, in Morocco, overlooks the Strait of Gibraltar to Spain and is a **free port.** Almost no taxes are charged on goods sold there.

The countries of North Africa share similar economies and challenges. Until 2011 Muammar Gaddafi was Libya's dictator. His crackdown on protesters led to a civil war in which his regime

> Who was Libya's dictator until 2011?
>
> _____

toppled. The country's economy suffered after the civil war, but OPEC allowed Libya to increase oil production. The country's economy seems to be back on its way to recovery.

After a series of protests in 2011, Algeria's government has made reforms. It eased restrictions on the media, political parties, and the ability of women to serve in elected office. Since forcing longtime President Zine al-Abidine Ben Ali from power, Tunisia has held democratic elections and struggled with the role of Islam in government and society. Morocco is the only North African country with little oil, but it is an important producer and exporter of fertilizer.

CHALLENGE ACTIVITY

Critical Thinking: Categorize Create a chart that lists four cities in North Africa, and include facts about each one.

DIRECTIONS Read each sentence and fill in the blank with the word in the word pair that best completes the sentence.

1. Someone who rules a country with complete power is a _____. **(dictator/berber)**

2. Western Libya, Tunisia, Algeria, and Morocco make up the _____. **(Algiers/Maghreb)**

3. In the Casbah, _____ sell spices, carpets, copper teapots, and other goods. **(free ports/souks)**

4. Tangier is known as a _____, a city in which almost no taxes are placed on the goods it sells. **(free port/souk)**

5. The _____ was a wave of pro-democracy protests that occurred in 2011 in North Africa. **(Arab Spring/Nile delta)**

Algiers	Arab Spring	carpets	Casbah
dictator	free port	Maghreb	souks

DIRECTIONS Choose five of the terms from the word bank. Use these words to write a summary of what you learned in the section.

_____

_____

_____

_____

_____

_____

_____

_____

_____

History of Sub-Saharan Africa

MAIN IDEAS
1. The remains of early humans have been found at sites all around Africa.
2. During the Stone and Iron Ages, people learned to make increasingly complex tools and formed Africa's first societies.
3. Anthropologists have learned how early Africans adapted to different environments by studying modern cultures.

Key Terms and Places

Olduvai Gorge famous Stone Age site, located on the Serengeti Plain in Tanzania

hominids early ancestors of humans

hunter-gatherers people who hunted animals and gathered plants, seeds, and nuts for food

rock art drawings and paintings left on stone

nomads people who move from place to place in search of food or other needs

Lesson Summary

EARLY HUMAN SITES

Prehistory is the word historians use for the time before written records. The Stone Age was a very long period of prehistory. During the Stone Age, people made their tools and weapons from stone or bone. The **Olduvai Gorge** is perhaps the most famous Stone Age site in Africa. There, anthropologists have discovered the fossil remains of more than 60 **hominids.** These discoveries have helped scientists see how early humans developed and changed.

The first hominid discovery at Olduvai Gorge was made by anthropologist Mary Leakey in 1959. She found pieces of a skull belonging to an Australopithecus. About a year later, Mary and her husband Richard found bones from a different type of hominid. Scientists have also found the remains of two other hominid species at Olduvai Gorge. A species called *Homo erectus,*

> Circle the name of what is perhaps the most famous Stone Age site in Africa.

or "upright man," may have appeared in Africa about 1.5 million years ago. Scientists think these people walked completely upright and knew how to control fire. They used it to cook food, for heat, and as protection against wild animals. Modern humans are called *Homo sapiens*, or "wise man." Another Australopithecus was found in Ethiopia in 1974 by Donald Johanson. He named his find Lucy. In 1976, Mary Leakey found fossilized hominid footprints in Tanzania. Most of these finds were in East Africa, but hominid remains have been found in other parts of Africa. These discoveries have helped scholars trace the spread of early people across Africa.

> **How was Lucy similar to Mary Leakey's 1959 find?**
>
> _____
>
> _____
>
> _____

THE STONE AND IRON AGES

The Stone Age lasted more than 2.5 million years in some places. To make this long period of time easier to understand, scientists have divided it into three periods. In the Early Stone Age, people learned to shape stone into tools. They used these tools for tasks such as digging up roots and hunting small animals. The tools became more complex as time went by. The hand ax, usually made of flint, was shaped into a rough oval. One side of the oval was sharpened for cutting. The other side was rounded, making it easier to hold. Early Stone Age people were **hunter-gatherers** who lived in caves for protection from weather and animals. At times, they decorated these caves with scenes of hunting or other activities. This **rock art** can be found throughout Africa.

> **Why was the hand ax easier to use than the first stone tools?**
>
> _____
>
> _____
>
> _____
>
> _____

The Middle Stone Age began at different times in different parts of Africa. Tools made in the Middle Stone Age were smaller and had sharper edges. People attached handles of bone or wood to these tools to make spears, axes, and other useful tools. New tools helped people adapt to new environments and settle in other parts of Africa.

In the Later Stone Age, people made advanced tools, including knives and saws. They also used the bow and arrow for hunting. They wove baskets and made pottery containers for cooking and storage. People all over Africa learned to plant crops and herd animals. This provided a steady supply of food and allowed people to settle in permanent communities. People in these communities developed distinct lifestyles.

The Stone Age ended when people learned how to make tools out of metal. Iron was the most common metal used to make tools in Africa. Iron tools are very strong and sharp. Evidence shows that Africans had begun making iron tools in some places by about 600 BC.

> **Underline the sentence that describes iron tools.**

AFRICANS ADAPT TO DIFFERENT ENVIRONMENTS

As people settled various parts of Africa during the Stone Age, they developed distinct cultures. These cultures were influenced by the surrounding environment. Some African cultures remained in the Stone Age until modern times. Anthropologists have studied the traditional ways of these modern Stone Age cultures, and this has helped them understand how people lived thousands of years ago. The Bambuti people live in the tropical rain forests of the Congo Basin. They are **nomads** who use bows, arrows, and spears to hunt animals. They gather wild yams, fruits, berries, and other plants. The San people of the Kalahari Desert are also hunter-gatherers. They use tools of wood, bone, reeds, and stone. They hunt with snares, by throwing sticks, and with bows and arrows. They have learned to adapt to their dry environment. The Maasai people in the savanna of East Africa have also adapted to their environment. They herd cattle and other animals instead of hunting and gathering. They are known as fierce warriors.

> **Circle the names of three Stone Age cultures. Underline the words that describe their environments.**

Guided Reading Workbook

CHALLENGE ACTIVITY

Critical Thinking: Explain In what ways did humans develop during the Stone Age? Write a short paragraph to explain your answer.

DIRECTIONS Read each sentence and fill in the blank with the word in the word pair that best completes the sentence.

1. One of the most famous Stone Age sites in Africa is the _____.
   (Congo Basin/Olduvai Gorge)

2. Both Mary Leakey and Donald Johanson discovered bones of a _____, an early human ancestor. **(hominid/hunter-gatherer)**

3. The Bambuti people live in temporary homes because they are _____. **(hominids/nomads)**

4. Stone Age people sometimes decorated their shelters with _____ showing scenes of hunting. **(rock art/Olduvai Gorge)**

5. Early Stone Age people were _____ who ate game and wild plants. **(Australopithecus/hunter-gatherers)**

DIRECTIONS Write two words or phrases that describe each term.

6. Olduvai Gorge

_____

7. Stone Age people

_____

8. rock art

_____

_____

History of Sub-Saharan Africa

MAIN IDEAS

1. Christianity became the major religion in Aksum and Ethiopia.
2. Through its control of trade, Ghana built an empire.
3. The empire of Mali built upon the foundation laid by Ghana, but the empire fell to invaders in the 1400s.
4. Songhai took over West Africa and built a new Islamic empire, conquering many of the lands that were once part of Mali.
5. Bantu peoples established several kingdoms as they migrated through Africa.

Key Terms and Places

Coptic Christianity new form of Christianity that blended local African customs with Christian teachings

silent barter process in which people exchange goods without ever contacting each other directly

Timbuktu important trade city in Mali

mosque building for Muslim prayer

Gao capital of Songhai

Djenné city that was a center of learning in Songhai

Bantu migration widespread movement of Bantu people out of West Africa between 5,000 and 2,000 years ago

Lesson Summary

CHRISTIAN KINGDOMS IN AFRICA

New kingdoms developed in Africa. One of those kingdoms was Aksum (AHK-soom), located near the Red Sea in northeast Africa. As Aksum became a major trading power, people from various cultures gathered there. As these people met to trade goods, they also traded ideas and beliefs. One of the beliefs brought to Aksum by traders was Christianity. In the late 300s, Aksum's most famous ruler, King Ezana (AY-zah-nah), made Christianity the kingdom's official religion.

Aksum developed ties with other Christian states and became an ally of the Byzantine

> Circle the name of the Aksum ruler who made Christianity the kingdom's official religion.

Empire. However, in the 600s and 700s, Muslim armies from Southwest Asia conquered most of North Africa. Though Aksum itself was never conquered, it became isolated from other lands. The descendants of the Aksum people formed a new kingdom called Ethiopia. By about 1150, Ethiopia had become a powerful kingdom. Like Aksum, Ethiopia was a Christian kingdom. Shared beliefs helped unify Ethiopians, but their isolation from other Christians led to changes in their beliefs. Some local African customs blended with Christian teachings. This resulted in a new form of Christianity called **Coptic Christianity.** Most Christians who live in North Africa today belong to Coptic churches.

When did Ethiopia become a powerful kingdom?
_____
_____

GHANA CONTROLS TRADE

Ghana's territory lay between the Sahara Desert to the north and deep forests to the south. Salt was found in the Sahara, and gold was mined in the south. Ghana was in a good position to control trade in these items. This trade often followed the process of **silent barter.** This ensured peaceful trading and kept the location of the gold mines secret from the salt traders. The power of Ghana and its rulers grew as trade increased.

What made Ghana powerful?
_____
_____

By 800 Ghana controlled West Africa's trade routes. Ghana's army protected traders. Traders paid taxes on goods they brought into Ghana and goods they took out. The people of Ghana also paid taxes. The kings conquered more territory and became rich. The empire of Ghana reached its peak under the ruler Tunka Manin.

By the end of the 1200s, Ghana had collapsed. Three major factors contributed to its decline. First, a Muslim group called the Almoravids invaded and weakened the empire. Second, the Almoravids brought herds of animals that overgrazed pastures. This ruined the farmland and caused many farmers to leave. The third

List three reasons for the decline of Ghana's empire.
_____
_____
_____
_____

factor was a rebellion by people Ghana had conquered.

MALI BUILDS ON GHANA'S FOUNDATION

Once Ghana's empire fell, Mali took control of the trade routes. Mali became powerful under a ruler named Sundiata (soohn-JAHT-ah). He freed Mali from a cruel ruler. Then he conquered nearby kingdoms, including Ghana, and took over the salt and gold trades and the religious and political authority. Mali reached its peak under a Muslim named Mansa Musa. Musa ruled Mali for about 25 years and captured many important trading cities, including **Timbuktu.** On his pilgrimage to Mecca, he brought attention to Islam throughout West Africa by building **mosques.** After Mansa Musa died, invaders destroyed the schools and mosques of Timbuktu. By 1500 nearly all the lands of the Mali empire were lost.

> Name two important things Mansa Musa did as leader of Mali.
>
> _____
>
> _____
>
> _____
>
> _____

SONGHAI TAKES OVER

As the empire of Mali reached its height, the Songhai (SAHNG-hy) kingdom was growing strong. From their capital at **Gao,** the Songhai participated in the same trade that had made Ghana and Mali rich. When Mali control weakened, the Songhai broke free. Songhai leader Sunni Ali strengthened and enlarged the Songhai empire. Songhai reached its peak under a ruler named Askia the Great. Muslim culture and education blossomed during Askia's reign. Timbuktu's universities, schools, libraries, and mosques attracted thousands of people. **Djenné** was an important center of learning. In 1591, Morocco invaded Songhai and destroyed Gao and Timbuktu. Changes in trade patterns completed Songhai's fall. Port cities became more important and replaced trading over land routes.

> Circle the names of two cities that were important centers of learning in the Songhai empire.

Guided Reading Workbook

The period of great West African empires came to an end.

BANTU KINGDOMS

The name *Bantu* describes 400 ethnic groups with origins in West Africa. The word *bantu* means "people." Between 5,000 and 2,000 years ago, the Bantu people began spreading out from West Africa. Historians call this widespread movement of people the **Bantu migration.** No one is certain why the Bantu migrated. By about AD 300, Bantu peoples had conquered and settled much of Africa south of the Sahara.

Some Bantu groups formed kingdoms. One such kingdom was Great Zimbabwe, founded by the Shona people about the year 1,000. Great Zimbabwe was a trading center. Merchants carried valuable products, especially gold. It is estimated that traders carried more than 2,000 pounds of gold through the city every year. In the 1400s, Great Zimbabwe began to decline. Scholars are not sure why, but some believe that drought and environmental issues could have contributed to its fall. By 1500 Great Zimbabwe was abandoned.

> Underline the sentence that explains the amount of gold traded each year in Great Zimbabwe.

Another powerful Bantu kingdom, the Kongo Kingdom, formed in Central Africa in the 1300s along the Congo river. From their capital at Mbanza, Kongo's rulers oversaw the growth of a profitable trade network. In the 1400s, Portuguese traders arrived in Kongo. At first, relations between the two groups were good. Soon, however, the Portuguese became more interested in trading slaves. Kongo's rulers became alarmed and tried to stop the slave trade, but met with little success. In response, they cut off ties with Portugal. Without this wealthy trade partner, Kongo began to decline. The Portuguese later returned and took over the struggling kingdom.

> When was the Kongo Kingdom formed?
>
> _____
>
> _____

CHALLENGE ACTIVITY

Critical Thinking: Draw Conclusions Re-create
the silent barter system in the classroom. Work
with a partner to simulate a gold trader and a salt
trader exchanging goods in the silent barter
system. Then, with your partner, write a one-page
paper detailing the advantages and disadvantages
of the silent barter system.

Bantu migration	Coptic Christianity	Djenné
Gao	mosque	silent barter
Timbuktu		

DIRECTIONS Answer each question by writing a sentence that
contains at least one word from the word bank.

1. What "new" religion was formed in North Africa?

   _____

   _____

2. How was trade conducted in Ghana?

   _____

   _____

3. What was one way Mansa Musa spread Islam throughout West Africa?

   _____

4. What was the capital of Songhai?

   _____

5. Describe two cities of cultural importance during the reign of Askia.

   _____

   _____

6. What was the widespread movement of people out of West Africa called?

   _____

   _____

History of Sub-Saharan Africa

MAIN IDEAS
1. Trade led to the spread of Islam in East Africa.
2. Europeans arrived in Africa in search of valuable trade goods.
3. The slave trade had terrible effects in Africa.
4. Many European countries established colonies in Africa.

Key Terms and Places

Swahili language and culture created from blending African and Arab influences

Middle Passage brutal trip to take slaves across the Atlantic

Gold Coast first European colony in West Africa

Lesson Summary

TRADE IN EAST AFRICA

In the 1100s farmers and fishers lived in small villages along Africa's eastern coast. Their lives changed when traders from Asia traveled to Africa. Some traders were Muslims from India, Persia, and Arabia. They were looking for new kinds of goods they could sell at home. They also wanted Africans to buy goods from their homelands. African traders became rich by selling ivory, gold, and other items.

Growing trade caused coastal villages to become busy seaports. By 1300 they became major trading cities. Merchants from many countries brought manufactured goods, porcelain, and cotton. They traded their goods for East African cloth and iron. Muslim traders settled in many cities. Africans, Arabs, and Persians lived and worked together. As a result, Islam spread throughout East Africa.

The contact between cultures caused other changes in East Africa. For example, architecture changed. People combined traditional materials with Arabic designs for their houses. Language

> Circle the words that tell why coastal villages became busy seaports.

> List two things that changed because of the contact between cultures.
>
> _____
> _____

also changed. Africans who spoke Bantu adopted Arabic and Persian words. The languages combined to form **Swahili,** a new language. Swahili also refers to the blended African-Arab culture.

THE ARRIVAL OF EUROPEANS

In the late 1400s, many European explorers searched for new trade routes to India and China. The Portuguese sailed around Africa. Europeans had heard rumors about gold in Africa. The stories were about Mansa Musa, the ruler of Mali. In the 1300s he traveled to Mecca. He gave away gifts of gold as he traveled. The Portuguese reached the coasts of West Africa. They learned that the stories were true.

Ivory was another valuable product in Africa. Europeans used it for furniture, jewelry, statues, and other items. The Portuguese traded mostly in gold and ivory. Soon they found they could make more money by selling slaves.

> Underline the sentence that tells what Europeans had heard about Africa.

THE ATLANTIC SLAVE TRADE

Slavery had existed in Africa for centuries. Most slaves had been captured in battle or from attacks on enemies. The arrival of Europeans in West Africa increased the demand for slaves. Europeans wanted Africans to work as slaves on their large farms in the Americas. They bought the captured slaves and put them on ships. The brutal trip to take slaves across the Atlantic was called the **Middle Passage.** Slave traders made a lot of money. Some Europeans argued against it, but it continued for more than 300 years. European governments finally stopped the slave trade in the 1800s.

The slave trade had terrible effects in Africa. It caused a sharp drop in Africa's population. Many millions of Africans were taken to the Americas, Europe, Asia, and the Middle East. The push to

> When did the European governments stop the slave trade?
>
> _____
> _____

> Underline the sentences that describe the slave trade's effects on Africa.

capture slaves also caused years of war between African kingdoms. The wars reduced the population and caused mistrust between Africans.

EUROPEAN COLONIES IN AFRICA

Portuguese merchants became very rich by trading in gold, ivory, and slaves. Other European countries envied Portugal. Several countries competed to establish colonies in Africa.

The Portuguese established the **Gold Coast** in 1482. It was the first European colony in West Africa. Europeans established other West African colonies in the 1500s. Most colonies were named for the products traded there, such as the Ivory Coast. Europeans built forts that were trading centers and military outposts.

> **What was the first European colony in West Africa?**
>
> _____
> _____

Only the Portuguese were interested in East Africa. They persuaded the rulers of strong kingdoms there to go to war with each other. Then the Portuguese made the winners their allies. Later, Muslims arrived. They forced the Portuguese out of most of the region.

CHALLENGE ACTIVITY

Critical Thinking: Identify Cause and Effect Africa became an important region for global trade. Merchants from many countries arrived. Trade changed its land and people. Write a short paragraph describing the causes and effects of trade in Africa.

DIRECTIONS Read each sentence and fill in the blank with the word in the word pair that best completes the sentence.

1. The contact between Africans, Arabs, and Persians resulted in
   _____. (**colonies/Swahili**)

2. _____ had existed in Africa for centuries. (**Slavery/ Warfare**)

3. Europeans put slaves on ships and took them to the Americas by the
   _____. (**Gold Coast/Middle Passage**)

4. The _____ persuaded rulers of African kingdoms to go to war with each other. (**Portuguese/Muslims**)

5. The Portuguese established the _____ in West Africa in 1482. (**Gold Coast/Ivory Coast**)

DIRECTIONS Write two words or phrases that describe each term.

6. Swahili

   _____

   _____

7. Middle Passage

   _____

   _____

8. Gold Coast

   _____

   _____

History of Sub-Saharan Africa

MAIN IDEAS
1. The search for raw materials led to a new wave of European involvement in Africa.
2. The Scramble for Africa was a race by Europeans to form colonies there.
3. Some Africans resisted rule by Europeans.
4. Nationalism led to independence movements in Africa.

Key Terms and Places

entrepreneurs independent businesspeople

imperialism attempt to dominate a country's government, trade, or culture

ethnocentrism belief that your own group or culture is better or more important than others

Suez Canal waterway built in Egypt in the 1860s to connect the Mediterranean and Red Seas

Berlin Conference meeting of European leaders that led to the division of Africa among European powers

Boers Dutch farmers in South Africa

nationalism devotion or loyalty to a country

Lesson Summary
NEW INVOLVEMENT IN AFRICA

After the slave trade ended in the early 1800s, Europeans lost interest in Africa. However, factory owners needed raw materials. The huge open spaces and mineral wealth of Africa drew new colonists. Most were **entrepreneurs** who built mines, plantations, and trade routes with the dream of becoming rich. They often tried to dominate the government, trade, or culture of a country, a practice called **imperialism.** They believed that their own government and culture were better than native African ways. Because of this European **ethnocentrism,** Africans were forced to adopt many elements of European culture.

What did entrepreneurs hope to gain in Africa?
_____
_____

European governments also became involved in Africa. This was often an extension of national rivalries. Each country wanted to control more land and more colonies than its rivals did. The English government got involved in Africa to protect British investments in the **Suez Canal.** Egypt's government was unstable in the 1880s. This made the British fear they would lose access to the canal. The British moved into Egypt and took partial control of the country to protect their shipping routes. In South Africa, diamonds were discovered. The De Beers Consolidated Mine Company, owned by Englishman Cecil Rhodes, came to control the diamond market.

> **In what way did European rivalries extend to Africa?**
>
> _____
> _____
> _____
> _____
> _____
> _____

THE SCRAMBLE FOR AFRICA

European countries rushed to claim as much land in Africa as they could. Conflicts arose as countries tried to claim the same area. To prevent these conflicts from developing into wars, Europe's leaders met in the **Berlin Conference** to divide up Africa. The boundaries they drew for their colonies often divided kingdoms, clans, and families. In time, the Europeans' disregard for Africans led to problems for Europeans and Africans alike. In South Africa, war broke out between British and Dutch settlers. The **Boers** had been in South Africa since the late 1600s. In 1899, the British tried to make the Boers' land part of the British Empire. The Boers fought a guerrilla war, but the British dealt harshly with them. South Africa became a British colony.

> **What was the purpose of the Berlin Conference?**
>
> _____
> _____
> _____

AFRICAN RESISTANCE

The African people fought against rule by Europeans and against adopting European ways. Especially strong resistance came from the Zulu of South Africa and the Ethiopians. A Zulu leader named Shaka brought together various tribes to form a single nation. This nation was so

> **How did Shaka make the Zulu people especially strong?**
>
> _____
> _____
> _____
> _____
> _____

strong that Europeans were hesitant to enter Zulu territory. Shaka's death weakened the Zulu, but they continued to fight off the British for more than 50 years. In the end, however, the superior weapons of the British helped them defeat the Zulu. Zulu lands were made into a new British colony.

While other African lands fell to European control, the kingdom of Ethiopia remained free. It is the only country in Africa that was never a European colony. It was successful fighting the Europeans mainly because of one man, Emperor Menelik II. He saw that European strength was based on modern weapons, so he created a powerful Ethiopian army equipped with modern weapons. As a result, when Italy invaded Ethiopia in 1895, the Ethiopian army was victorious. This victory in the Battle of Adwa is celebrated as a high point in Ethiopian history.

> **Underline the sentence that explains how Emperor Menelik II made Ethiopia strong?**

NATIONALISM AND INDEPENDENCE

In the early 20th century, many Africans grew increasingly unhappy with European rule. African soldiers fought alongside Europeans in World War II. The experience made them less willing to accept colonial rule at home. Across Africa, Africans began to call for political independence. A growing sense of **nationalism** fueled independence movements. South Africa was one of the first African colonies to gain independence in 1909, followed by Nigeria in 1960 and Kenya in 1963.

CHALLENGE ACTIVITY

Critical Thinking: Analyze How was nationalism a result of imperialism and ethnocentrism?

DIRECTIONS Read each sentence and fill in the blank with the word in the word pair that best completes the sentence.

1. The quest for raw materials led _____ to Africa. **(entrepreneurs/imperialists)**

2. _____ led Europeans to force Africans to adopt many elements of European culture. **(Nationalism/Ethnocentrism)**

3. Concern over the safety of the Suez Canal in the late 1880s led _____ to take partial control of Egypt. **(Britain/France)**

4. The De Beers Consolidated Mine Company controlled the market in _____. **(gold/diamonds)**

5. The only African country that was never a European colony is _____. **(Zulu/Ethiopia)**

Berlin Conference	Boers	entrepreneur
ethnocentrism	imperialism	nationalism
Suez Canal		

DIRECTIONS Answer each question by writing a sentence that contains at least one word from the word bank.

6. How and why did the Europeans divide up Africa?

_____

_____

7. What happened before South Africa could become a British colony?

_____

_____

_____

8. How did African soldiers help the cause for independence in Africa after World War II?

_____

_____

_____

Guided Reading Workbook

West and Central Africa

MAIN IDEAS
1. West Africa's key physical features include plains and the Niger River.
2. West Africa has distinct climate and vegetation zones, such as arid and tropical.
3. Central Africa's major physical features include the Congo Basin and plateaus surrounding the basin.
4. Central Africa has a humid tropical climate and dense forest vegetation.

Key Terms and Places

Niger River most important river in West Africa

zonal organized by zone

Sahel strip of land that divides the desert from wetter areas

desertification spread of desert-like conditions

savanna area of tall grasses and scattered trees and shrubs

Congo Basin basin near the middle of Central Africa

basin generally flat region surrounded by higher land such as mountains and plateaus

Congo River river that drains the Congo Basin and empties into the Atlantic Ocean

Zambezi River river that flows eastward toward the Indian Ocean

Lesson Summary
PHYSICAL FEATURES OF WEST AFRICA

The main physical features in West Africa are plains and rivers. Most of the region's cities are on the plains along the coast. People on inland plains usually farm or raise animals. The **Niger River** is the most important river in the region. It provides water for farming, fishing, and transportation.

> Underline the sentence that describes the importance of the Niger River to the region.

CLIMATE AND VEGETATION

West Africa has four **zonal** climate regions that run in east to west bands. The zone farthest north is part of the largest desert in the world, the Sahara. The **Sahel,** south of the Sahara, has a steppe climate where enough plants grow to support some grazing animals. Overgrazing and cutting trees for firewood have caused **desertification.** The third zonal area, the **savanna,** is a good area for farming. The coastal areas have a humid tropical climate with tropical forests. The climate of the savanna is milder than other parts of Africa. The fourth climate zone lies along the coasts of the Atlantic and the Gulf of Guinea. This zone has a humid tropical climate with plentiful rainfall.

What are two causes of desertification?
_____
_____

PHYSICAL FEATURES OF CENTRAL AFRICA

The **Congo Basin** lies near the middle of the region. Plateaus and low hills surround the **basin.** A basin is shaped like a big soup bowl with a wide brim. The highest mountains in Central Africa lie east along the Western Rift Valley. The **Congo River** drains the Congo Basin and has hundreds of smaller rivers flowing into it. The many rapids and waterfalls prevent ships sailing from the interior to the Atlantic. Many rivers join the **Zambezi River** before it reaches the Indian Ocean. Victoria Falls is the most famous falls on the Zambezi River.

Where are the tallest mountains in the region found?
_____
_____
_____

CLIMATE, VEGETATION, AND ANIMALS

The Congo Basin and much of the Atlantic coast have a humid tropical climate. The dense tropical forests that grow in this climate are home to gorillas, elephants, wild boars, and okapis. Since little sunlight shines through the canopy, only a few animals live on the forest floor. Birds, monkeys, bats, and snakes live in the trees. Areas north and south of the Congo Basin have a tropical savanna climate. The mountains in the east have a highland climate. The southern part of the region has dry steppe and desert climates.

Name four animals that make their home in the tropical forests.
_____
_____
_____

CHALLENGE ACTIVITY

Critical Thinking: Draw Conclusions Describe
how desertification and deforestation are
impacting West and Central Africa. What
conclusions can be drawn about these issues?

DIRECTIONS Read each sentence and fill in the blank with the
word in the word pair that best completes the sentence.

1. _____ in the Sahel is causing the expansion of the
   Sahara. (**Deforestation/Desertification**)

2. The _____ brings life-giving water to West Africa.
   (**Niger River/Zambezi River**)

3. The Congo River drains the _____. (**Congo Basin/Sahel**)

4. Victoria Falls is on the _____. (**Niger River/Zambezi
   River**)

DIRECTIONS Write three words or phrases that describe each term.

5. savanna

   _____

   _____

6. zonal

   _____

   _____

7. basin

   _____

   _____

West and Central Africa

MAIN IDEAS

1. In West Africa's history, trade made great kingdoms rich, but this greatness declined as Europeans began to control trade routes.
2. The culture of West Africa includes many different ethnic groups, languages, religions, and housing styles.
3. Most coastal countries of West Africa have struggling economies and weak or unstable governments.
4. Lack of resources in the Sahel countries is a main challenge to economic development.

Key Terms and Places

Timbuktu cultural center of the Songhai Empire in the 1500s

animism belief that bodies of water, animals, trees, and other natural objects have spirits

extended family group of family members that includes the father, mother, children, and close relatives in one household

Lagos former capital of Nigeria and the most populous city in West Africa

famine extreme shortage of food

Lesson Summary

HISTORY

Ghana became rich and powerful by controlling trade in gold and salt across the Sahara. Later, the empire of Mali controlled the trade routes and supported artists and scholars. **Timbuktu** was the cultural center of the empire of Songhai. Europeans began the Atlantic slave trade in the 1500s. By the time the slave trade ended in the 1800s, millions of Africans had been taken from their homes. European countries claimed colonies in the late 1800s so they could have access to West African resources. Europeans built schools, roads, and railroads, but they also created problems for West Africans. All the countries in West Africa were independent by 1974.

> Underline the names of the three African trading empires.

Guided Reading Workbook

CULTURE

West Africa is the world's fastest growing region. Its culture reflects traditional African cultures, European culture, and Islam. There are hundreds of ethnic groups and languages in the region. Europeans drew the national boundaries without considering these ethnic groups or their rivalries, so many West Africans are more loyal to their ethnic group than to their country. Traditional religions are forms of **animism.** Islam and Christianity are also practiced. Some people in the region wear Western-style clothing. Others wear traditional cotton clothing, which is loose and flowing. Rural homes are made from mud or straw and have straw or tin roofs. **Extended families** often live close together in a village. An extended family includes the father, mother, children and close relatives in one household.

> Circle three influences on West African societies.

COASTAL COUNTRIES

Nigeria has the largest population in Africa and the region's strongest economy. There is conflict among the many different ethnic groups within Nigeria. After many years of military rule, Nigeria is now a democracy. Its most important resource is oil, which accounts for 95 percent of the country's export earnings. The main industrial center is **Lagos.** Nigeria has many resources but poverty is a problem. This is due partly to the high birthrate and corrupt government.

> What are two causes of poverty in Nigeria?
>
> _____
>
> _____

Small countries along the coast struggle to develop their economies and stabilize their governments. Senegal and Gambia produce peanuts and offer tourism sites. Guinea has some bauxite reserves. Guinea-Bissau has undeveloped mineral resources. Cape Verde is West Africa's only island country and has a democratic government. Liberia was founded for freed slaves. Both Liberia and Sierra Leone have suffered

> What two countries produce peanuts and offer tourism?
>
> _____
>
> _____

from violent civil war. They are now trying to rebuild. Ghana and Côte d'Ivoire have rich natural resources. Unstable governments and poor farming economies have hurt Togo and Benin.

SAHEL COUNTRIES

Drought and the expanding desert challenge the Sahel countries. Former nomads in Mauritania are now crowded into cities. Ethnic tensions continue to cause problems there. Niger has a very small amount of farmland where people grow staple crops. Drought and locusts created **famine** there in the early 2000s. Chad depends on fishing in Lake Chad and farming. Much of Lake Chad's water has evaporated in recent years, creating conflict over control of the remaining water. Chad began exporting oil in 2004. Much of Mali is desert with some farming in the south. It is one of the poorest countries in the world, but its economy is improving. Burkina Faso is also very poor and has few resources. Conflicts in the region have hurt its economy.

> Underline the causes of famine in Niger.

CHALLENGE ACTIVITY

Critical Thinking: Draw Inferences Write a letter to a newspaper to explain the problems that could arise from creating borders that put different ethnic groups in one country or separating ethnic groups into different countries.

animism	extended family	famine
Lagos	Timbuktu	

DIRECTIONS On the line provided before each statement, write **T** if a statement is true and **F** if a statement is false. If the statement is false, write the correct term from the word bank on the line after each sentence to make the sentence a true statement.

_____ 1. The city of <u>Lagos</u> served as a cultural center in the empire of Songhai.

_____

_____ 2. Traditional African religions are forms of <u>animism</u>.

_____

_____ 3. Family members—father, mother, children, and close relatives—living in one household are known as <u>ancestors</u>.

_____

_____ 4. The most populous city in West Africa is <u>Lagos</u>.

_____

_____ 5. Drought and locusts created <u>civil war</u> in Niger.

_____

West and Central Africa

> **MAIN IDEAS**
> 1. Great African kingdoms and European colonizers have influenced the history of Central Africa.
> 2. The culture of Central Africa includes many ethnic groups and languages, but it has also been influenced by European colonization.
> 3. The countries of Central Africa are mostly poor, and many are trying to recover from years of civil war.
> 4. Challenges to peace, health, and the environment slow economic development in Central Africa.

Key Terms and Places

Kongo Kingdom one of the most important kingdoms in Central Africa, founded in the 1300s near the mouth of the Congo River

dialects regional varieties of a language

period market open-air trading market that is set up once or twice a week

copper belt area where copper is found in northern Zambia and southern Democratic Republic of the Congo

Kinshasa capital of the Democratic Republic of the Congo

inflation rise in prices that occurs when currency loses its buying power

malaria disease spread by mosquitoes that causes fever and pain

malnutrition condition of not getting enough nutrients from food

Lesson Summary
HISTORY

People of the **Kongo Kingdom** set up trade routes and grew rich from trade in animal skins, shells, slaves, and ivory. Europeans arrived in the 1400s and traded for these forest products and for slaves. In the late 1800s France, the United Kingdom, Belgium, Germany, Spain, and Portugal divided Central Africa into colonies. These colonial borders ignored the homelands of different groups and put groups with different languages and customs together, which created conflict. These colonies gained independence after World War II. The last was Angola, which won its freedom from Portugal in 1975. After

What problems did colonial borders create for the people of the region?
_____
_____
_____
_____
_____

Guided Reading Workbook

independence, fighting continued among ethnic groups within the new countries. During the Cold War, the Soviet Union and the United States supported different groups in small wars that killed many people.

CULTURE

Many different languages and **dialects** are spoken in Central Africa. Most countries also have official European languages because of the influence of the European colonial powers. The colonial powers also brought Christianity to the region. Many Muslims live near the Sahel, and Muslims and Hindus live in Zambia.

The traditional cultures of Central Africa's ethnic groups have influenced the arts. The region is famous for sculpture, carved wooden masks, and colorful cotton gowns. The region is also the birthplace of a popular musical instrument called the *likembe*, or thumb piano, and a type of dance music called *makossa*.

> **What impact did colonial powers have on the culture of Central Africa?**
>
> _____
> _____
> _____
> _____
> _____
> _____

RESOURCES AND COUNTRIES OF CENTRAL AFRICA

Most Central African countries are very poor. Because of colonial rule and civil wars, they have had problems building stable governments and strong economies.

Most people are subsistence farmers but are beginning to grow crops for sale. Common crops are coffee, bananas, and corn. In rural areas people sell goods at **periodic markets.** Rivers are important for travel, trade, and production of hydroelectricity. Timber, oil, natural gas, coal, copper, uranium, tin, zinc, diamonds, gold, and cobalt are found in the region. Most of Africa's copper is in the **copper belt.** However, political problems and poor transportation have kept these resources from being fully developed. Civil war, bad government, and crime have scared away foreign businesses.

Many people live in rural areas, but many are moving to the capital, **Kinshasa.** The city is crowded and has many slums. The Democratic Republic of the Congo was a Belgian colony until 1960. A military leader named Joseph Mobutu came to power in 1965 and ruled as a dictator. In 1997, after a civil war, a new government took over. The country has many mineral resources and is part of Centra Africa's rich copper belt.

Central African Republic has had military coups, corrupt leaders, and improper elections. Civil wars in the Republic of the Congo and Angola have hurt their governments and economies. Angola is troubled also by land mines left from its civil war, high **inflation,** and corrupt officials. The economies of many countries depend heavily on the sale of natural resources like oil, copper, and diamonds, or on export crops like coffee and cocoa. The Republic of the Congo has oil and forest products. Angola has diamonds and large oil deposits. Zambia's economy depends on copper mining. Malawi relies on farming and foreign aid. Oil discoveries in Equatorial Guinea and São Tomé and Príncipe may help their economies improve. Cameroon's stable government has helped its economy grow. It has good roads and railways. Gabon also has a stable government. Its economy is the strongest in the region. Half of its income comes from oil.

> Circle the issues that make progress difficult for Angola.

ISSUES AND CHALLENGES

The region faces serious challenges from wars, diseases such as **malaria** and AIDS, and threats to the environment. Deaths from wars and diseases have resulted in fewer older, more skilled workers. Other issues include food shortages and **malnutrition.** The region is also threatened by the destruction of tropical forests and the open-pit mining of diamonds and copper, which destroys the land.

> What diseases are creating challenges in Central Africa?
>
> _____
>
> _____

Guided Reading Workbook

CHALLENGE ACTIVITY

Critical Thinking: Evaluate Do you
think colonial rule helped or hurt
the people of Central Africa?
Explain your answer in a paragraph.

DIRECTIONS Read each sentence and fill in the blank with the
word in the word pair that best completes the sentence.

1. _____ grew rich from trade in animal skins, shells, slaves, and
   ivory. (**Kinshasa/Kongo Kingdom**)

2. _____ are regional varieties of a language. (**Dialects/Makossa**)

3. _____, the capital of the Democratic Republic of the Congo,
   is a crowded city that consists mostly of poor slums. (**Cabinda/Kinshasa**)

4. A rise in prices that occurs when currency loses its buying power is called
   _____. (**debt/inflation**)

5. _____ is a disease spread by mosquitoes.
   (**Malaria/Malnutrition**)

6. The condition of not getting enough nutrients from food is called
   _____. (**malaria/malnutrition**)

East and Southern Africa

MAIN IDEAS
1. East and Southern Africa's physical features range from rift valleys to sweeping plateaus.
2. Location and elevation shape East and Southern Africa's climate and vegetation.
3. Water and minerals are vital resources in East and Southern Africa.

Key Terms and Places

Great Rift Valley largest rift on Earth, made up of the eastern rift and the western rift

rift valley long narrow valley with flat floors and steep walls

escarpment steep slope at the edge of a plateau or other raised area

Mount Kilimanjaro highest mountain in Africa

Serengeti Plain one of Tanzania's largest plains; home to abundant wildlife

veld open grassland areas of South Africa

Namib Desert desert located on the Atlantic coast of Southern Africa

droughts periods when little rain falls and crops are damaged

Lesson Summary
PHYSICAL FEATURES

Geographically, East and Southern Africa is a vast region with spectacularly varied landscapes and wildlife. The **Great Rift Valley** cuts across Africa from the Red Sea to Mozambique. **Rift valleys** are formed when tectonic plates pull away from one another along parallel fault lines. Rift walls are often steep cliffs that can rise as much as 6,000 feet. The Great Rift Valley is the largest rift on Earth.

The region also has many high plateaus. These are often bound by an **escarpment** or by mountains. Most of Southern Africa lies on a plateau that drops sharply towards coastal areas.

> Underline the sentence that describes the walls of rift valleys.

Guided Reading Workbook

The East Africa Plateau is cut by rift valleys. East Africa has many volcanic mountains. The tallest of these is **Mount Kilimanjaro.** Although the mountain is located near the equator, its peak is covered with ice and snow. Another area of high elevation is the Ethiopian Highlands.

Grassy plains cover wide areas of the plateaus in East and Southern Africa. The **Serengeti Plain** in Tanzania is one of the largest. Many kinds of wildlife live here, including elephants, giraffes, lions, and zebras. Tanzania established much of the plain as a national park. The flat plains of Southern Africa are home to animals such as lions, leopards, elephants, baboons, and antelope.

The Nile, the world's longest river, begins in East Africa. It is formed by the White Nile and the Blue Nile. The White Nile flows from Lake Victoria. The Blue Nile begins in the Ethiopian Highlands. Both rivers meet in Sudan to form the Nile. Many large rivers cross Southern Africa's plains. The Okavango flows from Angola into a huge basin in Botswana. There, it forms a swampy inland delta that is home to crocodiles, zebras, hippos, and other animals. The Orange River passes through the Augrabies Falls and flows into the Atlantic Ocean.

CLIMATE AND VEGETATION

East Africa is cooler and dryer than other equatorial regions. This is because of the high elevations and the rain shadow effect that blocks wet weather from the region. The plateaus and mountains north of the equator have a cool highland climate and dense forests. A large savanna region extends south from the Equator and covers much of East and Southern Africa. In South Africa, these grasslands are known as the **veld.** The Kalahari Desert has grasses and shrubs in the north, but in the southwest it merges with

> **What is surprising about Mount Kilimanjaro?**
> _____
> _____
> _____
> _____

> **Underline examples of wildlife that can be found on the Serengeti Plain.**

> **Where is the veld located?**
> _____

the **Namib Desert.** Parts of the Namib Desert get as little as half an inch of rainfall in a year. Madagascar, off the mainland, has lush vegetation and tropical forests. It also has many animals that are found only in Madagascar. Unfortunately, rain forest destruction has endangered many of Madagascar's animals.

RESOURCES

Water is a vital resource in East and Southern Africa. Rivers supply hydroelectricity and water for irrigation. Where there is enough rain or where irrigation is possible, farmers can grow a wide range of crops. However, seasonal **droughts** are common. During a drought, crops and the grasses for cattle die, and people begin to starve. Important discoveries of gas and oil resources have been made in Mozambique, Tanzania, Uganda, and Kenya. Madagascar's forests provide timber. Most of the world's gold is mined in South Africa. Other mineral resources include diamonds, platinum, copper, uranium, coal, and iron ore. Mining is very important to Southern Africa's economy. However, mining can harm the surrounding natural environments.

> **What happens during a drought?**
> _____
> _____
> _____
> _____

CHALLENGE ACTIVITY

Critical Thinking: Summarize Write a booklet for tourists to read before they embark on a helicopter tour of East and Southern Africa. What might they find most interesting about the region?

DIRECTIONS Read each sentence and fill in the blank with the word
in the word pair that best completes the sentence.

1. _____ are formed when two tectonic plates move
   away from each other, stretching and breaking Earth's crust.
   (Rift valleys/Savannas)

2. _____ is the source of the White Nile.
   (Lake Victoria/Mount Kilimanjaro)

3. Many plateaus are bound by _____ that separate
   them from the land below. **(escarpments/veld)**

4. _____ is the highest point in Africa.
   (Lake Victoria/Mount Kilimanjaro)

5. The _____, Botswana's major river, flows into a
   huge basin and forms a swampy inland delta that is home to many animals.
   (Okavango River/Blue Nile)

6. The _____ in Tanzania is home to a great variety of
   wildlife. **(Serengeti Plain/Great Rift Valley)**

7. The open grassland areas of South Africa are known as the
   _____. **(veld/Namib Desert)**

8. The _____ has sandy plains, grasses, and scattered
   shrubs in its northern area. **(Kalahari Desert/Namib Desert)**

9. During a _____, little rain falls, and crops and
   animals die as a result. **(savanna/drought)**

East and Southern Africa

MAIN IDEAS
1. Religion, trade, and European imperialism have shaped East Africa's history.
2. East Africa is home to a diversity of languages and religions.
3. Though resource rich, nations in East Africa have suffered conflicts, poverty, and drought.
4. The Horn of Africa is one of the most troubled regions of the world.

Key Terms and Places

Zanzibar East African island that became an international slave-trading center in the late 1700s

imperialism practice that tries to dominate other countries' government, trade, and culture

safari overland journey to view African wildlife

geothermal energy energy produced from the heat of Earth's interior

Darfur region of Sudan

genocide intentional destruction of a people

Mogadishu port city in Somalia

Lesson Summary
HISTORY
Religion, imperialism, and independence movements have shaped the history of East Africa. Ethiopia was an early center of Christianity. A Christian emperor in Ethiopia named Lalibela built 11 rock churches in the early 1200s. Muslim Arabs from Egypt brought Islam into northern Sudan. Islamic trading centers on the East African coast exchanged products from overseas for coconut oil, copper, leopard skins, ivory, and gold from the interior. Enslaved Africans were also exported. The island of **Zanzibar** became a center of the international slave trade in the late 1700s. Industrialization in

European nations increased their need for raw materials. European powers claimed lands and set up colonies, a process called **imperialism.** They competed in Africa to get natural resources such as gold, ivory, and rubber. The British controlled much of East Africa. The boundaries European leaders drew split ethnic groups apart and combined unfriendly groups. Most colonial rulers used African deputies to control the countries. Many deputies were traditional chiefs who often favored their own peoples. This caused conflict between ethnic groups. After 1945, nationalist movements formed throughout Africa. Most East African countries gained independence in the early 1960s.

> Underline the sentence that explains the meaning of imperialism in Africa.

CULTURE

East Africa's history has contributed to its great diversity of people and ways of life. As a result, East Africans speak many different languages and practice several religions. French is the official language in Rwanda, Burundi, and Djibouti. English is spoken in Uganda, Kenya, and Tanzania. Swahili is an African language spoken by about 80 million East Africans. The largest religious groups are Christian and Muslim, but many East Africans follow traditional animist religions. Some people combine animist worship with religions such as Christianity.

> Circle the three main languages spoken in East Africa.

EAST AFRICA TODAY

Tanzania and Kenya are popular tourist destinations. Tourists take **safaris** to see the wildlife. Much of Kenya has been set aside as national parkland to protect wildlife. Tanzania is rich in gold and diamonds, but most of its people are subsistence farmers. Coffee, flowers, and tea grow well in the rich volcanic soil of Kenya. **Geothermal energy** is another important resource.

> Circle the crops grown in Kenya.

Guided Reading Workbook

Both nations have modern cities. Kenya's capital, Nairobi, is an industrial and railroad center. Tanzania's largest city, Dar es Salaam, is a business center with a busy port.

Sudan is a mix of Arab, Afro-Arab, and African cultures. Sudan's government has abused the human rights of ethnic and religious minorities. An Arab militia group has killed hundreds of thousands of people in a region of Sudan called **Darfur.** Uganda was a military dictatorship for several decades. It has been more democratic since 1986. About 80 percent of Ugandans work in agriculture. Coffee is the country's main export. Rwanda and Burundi have experienced conflict between ethnic groups, the Tutsi and Hutu. This conflict led to **genocide** in Rwanda in the 1990s, as the Hutu tried to completely wipe out the Tutsi.

> Underline the names of two ethnic groups in Rwanda and Burundi.

THE HORN OF AFRICA

Eritrea, Djibouti, Somalia, and Ethiopia make up the Horn of Africa. Eritrea was controlled by Italy, Great Britain, and Ethiopia. In 1992, after 32 years of armed conflict with Ethiopia, Eritrea gained independence. However, conflict and human rights abuses continue there. Djibouti is a small, desert country. It lies on an important shipping route, and its port is a major source of income. The Issa and the Afar people of Djibouti fought a civil war that ended in 2001.

> What four countries make up the Horn of Africa?
> _____
> _____
> _____
> _____

Somalia's deserts and dry savannas make poor farmland, but the economy still depends heavily on agriculture. Most Somalians are Muslim and share the same language and ethnic background. Still, the country is torn by chaos and violence, and there is no central government. Clans fight over grazing rights and control of port cities such as **Mogadishu.** Ethiopia is the only nation in the Horn of Africa that escaped European colonization. Ethiopia's mountains and

> Underline the descriptions of the land in Somalia and Ethiopia.

Guided Reading Workbook

highlands provide rich volcanic soil for
agriculture. Top exports include coffee,
vegetables, livestock, and oilseeds.

CHALLENGE ACTIVITY

Critical Thinking: Draw Conclusions Suppose
you joined a United Nations delegation in
East Africa. Propose ways the UN could
help people in the region.

Darfur	genocide	geothermal energy	imperialism
Mogadishu	safari	Zanzibar	

DIRECTIONS On the line provided before each statement, write **T** if
a statement is true and **F** if a statement is false. If the statement is
false, write the correct term from the word bank on the line after
each sentence to make it a true statement.

_____ 1. The English practiced <u>genocide</u> in East Africa as they tried to claim
   lands and set up colonies.

_____

_____ 2. The island of <u>Zanzibar</u> was once a slave-trading center.

_____

_____ 3. In Tanzania and Kenya, tourists can enjoy the wildlife on a <u>Darfur</u>.

_____

_____ 4. Energy that is produced from the heat of Earth's interior is called
   <u>geothermal energy</u>.

_____

_____ 5. Hatred between the Tutsi and the Hutu led to <u>imperialism</u> in Rwanda.

_____

_____ 6. Ethnic conflict in <u>Tanzania</u> led to hundreds of thousands of people
   being killed by an Arab militia group.

_____

_____ 7. In Somalia, different clans have fought for control of the port city of
   <u>Zanzibar</u>.

_____

East and Southern Africa

MAIN IDEAS
1. Southern Africa's history began with hunter-gatherers, followed by great empires and European settlements.
2. The cultures of Southern Africa are rich in different languages, religions, customs, and art.
3. The countries of Southern Africa are diverse in their resources and governments.
4. Today, the people of Southern Africa face economic, environmental, and health challenges.

Key Terms and Places

Great Zimbabwe stone-walled capital built by the Shona in the late 1000s

Cape of Good Hope area at the tip of Africa near where a trade station was set up by the Dutch in 1652

Boers Dutch farmers who had spread out from the original Cape colony

Afrikaners Dutch, French, and German settlers and their descendants living in South Africa

apartheid policy of racial separation set up by South Africa's government

townships separate areas where blacks had to live under apartheid

sanctions economic or political penalties imposed by one country on another to force a change in policy

Cape Town city in South Africa that attracts many tourists

enclave small territory surrounded by a foreign territory

Lesson Summary

HISTORY

The Shona, a Bantu group, farmed, raised cattle, and traded gold with other groups. Their capital, **Great Zimbabwe,** was the center of a large trading network. Later, Portuguese traders set up bases on the Southern African coast. In 1652 the Dutch built a trade station near the **Cape of Good Hope.** Some settlers became farmers and were known as **Boers.** European settlers on the Cape, called **Afrikaners,** eventually controlled rich deposits of gold and diamonds in the

Who were the Boers?
_____
_____

interior. The British fought and defeated the
Boers and the Zulu to control the Cape.

In 1910, South Africa gained independence
from Great Britain. The struggle for
independence in some other Southern African
nations was long and violent. South Africa was
ruled by whites. Black South Africans who
opposed them formed the African National
Congress (ANC). The white government set up a
policy called **apartheid,** which separated whites
and nonwhites. Blacks had to live in separate
areas called **townships** and had few rights. The
United States and other countries applied
sanctions on South Africa. In the 1990s, South
Africa ended its apartheid laws. ANC leader
Nelson Mandela was elected president.

Who formed the ANC?
_____
_____
_____
_____

CULTURE

Southern Africa's people belong to hundreds
of different ethnic groups. They speak many
languages, most of which are related to Khoisan
or Bantu. They practice different religions,
including Christianity and traditional African
religions. Southern Africa's arts reflect its many
cultures, using traditional ethnic designs and
crafts.

Most of Southern Africa's languages are related to what two languages?
_____
_____

SOUTHERN AFRICA TODAY

South Africa is a republic with an elected
president. It has a strong economy with valuable
mineral resources and industry. Johannesburg is
Africa's largest industrial area. **Cape Town**
attracts many tourists. Surrounded by South
Africa, Lesotho and Swaziland are both **enclaves.**
Both are also kingdoms, with a king and an
elected prime minister and parliament. Namibia
is a republic. Most of its income comes from
mineral resources. Fishing and ranching are also
important. Botswana is rich in mineral resources

What two things do Lesotho and Swaziland have in common?
_____
_____
_____
_____

and has a stable, democratic government. Cattle ranching and diamond mining are its main economic activities.

   Zimbabwe has suffered from a poor economy, political instability, and inequality. In 2000, the president began a land reform program, taking land from white farmers and giving it to black residents. However, white farmers left the country and food shortages resulted. Mozambique is one of the world's poorest countries. The economy was damaged by a civil war. It relies on taxes collected on products from the interior of Africa that are shipped out of its ports. Madagascar has a struggling economy. The country is popular with tourists because of its unique plants and animals. Comoros is made up of four tiny islands. It is politically unstable and lacks resources. However, the government hopes to improve education and promote tourism.

What makes Madagascar a tourist destination?
_____
_____

ISSUES AND CHALLENGES

Southern Africa faces many challenges, especially poverty, disease, and environmental destruction. The African Union (AU) is working to promote cooperation among African countries to try to solve these problems.

What is the AU and what is its purpose?
_____
_____
_____
_____

CHALLENGE ACTIVITY

Critical Thinking: Contrast Contrast the economies and governments of Botswana and Zimbabwe. Write one or two sentences to explain how they are different from one another.

Afrikaners	apartheid	Boers
Cape of Good Hope	Cape Town	enclave
Great Zimbabwe	sanctions	townships

DIRECTIONS On the line provided before each statement, write **T** if a statement is true and **F** if a statement is false. If the statement is false, write the correct term from the word bank on the line after each sentence to make the sentence a true statement.

_____ 1. The Shona built a large empire and constructed stone-walled towns, including <u>Mozambique</u>, the Shona capital.

_____

_____ 2. Dutch, French, and German settlers and their descendants in South Africa were called <u>Afrikaners</u>.

_____

_____ 3. The <u>Zulu</u> were Dutch farmers who resisted British authority in the Cape area.

_____

_____ 4. During apartheid, many blacks were forced to live in separate, crowded areas called <u>colonies</u>.

_____

DIRECTIONS Answer each question by writing a sentence or two that contains at least one term from the word bank.

_____ 5. How did other countries pressure South Africa to end apartheid?

_____

_____

_____ 6. How do South Africa's large cities contribute to its economy?

_____

_____

_____ 7. Why are Lesotho and Swaziland influenced by South Africa?

_____

_____

Guided Reading Workbook

Indian Early Civilizations, Empires, and World Religions

MAIN IDEAS
1. Located on the Indus River, the Harappan civilization also had contact with people far from India.
2. Harappan achievements included a writing system, city planning, and art.
3. The rise of the Aryan tribes changed India's civilization.
4. The Vedas were the basis of religion in the Vedic era and moving forward.
5. Indian society divided into distinct groups.

Key Terms and Places

Indus River major river in India along which the Harappan civilization developed

Harappa city in ancient India

Mohenjo-Daro city in ancient India

Sanskrit most important language of ancient India

caste system division of Indian society into groups based on a person's birth, wealth, or occupation

Lesson Summary
HARAPPAN CIVILIZATION

India's first civilization, the Harappan civilization, developed along the **Indus River.** Harappan settlements were scattered over a huge area, but most lay next to rivers. The largest cities were **Harappa** and **Mohenjo-Daro.** Archaeologists currently estimate that Harappan civilization thrived between 2600 and 1700 BC. They had a farming economy and used irrigation canals to bring water to their fields. They grew cotton and food crops. The Harappans may have traded with people as far away as southern India and Mesopotamia.

> Circle the names of the two largest Harappan cities.

HARAPPAN ACHIEVEMENTS

The Harappans developed India's first writing system, but scholars have not been able to read it. Most of what is known about Harappans comes from studying the ruins of their cities, especially

> Underline the phrase that explains why we know so little about the Harappans.

Harappa and Mohenjo-Daro. These cities were well-planned and built in the shadow of a fortress that could easily oversee the city streets. The streets themselves were built at right angles and had drainage systems. Buildings were made of kiln-fired mud brick. These bricks were uniform in size across Harappan civilization. The Harappans also developed beautiful artisan crafts, some of which have helped historians draw conclusions about Harappan society.

A NEW CULTURE ARISES

The Aryan people may have arrived in India in the 2000s BC. Historians do not know where they came from, but over many centuries, they spread into central India. They became the dominant society in India during a time known as the Vedic period or Vedic age. Much of what is known about the Aryans comes from a collection of religious writings called the Vedas. Unlike the Harappans, Aryans lived in small communities run by a local leader, or raja. Aryan groups fought each other as often as they fought outsiders. The Aryans spoke **Sanskrit** and memorized poems and hymns that survived by word of mouth. People later figured out how to write Sanskrit. Today Sanskrit is the root of many modern South Asian languages.

> How did the early Aryans preserve their poems and their history without writing?
>
> _____
>
> _____
>
> _____
>
> _____

VEDIC RELIGION AND EARLY HINDUISM

Religion was important during the Vedic age. Many scholars call the early Hinduism of this period Vedic religion or Brahmanism. This is because of the religion's emphasis on the Vedas and the belief in a divine reality known as Brahman. The oldest of the Vedas is the Rigveda. Over time, the Aryans wrote down their poems and hymns in Sanskrit. These were compiled into collections called Vedic texts. The texts described rituals, such as how to perform sacrifices, and

> Underline the sentence that explains why early Hinduism is called Vedic religion or Brahmanism.

offered reflections from religious scholars. By the later Vedic period, powerful chiefs became rulers over larger areas. Religious ceremonies provided more power and status to these rulers, or kings. The priests and upper class grew in importance and wealth. This led to greater divisions in ancient Indian society.

INDIAN SOCIETY DIVIDES

According to the Vedas, there were four main *varnas*, or social divisions. The Brahmins were priests. They were the highest-ranking varna. The Kshatriyas were rulers or warriors. The Vaisyas were commoners, including farmers, craftspeople, and traders. The Sudras were workers and servants. Another kind of division, called *jatis*, was based on birth and had rules about how these groups interacted with each other. The varnas and the jatis developed into the **caste system.** Castes were family based. A person's caste determined his or her place in society, but at first there was some social mobility among the castes. Each caste had its own norms that people in that caste followed. The Dalits, or Untouchables, did not belong to any caste. In ancient India, women had the same rights as men, but over time, laws were passed to limit these rights.

> **What are the four main *varnas*, or social divisions, in Indian society?**
>
> _____
> _____
> _____
> _____

CHALLENGE ACTIVITY

Critical Thinking: Draw Inferences Do you think
we know more about the Harappans or the
Aryans? Explain your answer.

DIRECTIONS Write a word or phrase that describes the term given.

1. Sanskrit _____

2. caste system _____
   _____

3. Harappa _____

DIRECTIONS Read each sentence and fill in the blank with the
word in the word pair that best completes the sentence.

4. The _____ civilization along the Indus River was India's
   first civilization. (**Aryan/Harappan**)

5. Ancient writings known as the _____ are collections of
   poems, hymns, myths, and rituals. (**Sanskrit/Vedas**)

6. The leader of each village was given the title of _____.
   (**Vedas/raja**)

7. The Vedic texts were written in _____. (**Aryan/Sanskrit**)

8. Mohenjo-Daro and _____ were the largest ancient
   settlements along the Indus River. (**Harappa/Rigveda**)

9. The _____ divided Indian society into groups based on
   birth, wealth, or occupation. (**caste system/Vedic texts**)

Guided Reading Workbook

Indian Early Civilizations, Empires, and World Religions

Lesson 2

MAIN IDEAS
1. Hinduism developed out of Brahmanism and influences from other cultures.
2. Jainism is another religion that arose in ancient India.

Key Terms and Places

reincarnation the belief that the soul, once a person dies, is reborn in a new body

karma the effects that good or bad actions have on a person's soul

nonviolence the avoidance of violent actions

Lesson Summary

HINDUISM DEVELOPS

The Vedic texts became the basis for Hinduism. These sacred texts blended with ideas from other cultures. Hinduism was also influenced by other religious texts. Since Hinduism is a blending of ideas, it does not have a single founder. It also does not have one set of teachings that all Hindus agree on. It is now the third-largest religion in the world. Most Hindus are in India.

Most Hindus believe in a single universal spirit called Brahman. They worship many other gods and goddesses, particularly Brahma the Creator, Siva the Destroyer, and Vishnu the Preserver. However, Hindus believe that each god and goddess is part of Brahman. They believe Brahman created the world and preserves it and that everything in the world is part of Brahman.

Hindus believe everyone has a soul, or *atman,* and the soul will eventually join Brahman. This happens when the soul recognizes that the world we live in is an illusion. Hindus believe this understanding takes several lifetimes, so **reincarnation,** or rebirth, is necessary. Your **karma,** or the effects of good or bad actions on your soul, controls your rebirth. People with bad

Why is there not one set of teachings that all Hindus agree on?
_____
_____
_____
_____

Underline the sentence that explains how Hindus believe gods and goddesses relate to Brahman.

According to Hindu belief, what is the effect of good karma?
_____
_____
_____
_____
_____

Guided Reading Workbook

karma will pay for their actions in a future birth. People with good karma will eventually be liberated from life's worries and the cycle of rebirth. Hinduism also teaches that each person has a *dharma*, which is a set of spiritual guidelines for living a moral life. Dharma includes nonviolence, self-restraint, and honesty. Karma and dharma promote good behavior and social order.

Rituals and ceremonies are important parts of Hinduism. Rites of passage, which are called *samskaras*, prepare a person for an event or the next stage of life. Many rituals revolve around birth. Wedding ceremonies also have special rituals, although these may vary depending on the cultural group and sect of Hinduism. Many Hindus also make pilgrimages to different shrines, temples, and sacred places. The most sacred of all pilgrimage sites in India is the Ganges River. Hindus believe the river's water is holy and bathing in it will remove some of their bad karma. Trade and the influence of Hindu kingdoms helped spread Hinduism throughout Southeast Asia. European colonization also helped spread Hinduism because Hindus were taken to British and Dutch colonies to work as indentured servants.

What are *samskaras*?
_____
_____
_____
_____
_____

JAINISM

Hinduism was not the only religion to influence how Indians lived. Jains were another religious group. They follow the religion called Jainism. Jainism is an ancient religion that may be even older than Hinduism. Jainism spread through the teachings of a man named Mahavira. He was an Indian prince who gave up his possessions to become a monk. Jains try to live by four principles: injure no life, tell the truth, do not steal, and own no property. Jains also practice **nonviolence,** or *ahimsa*. This emphasis on nonviolence comes from the belief that everything in nature is part of the cycle of

Circle the four principles of Jainism.

rebirth. Since they do not want to hurt any living
creature, Jains are vegetarians.

CHALLENGE ACTIVITY

Critical Thinking: Summarize Create a glossary
of at least ten terms from this section. Place the
words in alphabetical order and write a
definition.

atman	Brahman	Hinduism	Jainism
karma	nonviolence	reincarnation	

DIRECTIONS On the line provided before each statement, write **T** if
a statement is true and **F** if a statement is false. If the statement is
false, write the correct term on the line after each sentence to make
the sentence a true statement.

_____ 1. <u>Hinduism</u> is based on four major principles: injure no life, tell the
truth, do not steal, and own no property.

_____

_____ 2. Brahma the Creator, Siva the Destroyer, and Vishnu the Preserver are
the three major gods of <u>Hinduism</u>, the largest religion in Indian society.

_____

_____ 3. <u>Karma</u> is the avoidance of violent actions, which was practiced by the
Jains.

_____

_____ 4. Hindus believe that souls are born and reborn many times, each time
into a new body, which is a process called <u>reincarnation</u>.

_____

_____ 5. According to Hindu teachings, everyone has a soul, or <u>atman</u>,
inside them.

_____

_____ 6. Hindus believe that a person's ultimate goal should be to reunite their
soul with <u>karma</u>, the universal spirit.

_____

Indian Early Civilizations, Empires, and World Religions

Lesson 3

MAIN IDEAS
1. Siddhartha Gautama searched for wisdom in many ways.
2. The teachings of Buddhism deal with finding peace.
3. Buddhism spread far from where it began in India.

Key Terms and Places

fasting going without food

meditation focusing of the mind on spiritual ideas

nirvana state of perfect peace

missionaries people who work to spread their religious beliefs

Lesson Summary
SIDDHARTHA'S SEARCH FOR WISDOM

In the late 500s BC, a major new religion began to develop from questions posed by a young prince named Siddhartha Gautama (si-DAHR-tuh GAU-tuh-muh). Siddhartha was born to a wealthy family and led a life of comfort, but he questioned the pain and suffering he saw all around him. Before the age of 30, Siddhartha left his home and family to look for answers about the meaning of life. He talked to many priests and wise men, but he was not satisfied with their answers.

Siddhartha did not give up. He wandered for years through the forests trying to free himself from daily concerns by **fasting** and **meditating.** After six years, Siddhartha sat down under a tree and meditated for seven weeks. He came up with an answer to what causes human suffering. Suffering is caused by wanting what one does not have, wanting to keep what one likes and already has, and not wanting what one dislikes but has. He began to travel and teach his ideas and was soon called the Buddha, or "Enlightened One."

> **Why did Siddhartha leave his life of luxury?**
> _____
> _____
> _____
> _____

> **What was Siddhartha called after he attained wisdom?**
> _____
> _____

Lesson 3, *continued*

TEACHINGS OF BUDDHISM

Buddhism is based upon the Four Noble Truths. These truths are as follows: suffering and unhappiness are part of life; suffering stems from our desire for pleasure and material goods; people can overcome their desires and reach **nirvana,** a state of perfect peace, which ends the cycle of reincarnation; and people can follow an eightfold path to nirvana, overcoming desire and ignorance.

These teachings were similar to some Hindu concepts, but went against some traditional Hindu ideas. Buddhism challenged the authority of the Brahmins. The Buddha said that each individual could reach salvation on his or her own. Buddhism also opposed the caste system.

> **What are the central teachings of Buddhism called?**
> _____
> _____

> **What traditional Hindu ideas did Buddhism challenge?**
> _____
> _____
> _____

BUDDHISM SPREADS

Buddhism spread quickly throughout India. With the help of Indian king Asoka, Buddhist **missionaries** were sent to other countries to teach their religious beliefs. Missionaries introduced Buddhism to Sri Lanka and other parts of Southeast Asia, as well as Central Asia and Persia. It spread to China, Japan, and Korea. Eventually, Buddhism split into two major branches. Both branches have millions of believers today. Buddhists observe many holidays. Pilgrimage to holy sites is one of Buddhism's most important rituals.

> **Who sent missionaries to other countries?**
> _____
> _____

CHALLENGE ACTIVITY

Critical Thinking: Compare Compare the roles of Constantine and Asoka in spreading Christianity and Buddhism. Write a paragraph to explain how they were alike.

| the Buddha | Buddhism | fasting |
| meditation | missionaries | nirvana |

DIRECTIONS Answer each question by writing a sentence that contains at least one term from the word bank.

1. According to Buddhist teachings, if people can overcome their desire and ignorance, they will reach what?

_____

_____

2. What did Siddhartha do to free his mind from daily concerns?

_____

_____

3. Who did the king Asoka send to spread the religious beliefs of Buddhism?

_____

_____

4. What is the term that means "Enlightened One?"

_____

_____

5. What is the religion based on the teachings of Siddhartha?

_____

_____

Indian Early Civilizations, Empires, and World Religions

MAIN IDEAS
1. Sikhs believe in equality and generally reject the caste system.
2. Sikhs have responded to historical and modern-day challenges.

Key Terms and Places

langar Sikh kitchen

gurdwara Sikh place of worship

Lesson Summary
SIKH RELIGION

Sikhism is the world's fifth largest religion. It began in the Punjab region in the late 15th century. Its founder was Guru Nanak. *Guru* is a Sanskrit title for "teacher." *Sikh* means "learner" in the language of the Punjab. In Punjabi, Sikhism is called Gurmat, which means "the way of the Guru." Guru Nanak was the first of ten gurus who established the core beliefs of Sikhism. He was brought up as a Hindu, but he disagreed with some of the Hindu teachings. His teachings blended ideas from Hinduism with ideas from Islam, but Sikhism is separate from both of these religions. Nanak thought people from different social classes should be treated equally.

Sikhs believe the first ten gurus were inhabited by a single spirit. When one of these gurus died, this spirit, or eternal Guru, was reincarnated into the next human guru. Sikhs believe that when Guru Gobind Singh, the tenth guru, died in 1708, the spirit transferred itself to the sacred scripture of the Sikhs. This scripture is called Guru Granth Sahib. It contains the actual words spoken by the Sikh gurus. Sikhs believe it is the word of Wahegure, or God. It also contains passages from Hindu and Muslim teachers. Sikhs believe that there is one God and everyone has equal

> Underline the sentence that explains the relationship of Sikhism to Hinduism and Islam.

access to God and is equal before God. They also believe in the cycle of life, death, and reincarnation, and in karma.

Sikh equality is seen in the **langar,** or kitchen, of their places of worship. There, food is served without charge and everyone sits together on the floor to eat. This is a symbol of social equality. Sikhs do observe the caste system in marriage and in some **gurdwaras,** or places of worship. Sikhs are expected to marry someone of their own caste. Some castes have also created gurdwaras for their caste only. A goal of Sikhism is to become one with God. To do this, Sikhs have three duties: to pray, to work, and to give. This means keeping God in mind at all times. God is kept in mind through prayer and meditation, earning an honest living, and giving to others. Sikhs also keep God in mind by wearing special articles that signify their faith. These articles include a turban, a sword, a metal bracelet, and a wooden comb. In their quest for spiritual liberation, Sikhs try to avoid five vices: lust, greed, attachment to worldly things, anger, and pride. Like other religions, Sikhs celebrate special times for individuals and important holidays for the community. An especially important ceremony is Khalsa, when an adult formally joins the Sikh community. Anniversaries of events in the lives of the ten gurus are also celebrated.

What beliefs are shared by Sikhs and Hindus?
_____
_____
_____
_____
_____

Underline the three Sikh duties and circle the five vices.

SIKH HISTORY

Many Sikhs lived in the Punjab region of India, which was under the control of the Mughal Empire. Sikhs were unfairly taxed and otherwise mistreated. When they protested, the Mughal Empire reacted harshly. Sikh resistance grew stronger as the Mughal Empire weakened. In 1799, a man named Ranjit Singh declared himself maharaja, or ruler of the Punjab. For the

Who was Ranjit Singh?
_____
_____
_____
_____

Guided Reading Workbook

next 50 years, the Sikhs ruled much of what is now northwestern India and eastern Pakistan. During this time, a gurdwara in northwestern India was rebuilt using marble and gold as a symbol of Sikh power. It became known as the Golden Temple. Ranjit Singh was a strong ruler, and the Sikh Empire thrived during his life. However, when he died in 1839, the Sikh Empire began to weaken. The Punjab became a part of British India in 1849.

There are nearly 25 million Sikhs worldwide today. Most live in India. For many years, most migrant Sikhs were traders. After the British took control of India, Sikhs served as soldiers in British colonies in Malaya and Hong Kong. Sikhs began to migrate to other parts of the world. Living outside India has presented struggles and opportunities for Sikhs. There are now large Sikh communities in the United States and Canada. Their unique dress makes them very visible in their adopted homelands.

> **How did British control of India spread Sikhism?**
> _____
> _____
> _____
> _____
> _____

CHALLENGE ACTIVITY

Critical Thinking: Analyze Analyze Sikhism's belief that all people are equal before God. How do Sikhs demonstrate this belief, and yet also observe the caste system? Write a short paragraph explaining your answer.

DIRECTIONS Look at each set of four terms. On the line provided, write the letter of the term that does not relate to the others.

_____ 1. a. gurdwara
      b. place of worship
      c. Golden Temple
      d. Mughal

_____ 2. a. Nanak
      b. ten gurus
      c. Ranjit Singh
      d. Gobind Singh

_____ 3. a. langar
      b. Khalsa
      c. kitchen
      d. equality

_____ 4. a. gurdwara
      b. death
      c. reincarnation
      d. karma

_____ 5. a. lust
      b. pray
      c. work
      d. give

_____ 6. a. Granth Sahib
      b. ten gurus
      c. Wahegure
      d. langar

_____ 7. a. Sikh Empire
      b. Hong Kong
      c. Ranjit Singh
      d. maharaja

Indian Early Civilizations, Empires, and World Religions

MAIN IDEAS
1. The Mauryan Empire unified most of India.
2. Gupta rulers promoted Hinduism in their empire.
3. The Mughal Empire reunited much of India during the 16th century.
4. The people of ancient India made great contributions to the arts and sciences.

Key Terms and Places

mercenaries hired soldiers

edicts laws

metallurgy the science of working with metals

alloys mixtures of two or more metals

inoculation a method of injecting a person with a small dose of a virus to help him or her build up defenses to a disease

Hindu-Arabic numerals the numbering system invented by Indian mathematicians and brought to Europe by Arabs; the numbers we use today

Lesson Summary
MAURYAN EMPIRE UNIFIES INDIA

In the 320s BC a military leader named Chandragupta Maurya and his army of **mercenaries** took control of the northern part of India. He founded the Mauryan Empire, which lasted about 150 years. Chandragupta's complex government included a huge army and a network of spies. He taxed the population heavily for the protection he offered. When he became a Jainist monk, Chandragupta gave the throne to his son. Chandragupta's grandson, Asoka, was the strongest ruler of the Mauryan dynasty. He extended Mauryan rule over most of India. At last, tired of killing and war, Asoka converted to Buddhism. He sent Buddhist missionaries to other countries and devoted the rest of his rule to improving the lives of his people. He had workers build wells, tree-shaded roads, and rest houses, and

> How did Asoka's conversion to Buddhism affect his philosophy of leadership?
>
> _____
>
> _____
>
> _____
>
> _____

raised large stone pillars carved with Buddhist
edicts, or laws. When Asoka died, however, his
sons struggled for power and foreign invaders
threatened the country. The Mauryan Empire fell
in 184 BC. India divided into smaller states once
again.

GUPTA RULERS PROMOTE HINDUISM

During the AD 300s, the Gupta dynasty united
and built the prosperity of India. The Guptas
were devout Hindus and encouraged the revival
of Hindu traditions and writings. They also
supported Jainism and Buddhism. Indian
civilization reached a high point under Chandra
Gupta II. He strengthened the empire's economy
and borders. He also promoted the arts,
literature, and religion. The Guptas believed the
caste system supported stability. The role of
women was very restricted. Women were expected
to marry and raise children. A woman had to
obey her husband and had few rights. The Gupta
dynasty lasted until it was invaded by Huns from
Central Asia. India broke up once again into a
patchwork of small states.

What religions did the Gupta rulers encourage and support?
_____
_____
_____

THE MUGHAL EMPIRE

About 1,000 years after the end of the Gupta
Empire, Turkish Muslims from Central Asia built
the Mughal Empire. An emperor named Akbar
instituted a tolerant religious policy. The
Mughals spread Islam through the lands they
conquered, but Akbar encouraged members of
all religions to live and work together. Under
Akbar, Muslims and Hindus in the empire lived
in peace. Their cooperation created a unique
Mughal culture that blended Persian, Islamic,
and Hindu elements. The Mughals were known
for their architecture, particularly the Taj Mahal.
A later Mughal emperor reversed Akbar's

Underline the sentence that describes Mughal culture.

tolerant policies, and violent revolts led to the end of the Mughal Empire.

INDIAN ACHIEVEMENTS

During the Gupta and Mauryan periods, religion influenced the arts. Many paintings and sculptures illustrated the teachings of either Hinduism or Buddhism. Beautiful Hindu and Buddhist temples were built during this time and decorated with elaborate wood and stone carvings. Great works of literature were written in Sanskrit during the Gupta dynasty. The best-known works are the *Mahabharata* and the *Ramayana*. Both of these works are still popular across the world.

> Which religions influenced the arts during the Gupta and Mauryan periods?
> _____
> _____

The ancient Indians were pioneers of **metallurgy,** the science of working with metals. Their knowledge allowed them to create high-quality tools and weapons. They also used processes for creating **alloys.** Alloys can be stronger or easier to work with than pure metals. Indian iron was very hard and pure, and Indian steel has been a valued export for centuries. In medicine, Indians developed the technique of **inoculation.** Doctors also performed some surgeries. The numbers we use today, called **Hindu-Arabic numerals,** were first developed by Indian mathematicians. They also created the concept of zero, upon which all modern math is based.

> What are two ways that early Indian mathematicians influenced modern mathematics?
> _____
> _____
> _____
> _____

CHALLENGE ACTIVITY

Critical Thinking: Draw Conclusions Why do you think so much of the art and literature from this period is religious? Write a paragraph to explain your answer.

DIRECTIONS Read each sentence and fill in the blank with the word in the word pair that best completes the sentence.

1. The Mauryan Empire began after an army of _____ seized control of northern India. (**edicts/mercenaries**)

2. _____ was a strong ruler who converted to Buddhism and swore that he would not fight any more wars. (**Akbar/Asoka**)

3. Under the _____, Hinduism became popular again, but the rulers also supported Buddhism and Jainism. (**Gupta dynasty/Mughal Empire**)

4. Asoka had stone pillars built and carved with Buddhist _____. (**edicts/inoculations**)

5. Their knowledge of _____ enabled ancient Indians to create high-quality tools and weapons. (**inoculations/metallurgy**)

6. Indian metal workers knew processes for mixing metals to create
_____ . (**alloys/edicts**)

7. Indian doctors knew how to protect people against disease through
_____ . (**alloys/inoculations**)

8. The numbers we use today are called _____ because they were created by Indian scholars and brought to Europe by the Arabs. (**Hindu-Arabic numerals/mercenaries**)

The Indian Subcontinent

MAIN IDEAS
1. Towering mountains, large rivers, and broad plains are the key physical features of the Indian Subcontinent.
2. The Indian Subcontinent has a great variety of climate regions and resources.

Key Terms and Places

subcontinent large landmass that is smaller than a continent

Mount Everest world's highest mountain, located between Nepal and China

Ganges River India's most important river that flows across northern India into Bangladesh

delta landform at the mouth of a river created by sediment deposits

Indus River river in Pakistan that creates a fertile plain known as the Indus River Valley

monsoons seasonal winds that bring either moist or dry air to an area

Lesson Summary
PHYSICAL FEATURES

The Indian Subcontinent is made up of the countries Bangladesh, Bhutan, India, Maldives, Nepal, Pakistan, and Sri Lanka. This subcontinent is also known as South Asia. A **subcontinent** is a large landmass that is smaller than a continent. Huge mountains separate the Indian Subcontinent from the rest of Asia—the Hindu Kush in the northwest and the Himalayas along the north. Lower mountains, called the Ghats, run along India's eastern and western coasts. The Himalayas stretch about 1,500 miles across and are the highest mountains in the world. The highest peak, **Mount Everest,** rises 29,035 feet (8,850 m) above sea level. Pakistan's K2 is the world's second tallest peak. Two major river systems originate in the Himalayas. They have flooded the surrounding land, creating fertile plains. The **Ganges River**

Circle the names of the seven countries in South Asia.

Underline the world's two highest mountain peaks.

flows across northern India. The area along the Ganges is called the Ganges Plain. It is India's farming heartland. In Bangladesh the Ganges River joins other rivers to form a huge **delta,** a landform created by sediment deposits. Pakistan's **Indus River** also forms a fertile plain, the Indus River Valley. This region was once home to the earliest Indian civilizations. Now, it is the most heavily populated area in Pakistan.

> **Which river forms a fertile plain in Pakistan?**
> _____

The Deccan is a hilly plateau south of the Ganges Plain. East of the Indus Valley is the Thar, or Great Indian Desert. In southern Nepal, the Tarai region is known for its fertile farmland and tropical jungles.

CLIMATES AND RESOURCES

Nepal and Bhutan, located in the Himalayas, have a highland climate which brings cool temperatures. In the plains south of the Himalayas, the climate is humid subtropical. The rest of the subcontinent has mainly tropical climates. Central India and Sri Lanka have a tropical savanna climate, with warm temperatures year round. Bangladesh, Sri Lanka, Maldives, and parts of southwest India have a humid tropical climate, with warm temperatures and heavy rains. Southern and western India and most of Pakistan have desert and steppe climates. **Monsoons** greatly affect the subcontinent's climate. From June to October, summer monsoons from the Indian Ocean bring heavy rains. In winter, monsoons change direction and bring in dry air from the north.

> **Underline the type of climate found in Nepal and Bhutan.**

The subcontinent's fertile soil is a vital resource for the region. It allows farmers to produce tea, rice, nuts, and jute. Other important resources are timber, livestock, iron ore, coal, natural gas, and gemstones.

> **Circle the resources of the Indian Subcontinent.**

Lesson 1, *continued*

CHALLENGE ACTIVITY

Critical Thinking: Summarize Make a two-column table showing major mountain ranges and river valleys of the Indian subcontinent and their locations.

DIRECTIONS Read each sentence and fill in the blank with the word in the word pair that best completes the sentence.

1. A _____ is a large landmass that is smaller than a continent. **(delta/subcontinent)**

2. The _____ creates a fertile plain, which is Pakistan's most densely populated region. **(Indus River/Ganges River)**

3. Summer _____ bring moist air up from the Indian Ocean, causing heavy rains. **(monsoons/Himalayas)**

4. The most important river in India is the _____. **(Indus River/Ganges River)**

5. The world's highest mountain is _____. **(Hindu Kush/Mount Everest)**

delta	Ganges River	Himalayas	Hindu Kush
Indus River	monsoons	Mount Everest	subcontinent

DIRECTIONS Choose five terms from the word bank. On a separate sheet of paper, use these terms to write a summary of what you learned in the lesson.

Guided Reading Workbook

The Indian Subcontinent

MAIN IDEAS

1. Advanced civilizations and powerful empires shaped the early history of India.
2. Powerful empires controlled India for hundreds of years.
3. Independence from Great Britain led to the division of India into several countries.
4. Indian culture is shaped by many things, including religion and a caste system.
5. Daily life in India is centered around cities, villages, and religion.
6. Today India faces many challenges, including a growing population and economic development.

Key Terms and Places

Delhi site of former Muslim kingdom in northern India

colony territory inhabited and controlled by people from a foreign land

partition division

Hinduism one of the world's oldest religions; the dominant religion of India

Buddhism religion based on the teaching of Siddhartha Gautama, the Buddha

Jainism ancient religion that teaches nonviolence as a way of life

Sikhism religion blending Hinduism and Islam and teaching equality for all

caste system divides Indian society into groups based on birth or occupation

Mumbai (Bombay) one of India's largest cities

Kolkata (Calcutta) one of India's largest cities

urbanization increase in the percentage of people who live in cities

green revolution program that encouraged farmers to adopt modern agricultural methods

Lesson Summary
EARLY CIVILIZATIONS AND EMPIRES

The Harappan civilization flourished in Pakistan's Indus River Valley between 3000 and 1700 BC. Later, an Aryan language called Sanskrit became the basis for many languages in northern India. Most of the subcontinent was conquered by the Mauryan people. After the death of Asoka, one of the greatest Mauryan

> Underline the name of one of the greatest Mauryan emperors.

rulers, the empire split up. The Gupta Empire united most of northern India. Trade and culture thrived under the Gupta rulers.

POWERFUL EMPIRES

Powerful empires controlled India for much of its history. First the Mughal Empire and then the British Empire ruled India for hundreds of years. Turkish Muslims set up a kingdom at **Delhi** in northern India and formed the Mughal Empire. Trade and culture flourished during this period, especially under Akbar, one of India's greatest rulers. As Mughal power faded, Great Britain's presence in the region increased. By the mid-1800s, India was a British **colony.**

INDEPENDENCE AND DIVISION

Under British rule, Indians were treated as second-class citizens. Mohandas Gandhi led nonviolent protests to gain Indian independence. Muslims were afraid they would have little say in a Hindu-controlled India. To avoid civil war, the British agreed to the **partition** of India. Two independent countries, India and Pakistan, were formed in 1947. Later, Sri Lanka and Maldives gained their independence from Great Britain and Bangladesh broke away from Pakistan.

> Why was India divided into two independent countries?
>
> _____
> _____
> _____
> _____

INDIAN CULTURE

India is the birthplace of several major religions. These include **Hinduism, Buddhism, Jainism,** and **Sikhism.** India's **caste system** began to develop in ancient times. The castes had rules about how their members interacted with people from other castes. Although caste discrimination is banned in India today, the Untouchables, or Dalits, still face obstacles.

> How does the caste system impact Dalits today?
>
> _____
> _____
> _____

DAILY LIFE IN INDIA

India's three largest cities, **Mumbai (Bombay),** Delhi, and **Kolkata (Calcutta),** are among the world's most populous. Most city dwellers have a hard time making a living. More than 70 percent of India's people live in villages. Most work on farms and live with extended families in simple homes. Religion plays a key role in Indian villages and cities.

> **Where do most of India's people live?**
> _____
> _____
> _____
> _____
> _____

INDIA'S CHALLENGES

India's population has grown rapidly. It is the world's second most populous country. This population growth has impacted India's environment and resources. Population growth and industrialization led to dangerous levels of air pollution. Millions of people have moved to India's cities in search of jobs, creating **urbanization.** Population growth strains the food supply and millions live in poverty. India's government began a program called the **green revolution,** which helped farmers produce more food. The government has also brought information technology (IT) businesses to India and Indian entrepreneurs now export IT to other countries.

> **Why have millions of Indians moved to cities?**
> _____
> _____

CHALLENGE ACTIVITY

Critical Thinking: Analyze Analyze the connection between India's population growth and the challenges the nation faces today.

Buddhism	caste system
colony	Delhi
green revolution	Hinduism
industrialization	Jainism
Kolkata (Calcutta)	Mumbai (Bombay)
partition	Sikhism
urbanization	

DIRECTIONS On the line provided before each statement, write **T** if a statement is true and **F** if a statement is false. If the statement is false, write the correct term from the word bank on the line after each sentence to make the sentence a true statement.

_____ 1. The <u>urbanization</u> was a program of the Indian government to encourage modern agricultural methods.

_____

_____ 2. Rapid <u>industrialization</u> has taken place in India as people have moved to cities seeking jobs.

_____

_____ 3. By the mid-1880s, India was a <u>colony</u> of Britain.

_____

_____ 4. The <u>partition</u> of India divided society into groups based on birth or occupation.

_____

DIRECTIONS Answer each question with a sentence that uses terms from the lesson.

5. What are India's three largest cities?

_____

6. India is the birthplace of which four major religions?

_____

_____

The Indian Subcontinent

Lesson 3

MAIN IDEAS

1. Many different ethnic groups and religions influence the culture of India's neighbors.
2. Rapid population growth, ethnic conflicts, and environmental threats are major challenges to the region today.

Key Terms and Places

Sherpas ethnic group from the mountains of Nepal

Kashmir region which both India and Pakistan claim control over

Dhaka capital of Bangladesh and its largest city

Kathmandu capital of Nepal and its largest city

Lesson Summary
CULTURE

India's neighbors have different ways of life. Their cultures reflect the customs of many ethnic groups. For example, the **Sherpas** in Nepal often serve as guides through the Himalayas. Many of the Tamils in Sri Lanka came from India to work on plantations.

People of the region also have different religious beliefs. Like India, most of its neighbors have one major religion. For example, most people in Pakistan and Bangladesh practice Islam. Hinduism is the major religion in Nepal while Buddhism is the major religion in Sri Lanka and Bhutan.

> Circle the countries of the Indian subcontinent where most people practice Islam.

THE REGION TODAY

Since its creation in 1947, Pakistan has not had a stable government. Rebellions and assassinations have hurt the country. Pakistan also faces the challenges of overpopulation and poverty. These challenges could cause even more instability. Pakistan has also clashed with India over control of the territory of **Kashmir.** Pakistan controls

> What challenges does Pakistan face?
>
> _____
> _____
> _____
> _____
> _____

western Kashmir and India controls the east, but both countries claim control over the whole region.

Since 2001 Pakistan has helped the United States fight terrorism. Many people, though, think terrorists still remain in Pakistan.

Bangladesh is a small country but one of the world's most densely populated. It has about 3,279 people per square mile (1,266 per square km). More than 17 million people live in Bangladesh's capital, **Dhaka.** One of the country's main challenges is flooding from rivers and monsoons, which often causes heavy damage. For example, one flood left over 25 million people homeless.

> Underline the sentence that tells one of Bangladesh's main challenges.

Nepal's population is growing rapidly. Its largest city and capital, **Kathmandu,** is poor and overcrowded. Nepal also faces environmental threats. Land cleared to grow food causes deforestation. This leads to soil erosion and harms wildlife. Tourists harm its environment by leaving trash behind and using valuable resources.

> What are two causes of damage to Nepal's environment?
> _____
> _____
> _____

Bhutan is a small, isolated mountain kingdom between India and China. After years of isolation, Bhutan formed ties with Great Britain and India in the 1900s. Bhutan has begun to modernize, building new roads, schools, and hospitals. Most of its people are farmers, growing rice, potatoes, and corn. To protect its environment and way of life, Bhutan limits the number of tourists who may visit.

> Underline the crops Bhutan's farmers grow.

Sri Lanka has been greatly influenced by its close neighbor, India. Two of Sri Lanka's main ethnic groups—the Tamil and the Sinhalese— have Indian roots. The Tamil minority has fought for years to create a separate state. The fighting ended in 2009 when the government defeated the Tamils. In 2004, an Indian Ocean tsunami struck Sri Lanka, killing thousands. More than 500,000

> Circle the two main ethnic groups in Sri Lanka.

were left homeless. Sri Lanka is still trying to rebuild its fishing and agricultural industries.

CHALLENGE ACTIVITY

Critical Thinking: Analyze Make a chart to compare the challenges faced by Nepal, Bhutan, and Sri Lanka.

Bhutan	Dhaka	Kashmir
Kathmandu	Sherpas	Tamils

DIRECTIONS Read each sentence and choose the correct term from the word bank to replace the underlined phrase. Write the term in the space provided and then define the term in your own words.

1. They have provided many guides for Himalayan expeditions.

   _____

   Your definition: _____

2. This city is the capital of Nepal.

   _____

   Your definition: _____

   _____

3. This region is the source of conflict between India and Pakistan.

   _____

   Your definition: _____

4. They came from India to work on Sri Lanka's plantations.

   _____

   Your definition: _____

   _____

5. This city in Bangladesh is home to more than 17 million people.

   _____

   Your definition: _____

Early Civilizations of China

MAIN IDEAS
1. Chinese civilization began along two rivers.
2. The Zhou and Qin dynasties changed Chinese society and made great advances.
3. Under the Han dynasty, China's government and society were largely based on the ideas of Confucius.
4. The Han made many achievements in art, literature, and learning and began trade with distant lands.

Key Terms and Places

Chang Jiang river in China

Huang He river in China

mandate of heaven idea that heaven chose China's ruler and gave him or her power

Xi'an present name of the capital city of the Qin dynasty

Great Wall barrier that linked earlier walls that stood near China's northern border

sundial device that uses the position of shadows cast by the sun to tell the time of day

seismograph device that measures the strength of earthquakes

acupuncture practice of inserting fine needles through the skin at specific points to cure disease or relieve pain

Silk Road network of overland trade routes stretching from China to the Mediterranean Sea

Lesson Summary
CHINESE CIVILIZATION BEGINS

By 7000 BC farmers were cultivating rice in the **Chang Jiang** valley and millet and wheat along the **Huang He**. The population grew in these river valleys. Villages became large towns, with pottery makers and silk weavers. Some people grew rich and became nobles. These powerful families, or dynasties, began to rule China.

By the 1500s BC China's first known dynasty, the Shang, was in power. The Shang created

> **Where did the Chinese first cultivate rice?**
>
> _____
>
> _____

made the route dangerous. However,
China grew rich from this trade.

CHALLENGE ACTIVITY

Critical Thinking: Analyze Create a timeline to
show the events and eras discussed in this lesson.

DIRECTIONS Read each sentence and fill in the blank with the
word in the word pair that best completes the sentence.

1. The land along the _____ was good for growing millet and
   wheat. (**Chang Jiang/Huang He**)

2. The Zhou dynasty claimed they had the _____ to rule China.
   (**mandate of heaven/Huang He**)

3. Shi Huangdi ordered nobles to move to the capital city of _____.
   (**Qin/Xi'an**)

4. During the_____ dynasty, systems of laws, money, and writing
   were developed. (**Qin/Zhou**)

5. The _____ was built to keep invaders out of China.
   (**Chang Jiang/Great Wall**)

6. Under the _____ dynasty, the Chinese made several advances in
   art, literature, science, and medicine. (**Qin/Han**)

7. A _____ is a device that measures the strength of an earthquake.
   (**seismograph/sundial**)

8. The practice of inserting fine needles through the skin at specific points to
   cure disease or relieve pain is called _____.
   (**seismograph/acupuncture**)

9. A _____ is an early type of clock. (**seismograph/sundial**)

10. Chinese traders used the _____ to take Chinese goods to
    Central Asia. (**Silk Road/Chang Jiang**)

Early Civilizations of China

MAIN IDEAS
1. After the Han dynasty, China fell into disorder but was reunified by new dynasties.
2. Cities and trade grew during the Tang and Song dynasties.
3. The Tang and Song dynasties produced fine arts and inventions.
4. Confucianism influenced the Song system of government.
5. Scholar-officials ran China's government during the Song dynasty.

Key Terms and Places

Grand Canal canal linking northern and southern China

Kaifeng capital during the Song dynasty

porcelain thin, beautiful pottery invented by the Chinese

woodblock printing form of printing in which an entire page is carved into a block of wood that is covered with ink and then pressed against paper to make a printed page

gunpowder mixture of powders used in guns and explosives

compass instrument that uses Earth's magnetic field to show direction

civil service service as a government official

bureaucracy body of unelected government officials

scholar-official educated member of the government

Lesson Summary
DISORDER AND REUNIFICATION

When the Han dynasty collapsed, China split into several rival kingdoms. During the violence and uncertainty, Chinese people found comfort in Buddhism. It taught that people can escape suffering and achieve a state of peace. This time of violence and uncertainty was called the Period of Disunion. It ended with the rise of the Sui dynasty. Although the Sui did not rule long, Sui rulers restored order and began the **Grand Canal** to link northern and southern China. The Tang dynasty followed, ruling China for nearly 300 years. The Tang conquered many lands, reformed the military, and created law codes. Tang empress

During which dynasty did work on the Grand Canal begin?

_____

Wu was the only woman to rule China. After the
fall of the Tang dynasty, separate kingdoms
competed for power. This period, called the Five
Dynasties and Ten Kingdoms, was ended by the
Song dynasty. The Song ruled for about 300
years. This was a time of great economic and
cultural achievements.

CITIES AND TRADE

China's growing cities were crowded with people,
shops, artisans, and government officials. The
largest city of the Tang dynasty, Chang'an (now
called Xi'an), was a major trade center. Growth
continued during the Song dynasty. **Kaifeng** (KY-
fuhng), the Song capital, had about a million
people. Traders used the Grand Canal to ship
goods and agricultural products throughout
China. Foreign trade traveled over both land
routes and sea routes.

Chinese exports included tea, rice, spices, and
jade. Silk and **porcelain** were especially popular in
other countries. The Chinese kept the method of
making silk a secret for centuries.

> **Why do you think the Chinese kept the method for making silk a secret?**
>
> _____
> _____
> _____

ARTS AND INVENTIONS

The Tang and Song dynasties produced great
artists and writers. In addition, some of the most
important inventions in human history were
created. A Tang invention called **woodblock
printing** produced the world's first known printed
book. Later, during the Song dynasty, the
Chinese invented movable type for printing.
Movable type can be rearranged and reused to
create new lines of text and different pages. The
Song dynasty also introduced the world's first
paper money. Two other Tang dynasty inventions
include **gunpowder** and the **compass**. The compass
revolutionized travel, and gunpowder
dramatically changed how wars were fought.

> **Circle the invention that replaced woodblock printing.**

CONFUCIANISM

Confucius's teachings focused on ethics, or proper behavior, of individuals and governments. During the Period of Disunion, Buddhism overshadowed Confucianism. However, late in the Tang dynasty, scholars again turned to Confucianism. They wanted to improve Chinese government and society. During and after the Song dynasty, a new version of Confucianism developed, known as Neo-Confucianism. In addition to teaching proper behavior, Neo-Confucianism emphasized spiritual matters. These ideas became official government teachings after the Song dynasty.

> Underline the sentence that explains what Neo-Confucianism emphasized.

SCHOLAR-OFFICIALS

The Song dynasty improved the government workforce. Workers had to pass a series of written **civil service** examinations to work for the government **bureaucracy**. The tests covered both the teachings of Confucius and related ideas. In this way, government officials were chosen by ability instead of wealth or influence. The tests were very difficult, and students spent years preparing for them. Passing the tests meant life as a **scholar-official**. Benefits included people's respect and reduced penalties for breaking the law. The civil service examination system helped ensure that talented, intelligent people became scholar-officials. This system was a major factor in the stability of the Song government.

> How did the civil service examinations contribute to government stability?
> _____
> _____
> _____
> _____
> _____

CHALLENGE ACTIVITY

Critical Thinking: Make Judgments Which do you think is better: a government that gives people jobs based on test scores or one that gives people jobs based on their family connections? Explain your answer.

Guided Reading Workbook

DIRECTIONS Write a word or phrase that has the same meaning as the term given.

1. compass _____

2. gunpowder _____

3. porcelain _____

4. woodblock printing _____

_____

_____

5. Grand Canal _____

6. Kaifeng _____

DIRECTIONS Read each sentence and fill in the blank with the word in the word pair that best completes the sentence.

7. _____ means working as a government official.
   (Bureaucracy/Civil service)

8. People who went to work for the government formed a large _____, a body of government officials. **(bureaucracy/scholar-official)**

9. A _____ was an elite member of society who received people's respect and reduced penalties for breaking the law.
   (scholar-official/bureaucracy)

Guided Reading Workbook

Early Civilizations of China

> **MAIN IDEAS**
> 1. The Mongol Empire included China, and the Mongols ruled China as the Yuan dynasty.
> 2. The Ming dynasty was a time of stability and prosperity.
> 3. The Ming brought great changes in government and relations with other countries.

Key Terms and Places

Beijing present-day city near the capital of the Yuan dynasty

Forbidden City huge palace complex that included hundreds of imperial residences, temples, and other government buildings

isolationism policy of avoiding contact with other countries

Lesson Summary

THE MONGOL EMPIRE

In 1206 a powerful Mongol leader known as Genghis Khan (JENG-guhs KAHN) led huge armies through much of Asia and Eastern Europe. He first led his armies into northern China in 1211, then headed south. By the time of Genghis Khan's death in 1227, all of northern China was under Mongol control.

Genghis Khan's grandson, Kublai Khan (KOO-bluh KAHN), completed the conquest of China and declared himself emperor in 1279. This began the Yuan dynasty, a period also known as the Mongol Ascendancy.

Kublai Khan did not force the Chinese to accept Mongol customs, but he did try to control them. One way was by having the Chinese pay heavy taxes, which were used to pay for building projects. One such project was the building of a new capital, Dadu, near the present-day city of **Beijing**.

Mongol emperors protected overland trade routes and continued sea trade. They welcomed foreign visitors. The Italian merchant

> When did Mongol armies complete the conquest of China?
>
> _____

Marco Polo, who traveled in China between 1271 and 1295, wrote of his travels and sparked Europeans' interest in China.

Two failed campaigns against Japan and expensive public works projects weakened the Yuan dynasty. Many Chinese groups rebelled, and in 1368 Zhu Yuanzhang (JOO yoo-ahn-JAHNG) took control and founded the Ming dynasty.

> **What weakened the Yuan dynasty?**
> _____
> _____
> _____
> _____

THE MING DYNASTY

The Ming dynasty lasted nearly 300 years, from 1368 to 1644. Ming China proved to be one of the most stable and prosperous times in Chinese history. Great Ming achievements include developing the remarkable ships and voyages of Zheng He (juhng HUH), restoring the Great Wall of China, and building the **Forbidden City** in Beijing. The Forbidden City was a massive palace of residences, temples, and government buildings. It symbolized China's glory. Common people were not allowed to enter the Forbidden City.

> **Who was not allowed to enter the Forbidden City?**
> _____

CHINA UNDER THE MING

Emperors during the Ming dynasty worked to eliminate foreign influences from Chinese society. In the early 1400s China entered a period of **isolationism**. This isolationism separated China from the leaps in technological progress made in the Western world. By the late 1800s Westerners took power in some parts of China, and China was too weak to stop them. Gradually, China's glory faded.

> **What did Ming emperors try to eliminate from Chinese society?**
> _____
> _____

Guided Reading Workbook

Lesson 3, *continued*

CHALLENGE ACTIVITY

Critical Thinking: Compare Create a graphic
organizer to compare the causes for the
downfall of the Yuan and Ming dynasties.

Beijing	Forbidden City	isolationism
Kublai Khan	Marco Polo	

DIRECTIONS Answer each question by writing a sentence that
contains at least one word from the word bank.

1. Who sparked Europeans' interest in China?

    _____

    _____

    _____

2. What huge palace complex was a symbol of China's glory?

    _____

    _____

    _____

3. What policy did Ming China follow in terms of contact with other countries?

    _____

    _____

    _____

4. Who became the ruler of the Mongol Empire and completed his
   grandfather's conquest of China?

    _____

    _____

    _____

5. Near what present-day city was the Yuan capital built?

    _____

    _____

    _____

China, Mongolia, and Taiwan

MAIN IDEAS
1. Physical features of China, Mongolia, and Taiwan include mountains, plateaus and basins, plains, and rivers.
2. China, Mongolia, and Taiwan have a range of climates and natural resources.

Key Terms and Places

Himalayas world's tallest mountain range

Plateau of Tibet world's highest plateau, located in southwest China

Gobi world's coldest desert, located in Mongolia

North China Plain fertile plain in east China

Huang He Yellow River, a river in northern China that often floods

loess fertile, yellowish soil

Chang Jiang Yangzi River, Asia's longest river, flows across central China

Lesson Summary
PHYSICAL FEATURES

China has a range of physical features. These include the world's tallest mountains, as well as some of the world's driest deserts and longest rivers. Mongolia and Taiwan are two of China's neighbors. Mongolia is north of China. It is a dry, landlocked country with vast grasslands and desert. Taiwan is a green tropical island.

There are mountains in much of the region. The **Himalayas** run along the border of southwest China. They are the tallest mountains in the world. Mount Everest is located in this mountain range. Many of the mountain ranges are separated by plateaus, basins, and deserts. North of the Himalayas is the **Plateau of Tibet**. It is the highest plateau on Earth and is called the Roof of the World.

North of this area is the Taklimakan Desert. It is a barren land with sand dunes and sandstorms.

> **How are Mongolia and Taiwan different?**
> _____
> _____
> _____

> **Where in China are the Himalayas located?**
> _____
> _____

Another desert, the **Gobi**, is located in Mongolia. It is the world's coldest desert.

Most Chinese live in east China, where there are low plains and river valleys, such as the **North China Plain**. This fertile area has farmlands and population centers. In Taiwan, most people live on a plain on the west coast.

Two long rivers run west to east across China. The **Huang He**, or the Yellow River, picks up a fertile, yellowish soil called **loess**. The river often floods in summer and deposits the loess, enriching farmland along the banks. Many people are killed by these floods. Another river, the **Chang Jiang**, or the Yangzi River, flows across central China. It is Asia's longest river and a major transportation route.

CLIMATE AND RESOURCES

Climate varies widely across the region. The tropical southeast is warm to hot. There, monsoons bring heavy rains in the summer. Violent storms called typhoons bring high winds and rain in the summer and fall. The climate in the north and west is mainly dry. Temperatures across this area vary. The climate in the northeast is quite different. It is drier and colder. In the winter, temperatures can drop below 0°F (–18°C).

The region has a variety of natural resources. China has many resources, including minerals and metals. It is a leading producer of coal. Farmland and forestland are also important. Mongolia's natural resources include minerals and livestock. Taiwan's main resource is farmland. It grows crops such as sugarcane, tea, and bananas.

Underline the region where most Chinese live.

Why is the Chang Jiang a major transportation route?
_____
_____
_____

What is a typhoon?
_____
_____
_____

Circle an important resource in both China and Taiwan.

CHALLENGE ACTIVITY

Critical Thinking: Make Generalizations Write a
journal entry describing your travels through a
part of the region, such as hiking in the
Himalayas, traveling with nomads across the
Gobi, or traveling a river by boat. What are your
general impressions?

DIRECTIONS Read each sentence and fill in the blank with the
word in the word pair that best completes the sentence.

1. Asia's longest river, the _____, flows through central
China. (**Chang Jiang/Huang He**)

2. The _____ is the world's coldest desert.
(**North China Plain/Gobi**)

3. The Roof of the World is another name for the _____.
(**Plateau of Tibet/Himalayas**)

4. The Yellow River picks up large amounts of fertile, yellowish soil called
_____. (**loess/Gobi**)

5. Mount Everest, the world's highest mountain, is located in the
_____. (**North China Plain/Himalayas**)

Chang Jiang (Yangzi River)	Gobi	Himalayas
Huang He (Yellow River)	loess	North China Plain
Plateau of Tibet		

DIRECTIONS Answer each question by writing a sentence
that contains at least one word from the word bank.

6. Where are many of China's main population centers?

_____

_____

7. How do China's rivers both help and hurt the country's people?

_____

_____

China, Mongolia, and Taiwan

MAIN IDEAS
1. In China's modern history, revolution and civil war led to a Communist government.
2. China's booming economy is based on agriculture and manufacturing.
3. China has a massive population and its urban areas are growing.
4. China's environment faces a number of serious problems.
5. China has a rich culture shaped by ancient traditions.

Key Terms and Places

Beijing China's capital

Tibet Buddhist region in southwest China

command economy an economy in which the government owns all businesses and makes all decisions

Shanghai China's largest city

Hong Kong important center of trade and tourism in southern China

dialect regional version of a language

Daoism belief system that stresses living simply and in harmony with nature

Confucianism philosophy based on the ideas and teachings of Confucius

pagodas Buddhist temples that have multistoried towers with an upward curving roof at each floor

Lesson Summary
MODERN HISTORY

In 1644 a group called the Manchu from northeastern Asia took control of China. They founded the Qing (CHING) dynasty. Qing rule was peaceful until the 1800s, when European nations spread their empires into Asia.

In 1911 rebels ended 2,000 years of rule by dynasties and founded a republic. Soon, two groups fought a civil war. The Nationalists wanted China to remain a republic. The Communists, led by Mao Zedong, won in 1949 and founded the People's Republic of China.

Who won China's civil war?
_____
_____
_____

The Nationalists fled to Taiwan, where they founded the Republic of China.

Mao Zedong led the new Communist government. In a Communist system, the government owns most businesses and land and controls all areas of life. Some people's lives improved, but freedoms were limited. Many economic programs failed.

Mao died in 1976. China's next leader was Deng Xiaoping. Deng worked to modernize and improve the economy. He allowed some private businesses and let other countries invest in China. The economy began growing rapidly. Leaders after Deng continued economic reforms, but economic freedom did not lead to political freedom.

China punishes people who disagree with the government. In 1989 a huge protest took place in China's capital, **Beijing**. About 100,000 people gathered in Tiananmen Square to demand more political rights and freedoms. The government used force to make people leave the square. Many protesters were killed or imprisoned.

China has also put down ethnic rebellions. Since 1950 China has controlled **Tibet**, a Buddhist region. When Tibetans rebelled, China crushed the revolt. Tibet's Buddhist leader, the Dalai Lama, fled to India.

ECONOMY

Until the 1980s China's Communist government had a **command economy**, in which the government owns all the businesses and makes all decisions. In the 1970s China began allowing a limited market economy. In a market economy, people can decide what to make or sell and keep the profits they earn. This mixed economic approach helped China become the world's second-largest economy.

> **How did Deng Xiaoping change China's economy?**
> _____
> _____
> _____
> _____
> _____

> **What is China's capital city?**
> _____
> _____

> **What is the government's role in a command economy?**
> _____
> _____
> _____

Only about 11 percent of China's land is good for farming. However, more than a third of workers are farmers. China is a leading producer of food crops.

China is also the largest manufacturing economy in the world. Economic growth has improved wages and living standards. More Chinese can now afford TVs, computers, and cars. Still, many rural Chinese remain poor and many cannot find work.

> **What are the two most important parts of China's economy?**
>
> _____
> _____

POPULATION

China has the world's largest population, with more than 1.3 billion people. Most people live in eastern China. The population grows by about 6 million people each year. The Chinese government has worked to slow this growth by urging people to delay having children and to have only one child.

Most Chinese live in small, rural villages, where farmers work the fields. Villages have small shops or people selling food and goods along the streets. Many people are moving to cities, which are growing rapidly. Most large cities are on the coast or along major rivers. Industry and trade contribute to their growth.

China's largest city is **Shanghai**, located where the Chang Jiang meets the East China Sea. Shanghai is China's leading seaport and an industrial and commercial center. Beijing is the second-largest city. It is China's political and cultural center. **Hong Kong** and Macao (muh-KOW) are important port cities in southern China. They are modern centers of trade and tourism.

> **Why is Shanghai a leading seaport?**
>
> _____
> _____
> _____

ENVIRONMENT

China's growth has created serious environmental problems. The country's growing number of cars and factories pollute the air and water. Burning

coal for electricity has the worst effect. China's
government is working to reduce pollution. It is
using more hydroelectric power, electricity
produced from dams. The Three Gorges Dam on
the Chang Jiang is the world's largest dam.

CULTURE

Most Chinese belong to the Han ethnic group.
Many speak Mandarin, one of China's official
languages. Others speak a **dialect**, the version of
a language spoken in a region. China has 55
other ethnic groups that have their own cultures.

> Circle the name of one of
> China's official languages.

The Communist government does not want
people to practice religion. However, many
people in China are influenced by religious values
and beliefs. The main belief systems are
Buddhism and Daoism. **Daoism** stresses living
simply and in harmony with nature. Buddhists
believe moral behavior, kindness, and meditation
lead to peace.

Many Chinese blend elements of these
religions with **Confucianism**. This philosophy is
based on the ideas and teachings of Confucius. It
stresses the importance of family, moral values,
and respect for one's elders.

> What values does
> Confucianism stress?
>
> _____
> _____
> _____
> _____

China has a rich artistic tradition. Crafts are
made from materials such as bronze, jade, ivory,
silk, wood, and porcelain. Chinese painting and
calligraphy, or decorative writing, are done on
silk or fine paper. The Chinese are known for
their poetry and opera. Buddhist temples called
pagodas have towers with many floors. Popular
culture includes sports such as martial arts and
table tennis.

CHALLENGE ACTIVITY

Critical Thinking: Draw Conclusions Imagine you
are living in China. Write a brief letter to a friend
back in the United States describing life in China.

Beijing	command economy	Confucianism
Daoism	Hong Kong	market economy
pagodas	Shanghai	Tibet

DIRECTIONS On the line provided before each statement, write **T** if
the statement is true and **F** if the statement is false. If the statement
is false, write the term from the word bank that makes the sentence a
true statement on the line after each sentence.

_____ 1. Confucianism stresses living simply and in harmony with nature.

_____

_____ 2. Many pagodas, or Buddhist temples, can be seen throughout China.

_____

_____ 3. A market economy is a system in which the government owns all
businesses and makes all economic decisions.

_____

_____ 4. Beijing and Macao are important port cities in southern China.

_____

_____ 5. Shanghai is a Buddhist region located in southwest China that China
has controlled since 1950.

_____

_____ 6. China's modern command economy benefits from international trade.

_____

DIRECTIONS Write three words or phrases that describe each term.

7. Shanghai _____

_____

8. Beijing _____

_____

China, Mongolia, and Taiwan

Lesson 3

MAIN IDEAS

1. Mongolia is a sparsely populated country where many people live as nomads.

2. Taiwan is a small island with a dense population and a highly industrialized economy.

Key Terms and Places

gers large, circular, felt tents that are easy to put up, take down, and move

Ulaanbaatar Mongolia's capital and only large city

Taipei Taiwan's capital and main financial center

Kao-hsiung Taiwan's main seaport and a center of heavy industry

Lesson Summary
MONGOLIA

The people of Mongolia have a proud and fascinating history. About 700 years ago, Mongolia was perhaps the greatest power in the world. Under the ruler Genghis Khan, Mongols conquered much of Asia, including China. Eventually, their empire stretched from Europe eastward to the Pacific Ocean. Over time, the empire declined. China conquered Mongolia in the late 1600s.

Who was the leader who built Mongolia's empire?

Mongolia declared independence from China in 1911. The Communists gained control in 1924. The Soviet Union helped Mongolia economically and was a strong influence. This help ended after the Soviet Union collapsed in 1991. Since then, Mongolians have tried to build a democratic government and a free-market economy.

Circle the name of the country that strongly influenced Mongolia.

Many Mongolians follow a traditional way of life. Nearly half live as nomads, herding livestock. Many live in **gers**. These large, circular, felt tents are easy to put up, take down, and move. Horses play a major role in nomadic life.

How do about half of Mongolians live?

Mongolia is large but has a small population of only about 3 million people. More than a quarter of them live in **Ulaanbaatar**, Mongolia's capital and only large city. It is the main industrial and commercial center.

The country's main industries include textiles, carpets, coal, copper, and oil. Mongolia produces livestock but very little other food.

What is Mongolia's capital city?

TAIWAN

Both China and Japan controlled Taiwan at different times. In 1949 the Chinese Nationalists took over the island. Led by Chang Kai-shek, they fled the Chinese mainland when the Communists took control. The Nationalists ruled Taiwan under martial law, or military rule, for 38 years. Today, Taiwan's government is a multiparty democracy.

What group came to Taiwan after the Communists took over mainland China?

Taiwan functions as an independent country, but there is still tension between China and Taiwan. China claims Taiwan is a rebel part of China. Taiwan claims to be China's true government.

Taiwan's population is about 85 percent native Taiwanese. They are descended from Chinese people who came to Taiwan in the 1700s and 1800s. As a result, Chinese ways are an important part of Taiwan's culture. In larger cities, some people follow European and American customs.

What is the major cultural influence in Taiwan?

Taiwan is a modern country with about 23 million people. Most Taiwanese live in cities on the island's western coastal plain. The rest of the country is mountainous. The two largest cities are **Taipei** and **Kao-hsiung**. Taipei is Taiwan's capital and main financial center. Kao-hsiung is a center of heavy industry and Taiwan's main seaport.

Underline the place where most Taiwanese live.

Taiwan is one of Asia's richest countries. It has a lot of industries, including making computers and sports equipment. Farmers grow many crops, including sugarcane.

Guided Reading Workbook

CHALLENGE ACTIVITY

Critical Thinking: Make Judgments Imagine you
are a government official from Taiwan visiting
Mongolia. Write a report explaining why
Mongolia and Taiwan should or should not
become trade partners.

DIRECTIONS Read each sentence and fill in the blank with the
word in the word pair that best completes the sentence.

1. _____ is Taiwan's capital and main financial center.
   (Taipei/Kao-hsiung)

2. The Mongol ruler _____ conquered much of Asia to
   create a Mongolian Empire. **(Chang Kai-shek/Genghis Khan)**

3. The coastal city of _____ is Taiwan's main seaport.
   (Kao-hsiung/Ulaanbaatar)

4. The capital city of _____ is home to more than a
   quarter of Mongolia's population. **(Ulaanbaatar/Taipei)**

5. _____ served as leader of the Chinese Nationalists
   in 1949. **(Genghis Khan/Chang Kai-shek)**

DIRECTIONS Write three words or phrases that describe each term.

6. gers _____

   _____

7. nomads _____

   _____

Name _____ Class _____ Date_____

MAIN IDEAS
1. The main physical features of Japan and the Koreas are rugged mountains.
2. The climates and resources of Japan and the Koreas vary from north to south.

Key Terms and Places

Fuji Japan's highest mountain

Korean Peninsula Asian peninsula that includes both North Korea and South Korea

tsunamis destructive waves caused by large underwater earthquakes

fishery place where lots of fish and other seafood can be caught

Lesson Summary
PHYSICAL FEATURES

Japan is made up of four large islands and more than 3,000 smaller ones. Its land area is slightly smaller than the state of California, but it stretches across 1,500 miles of ocean—about the length of the eastern United States coastline. Most people live on the four largest "home" islands, which are Hokkaido, Honshu, Shikoku, and Kyushu.

Mountains cover about 75 percent of Japan. The Japanese Alps are Japan's largest mountain range. They are very steep and rocky. Japan's highest mountain, **Fuji**, is not in a mountain range. It is a volcanic peak that rises above a flat area in eastern Honshu. It has become a symbol of Japan and is considered sacred by some people. Many shrines and temples have been built around it.

The **Korean Peninsula** juts south from the Asian mainland. It is divided between North and South Korea. Rugged mountains run along the eastern coast. The western coast has plains and river valleys. The Koreas have more rivers than

> Circle the names of Japan's four largest islands.

> Where is the mountain range located in the Korean Peninsula?
>
> _____
>
> _____

Guided Reading Workbook

Japan. Most of them flow westward and empty into the Yellow Sea.

Japan is subject to volcanic eruptions, earthquakes, and **tsunamis**, which are destructive waves caused by large underwater earthquakes. The Korean Peninsula does not have many earthquakes or volcanoes. Both Japan and the Koreas are subject to huge storms, called typhoons, that sweep in from the Pacific Ocean.

| Underline the definition of a tsunami. |

CLIMATE AND RESOURCES

Besides having similar physical features, Japan and the Koreas also have similar climates. In both places, climate varies from north to south. The northern regions have a humid continental climate. It brings cool summers, long, cold winters, and a short growing season. In the south, a humid subtropical climate brings mild winters and hot, humid summers. Heavy rains and typhoons in the summer can bring as much as 80 inches of rain each year.

| In a humid subtropical climate, when does most of the rain fall? _____ |

There are few natural resources in Japan or South Korea, but North Korea is rich in mineral resources such as iron and coal. Both of the Koreas use their quick-flowing rivers to generate hydroelectric power. Japan has one of the world's strongest fishing economies. The islands lie near one of the world's most productive fisheries. A **fishery** is an area where lots of fish and seafood can be caught. Swift ocean currents near Japan carry numerous fish to the islands. Huge fishing nets are used to catch the large number of fish needed to serve Japan's busy fish markets.

| Which country in this region has mineral resources? _____ |

CHALLENGE ACTIVITY

Critical Thinking: Analyze Write a paragraph describing the physical features and climate of Japan.

DIRECTIONS Read each sentence and fill in the blank with the word in the word pair that best completes the sentence.

1. The northern parts of the region have a _____ climate, in which the summers are cool but the winters are long and cold. (**humid continental/humid subtropical**)

2. The _____ along the eastern coast is covered with rugged mountains. (**tsunami/Korean Peninsula**)

3. A _____ can be brought on by underwater earthquakes. (**tsunami/fishery**)

4. Swift ocean currents provide a productive _____ area for Japan. (**fishery/humid subtropical**)

5. Many Japanese consider _____ a sacred place. (**Fuji/the Korean Peninsula**)

fishery	Fuji	humid continental
humid subtropical	Korean Peninsula	tsunamis

DIRECTIONS Choose four of the vocabulary terms from the word bank to write a summary of what you learned in the lesson.

_____

_____

_____

_____

_____

_____

Japan and the Koreas

MAIN IDEAS
1. Japan's early government was ruled by emperors and shoguns.
2. Japanese culture blends traditional customs with modern innovations.
3. Since World War II, Japan has developed a democratic government.
4. Japan has become one of the world's strongest economies.
5. A shortage of open space shapes daily life in Japan.
6. Crowding, competition, and pollution are among Japan's main issues and challenges.

Key Terms and Places

Kyoto Japan's imperial capital, known before as Heian

shoguns powerful military leaders of imperial Japan

samurai highly trained warriors

kimonos traditional Japanese robes

Diet Japan's elected legislature

Tokyo capital of Japan

work ethic belief that work in itself is worthwhile

trade surplus exists when a country exports more goods than it imports

tariff fee a country charges for exports or imports

Osaka Japan's second-largest city

Lesson Summary

HISTORY

Japan lies across the sea from China, so Chinese culture has been an important influence. One example is Buddhism, which became Japan's main religion. Japan's first government was modeled after China's. Both countries were ruled by emperors. Japan's emperors made their capital in Heian (now called **Kyoto**), a center for the arts.

Eventually, the emperors' power slipped away. Japan fell under the control of powerful generals called **shoguns**. One shogun would rule in the emperor's name. Shoguns had armies of fierce warriors called **samurai**. The shoguns ruled Japan

> Who took government power away from the emperors of Japan?
>
> _____

until 1868, when a group of samurai gave power back to the emperor.

During World War II, Japan sided with Germany and Italy. It wanted to build an empire in Southeast Asia and the Pacific. Japan brought the United States into the war in 1941, when it bombed the naval base at Pearl Harbor. To end the war, the Americans dropped atomic bombs on the Japanese cities of Hiroshima and Nagasaki. These powerful weapons caused Japan to surrender.

> **How did Japan bring the U.S. into World War II?**
> _____
> _____
> _____

JAPANESE CULTURE

Some Japanese culture is influenced by China, but many elements are native to Japan. Western culture is also an important influence.

Nearly everyone in Japan speaks Japanese, a difficult language to learn. The Japanese writing system uses two types of characters. Some characters, called kanji, represent a single word. About 2,000 kanji characters are commonly used. Other characters, called kana, stand for a part of a word.

> **Circle the names of the kinds of characters used to write Japanese.**

Most Japanese people combine elements of Shinto and Buddhism in their religious practices. Shinto is native to Japan. In the Shinto religion, everything in nature is believed to have a spirit, or *kami*. Buddhism encourages people to seek enlightenment and peace. There are many Shinto and Buddhist shrines and temples in Japan.

Most people in Japan wear Western-style clothing, but many also wear traditional **kimonos** on special occasions. Traditional forms of art include Noh and Kabuki plays.

> **What do Japanese people wear most of the time?**
> _____

GOVERNMENT

Japan's government has changed since World War II, and it is now a democracy. Although Japan's emperor is the country's official leader, he has little power. His main role is to act as a

Lesson 2, *continued*

symbol of Japan. In Japan today, power rests
with an elected legislature called the **Diet**. The
Diet chooses a prime minister. The seat of
government and capital of Japan is **Tokyo**.

> **Circle the words that explain who has power in Japan.**

ECONOMY

Until the 1950s the Japanese economy was not
strong. But within a few decades, Japan became
an economic powerhouse. It is the home of
successful companies like Honda, Toyota, and
Sony. Japanese companies are known for
manufacturing high-quality products, and they
are leaders in creating new technology.

The government has helped Japanese
companies succeed by controlling production and
planning for the future. Workers are highly
trained and have a strong **work ethic**, which also
helps.

Japan's economy depends on trade. Many
goods made in Japan are intended for export to
other countries. The United States is Japan's
main trading partner. Japan exports much more
than it imports, causing a huge **trade surplus**. This
has added to Japan's wealth. Japanese people do
not buy many imported goods because a high
tariff, or fee, makes them expensive.

> **What happens to many of the goods manufactured in Japan?**
> _____
> _____

Japan's economic success is due to its
manufacturing, not natural resources. Japan must
import most of the raw materials it uses to make
goods. Since there is little farmland, Japan must
also import much of its food from countries like
China and the United States.

DAILY LIFE

Tokyo is the center of Japan's banking and
communication industries. Like most Japanese
cities, it is densely populated and very crowded.
Almost 36 million people live in the Tokyo area,
making land scarce and expensive.

> **About how many people live in the Tokyo area?**
> _____

Guided Reading Workbook

Tokyo has tall, narrow buildings that use less land area. There are shops and restaurants in subway stations underground. Some hotels save space by housing guests in tiny sleeping chambers rather than rooms. Many people commute to Tokyo from outside the city. Trains are often jammed with commuters.

Other cities include **Osaka**, Japan's second-largest city located in western Honshu, and Kyoto, the former capital. Kyoto is full of historic buildings. Japan's major cities are linked by efficient, high-speed trains called bullet trains, which can reach more than 160 miles per hour (260 kph). Most people live in cities, but some live in villages or on farms. Many farmers have left rural areas to find jobs in cities.

ISSUES AND CHALLENGES

Japan's lack of space is a growing problem. Housing is crowded, commutes are long, and new tall buildings must withstand earthquakes.

> Underline three reasons lack of space is a challenge.

Japan also faces economic competition from countries such as China and South Korea, whose companies have taken away Japanese business. Many Japanese companies are decades old. To compete, the country must create new businesses.

There are also environmental concerns. Pollution is a problem. In 1997 the Kyoto Protocol agreement was signed by 150 countries to help cut pollution and improve air quality. And in 2011 a massive earthquake struck Japan, causing a tsunami that killed more than 18,000 people. It created a dangerous meltdown in a nuclear power plant. Today, the Japanese continue to rebuild their nation.

> What is the Kyoto Protocol?
>
> _____
> _____
> _____
> _____

CHALLENGE ACTIVITY

Critical Thinking: Sequence Write a paragraph describing three periods or events in Japan's history.

Diet	kana	kanji	kimonos
Kyoto	Osaka	samurai	Shinto
shoguns	tariff	Tokyo	trade surplus

DIRECTIONS On the line provided before each statement, write **T** if the statement is true and **F** if the statement is false. If the statement is false, write the correct term from the word bank on the line after each sentence to make the sentence a true statement.

_____ 1. The emperors made their capital at Heian, now called <u>Shinto</u>.

_____

_____ 2. Many Japanese wear traditional robes called <u>kimonos</u> on special occasions.

_____

_____ 3. <u>Kana</u> characters represent a single word.

_____

_____ 4. Because Japan exports more than it imports, it has a large <u>tariff</u>.

_____

_____ 5. <u>Kyoto</u> is Japan's modern seat of government.

_____

_____ 6. Located in western Honshu, <u>Tokyo</u> is Japan's second-largest city.

_____

_____ 7. In Japan, the <u>Diet</u> and the prime minister make the laws.

_____

Japan and the Koreas

Lesson 3

MAIN IDEAS
1. Korea was one state with a shared history until the Korean War.
2. Korean culture reflects its long history, and traditions continue into today.
3. The people of South Korea today have freedom and economic opportunities.
4. The people of North Korea today have little freedom or economic opportunity.
5. Some people in both South and North Korea support the idea of Korean reunification.

Key Terms and Places

Silla early kingdom that unified and ruled Korea

kimchi Korean dish made from pickled cabbage and spices

Seoul the capital of South Korea

demilitarized zone empty buffer zone created to keep two countries from fighting

Pyongyang capital of North Korea

Lesson Summary
HISTORY

In its early history, Korea was ruled by several different kingdoms. Later, three powerful kingdoms competed for control. Eventually, the kingdom of **Silla** unified the Three Kingdoms and ruled Korea. Silla leaders fought the Chinese for many years. During this time, the Silla adapted the Chinese system of governing and the religions of Buddhism and Confucianism. The Goryeo dynasty was the next to rule Korea. The English name *Korea* comes from *Goryeo*. In 1392 the Joseon took over and became Korea's last dynasty.

Later, the Japanese invaded. They were harsh rulers, and the Korean people resented them. After World War II, Korea became independent from Japan. However, the country was divided into two countries.

> **What parts of Chinese culture did the Silla adopt?**
>
> _____
> _____
> _____
> _____

The Soviet Union helped Communists take control in North Korea, while the United States helped to form a democratic government in South Korea. In 1950 North Korea invaded the south, starting the Korean War. North Korea wanted to unite Korea under a Communist government. The United States helped South Korea remain separate.

What action started the Korean War?
_____
_____

KOREAN CULTURE

People in both North and South Korea speak Korean. Unlike Japanese, written Korean uses an alphabet. Korea's traditional religion is shamanism. However, today, Christianity is the most widely practiced religion in South Korea. Buddhism is second. Communist North Korea discourages people from practicing any religion.

The people of Korea have kept many old customs. **Kimchi**, a spicy dish made from pickled cabbage, has been eaten for centuries. Traditions are especially important in North Korea, where the Communists want to preserve the country's customs and culture. In South Korea, people in rural areas keep their traditional ways. However, people in cities have adopted modern ways of life.

What parts of North and South Korea are more likely to keep traditions?
_____
_____
_____

SOUTH KOREA TODAY

The official name of South Korea is the Republic of Korea. It is a democracy, headed by a president and an assembly. Both are elected by the people. After World War II, the United States helped create South Korea's government and gave it economic support. In the first half of the 20th century, South Korea was poor. Today, it has one of the strongest economies in East Asia. It is a major manufacturing country that exports goods around the world.

Like Japan, South Korea is densely populated. Its capital, **Seoul**, is one of the most densely populated cities in the world. It has more than

Underline the official name of South Korea.

Lesson 3, *continued*

44,000 people per square mile. The most crowded part of the country is on the western coast.

In the cities, people live in small apartments. Housing is expensive, and there is pollution. In the country, many South Koreans live on small farms, grow rice, beans, and cabbage, and are more traditional.

Although South Korea has a strong economy, many people feel that its government is corrupt. For many years, four families controlled much of the country's industry, which gave them wealth and power. In 2016 the president was impeached due to a scandal related to these businesses.

A big challenge for South Korea is its relationship with North Korea. Since the end of the Korean War in the 1950s, the countries have been separated by a **demilitarized zone**. This empty area has no soldiers but is patrolled by guards on both sides to keep the countries from fighting.

> Why is there a demilitarized zone between North and South Korea?
>
> _____
> _____
> _____

NORTH KOREA TODAY

North Korea's official name, the Democratic People's Republic of Korea, is misleading. The country is not democratic. It is a totalitarian, Communist state.

From 1948 until 1994, it was led by the dictator Kim Il Sung. At Kim's death, his son, Kim Jong Il, became ruler. He was called "Dear Leader" by North Koreans, but he was a brutal dictator. Under his rule, North Koreans suffered human rights abuses, poverty, and widespread hunger. He developed weapons to threaten neighboring countries. After Kim Jong Il's death in 2011, his son Kim Jong Un took over. There was hope he would improve life for North Koreans. However, he followed his father's policies.

> When did Kim Il Sung rule North Korea?
>
> _____

North Korea has a command economy. In this economy, the government makes all economic decisions. It also owns all land and controls all access to jobs. North Korea uses much of its rich mineral resources to make machinery and military supplies. However, its factories are out of date, so the country stays poor. There is little farmland because the country is so rocky. Usable farmland is owned by the government. Farms are not able to produce enough food to feed the country, so the government must import food.

As in Japan and South Korea, most people in North Korea live in cities. The largest city is the crowded capital **Pyongyang**. Life there is different from life in Seoul or Tokyo. Only top government officials can have cars, so most people must use bicycles or public transportation. Many streets are dark because of electricity shortages. People are denied the rights of freedom of the press, speech, and religion.

North Korea has isolated itself since the fall of the Soviet Union. It does not allow other countries to sell goods there. It also does not have the technology to use its own resources effectively.

Many countries worry about North Korea's possession of nuclear weapons. It has conducted nuclear tests, which concerns countries in Asia and around the world.

KOREAN REUNIFICATION

For years, many North and South Koreans wanted their countries to be reunited. The two countries split up many families. People who shared a common culture were separated. At times, the North and South Korean governments have expressed support for reunification. In 2000 leaders met for the first time since the Korean War to discuss ways to improve relations.

However, the system of government remains an obstacle to reunification. South Korea prefers democracy, and North Korea insists on communism.

> **Why does North Korea have to import food?**
> _____
> _____
> _____

> **Why do both North and South Korean governments want to reunite their countries?**
> _____
> _____
> _____
> _____

Lesson 3, *continued*

CHALLENGE ACTIVITY

Critical Thinking: Compare and Contrast Draw a
Venn diagram to compare and contrast South
Korea and North Korea.

| demilitarized zone | kimchi | Pyongyang |
| Seoul | Silla | |

DIRECTIONS Read each sentence and choose the correct term from
the word bank to replace the underlined phrase. Write the term in
the space provided and then define the term in your own words.

1. <u>This dish</u> is a traditional Korean food that has been eaten for centuries.

   _____

   Your definition: _____

   _____

2. <u>This densely populated city</u> is the capital of South Korea. _____

   Your definition: _____

   _____

3. <u>This area</u> lies between North and South Korea to keep the two countries
   from fighting. _____

   Your definition: _____

   _____

4. Few people in <u>this crowded city</u> own private cars because the North Korean
   government allows only top Communist officials to own cars. _____

   Your definition: _____

   _____

Guided Reading Workbook

Southeast Asia

MAIN IDEAS

1. Southeast Asia's physical features include peninsulas, islands, rivers, and many seas, straits, and gulfs.
2. The tropical climate of Southeast Asia supports a wide range of plants and animals.
3. Southeast Asia is rich in natural resources such as wood, rubber, and fossil fuels.

Key Terms and Places

Indochina Peninsula peninsula that makes up part of Mainland Southeast Asia

Malay Peninsula peninsula that makes up part of Mainland Southeast Asia

Malay Archipelago island group that makes up part of Island Southeast Asia

archipelago large group of islands

New Guinea Earth's second-largest island

Borneo Earth's third-largest island

Mekong River most important river in Southeast Asia

Lesson Summary
PHYSICAL FEATURES

Two peninsulas and two large island groups make up the Southeast Asia region. Mainland Southeast Asia is made up of the **Indochina Peninsula** and the **Malay Peninsula**. Island Southeast Asia is made up of the many islands of the Philippines and the **Malay Archipelago**. An **archipelago** is a large group of islands.

> Underline the two peninsulas that make up Mainland Southeast Asia.

Mainland Southeast Asia includes the countries of Myanmar, Thailand, Laos, and Vietnam. This region has rugged mountains, low plateaus, and river floodplains. Island Southeast Asia has more than 20,000 islands. These include **New Guinea**, the world's second-largest island, and **Borneo**, the world's third-largest island. Some of the larger islands have high mountains with snow and glaciers.

Island Southeast Asia is part of the Ring of Fire, where earthquakes and volcanoes often occur. Underwater earthquakes can cause giant waves called tsunamis. In 2004 a tsunami in the Indian Ocean killed hundreds of thousands of people, many in Southeast Asia.

Southeast Asia has many water bodies, such as seas, straits, and gulfs. Several major rivers drain the mainland's peninsulas. The **Mekong River** is the most important river. The region's fertile river valleys and deltas support farming and are home to many people.

What is the Ring of Fire?
_____ _____ _____

CLIMATE, PLANTS, AND ANIMALS

Southeast Asia is in the tropics, the area on and around the equator. This region is generally warm to hot all year round. It is cooler in the north and in the mountains.

Much of the mainland has a tropical savanna climate. Savannas—areas of tall grasses and some trees and shrubs—grow here. Monsoon winds from the ocean bring heavy rain in summer and drier weather in winter. Wet seasons often have severe flooding.

Where do monsoon winds come from?
_____

The islands and the Malay Peninsula have a mostly humid tropical climate. It is hot, muggy, and rainy all year, with daily storms. Huge storms, called typhoons, can bring heavy rain and powerful winds.

This humid climate supports tropical rain forests. These forests are home to many different plants and animals. Indonesia alone has about 40,000 kinds of flowering plants. There are also many animals, including elephants, monkeys, tigers, and birds. Animals such as orangutans and Komodo dragons are found only in this region. Many of these plants and animals are endangered. Their habitat, the rain forest, is being cut down for timber, farming, and mining.

Why are the plants and animals of the rain forest endangered?
_____ _____ _____

NATURAL RESOURCES

Southeast Asia is rich in natural resources. Farming is very productive here thanks to the region's climate and rich soil. Rice, coconuts, coffee, sugarcane, palm oil, and spices are major crops. Rubber tree plantations are found in Indonesia and Malaysia. The rain forests supply hardwoods and medicines. The region also has fisheries, minerals, and fossil fuels.

> **What natural resources come from rain forests?**
>
> _____
>
> _____

CHALLENGE ACTIVITY

Critical Thinking: Draw Inferences Write an essay explaining the advantages and disadvantages of Southeast Asia's water resources for its people.

DIRECTIONS On the line provided before each statement, write **T** if the statement is true and **F** if the statement is false. If the statement is false, write the correct term on the line after each sentence to make the sentence a true statement.

_____ 1. New Guinea and the Philippines are the world's second- and third-largest islands, respectively.

_____

_____ 2. The most important river in Southeast Asia is the Mekong River.

_____

_____ 3. Mainland Southeast Asia is made up of the Malay Archipelago and the Indochina Peninsula.

_____

_____ 4. The two large island groups in Southeast Asia are the Philippines and the New Guinea Archipelago.

_____

_____ 5. Southeast Asia lies in the archipelago, the area on and around the equator.

_____

archipelago	Borneo	Indochina Peninsula
Malay Archipelago	Malay Peninsula	Mekong River
New Guinea	Philippines	tropics

DIRECTIONS Choose four of the terms from the word bank. On a separate piece of paper, use these terms to write a summary of what you learned in the lesson.

MAIN IDEAS
1. Southeast Asia's early history includes empires, colonial rule, and independence.
2. The modern history of Southeast Asia involves struggles with war and communism.
3. Southeast Asia's culture reflects its Chinese, Indian, and European heritage.
4. The area today is largely rural and agricultural, but cities are growing rapidly.
5. Myanmar is poor with a harsh military government, while Thailand is a democracy with a strong economy.
6. The countries of Indochina are poor and struggling to rebuild after years of war.

Key Terms and Places

Timor small island that stayed under Portugal's control after the Dutch took over the region

domino theory idea that if one country fell to communism, other countries nearby would follow like falling dominoes

wats Buddhist temples that also serve as monasteries

Yangon Myanmar's capital and major seaport

human rights rights that all people deserve, such as rights to equality and justice

Bangkok capital and largest city of Thailand

klongs canals

Phnom Penh Cambodia's capital and chief city

Hanoi capital of Vietnam, located in the north

Lesson Summary
EARLY HISTORY

China and India lie close to Southeast Asia and have had a strong role in its history. Many people from China and India settled in Southeast Asia, creating trade between the countries.

According to recent research, humans lived in Southeast Asia's rain forests as long as 11,000 years ago. The most advanced early civilization was the Khmer. Their empire lasted from the AD 800s to the mid-1200s in what is now Cambodia. The Khmer built a huge temple, Angkor Wat. This temple is an example of their advanced civilization and Hindu religion. In the 1200s the Thai came from southern China and settled in the Khmer area. Buddhism began to replace Hinduism in the region.

Starting in the 1500s, European countries came to the area to colonize, trade, and spread their religion. Portugal led the way. Spain claimed the Philippines and spread Roman Catholicism there. Later, the Dutch drove Portugal out of much of the region. Portugal kept **Timor**, a small island, but the Dutch controlled the tea and spice trade in what is now Indonesia.

> **Why did European countries come to this region?**
> _____
> _____
> _____

In the 1800s the British and French set up colonies with plantations, railroads, and mines. People from China and India worked in the colonies. The British and French also spread Christianity. In 1898 the United States came into the region when it won the Philippines from Spain in the Spanish-American War. Colonial powers ruled all of the area except for Siam (now Thailand) by the early 1900s.

> **Circle the year the United States entered the region.**

During World War II, Japan invaded and occupied most of Southeast Asia. When the war ended, the United States granted the Philippines independence. Other countries in the region started to fight for independence, too. The French left Indochina in 1954 after a bloody war. The independent countries of Cambodia, Laos, and Vietnam were formed from this area. By 1970 most of Southeast Asia was free from colonial rule.

> **What three countries were formed from Indochina?**
> _____
> _____
> _____

MODERN HISTORY

In Vietnam, feelings of nationalism, or loyalty to the country, led to the fight against French colonialism. The Vietnamese were led by

Ho Chi Minh, a Communist. The fighting divided the country into North and South Vietnam. In South Vietnam, a civil war started.

In the 1960s the United States decided to send troops to South Vietnam to fight Communist forces. This decision was based on the **domino theory**—the idea that if one country fell to communism, other nearby countries would fall, too. Years of war led to millions of deaths and terrible destruction. Eventually, North and South Vietnam became one Communist country. About a million refugees fled. Many went to the United States.

Civil wars also broke out in Cambodia and Laos. In 1975 Communists took over both countries. Cambodia's government was brutal. Vietnam helped overthrow Cambodia's government in 1978. Fighting lasted until the mid-1990s.

> **Restate the domino theory in your own words.**
> _____
> _____
> _____
> _____
> _____
> _____

CULTURE

Southeast Asia blends native, Chinese, Indian, and European cultures. There are hundreds of ethnic groups in the region. There are also many languages and religions. Buddhism is the most popular religion on the mainland. The area is home to many beautiful Buddhist temples, or **wats**, which also serve as monasteries. Islam is the main religion in Malaysia, Brunei, and Indonesia. Indonesia has more Muslims than any other country. In the Philippines, most people are Roman Catholic. The island of Bali and Indian communities practice Hinduism.

Customs vary widely, yet there are some similarities. Religion and religious festivals are important parts of daily life. Traditional dances and music are still popular, especially in rural areas. Also, many people still wear traditional clothing such as sarongs, strips of cloth worn wrapped around the body.

> **Circle the four main religions practiced in Southeast Asia.**

MAINLAND SOUTHEAST ASIA TODAY

Mainland Southeast Asia includes the countries of Myanmar, Thailand, Cambodia, Laos, and Vietnam. Because of war, harsh governments, and other problems, progress has slowed in much of this area. However, the area's rich resources make the future promising. In 2010 most of the countries of Southeast Asia joined the Association of Southeast Asian Nations (ASEAN). It promotes political, economic, and social cooperation in the region.

Most of Mainland Southeast Asia is rural and most people are farmers. They live in small villages and grow rice. Most farm work is done using traditional methods.

Mainland Southeast Asia has several big cities. They are growing rapidly as people move to them in search of work.

MYANMAR AND THAILAND

Myanmar, also called Burma, is a poor country. It gained independence from Great Britain in 1948. **Yangon**, or Rangoon, is its capital, though the administrative capital is Naypyidaw. Most people in Myanmar are Burmese. Many live in small farming villages, with houses built on stilts. The main religion is Buddhism.

For about half a century, a harsh military government has ruled Myanmar. This government abuses **human rights**—rights that all people deserve. One woman, Aung San Suu Kyi, has led a movement for more democracy and rights. She and others have been repeatedly arrested. Her fight for reform resulted in the country's first free elections in 2016.

Thailand, once called Siam, has the area's strongest economy. Its capital and largest city is **Bangkok**. It is a modern, crowded city, which lies near the mouth of the Chao Phraya River. Bangkok is known for its palaces and Buddhist

Who is Aung San Suu Kyi?
_____
_____
_____
_____

wats. It is also famous for its **klongs**, or canals. Klongs are used for trade and travel and to drain floodwater.

Thailand is a constitutional monarchy. Its king has a ceremonial role. The real power is held by a prime minister and elected legislature. The democratically elected government and rich resources have helped Thailand's economy grow. Industries include manufacturing, farming, fishing, mining, and tourism.

Who governs Thailand?
_____
_____

THE COUNTRIES OF INDOCHINA

After decades of war, the countries of Indochina—Cambodia, Laos, and Vietnam—are working hard to improve their economies.

The capital and chief city of Cambodia is **Phnom Penh**. It lies in the Mekong River valley and is a center of trade. Cambodia endured 20 years of war, terror, and devastation, which finally ended in the early 1990s. Today, the country has a stable, elected government similar to Thailand's. However, years of war have left the country with little industry. Although farming has improved, many land mines still remain buried.

How has war affected Cambodia?
_____
_____
_____

Laos is the area's poorest country. It is landlocked by mountains, with few roads, no railroads, and little electricity. The Communist government is trying to improve the economy, which is based on farming. There is little good farmland, so most people are subsistence farmers. They grow just enough food for their families.

Vietnam is also mountainous. Its main cities include its capital in the north, **Hanoi**, and Ho Chi Minh City in the south. It is still a Communist country, but Vietnam's government has been allowing more economic freedom and private business.

CHALLENGE ACTIVITY

Critical Thinking: Understand Cause and Effect
Several European countries had colonies in
Southeast Asia for hundreds of years. Make a
two-column chart of cultural effects and political
effects of colonization on the region.

DIRECTIONS Read each sentence and fill in the blank with the
word in the word pair that best completes the sentence.

1. The small island that stayed under Portugal's control when the Dutch took
   over the region was _____. **(Timor/Khmer)**

2. _____ is now called Thailand. **(Burma/Siam)**

3. Southeast Asia has many _____, or Buddhist temples.
   (klongs/wats)

4. The United States sent troops to South Vietnam to prevent the spread of
   communism based on the _____.
   (domino theory/human rights)

5. _____ is the capital and largest city of Cambodia.
   (Phnom Penh/Yangon)

6. In Thailand, _____ are used for transportation, trade,
   and draining floodwaters. **(Yangon/klongs)**

7. Vietnam's capital, _____, is located in the north.
   (Hanoi/Ho Chi Minh City)

DIRECTIONS Write two words or phrases that describe the term.

8. Bangkok _____

9. human rights _____

10. Yangon _____

Guided Reading Workbook

Southeast Asia

MAIN IDEAS
1. The area today has rich resources and growing cities but faces challenges.
2. Malaysia and its neighbors have strong economies but differ in many ways.
3. Indonesia and the Philippines are diverse with growing economies, and East Timor is small and poor.

Key Terms and Places

Timor-Leste small island of Timor that declared independence from Indonesia in 1999

kampongs villages or city districts with traditional houses built on stilts; slums around cities

Jakarta capital of Indonesia

Kuala Lumpur Malaysia's capital and a cultural and economic center

free ports ports that place few, if any, taxes on goods

sultan supreme ruler of a Muslim country

Java Indonesia's main island

Manila capital of the Philippines

Lesson Summary
THE AREA TODAY
The six countries of Island Southeast Asia are Malaysia, Singapore, Brunei, Indonesia, **Timor-Leste**, and the Philippines. These countries could have bright futures. They have rich resources and skilled labor forces. Their economies are growing. All but Timor-Leste belong to ASEAN, which promotes cooperation in Southeast Asia.

However, these island countries still face challenges. Ethnic conflicts have hurt progress. Many people live in poverty, while much of the money is controlled by only a few leaders and businesspeople. There are many environmental problems, such as pollution.

> Underline three challenges facing Island Southeast Asia.

Many people in Island Southeast Asia live in rural areas. They fish or farm. Seafood is the main source of protein. Rice is the main crop, though they also grow coffee, spices, sugarcane, tea, and tropical fruit. Indonesia and Malaysia are the world's biggest producers of rubber.

As on the mainland, many people here are moving to cities for work. The capitals are the largest cities. They are modern and crowded. Common problems include smog, heavy traffic, and large slums. In some areas, people live in **kampongs**, places with traditional houses on stilts. The stilts protect houses from flooding. The term *kampong* also refers to slums in cities such as **Jakarta**, Indonesia's capital.

Why might people want to live in a house on stilts?

MALAYSIA AND ITS NEIGHBORS

Malaysia has two parts. One part is on the island of Borneo. The other is on the southern part of the Malay Peninsula. This is where most Malaysians live. Malaysia's capital, **Kuala Lumpur**, is also located there. Kuala Lumpur is the country's cultural and economic center.

Circle the two areas that make up Malaysia.

Malaysia is ethnically diverse. Malays are the main ethnic group, but many Chinese and other groups live there, too. This is why the country has many languages and religions. Bahasa Malay is the main language. Islam and Buddhism are the main religions.

Malaysia is a constitutional monarchy. Local rulers take turns being king, which is mostly a ceremonial position. A prime minister and elected legislature hold the real power. The country has one of the strongest economies in the region. It has well-educated workers and rich resources. It produces and exports natural rubber, palm oil, electronics, oil, and timber.

Singapore is on a tiny island at the tip of the Malay Peninsula. This location is on a major shipping route, which has made Singapore rich.

How does Singapore's location help its economy?

It is one of the world's busiest **free ports**—ports with few or no taxes on goods. Singapore is also an industrial center with many offices of foreign banks and high-tech firms. The city is modern, wealthy, orderly, and clean.

Singapore has a low crime rate, but that is because of strict laws. The government has cleaned up slums and improved housing. But it also gives fines for littering. People caught with illegal drugs can be executed. Politics and media are also controlled by the government.

Brunei is a tiny country on Borneo. It is ruled by a **sultan**, the supreme ruler of a Muslim country. Large oil and gas deposits have made Brunei wealthy. This wealth allows citizens to receive free health care and other benefits. They do not pay taxes. However, the oil is expected to run out around 2020, so the government is trying to find other ways to develop the economy.

> **Why does Singapore have a low crime rate?**
> _____
> _____
> _____

> **Underline the text that explains the economic problem soon facing Brunei.**

INDONESIA, TIMOR-LESTE, AND THE PHILIPPINES

Indonesia is the world's largest archipelago, with over 13,500 islands. It has the fourth-largest population of any country and the world's largest Muslim population. The country has more than 300 ethnic groups that speak over 250 languages.

Java is Indonesia's main island. The capital, Jakarta, is there. More than half the population live in Java, making it extremely crowded. To reduce the crowding, the government is moving people to less-populated islands. This is an unpopular policy.

Indonesia has rich resources, such as rubber, oil, gas, and timber. There is good farmland for rice and other crops. Factories and tourism also help the economy. But there are also problems. People are poor and unemployment is high. In some areas, religious and ethnic conflicts have led to violence.

Guided Reading Workbook

Timor-Leste is on the small island of Timor. In 1999 Timor-Leste declared independence from Indonesia, leading to years of violence. The United Nations sent in troops to end the war. The fighting left Timor-Leste poor. Most people farm, and coffee is the main export.

What led to the war in Timor-Leste?
_____
_____
_____

The Philippines has more than 7,000 islands. The largest is Luzon. It is the most populated island, and the capital, **Manila**, is there. The Philippines is one of the most diverse countries in the region. It is home to ten ethnic groups and many foreigners.

The country's many natural resources include metals, oil, and woods. Farming and manufacturing are also important for the economy. However, even though the economy has improved, there is a big gap between the rich and poor. Few Filipinos are wealthy. Most are poor farmers who do not own any land.

What is one of the main economic problems in the Philippines?
_____
_____
_____
_____

The country is mainly Roman Catholic, but some areas are mostly Muslim. These areas want independence. This has led to violent conflicts.

CHALLENGE ACTIVITY

Critical Thinking: Draw Inferences Choose two island countries of Southeast Asia and write a paragraph that compares two of the following categories: geography, people, government, economy.

DIRECTIONS On the line provided before each statement, write **T** if the statement is true and **F** if the statement is false. If the statement is false, write the correct term on the line after each sentence to make the sentence a true statement.

_____ 1. Singapore is one of the world's busiest <u>kampongs</u>.

_____

_____ 2. Malaysia's capital, <u>Java</u>, is also a cultural and economic center.

_____

_____ 3. The Philippines has many islands, including Luzon, which is where the capital city of <u>Manila</u> is located.

_____

_____ 4. <u>Kuala Lumpur</u>, the capital of Indonesia, is located on the country's largest island.

_____

_____ 5. The supreme ruler of Brunei, a Muslim country, is a <u>sultan</u>.

_____

_____ 6. <u>Timor-Leste</u> is on the small island of Timor.

_____

Oceania and Antarctica

MAIN IDEAS
1. The physical geography of Australia and New Zealand is diverse and unusual.
2. Native peoples and British settlers shaped the history of Australia and New Zealand.
3. Australia and New Zealand today are wealthy and culturally diverse countries.

Key Terms and Places

Great Barrier Reef largest coral reef in the world, off Australia's northeastern coast

coral reef collection of rocky material found in shallow, tropical waters

Aborigines first humans to live in Australia

Maori New Zealand's first settlers

Outback Australia's interior

Lesson Summary
PHYSICAL GEOGRAPHY

Australia has wide, flat stretches of dry land. Western Australia is home to Uluru, a rock formation also known as Ayers Rock. Uluru is one of Australia's best-known landforms. Low mountains, valleys, and a major river system make up the eastern part of the country. The **Great Barrier Reef**, the world's largest **coral reef**, is located off of Australia's northeastern coast.

New Zealand is made up of North Island and South Island. A large mountain range called the Southern Alps is a key feature of South Island. New Zealand also has green hills, volcanoes, hot springs, dense forests, deep lakes, and fertile plains. Narrow inlets called fjords create natural harbors along the coasts of both islands.

Most of Australia has warm, dry desert and steppe climates. The coastal areas are milder and wetter. New Zealand has a marine climate, with plenty of rainfall and mild temperatures. Native

> Underline the two islands that make up New Zealand.

animals include Australia's kangaroo and koala and New Zealand's kiwi, a flightless bird. Australia has many valuable mineral resources, and farms raise wheat, cotton, and sheep despite the poor soil. New Zealand has few mineral resources but plenty of rich soil.

Circle the region's native animals.

HISTORY

Aborigines, the first humans in Australia, came from Southeast Asia more than 40,000 years ago. Early Aborigines were nomads who gathered plants, hunted animals, and fished. The **Maori**, New Zealand's first settlers, came from other Pacific islands about 1,200 years ago. They hunted, fished, and farmed. Captain James Cook visited New Zealand in 1769. British settlers began arriving in Australia and New Zealand in the late 1700s and early 1800s. Many of the first settlers to arrive in Australia were British prisoners. Some early British settlers took over the lands inhabited by the Aborigines. In New Zealand, tensions between the Maori and British settlers led to a series of wars over land. Australia and New Zealand gained independence in the early 1900s. Both countries are in the British Commonwealth and are close allies of the United Kingdom.

Who were the first humans to settle in Australia and New Zealand? _____ _____

AUSTRALIA AND NEW ZEALAND TODAY

Most people in both countries are of British ancestry. Sydney and Melbourne are Australia's two largest cities. Auckland is New Zealand's largest city. Both countries produce wool, meat, and dairy products. Mining is important throughout the **Outback**. Other industries include steel, heavy machines, and computers. Manufacturing, banking, and tourism are important in New Zealand.

Today, Australia and New Zealand face the challenge of improving the political and economic status of their native populations.

Circle the name of New Zealand's largest city.

CHALLENGE ACTIVITY

Critical Thinking: Make Judgments How were the Aboriginal and Maori populations of Australia and New Zealand affected after British settlers arrived? Explain your answer in a short paragraph.

DIRECTIONS Read each sentence and fill in the blank with the word in the word pair that best completes the sentence.

1. The _____ were the first people to inhabit Australia.

    (Aborigines/Maori)

2. Melbourne and _____ are two large cities in Australia.

    (Auckland/Sydney)

3. A _____ is a collection of rocky materials found in shallow, tropical waters. **(coral reef/fjord)**

4. The_____ is a flightless bird unique to New Zealand.

    (koala/kiwi)

Aborigines	Auckland	coral reef	fjord
Great Barrier Reef	kiwi	koala	Maori
Melbourne	Outback	Sydney	Uluru

DIRECTIONS Choose five of the terms from the word bank. On a separate sheet of paper, use these terms to write a summary of what you learned in this lesson.

Name _____ Class _____ Date_____

Oceania and Antarctica

MAIN IDEAS
1. Unique physical features, tropical climates, and limited resources shape the physical geography of the Pacific Islands.
2. Native customs and contact with the Western world have influenced the history and culture of the Pacific Islands.
3. Pacific Islanders today are working to improve their economies and protect the environment.

Key Terms and Places

Micronesia region of Pacific Islands located east of the Philippines

Melanesia region of Pacific Islands stretching from New Guinea to Fiji

Polynesia largest region of Pacific Islands, east of Melanesia

atolls small, ring-shaped coral islands surrounding lagoons

territory area that is under the control of another government

Lesson Summary
PHYSICAL GEOGRAPHY

There are three regions of islands in the Pacific. **Micronesia**, consisting of about 2,000 small islands, is east of the Philippines. **Melanesia**, the most heavily populated region, stretches from New Guinea to Fiji. **Polynesia**, the largest region, is located east of Melanesia and includes Tonga, Samoa, and the Hawaiian Islands.

There are two kinds of islands in the Pacific: high islands and low islands. High islands are formed from volcanoes or continental rock. They tend to be mountainous and rocky. They have dense forests, rich soil, and many mineral resources. Low islands are much smaller; they have thin soil, little vegetation, few resources, and low elevations. Many low islands are **atolls**, small, ring-shaped coral islands surrounding lagoons.

Most high and low islands have a humid tropical climate. Temperatures are warm and rain falls all year.

> **What three regions make up the Pacific Islands?**
>
> _____
>
> _____
>
> _____

Guided Reading Workbook

Lesson 2, *continued*

HISTORY AND CULTURE

People began settling the Pacific more than 40,000 years ago. They arrived in Melanesia first. Polynesia was the last region to be settled. Europeans first encountered the Pacific Islands in the 1500s. James Cook, a captain in the British navy, visited all the main regions in the 1700s. By the late 1800s Britain, Spain, France, and other European nations gained control of most of the islands. When the United States defeated Spain in the Spanish-American War, it took Guam as a **territory**, an area that is under the authority of another government. After World War I, Japan gained control of many islands. After World War II, the United Nations placed some islands under the control of the United States and its Allies.

More than 9 million people of many cultures and ethnic groups live in the Pacific Islands. Most are descended from the original settlers. Some are ethnic Europeans and Asians. Most islanders are now Christian. Many, however, continue to practice traditional customs, ranging from architecture to art styles and various ceremonies.

| Circle the name of the Pacific Island region that was first to be settled. |

| About how many people live in the Pacific Islands? _____ _____ |

THE PACIFIC ISLANDS TODAY

The Pacific Islands face important challenges today. They are trying to build stronger economies through tourism, agriculture, and fishing. Some countries, including Papua New Guinea, export gold, copper, and oil. The islands also must cope with the potentially damaging effects of past nuclear testing in the area and global warming.

| Underline three ways the Pacific Islands are trying to improve their economies. |

CHALLENGE ACTIVITY

Critical Thinking: Drawing Conclusions Which island countries probably have stronger economies: those occupying high islands or those occupying low islands? Support your answer using details from the summary.

Guided Reading Workbook

atoll	Melanesia	Micronesia
Polynesia	territory	

DIRECTIONS On the line provided before each statement, write **T** if a statement is true and **F** if a statement is false. If the statement is false, write the term from the word bank on the line after each sentence to make the sentence a true statement.

_____ 1. <u>Melanesia</u>, which means "tiny islands," is a group of about 2,000 small islands in the Pacific.

_____

_____ 2. Tonga and Hawaii are part of <u>Polynesia</u>.

_____

_____ 3. <u>Micronesia</u> is the most heavily populated of the three Pacific island groups.

_____

DIRECTIONS Read each sentence and choose the correct term from the word bank to replace the underlined phrase. Write the term in the space provided and then define the term in your own words.

4. Wake Island, located west of the Hawaiian Islands, is an <u>unusual physical feature</u>. _____

Your definition: _____

5. When the United States defeated Spain in the Spanish-American War, Guam became a U.S. <u>political unit</u>. _____

Your definition: _____

Oceania and Antarctica

MAIN IDEAS
1. Freezing temperatures, ice, and snow dominate Antarctica's physical geography.
2. Explorations in the 1800s and 1900s led to Antarctica's use for scientific research.
3. Research and protecting the environment are key issues in Antarctica today.

Key Terms and Places

ice shelf ledge of ice that extends over the water

icebergs floating masses of ice that have broken off a glacier

Antarctic Peninsula peninsula that extends north of the Antarctic Circle

polar desert high-latitude region that receives very little precipitation

ozone layer layer of Earth's atmosphere that protects living things from the harmful effects of the sun's ultraviolet rays

Lesson Summary
PHYSICAL GEOGRAPHY

Ice covers more than 98 percent of Antarctica. Ice flows slowly toward the coasts of Antarctica. At the coast, it forms a ledge over the water called an **ice shelf**. Antarctica's largest ice shelf is the Ross Ice Shelf. Floating masses of ice that break off from ice shelves are called **icebergs**. The **Antarctic Peninsula** is on the western side of the continent.

Antarctica has a freezing ice cap climate. It is a **polar desert**, a high-latitude region that receives little precipitation. It is bitterly cold during the dark winter. Summer temperatures reach near freezing.

Tundra plant life grows in ice-free areas. Insects are the only animals on the land. Penguins, seals, and whales live in the nearby waters. Antarctica has many mineral resources.

> How is an iceberg related to an ice shelf?
>
> _____
>
> _____
>
> _____

EARLY EXPLORATIONS

Antarctica was first sighted in 1775. European explorations investigated Antarctica throughout the 1800s. A team of Norwegian explorers became the first people to reach the South Pole in 1911.

Several countries have claimed parts of Antarctica. In 1959 several countries signed the Antarctic Treaty, which bans military activity on the continent and sets it aside for scientific research.

> **What are the terms of the Antarctic Treaty of 1959?**
>
> _____
>
> _____
>
> _____
>
> _____

ANTARCTICA TODAY

Antarctica is the only continent with no permanent human population. Scientists use Antarctica to conduct research and study the environment. Several countries, including the United States, have bases there.

Antarctic research includes the study of plant and animal life, analysis of weather conditions and patterns, and examination of issues affecting Earth's environment. Scientists are concerned about the thinning of the **ozone layer**—the layer of Earth's atmosphere that protects living things from the harmful effects of the sun's ultraviolet rays.

Tourism, oil spills, and mining are real and potential threats to Antarctica's environment. An agreement reached in 1991 bans mining and drilling and limits tourism.

> **Underline three activities that threaten Antarctica's environment.**

CHALLENGE ACTIVITY

Critical Thinking: Make Judgments What do you think is the greatest threat to Antarctica's environment? Why? Explain your answer.

Antarctic Peninsula	Antarctic Treaty	glacier	ice shelf
icebergs	motive	ozone layer	polar desert

DIRECTIONS Answer each question by writing a sentence that contains at least one word from the word bank.

1. Describe the physical geography of Antarctica.

_____

_____

_____

2. What kinds of things are scientists studying in Antarctica?

_____

_____

_____

DIRECTIONS Write three words or phrases that describe the term.

3. icebergs _____

_____

4. polar desert _____

_____

5. Antarctic Peninsula _____

_____

6. ozone layer _____

_____